# MACDONALD ILLUSTRATED CLASSICS

### GENERAL EDITOR: MALCOLM ELWIN

5

# The Poetical Works
# of Shelley

SHELLEY

*From the painting by George Clint, after Amelia Curran. Now in the National Portrait Gallery, London.*

# THE POETICAL WORKS OF

# SHELLEY

SELECTED, WITH AN INTRODUCTION,
BY MORCHARD BISHOP

MACDONALD : LONDON

*First published in this series in February 1949*
*Second impression January 1958*

*Published by*
*Macdonald & Co. (Publishers) Ltd.*
*16 Maddox Street, W.1*
*Made and Printed in Great Britain by*
*Purnell and Sons, Ltd., Paulton*
*(Somerset) and London*

# INTRODUCTION

INCONGRUOUSLY, even slightly ignominiously, situated a brief trolley-bus ride from the brisk and dapper centre of Bournemouth, the old grey Norman priory-church of Christchurch stands on the very brink of a crimson jungle of desirable residential properties. At the western end of this noble building, surrounded as a rule by coveys of chattering tourists, may be observed a very large and pure white marble monument in the style of a Pietà—with the difference that the undraped male figure is that of a drowned poet, and the mourning female is, it is to be presumed and hoped, a representation of the poet's wife. This startling piece of sculpture, which no doubt is fine enough of its kind, has always seemed to the present writer a quite perfect symbol and epitome of the strange, the even somewhat unfortunate fate which, throughout the whole of the latter part of the last century, and some of this one too, has dogged the reputation of that very great man and very great poet, Percy Bysshe Shelley.

A poet, according to Victorian standards, was necessarily a romantic figure; poets who died young, by misadventure, after lives that were chequered by matrimonial misfortune and love-affairs that were conducted in a positive blaze of public solicitude, were naturally the most romantic of all. Together with Byron and Keats, who also fulfilled the whole of the requisite conditions, Shelley has tended to merge into the typical poet of the romanticists, a state of affairs that has not been made any better by the fact that the only well-known portrait of him—the one painted in Rome by the somewhat amateurish Amelia Curran, and now in the National Portrait Gallery—is a representation to say the least highly sentimentalized. When a sufficiently potent aura of association has been plastered round the figure of an eminent man, it becomes very nearly impossible to see him objectively, or even to judge dispassionately of his works. It is, we think, for this reason

vii

that, until quite lately, Shelley has been presented to the general reading public in terms almost more suited to the description of a fabulous monster than of a man. From Matthew Arnold's 'beautiful and ineffectual angel' down to Francis Thompson's godlike child who, in an admirably purple patch, takes the universe for his box of toys, 'dabbles his fingers in the day-fall' and is 'gold-dusty with tumbling amid the stars,' Shelley would seem to have become the intimate personal property of every poet who felt inclined to indulge himself in a bout of fine writing. The writing is, mostly, fine enough: the trouble is that, while an effect similar to that of a painting by Michelangelo is aimed at, the finished article tends, perversely and obstinately enough, to turn out much more like one of the portentous productions of George Frederick Watts. The fact is that nowadays we have rather lost the secret of the Grand Manner; perhaps, too, we are acquiring painfully the knowledge that the truest portraits of even the greatest men are those in which they are, at least, painted no larger than life.

Added to all this, of course, is the fact that Shelley's sad and even disastrous life-story presents an unrivalled opportunity to every writer who seeks to purvey, under the guise of biography, savoury and romantic myths such as the public loves. M. André Maurois's fascinating and very readable work, *Ariel*, is perhaps the best of such studies, which, while highly laudable in themselves as entertainment, and sovran for all such literary skirmishers as adore 'chatter about Harriet,' do perhaps nevertheless a little unduly distract the attention of readers from the real man, and his most real works. It now needs nothing but for the cinema to seize hold of Shelley, as it has already seized hold of the Brontës, the Brownings, Chopin and God knows who else beside, for the obfuscation to become entire.

Happily, however, for those who still really wish to 'see Shelley plain,' there yet remain two genuinely untainted sources of evidence as to what manner of man he was, the first of these being his works, of which a full and generous measure is here laid before the reader; while the second is the account not stintingly given of him by the men who were his actual contemporaries—by Hunt and Trelawny, Peacock and Hazlitt, Medwin and Byron. Later on we will consider the evidences of his poems, but here first let us look for a moment at what the people who really knew him, 'in his habit as he lived,' had to say.

First, Byron: 'Poor Shelley . . . is, to my knowledge, the *least* selfish and the mildest of men—a man who has made more sacrifices of his fortune and feelings for others than any I ever heard of. . . . You do not know how mild, how tolerant, how good he was in society; and as perfect a gentleman as ever crossed a drawing-room, when he liked, and where he liked.'

Trelawny: 'Shelley, one of the most benevolent and humane men of his time, was shunned (as if he had a pestilential disease) from his anti-Christian writings before he was twenty-one years of age. . . . He was habited like a boy, in a black jacket and trousers, which he seemed to have outgrown.'

Williams (who was drowned with him): 'Shelley is certainly a man of most astonishing genius, in appearance extraordinarily young, of manners mild and amiable, but withal full of life and fun. His wonderful command of language, and the ease with which he speaks on what are generally considered abstruse subjects, are striking; in short, his ordinary conversation is akin to poetry, for he sees things in the most singular and pleasing lights; if he wrote as he talked, he would be popular enough.'

It may be that a picture begins to emerge: a picture in which the salient characteristics are mildness and amiability. But this is Counsel for the Defence; these men were his friends, for all that it was Byron who nicknamed him 'The Snake.' Let us pass on to the verdict of a contemporary not so susceptible to his spell, Hazlitt: 'The author of *Prometheus Unbound* has a fire in his eye, a fever in his blood, a maggot in his brain, a hectic flutter in his speech, which mark out the philosophic fanatic. He is sanguine-complexioned and shrill-voiced. As is often observable in the case of religious enthusiasts, there is a slenderness of constitutional *stamina*, which renders the flesh no match for the spirit. . . . The shock of accident, the weight of authority make no impression on his opinions, which retire like a feather, or rise from the encounter unhurt through their own buoyancy. He is clogged by no dull system of realities, no earth-bound feelings, no rooted prejudices, by nothing that belongs to the mighty trunk and hard husk of nature and habit, but is drawn up by irresistible levity to the regions of mere speculation and fancy, to the sphere of air and fire, where his delighted spirit floats in "seas of pearl and clouds of amber." There is no *caput mortuum* of worn-out, threadbare experience to serve as ballast to his mind; it is all volatile intellectual salt of tartar, that refuses to combine its evanescent, inflammable essence with anything solid or anything lasting. Bubbles are to him the only realities:—touch them, and they vanish.'

An extension of this same line of thought is Carlyle's judgement, though it must be borne in mind that Carlyle was not strictly a contemporary, and had never met Shelley: 'There is something void, and Hades-like in the whole inner world of him; his universe is all vacant azure, hung with a few frosty mournful if beautiful stars; the very voice of him (his style, etc.) shrill, shrieky . . . as if a ghost were trying to "sing to us".'

Well, there, out of a great mass of testimony (for Shelley's astonishing personality had the effect of making most of those who came in contact with him set down their impressions on paper), we have the extremes of the case for and against; from which, I think, one inference at least may reasonably be drawn. This is, that to such as knew him intimately and had experienced his spell, Shelley as a man was quite irresistible, creating the impression both of great sensibility and goodness, and of overwhelming genius; whereas, on the other hand, to those who knew him only slightly, or only through his works, there was a certain quality of intangibility and unreality about him that was almost, if not quite, repellent. It is important that we, who can only know him through his works, should realize this and make due adjustment. It is for this reason that such a book as Trelawny's *Records of Shelley, Byron and the Author*, inaccurate and downright mendacious as it no doubt often is, is yet invaluable in assisting us to see in something like true perspective the figure of the author of *Adonais*, who, whatever manner of man he was, beyond peradventure resembled not at all the dripping, weed-girt, school-girl's dream of the effigy at Christchurch.

To turn to the other source of evidence: the poems. It is not easy at this time of the day to say anything new about the works of Shelley. There they are, his best poems, unchanged by time, serene, pure, permanent; poems which in their sparkling, icy, unearthly, ethereal quality are quite without parallel in the work of any other English writer, even if one may trace some vestiges of their peculiar splendours in two at least of his predecessors, Crashaw and Collins, and may name for him one reasonably legitimate successor in Francis Thompson. One rather feels about these poems that, had any trace remained of the songs which the morning stars sang together, or any least echo of the shouts of joy which on the same occasion proceeded from all the Sons of God, then these most melodious utterances might well have been like the poems of Shelley. Or again, his music is that of the 'thousand twangling instruments' which made sweet the enchanted air of Prospero's island. What, after all, is his secret? Though very great, his work is not quite of the greatest: it is magical, while the greatest is miraculous. The essence of the magical kind of poetry is incantation; the essence of the miraculous is evocation. The poet who specializes in magic casts a spell, presenting to his readers a strange and rare concatenation of ideas that engenders in their imaginations concepts such as, save for his invocation, would not have visited them. He superimposes, as it were, upon the minds of others, fantasies which are the exclusive property of his own individual vision. He is, in fact, precisely what is termed in the vernacular a spell-binder. But the poet who evokes, who deals in the miracle, works otherwise: as Browning so admirably puts it in *Abt Vogler*, 'Out of three sounds he frames, not a fourth sound, but a star.' How so? Nobody knows, save that it comes as a rule through some quite simple and purely concrete image drawn from actuality, which strikes a note that wakens to gigantic life a dormant, responsive chord in the reader's own imagination. Such lines as 'The great Vision of the guarded mount,' or 'And visited all night by troops of stars,' or 'Bright *shootes* of everlasting-nesse,' or even 'Erle Douglas on his milke-white steede' (happily they are not few in English poetry), are miracles of the highest order because they represent the known and the familiar transmuted by some lucky art or chance into the semblance of eternity.

With Shelley this faculty, though not entirely absent, is largely so; and the reason for its absence is singularly interest-ing. He lacked the concrete and the common touch because, we believe, his vision of existence was one totally different from that of the ordinary man, in so far as the phrase 'the ordinary man' can be said to apply, as we think it can without an undue wrenching of the sense of the words, to such poets as Wordsworth or Milton. Shelley's vision of life was pre-dominantly a bookish vision, a student's vision; it was that of a young man who was a great classical scholar and who had been thoroughly impregnated with the beauty and the strange-ness of the Greek view of life. It was also, and at the same time, on occasions the bookish vision of the man who had read widely and with evident relish in the 'Gothick' romances of his own day, in Mrs. Radcliffe's *Mysteries of Udolpho*, and Lewis's *Monk*, and Godwin's *St. Leon*, and who had himself, at an exceedingly early age, produced the two similar and unmemorable romances of *Zastrozzi* and *St. Irvyne; or, The Rosicrucian*. It is because of this that when, as will happen to the best of writers, his inspiration flagged, the true poetical and Attic splendours of his imagination were often succeeded by patches of imagery and mere fantasy which, to a present-day eye and ear, must seem simply stagey, unreal and melo-dramatic—rather like the transformation-scene at a really first-class pantomime. This is a blemish, but it is a blemish that may be easily borne when one reflects upon the many pages of the true gold that stand to his account. A poet does not need to write many *Hymns of Pan* or *Odes to the West Wind* to be assured of his immortality.

A few lines back we made use of the word 'imagery'; it

is an important one in the consideration of Shelley's poetry.
No English poet has ever been so addicted to this device, and
none has used it more splendidly. Yet what precisely does it
mean? The dictionary definition of the word is 'forms of
fancy'; and it is Fancy in the sense in which Coleridge uses
it, as the antithesis of Imagination. Opening a Shelley quite
at random, the first passage upon which my eye falls is the
following from *Prometheus Unbound*:

> 'My soul is an enchanted boat,
> Which, like a sleeping swan, doth float
> Upon the silver waves of thy sweet singing;
> And thine doth like an angel sit
> Beside a helm conducting it,
> Whilst all the winds with melody are ringing.'

It is beautiful; it lulls one, as Swinburne's meaningless cadences
lull one; so that one does not inquire overmuch whether it
means anything or nothing. Indeed, it may be said by all
except the hypercritical that it does not matter whether it
means anything or not, since beauty in sound is an end all-
sufficing in itself. Yet here is a tune of another kind:

> 'Therefore all seasons shall be sweet to thee,
> Whether the summer clothe the general earth
> With greenness, or the redbreast sit and sing
> Betwixt the tufts of snow on the bare branch
> Of mossy apple-tree, while the nigh thatch
> Smokes in the sun-thaw.'

That, which is from Coleridge's *Frost at Midnight*, is observed,
not 'made-up,' and therefore truly imaginative and evocative
verse. According to the Platonic doctrine, all knowledge is
merely recollection, and the scene which these lines conjure
up, being true to general and normal experience, is therefore
one in which, without his being aware of it, the reader's
imagination is given permanent and genuine material to feed
on. 'Men must be taught as if you taught them not, and things
unknown propos'd as things forgot.'

That Shelley should so often have fallen back upon the day-dreaming 'making-up' of fancy is, of course, largely attributable to the childlike quality that lived on in him so much longer than it does in most poets, since it is predominantly the child that sees things not so much as they are as in the semblance of some other thing that they are not, but which they resemble; in short, in the terms of myth or legend. Together with, and linked to, this fondness of his for imagery is also a very strong liking for personification (a device much favoured also by Collins), that is in itself a further proof, if one were needed, that he still adhered to the child's way of seeing things. One might, indeed, say that just as such a poet as Wordsworth rendered his concrete experiences of Nature doubly concrete by the fashion in which he kept them rigorously separated from his excursions into the abstract, so, in total contrast, Shelley succeeded in turning the concrete realities of Nature into something more insubstantial and evanescent than any poet has ever done, while at the same time presenting, as solid and tangible entities, each and every abstraction upon which his fancy lighted.

Very largely, no doubt, this mythopœic quality in Shelley derived from his deep knowledge of and admiration for the Greeks. Of all English poets it is he who stands most indebted to Homer and Sophocles and Æschylus, and it would indeed almost be true to say that, in this age when the study of the classics is at its ebb, the man who has no Greek cannot well hope to get nearer to the true essence of the Greek spirit than by way of the English poetry of Shelley. And as well as Greece there was, in the later years, Italy, of which Landor has written so truly:

> 'He who beholds the skies of Italy
> Sees ancient Rome reflected, sees beyond,
> Into more glorious Hellas, nurse of Gods
> And godlike men: dwarfs people other lands.'

Thus far these notes may seem to have inclined a little to the critical, in that they have touched somewhat upon the things that Shelley as a poet is *not*. Better now to stress the things that he is. He is, then, perhaps of all English poets the one whose rhythms most nearly approach to the condition of music, whose imagery most closely approximates to the pure outlines of sculpture. A poem of Shelley resembles the figures on that Grecian Urn of which his contemporary Keats wrote:

'Fair youth, beneath the trees, thou canst not leave
    Thy song, nor ever can those trees be bare.'

His figures are static, caught for ever in beautiful and unforgettable poses; in him it is Nature alone that moves: the clouds speed across the heavens, the thunder rolls, the torrents roar, while leaping lightning unseams the icy sky. But all this is remote, unfamiliar, afar; a sort of Salvator Rosa landscape. His pictures of Nature, beautiful as they are, are different from any Nature that we know, are spiritualized, refined, ideal. Shelley is completely the intellectual as poet. It is this which makes all the more poignant the comparatively few occasions upon which the singing-robe slips for a moment aside, and we see the man himself, not fainting, panting, expiring as he was so prone to do upon the set occasion, but really moved, really human. There is an instance of this in those most touching of all his lines, those written to Fanny Godwin after he had learnt of her self-destruction by poison at the Mackworth Arms in Swansea: *Her voice did quiver as we parted.* There is another, as it seems to me, in his little poem, *The Aziola*, in which there is a purity and a sincerity of feeling that is worth a whole waggon-load of the more obvious, and obviously histrionic, sufferings.

Shelley was histrionic because he was young, because he had really suffered deeply, and because he was a childlike genius and had all the child's exasperating, though reasonable, quality of crying out loudly and helplessly when it is hurt. In his poetry these qualities are distinctly noticeable. In his life it was quite otherwise. As Mr. Edmund Blunden has made very clear in his recent most penetrating study, Shelley, in himself, was a most charming and considerate, virile and far from incapable person. Leigh Hunt gives much the same account of him. He was, as a friend, intensely generous and thoughtful, and in no instance does he show as a man to better advantage than in his warm appreciation of Peacock's very amusing caricature of himself as Scythrop Glowry in *Nightmare Abbey*— a caricature which, in its sly way, contains a very considerable measure of the truth. As for his so much discussed relations with women, they were as they were, because his disposition was as it was. He was congenitally incapable of meeting a woman who attracted him without at once conferring upon her every virtue, both human and divine; and this, far from its being to his discredit, was really only the outward and visible sign of a noble (if slightly unworldly) generosity, which insisted on an absolute perfection in all to whom he was in any way attached. 'I think,' he once wrote, 'one is always in love with something or other; the error, and I confess it is not easy for spirits cased in flesh and blood to avoid it, consists in seeking in a mortal image the likeness of what is perhaps eternal.' Well, it is *not* easy; certainly was not so for Shelley.

In any assessment of his work and personality, it cannot too much be stressed that Shelley died young—he was still under thirty when the waters of the Mediterranean claimed him— and that a great deal of the work by which he is now best known was not issued by him in his lifetime, but was post-humously published by his wife. This means that a consider-able quantity of the poetry which is now for ever associated with his name is poetry which, if he had lived, he would not necessarily have published at all. The point is minor, though not without some interest. Similarly, there has been from time to time a marked tendency on the part of politically-minded persons to take Shelley's youthful and generous revolutionary fervour with extreme seriousness, and to elevate him to the status of a sort of Marxian Messiah. Because men are endlessly the captives of their own doctrines, it is natural that a genius so many-faceted as Shelley should seem to his various critics to exhibit so many, and such disparate, images; for they see in him only the qualities that reflect back what is in their own minds. So he has been claimed as the principal apostle of their creed by anarchists, republicans, vegetarians, atheists, æsthetes, free-lovers, by every sort and species of the intellectual Christopher Robins of this our time, and of other times. All of which may be very true; and without significance; for poets, as a rule, do best to steer a wide course of politics. Liberty is a great matter; and tyranny is a very bad thing; but the reiteration of either the one or the other of these eternal verities does not necessarily make for the best and most enduring verse. The ideas of men, like the men themselves, like 'Ozymandias, king of kings,' wear out in their good time and perish. Poetry is otherwise. The process of art is a miracle. No man knows how the thing is done, but every man knows when it is done. *Non omnis moriar*. And it is because Shelley, the poet, had this secret that his best work is as fresh and as strange to us to-day as upon the day of its creation.

So much for the immortal part of the man, which is our heritage. For the sake of completeness, for the adventitious interest inherent in them, and for the very real light which they sometimes throw upon the poems, it may be as well now briefly to recapitulate the facts of his life, even though they are, as we have stressed earlier, facts lamentably so much better known to most of us than are the really essential aspects of him to which his works bear witness.

Percy Bysshe Shelley, then, was born, the son of a baronet, at Field Place, Warnham, near Horsham in Sussex, on August 4, 1792. He was educated at Eton, and made the grievous mistake of proceeding thence to Oxford, that university which, as Augustine Birrell has pointed out in a devastating essay, is so very far from congenial to the poets of England. Oxford promptly sent him down for publishing at the tender age of nineteen a pamphlet with that most uncompromising of titles, *The Necessity of Atheism*; a move which Shelley at once countered by taking to himself a wife, the charming and pathetic Harriet Westbrook, then aged just sixteen. For the next three years they roamed the countryside, living chiefly at beauty-spots in Wales, the Lake District and Devonshire, though paying also a visit to Dublin where, from his balcony in Sackville Street, Shelley showered upon the passers-by his

pamphlet, *An Address to the Irish People*, now a great biblio-
philist's rarity, which besought the natives to cast off, as they
have always exhibited so apt a propensity for doing, the yoke
of tyranny. By this time Shelley had imbibed a full measure
of the exciting revolutionary doctrines of William Godwin, the
author of *Political Justice*, and was writing in *Queen Mab* a kind
of poetical version of the same, that came out in 1813. In the
following year, leaving his wife with two small children, he
eloped with Mary, the daughter of Godwin and Mary
Wollstonecraft, and went to Switzerland. Two years later,
in 1816, poor Harriet drowned herself, probably in the
Serpentine in Hyde Park, and Shelley married Mary Godwin
at the church of St. Mildred, Bread Street (now destroyed by
German bombers). In that same year, he had published
*Alastor*; and one year later came *The Revolt of Islam*. In
1818, he and his wife left England for ever and went to Italy,
living in Rome, Venice, Pisa and other places. Here they
resumed the threads of their friendship with Byron, whom
they had first met at Geneva in 1816. Almost the whole of
Shelley's finest work was composed under the congenial skies
of Italy, where, in just over four years, he completed *Prometheus
Unbound*, *The Cenci*, *Epipsychidion*, *Adonais* and *Hellas*, as well as
the majority of his best-known lyrics: truly a stupendous
achievement. Then on July 8, 1822, Shelley set out with his
friend, Edward Williams (the husband of the Jane of the later
poems), to sail his cockleshell of a boat, the *Don Juan*, from
Leghorn to Lerici. The weather was treacherous; his friends
anxiously watched the progress of the vessel till it was some
ten miles out to sea, off Via Reggio; then saw it vanish into
the mist. What happened in that mist no one will ever know:
whether the *Don Juan* capsized in the storm, or was run down
by accident by an Italian ship, or was run down by design by
pirates—as there is some evidence that it may have been
—for the sake of the money that was on board. What is certain
is that the bodies of Shelley, Williams, and their sailor
boy, Charles Vivian, were washed ashore about a fortnight
later, and were burnt on the beach at Via Reggio in the
presence of Byron, Leigh Hunt and Trelawny. In one pocket

of Shelley's jacket was found a small edition of Sophocles[1], in another the last volume of Keats's poems 'doubled back, as if the reader, in the act of reading, had hastily thrust it away'; his face, we are told, had been quite eaten by the fishes. Few events in literary history are more fully or movingly recorded than the burning of Shelley's body, in the accounts given in Hunt's *Autobiography* and Trelawny's *Record*. Later, Shelley's ashes were buried in the Protestant cemetery at Rome, close to the grave of Keats where he lies 'under the pyramid which is the tomb of Cestius.'

For many years after her husband's death, Mary Shelley collected all such scraps of his writings as could be found, and published them: a pious process that has continued almost until this present day, whether to the augmentation of Shelley's reputation, or otherwise, it is difficult to determine. Certainly, there are few major poets whose collected works contain so much that is fragmentary, in some cases even single lines having been carefully preserved.

Because of this somewhat piecemeal appearance of the Collected Works, it is at least arguable that the real stature of Shelley may better be revealed by a selection, such as the present volume. In making this selection I have been guided by one leading principle: that no poem should be mutilated. If a poem is included here, it is included in full, save for a very few exceptions where I have thought that a poem, in any case unfinished, would read more completely as a whole by the excision of the obviously unfinished portion. The only time I have departed from this rule is where certain sections of *Peter Bell the Third* have been included, more for the interest of their matter than for their actual poetic merit. Because of this solicitude not to wrench fine passages out of their proper context (an activity to which previous selectors, particularly in the case of *Hellas*, have been unduly prone), I have been obliged, for considerations of space, to omit altogether *The Revolt of Islam* and *Rosalind and Helen*. Both these poems contain fine lines and fine passages; which must be sought elsewhere

[1]This book may now be seen in the Bodleian Library. The volume of Keats was burnt with Shelley's body.

by those who wish to find them. But apart from these two long poems, I do not think that anything of really first quality written in verse by Shelley is absent from this book. Nothing of his prose, which is often very noble, has been included, however, and all lovers of his poetry are warmly recommended to turn, at least at some time, to his great *Defence of Poetry*, which explains and justifies better than any other writer can hope to do his practice of the craft. Nowhere else in his writings are the truly Titanic qualities of his intellect so well displayed as in this essay, of which it is a pleasure to transcribe here a few flawless lines:

'Poetry (he writes) redeems from decay the visitations of the divinity in man. Poetry turns all things to loveliness; it exalts the beauty of that which is most beautiful, and it adds beauty to that which is most deformed; it marries exultation and horror, grief and pleasure, eternity and change; it subdues to union, under its light yoke, all irreconcilable things. It transmutes all that it touches, and every form moving within the radiance of its presence is changed by wondrous sympathy to an incarnation of the spirit which it breathes: its secret alchemy turns to potable gold the poisonous waters which flow from death through life.'

And so, at the end, he comes to that last often-quoted, never to be too-much-quoted, triumphant valediction and vindication of himself and of his life's work:

'Poets are the hierophants of an unapprehended inspiration; the mirrors of the gigantic shadows which futurity casts upon the present; the words which express what they understand not; the trumpets which sing to battle and feel not what they inspire; the influence which is moved not, but moves. Poets are the unacknowledged legislators of the world.'

MORCHARD BISHOP

# CONTENTS

## Poems written in 1821.

TRANSLATIONS.

ILLUSTRATIONS

# ILLUSTRATIONS

Acknowledgments are due to *Picture Post* Library for permission
to reproduce the illustrations facing pages 67, 163, 259, 419.

# DEDICATION TO QUEEN MAB

## TO HARRIET * * * * *

WHOSE is the love that gleaming through the world,
Wards off the poisonous arrow of its scorn?
   Whose is the warm and partial praise,
   Virtue's most sweet reward?

Beneath whose looks did my reviving soul          5
Riper in truth and virtuous daring grow?
   Whose eyes have I gazed fondly on,
   And loved mankind the more?

HARRIET! on thine:—thou wert my purer mind;
Thou wert the inspiration of my song;          10
   Thine are these early wilding flowers,
   Though garlanded by me.

Then press into thy breast this pledge of love;
And know, though time may change and years may roll,
   Each floweret gathered in my heart        15
   It consecrates to thine.

# THE DÆMON OF THE WORLD

## A FRAGMENT

### PART I

Nec tantum prodere vati,
Quantum scire licet.  Venit aetas omnis in unam
Congeriem, miserumque premunt tot saecula pectus.

LUCAN, *Phars.* v. 176.

How wonderful is Death,
Death and his brother Sleep!
One pale as yonder wan and hornèd moon,
With lips of lurid blue,
The other glowing like the vital morn,          5
When throned on ocean's wave
It breathes over the world:
Yet both so passing strange and wonderful!

Hath then the iron-sceptred Skeleton,
Whose reign is in the tainted sepulchres,          10
To the hell dogs that couch beneath his throne
Cast that fair prey?  Must that divinest form,
Which love and admiration cannot view
Without a beating heart, whose azure veins
Steal like dark streams along a field of snow,          15
Whose outline is as fair as marble clothed
In light of some sublimest mind, decay?
Nor putrefaction's breath
Leave aught of this pure spectacle
But loathsomeness and ruin?—          20
Spare aught but a dark theme,
On which the lightest heart might moralize?

Or is it but that downy-wingèd slumbers
Have charmed their nurse coy Silence near her lids
    To watch their own repose?           25
    Will they, when morning's beam
    Flows through those wells of light,
Seek far from noise and day some western cave,
Where woods and streams with soft and pausing winds
    A lulling murmur weave?—          30
    Ianthe doth not sleep
    The dreamless sleep of death:
Nor in her moonlight chamber silently
Doth Henry hear her regular pulses throb,
    Or mark her delicate cheek          35
With interchange of hues mock the broad moon,
    Outwatching weary night,
    Without assured reward.
    Her dewy eyes are closed;
On their translucent lids, whose texture fine    40
Scarce hides the dark blue orbs that burn below
    With unapparent fire,
    The baby Sleep is pillowed:
    Her golden tresses shade
    The bosom's stainless pride,          45
Twining like tendrils of the parasite
    Around a marble column.

    Hark! whence that rushing sound?
    'Tis like a wondrous strain that sweeps
    Around a lonely ruin          50
When west winds sigh and evening waves respond
    In whispers from the shore:
'Tis wilder than the unmeasured notes
Which from the unseen lyres of dells and groves
    The genii of the breezes sweep.          55
Floating on waves of music and of light,
The chariot of the Dæmon of the World
    Descends in silent power:
Its shape reposed within: slight as some cloud

B

That catches but the palest tinge of day          60
   When evening yields to night,
Bright as that fibrous woof when stars indue
   Its transitory robe.
Four shapeless shadows bright and beautiful
Draw that strange car of glory, reins of light          65
Check their unearthly speed: they stop and fold
   Their wings of braided air:
The Dæmon leaning from the ethereal car
   Gazed on the slumbering maid.
Human eye hath ne'er beheld          70
A shape so wild, so bright, so beautiful,
As that which o'er the maiden's charmèd sleep
   Waving a starry wand,
   Hung like a mist of light.
Such sounds as breathed around like odorous winds          75
   Of wakening spring arose,
Filling the chamber and the moonlight sky.
Maiden, the world's supremest spirit
   Beneath the shadow of her wings
Folds all thy memory doth inherit          80
   From ruin of divinest things,
     Feelings that lure thee to betray,
     And light of thoughts that pass away.


For thou has earned a mighty boon,
   The truths which wisest poets see          85
Dimly, thy mind may make its own,
   Rewarding its own majesty,
     Entranced in some diviner mood
     Of self-oblivious solitude.


Custom, and Faith, and Power thou spurnest;          90
   From hate and awe thy heart is free;
Ardent and pure as day thou burnest,
   For dark and cold mortality
     A living light, to cheer it long,
     The watch-fires of the world among.          95

Therefore from nature's inner shrine,
  Where gods and fiends in worship bend,
Majestic spirit, be it thine
    The flame to seize, the veil to rend,
      Where the vast snake Eternity           100
      In charmèd sleep doth ever lie.

All that inspires thy voice of love,
  Or speaks in thy unclosing eyes,
Or through thy frame doth burn or move,
    Or think or feel, awake, arise!           105
      Spirit, leave for mine and me
      Earth's unsubstantial mimicry!

It ceased, and from the mute and moveless frame
  A radiant spirit arose,
All beautiful in naked purity.                 110
Robed in its human hues it did ascend,
Disparting as it went the silver clouds,
It moved towards the car, and took its seat
    Beside the Dæmon shape.

Obedient to the sweep of aëry song,           115
  The mighty ministers
Unfurled their prismy wings.
  The magic car moved on;
The night was fair, innumerable stars
    Studded heaven's dark blue vault;          120
    The eastern wave grew pale
    With the first smile of morn.
    The magic car moved on.
    From the swift sweep of wings
The atmosphere in flaming sparkles flew;       125
    And where the burning wheels
Eddied above the mountain's loftiest peak
    Was traced a line of lightning.
Now far above a rock the utmost verge
    Of the wide earth it flew,                  130

The rival of the Andes, whose dark brow
    Frowned o'er the silver sea.

Far, far below the chariot's stormy path,
    Calm as a slumbering babe,
    Tremendous ocean lay.          135
Its broad and silent mirror gave to view
    The pale and waning stars,
    The chariot's fiery track,
    And the gray light of morn
    Tingeing those fleecy clouds    140
That cradled in their folds the infant dawn.
    The chariot seemed to fly
Through the abyss of an immense concave,
Radiant with million constellations, tinged
    With shades of infinite colour,    145
    And semicircled with a belt
    Flashing incessant meteors.

As they approached their goal,
The wingèd shadows seemed to gather speed.
The sea no longer was distinguished; earth    150
Appeared a vast and shadowy sphere, suspended
    In the black concave of heaven
    With the sun's cloudless orb,
    Whose rays of rapid light
Parted around the chariot's swifter course,    155
And fell like ocean's feathery spray
    Dashed from the boiling surge
    Before a vessel's prow.

    The magic car moved on.
    Earth's distant orb appeared    160
The smallest light that twinkles in the heavens,
    Whilst round the chariot's way
Innumerable systems widely rolled,
    And countless spheres diffused
    An ever varying glory.    165

It was a sight of wonder! Some were horned,
And like the moon's argentine crescent hung
In the dark dome of heaven; some did shed
A clear mild beam like Hesperus, while the sea
Yet glows with fading sunlight; others dashed      170
Athwart the night with trains of bickering fire,
Like spherèd worlds to death and ruin driven;
Some shone like stars, and as the chariot passed
    Bedimmed all other light.


    Spirit of Nature! here      175
In this interminable wilderness
Of worlds, at whose involved immensity
    Even soaring fancy staggers,
    Here is thy fitting temple.
    Yet not the lightest leaf      180
That quivers to the passing breeze
    Is less instinct with thee,—
    Yet not the meanest worm,
That lurks in graves and fattens on the dead,
    Less shares thy eternal breath.      185
    Spirit of Nature! thou
Imperishable as this glorious scene,
    Here is thy fitting temple.


If solitude hath ever led thy steps
To the shore of the immeasurable sea,      190
    And thou hast lingered there
    Until the sun's broad orb
Seemed resting on the fiery line of ocean,
Thou must have marked the braided webs of gold
    That without motion hang      195
    Over the sinking sphere:
Thou must have marked the billowy mountain clouds,
Edged with intolerable radiancy,
    Towering like rocks of jet
    Above the burning deep:      200

And yet there is a moment
When the sun's highest point
Peers like a star o'er ocean's western edge,
When those far clouds of feathery purple gleam
Like fairy lands girt by some heavenly sea:               205
Then has thy rapt imagination soared
Where in the midst of all existing things
The temple of the mightiest Dæmon stands.


Yet not the golden islands
That gleam amid yon flood of purple light,               210
Nor the feathery curtains
That canopy the sun's resplendent couch,
Nor the burnished ocean waves
Paving that gorgeous dome,
So fair, so wonderful a sight                            215
As the eternal temple could afford.
The elements of all that human thought
Can frame of lovely or sublime, did join
To rear the fabric of the fane, nor aught
Of earth may image forth its majesty.                   220
Yet likest evening's vault that faëry hall,
As heaven low resting on the wave it spread
Its floors of flashing light,
Its vast and azure dome;
And on the verge of that obscure abyss                  225
Where crystal battlements o'erhang the gulf
Of the dark world, ten thousand spheres diffuse
Their lustre through its adamantine gates.


The magic car no longer moved;
The Dæmon and the Spirit                                 230
Entered the eternal gates.
Those clouds of aëry gold
That slept in glittering billows
Beneath the azure canopy,
With the ethereal footsteps trembled not;               235

While slight and odorous mists
Floated to strains of thrilling melody
Through the vast columns and the pearly shrines.


The Dæmon and the Spirit
Approached the overhanging battlement.                    240
Below lay stretched the boundless universe!
     There, far as the remotest line
That limits swift imagination's flight,
Unending orbs mingled in mazy motion,
     Immutably fulfilling                                  245
     Eternal Nature's law.
     Above, below, around,
     The circling systems formed
     A wilderness of harmony,
     Each with undeviating aim                             250
In eloquent silence through the depths of space
     Pursued its wondrous way.—


Awhile the Spirit paused in ecstasy.
Yet soon she saw, as the vast spheres swept by,
Strange things within their belted orbs appear.           255
Like animated frenzies, dimly moved
Shadows, and skeletons, and fiendly shapes,
Thronging round human graves, and o'er the dead
Sculpturing records for each memory
In verse, such as malignant gods pronounce,               260
Blasting the hopes of men, when heaven and hell
Confounded burst in ruin o'er the world:
And they did build vast trophies, instruments
Of murder, human bones, barbaric gold,
Skins torn from living men, and towers of skulls          265
With sightless holes gazing on blinder heaven,
Mitres, and crowns, and brazen chariots stained
With blood, and scrolls of mystic wickedness,
The sanguine codes of venerable crime.
The likeness of a thronèd king came by,                   270

When these had passed, bearing upon his brow
A threefold crown; his countenance was calm,
His eye severe and cold; but his right hand
Was charged with bloody coin, and he did gnaw
By fits, with secret smiles, a human heart          275
Concealed beneath his robe; and motley shapes,
A multitudinous throng, around him knelt,
With bosoms bare, and bowed heads, and false looks
Of true submission, as the sphere rolled by.
Brooking no eye to witness their foul shame,          280
Which human hearts must feel, while human tongues
Tremble to speak, they did rage horribly,
Breathing in self-contempt fierce blasphemies
Against the Dæmon of the World, and high
Hurling their armèd hands where the pure Spirit,          285
Serene and inaccessibly secure,
Stood on an isolated pinnacle,
The flood of ages combating below,
The depth of the unbounded universe
Above, and all around          290
Necessity's unchanging harmony.

# ALASTOR; OR,
# THE SPIRIT OF SOLITUDE

## PREFACE

THE poem entitled *Alastor* may be considered as allegorical
of one of the most interesting situations of the human mind.
It represents a youth of uncorrupted feelings and adventurous
genius led forth by an imagination inflamed and purified
through familiarity with all that is excellent and majestic, to
the contemplation of the universe. He drinks deep of the
fountains of knowledge, and is still insatiate. The magnificence

and beauty of the external world sinks profoundly into the frame of his conceptions, and affords to their modifications a variety not to be exhausted. So long as it is possible for his desires to point towards objects thus infinite and unmeasured, he is joyous, and tranquil, and self-possessed. But the period arrives when these objects cease to suffice. His mind is at length suddenly awakened and thirsts for intercourse with an intelligence similar to itself. He images to himself the Being whom he loves. Conversant with speculations of the sublimest and most perfect natures, the vision in which he embodies his own imaginations unites all of wonderful, or wise, or beautiful, which the poet, the philosopher, or the lover could depicture. The intellectual faculties, the imagination, the functions of sense, have their respective requisitions on the sympathy of corresponding powers in other human beings. The Poet is represented as uniting these requisitions, and attaching them to a single image. He seeks in vain for a prototype of his conception. Blasted by his disappointment, he descends to an untimely grave.

The picture is not barren of instruction to actual men. The Poet's self-centred seclusion was avenged by the furies of an irresistible passion pursuing him to speedy ruin. But that Power which strikes the luminaries of the world with sudden darkness and extinction, by awakening them to too exquisite a perception of its influences, dooms to a slow and poisonous decay those meaner spirits that dare to abjure its dominion. Their destiny is more abject and inglorious as their delinquency is more contemptible and pernicious. They who, deluded by no generous error, instigated by no sacred thirst of doubtful knowledge, duped by no illustrious superstition, loving nothing on this earth, and cherishing no hopes beyond, yet keep aloof from sympathies with their kind, rejoicing neither in human joy nor mourning with human grief; these, and such as they, have their apportioned curse. They languish, because none feel with them their common nature. They are morally dead. They are neither friends, nor lovers, nor fathers, nor citizens of the world, nor benefactors of their country. Among those who attempt to exist without human sympathy, the pure and tender-hearted perish through the intensity and passion of their search after its communities, when the vacancy of their spirit suddenly makes itself felt. All else, selfish, blind, and torpid, are those unforeseeing multitudes who constitute, together with their own, the lasting misery and loneliness of the world. Those who love not their fellow-beings live unfruitful lives, and prepare for their old age a miserable grave.

> 'The good die first,
> And those whose hearts are dry as summer dust,
> Burn to the socket!'

*December* 14, 1815.

———————

*Nondum amabam, et amare amabam, quaerebam quid amarem, amans amare.—Confess. St. August.*

EARTH, ocean, air, belovèd brotherhood!
If our great Mother has imbued my soul
With aught of natural piety to feel
Your love, and recompense the boon with mine;
If dewy morn, and odorous noon, and even,                5
With sunset and its gorgeous ministers,
And solemn midnight's tingling silentness;
If autumn's hollow sighs in the sere wood,
And winter robing with pure snow and crowns
Of starry ice the gray grass and bare boughs;            10
If spring's voluptuous pantings when she breathes
Her first sweet kisses, have been dear to me;
If no bright bird, insect, or gentle beast
I consciously have injured, but still loved
And cherished these my kindred; then forgive            15
This boast, belovèd brethren, and withdraw
No portion of your wonted favour now!

Mother of this unfathomable world!
Favour my solemn song, for I have loved
Thee ever, and thee only; I have watched          20
Thy shadow, and the darkness of thy steps,
And my heart ever gazes on the depth
Of thy deep mysteries. I have made my bed
In charnels and on coffins, where black death
Keeps record of the trophies won from thee,        25
Hoping to still these obstinate questionings
Of thee and thine, by forcing some lone ghost
Thy messenger, to render up the tale
Of what we are. In lone and silent hours,
When night makes a weird sound of its own stillness, 30
Like an inspired and desperate alchymist
Staking his very life on some dark hope,
Have I mixed awful talk and asking looks
With my most innocent love, until strange tears
Uniting with those breathless kisses, made          35
Such magic as compels the charmèd night
To render up thy charge: . . . and, though ne'er yet
Thou hast unveiled thy inmost sanctuary,
Enough from incommunicable dream,
And twilight phantasms, and deep noon-day thought, 40
Has shone within me, that serenely now
And moveless, as a long-forgotten lyre
Suspended in the solitary dome
Of some mysterious and deserted fane,
I wait thy breath, Great Parent, that my strain     45
May modulate with murmurs of the air,
And motions of the forests and the sea,
And voice of living beings, and woven hymns
Of night and day, and the deep heart of man.

There was a Poet whose untimely tomb                50
No human hands with pious reverence reared,
But the charmed eddies of autumnal winds
Built o'er his mouldering bones a pyramid
Of mouldering leaves in the waste wilderness:—

A lovely youth,—no mourning maiden decked        55
With weeping flowers, or votive cypress wreath,
The lone couch of his everlasting sleep:—
Gentle, and brave, and generous,—no lorn bard
Breathed o'er his dark fate one melodious sigh:
He lived, he died, he sung, in solitude.        60
Strangers have wept to hear his passionate notes,
And virgins, as unknown he passed, have pined
And wasted for fond love of his wild eyes.
The fire of those soft orbs has ceased to burn,
And Silence, too enamoured of that voice,        65
Locks its mute music in her rugged cell.

    By solemn vision, and bright silver dream,
His infancy was nurtured. Every sight
And sound from the vast earth and ambient air,
Sent to his heart its choicest impulses.        70
The fountains of divine philosophy
Fled not his thirsting lips, and all of great,
Or good, or lovely, which the sacred past
In truth or fable consecrates, he felt
And knew. When early youth had passed, he left        75
His cold fireside and alienated home
To seek strange truths in undiscovered lands.
Many a wide waste and tangled wilderness
Has lured his fearless steps; and he has bought
With his sweet voice and eyes, from savage men,        80
His rest and food. Nature's most secret steps
He like her shadow has pursued, where'er
The red volcano overcanopies
Its fields of snow and pinnacles of ice
With burning smoke, or where bitumen lakes        85
On black bare pointed islets ever beat
With sluggish surge, or where the secret caves
Rugged and dark, winding among the springs
Of fire and poison, inaccessible
To avarice or pride, their starry domes        90
Of diamond and of gold expand above

Numberless and immeasurable halls,
Frequent with crystal column, and clear shrines
Of pearl, and thrones radiant with chrysolite.
Nor had that scene of ampler majesty          95
Than gems or gold, the varying roof of heaven
And the green earth lost in his heart its claims
To love and wonder; he would linger long
In lonesome vales, making the wild his home,
Until the doves and squirrels would partake    100
From his innocuous hand his bloodless food,
Lured by the gentle meaning of his looks,
And the wild antelope, that starts whene'er
The dry leaf rustles in the brake, suspend
Her timid steps to gaze upon a form           105
More graceful than her own.
                              His wandering step
Obedient to high thoughts, has visited
The awful ruins of the days of old:
Athens, and Tyre, and Balbec, and the waste
Where stood Jerusalem, the fallen towers      110
Of Babylon, the eternal pyramids,
Memphis and Thebes, and whatsoe'er of strange
Sculptured on alabaster obelisk,
Or jasper tomb, or mutilated sphynx,
Dark Æthiopia in her desert hills             115
Conceals. Among the ruined temples there,
Stupendous columns, and wild images
Of more than man, where marble daemons watch
The Zodiac's brazen mystery, and dead men
Hang their mute thoughts on the mute walls around,  120
He lingered, poring on memorials
Of the world's youth, through the long burning day
Gazed on those speechless shapes, nor, when the moon
Filled the mysterious halls with floating shades
Suspended he that task, but ever gazed        125
And gazed, till meaning on his vacant mind
Flashed like strong inspiration, and he saw
The thrilling secrets of the birth of time.

Meanwhile an Arab maiden brought his food,
Her daily portion, from her father's tent,                    130
And spread her matting for his couch, and stole
From duties and repose to tend his steps:—
Enamoured, yet not daring for deep awe
To speak her love:—and watched his nightly sleep,
Sleepless herself, to gaze upon his lips                      135
Parted in slumber, whence the regular breath
Of innocent dreams arose: then, when red morn
Made paler the pale moon, to her cold home
Wildered, and wan, and panting, she returned.

The Poet wandering on, through Arabie                         140
And Persia, and the wild Carmanian waste,
And o'er the aërial mountains which pour down
Indus and Oxus from their icy caves,
In joy and exultation held his way;
Till in the vale of Cashmire, far within                      145
Its loneliest dell, where odorous plants entwine
Beneath the hollow rocks a natural bower,
Beside a sparkling rivulet he stretched
His languid limbs. A vision on his sleep
There came, a dream of hopes that never yet                   150
Had flushed his cheek. He dreamed a veilèd maid
Sate near him, talking in low solemn tones.
Her voice was like the voice of his own soul
Heard in the calm of thought; its music long,
Like woven sounds of streams and breezes, held               155
His inmost sense suspended in its web
Of many-coloured woof and shifting hues.
Knowledge and truth and virtue were her theme,
And lofty hopes of divine liberty,
Thoughts the most dear to him, and poesy,                     160
Herself a poet. Soon the solemn mood
Of her pure mind kindled through all her frame
A permeating fire: wild numbers then
She raised, with voice stifled in tremulous sobs
Subdued by its own pathos: her fair hands                     165

Were bare alone, sweeping from some strange harp
Strange symphony, and in their branching veins
The eloquent blood told an ineffable tale.
The beating of her heart was heard to fill
The pauses of her music, and her breath          170
Tumultuously accorded with those fits
Of intermitted song.  Sudden she rose,
As if her heart impatiently endured
Its bursting burthen: at the sound he turned,
And saw by the warm light of their own life       175
Her glowing limbs beneath the sinuous veil
Of woven wind, her outspread arms now bare,
Her dark locks floating in the breath of night,
Her beamy bending eyes, her parted lips
Outstretched, and pale, and quivering eagerly.     180
His strong heart sunk and sickened with excess
Of love.  He reared his shuddering limbs and quelled
His gasping breath, and spread his arms to meet
Her panting bosom: . . . she drew back a while,
Then, yielding to the irresistible joy,            185
With frantic gesture and short breathless cry
Folded his frame in her dissolving arms.
Now blackness veiled his dizzy eyes, and night
Involved and swallowed up the vision; sleep,
Like a dark flood suspended in its course,         190
Rolled back its impulse on his vacant brain.

  Roused by the shock he started from his trance—
The cold white light of morning, the blue moon
Low in the west, the clear and garish hills,
The distinct valley and the vacant woods,          195
Spread round him where he stood.  Whither have fled
The hues of heaven that canopied his bower
Of yesternight?  The sounds that soothed his sleep,
The mystery and the majesty of Earth,
The joy, the exultation?  His wan eyes             200
Gaze on the empty scene as vacantly
As ocean's moon looks on the moon in heaven.

The spirit of sweet human love has sent
A vision to the sleep of him who spurned
Her choicest gifts. He eagerly pursues      205
Beyond the realms of dream that fleeting shade;
He overleaps the bounds. Alas! Alas!
Were limbs, and breath, and being intertwined
Thus treacherously? Lost, lost, for ever lost,
In the wide pathless desert of dim sleep     210
That beautiful shape! Does the dark gate of death
Conduct to thy mysterious paradise,
O Sleep? Does the bright arch of rainbow clouds,
And pendent mountains seen in the calm lake,
Lead only to a black and watery depth,       215
While death's blue vault, with loathliest vapours hung,
Where every shade which the foul grave exhales
Hides its dead eye from the detested day,
Conducts, O Sleep, to thy delightful realms?
This doubt with sudden tide flowed on his heart,   220
The insatiate hope which it awakened, stung
His brain even like despair.
              While daylight held
The sky, the Poet kept mute conference
With his still soul. At night the passion came,
Like the fierce fiend of a distempered dream,    225
And shook him from his rest, and led him forth
Into the darkness.—As an eagle grasped
In folds of the green serpent, feels her breast
Burn with the poison, and precipitates
Through night and day, tempest, and calm, and cloud,
Frantic with dizzying anguish, her blind flight   231
O'er the wide aëry wilderness: thus driven
By the bright shadow of that lovely dream,
Beneath the cold glare of the desolate night,
Through tangled swamps and deep precipitous dells,  235
Startling with careless step the moonlight snake,
He fled. Red morning dawned upon his flight,
Shedding the mockery of its vital hues
Upon his cheek of death. He wandered on

Till vast Aornos seen from Petra's steep          240
Hung o'er the low horizon like a cloud;
Through Balk, and where the desolated tombs
Of Parthian kings scatter to every wind
Their wasting dust, wildly he wandered on,
Day after day a weary waste of hours,            245
Bearing within his life the brooding care
That ever fed on its decaying flame.
And now his limbs were lean; his scattered hair
Sered by the autumn of strange suffering
Sung dirges in the wind; his listless hand        250
Hung like dead bone within its withered skin;
Life, and the lustre that consumed it, shone
As in a furnace burning secretly
From his dark eyes alone. The cottagers,
Who ministered with human charity                255
His human wants, beheld with wondering awe
Their fleeting visitant. The mountaineer,
Encountering on some dizzy precipice
That spectral form, deemed that the Spirit of wind
With lightning eyes, and eager breath, and feet   260
Disturbing not the drifted snow, had paused
In its career: the infant would conceal
His troubled visage in his mother's robe
In terror at the glare of those wild eyes,
To remember their strange light in many a dream   265
Of after-times; but youthful maidens, taught
By nature, would interpret half the woe
That wasted him, would call him with false names
Brother, and friend, would press his pallid hand
At parting, and watch, dim through tears, the path 270
Of his departure from their father's door.

    At length upon the lone Chorasmian shore
He paused, a wide and melancholy waste
Of putrid marshes. A strong impulse urged
His steps to the sea-shore. A swan was there,     275
Beside a sluggish stream among the reeds.

It rose as he approached, and with strong wings
Scaling the upward sky, bent its bright course
High over the immeasurable main.
His eyes pursued its flight.—'Thou hast a home,      280
Beautiful bird; thou voyagest to thine home,
Where thy sweet mate will twine her downy neck
With thine, and welcome thy return with eyes
Bright in the lustre of their own fond joy.
And what am I that I should linger here,      285
With voice far sweeter than thy dying notes,
Spirit more vast than thine, frame more attuned
To beauty, wasting these surpassing powers
In the deaf air, to the blind earth, and heaven
That echoes not my thoughts?' A gloomy smile      290
Of desperate hope wrinkled his quivering lips.
For sleep, he knew, kept most relentlessly
Its precious charge, and silent death exposed,
Faithless perhaps as sleep, a shadowy lure,
With doubtful smile mocking its own strange charms.      295

Startled by his own thoughts he looked around.
There was no fair fiend near him, not a sight
Or sound of awe but in his own deep mind.
A little shallop floating near the shore
Caught the impatient wandering of his gaze.      300
It had been long abandoned, for its sides
Gaped wide with many a rift, and its frail joints
Swayed with the undulations of the tide.
A restless impulse urged him to embark
And meet lone Death on the drear ocean's waste;      305
For well he knew that mighty Shadow loves
The slimy caverns of the populous deep.

The day was fair and sunny, sea and sky
Drank its inspiring radiance, and the wind
Swept strongly from the shore, blackening the waves.      310
Following his eager soul, the wanderer
Leaped in the boat, he spread his cloak aloft

On the bare mast, and took his lonely seat,
And felt the boat speed o'er the tranquil sea
Like a torn cloud before the hurricane.                    315

As one that in a silver vision floats
Obedient to the sweep of odorous winds
Upon resplendent clouds, so rapidly
Along the dark and ruffled waters fled
The straining boat.—A whirlwind swept it on,               320
With fierce gusts and precipitating force,
Through the white ridges of the chafèd sea.
The waves arose.  Higher and higher still
Their fierce necks writhed beneath the tempest's scourge
Like serpents struggling in a vulture's grasp.             325
Calm and rejoicing in the fearful war
Of wave ruining on wave, and blast on blast
Descending, and black flood on whirlpool driven
With dark obliterating course, he sate:
As if their genii were the ministers                       330
Appointed to conduct him to the light
Of those belovèd eyes, the Poet sate
Holding the steady helm.  Evening came on,
The beams of sunset hung their rainbow hues
High 'mid the shifting domes of sheeted spray              335
That canopied his path o'er the waste deep;
Twilight, ascending slowly from the east,
Entwined in duskier wreaths her braided locks
O'er the fair front and radiant eyes of day;
Night followed, clad with stars.  On every side            340
More horribly the multitudinous streams
Of ocean's mountainous waste to mutual war
Rushed in dark tumult thundering, as to mock
The calm and spangled sky.  The little boat
Still fled before the storm; still fled, like foam         345
Down the steep cataract of a wintry river;
Now pausing on the edge of the riven wave;
Now leaving far behind the bursting mass
That fell, convulsing ocean: safely fled—

As if that frail and wasted human form,          350
Had been an elemental god.

                              At midnight
The moon arose: and lo! the ethereal cliffs
Of Caucasus, whose icy summits shone
Among the stars like sunlight, and around
Whose caverned base the whirlpools and the waves   355
Bursting and eddying irresistibly
Rage and resound for ever.—Who shall save?—
The boat fled on,—the boiling torrent drove,—
The crags closed round with black and jaggèd arms,
The shattered mountain overhung the sea,          360
And faster still, beyond all human speed,
Suspended on the sweep of the smooth wave,
The little boat was driven. A cavern there
Yawned, and amid its slant and winding depths
Ingulfed the rushing sea. The boat fled on        365
With unrelaxing speed.—'Vision and Love!'
The Poet cried aloud, 'I have beheld
The path of thy departure. Sleep and death
Shall not divide us long!'

                           The boat pursued
The windings of the cavern. Daylight shone        370
At length upon that gloomy river's flow;
Now, where the fiercest war among the waves
Is calm, on the unfathomable stream
The boat moved slowly. Where the mountain, riven,
Exposed those black depths to the azure sky,      375
Ere yet the flood's enormous volume fell
Even to the base of Caucasus, with sound
That shook the everlasting rocks, the mass
Filled with one whirlpool all that ample chasm;
Stair above stair the eddying waters rose,        380
Circling immeasurably fast, and laved
With alternating dash the gnarlèd roots
Of mighty trees, that stretched their giant arms
In darkness over it. I' the midst was left,
Reflecting, yet distorting every cloud,           385

A pool of treacherous and tremendous calm.
Seized by the sway of the ascending stream,
With dizzy swiftness, round, and round, and round,
Ridge after ridge the straining boat arose,
Till on the verge of the extremest curve,                390
Where, through an opening of the rocky bank,
The waters overflow, and a smooth spot
Of glassy quiet mid those battling tides
Is left, the boat paused shuddering.—Shall it sink
Down the abyss? Shall the reverting stress           395
Of that resistless gulf embosom it?
Now shall it fall?—A wandering stream of wind,
Breathed from the west, has caught the expanded sail,
And, lo! with gentle motion, between banks
Of mossy slope, and on a placid stream,                400
Beneath a woven grove it sails, and, hark!
The ghastly torrent mingles its far roar,
With the breeze murmuring in the musical woods.
Where the embowering trees recede, and leave
A little space of green expanse, the cove           405
Is closed by meeting banks, whose yellow flowers
For ever gaze on their own drooping eyes,
Reflected in the crystal calm. The wave
Of the boat's motion marred their pensive task,
Which nought but vagrant bird, or wanton wind,        410
Or falling spear-grass, or their own decay
Had e'er disturbed before. The Poet longed
To deck with their bright hues his withered hair,
But on his heart its solitude returned,
And he forbore. Not the strong impulse hid           415
In those flushed cheeks, bent eyes, and shadowy frame
Had yet performed its ministry: it hung
Upon his life, as lightning in a cloud
Gleams, hovering ere it vanish, ere the floods
Of night close over it.
                         The noonday sun              420
Now shone upon the forest, one vast mass
Of mingling shade, whose brown magnificence

A narrow vale embosoms. There, huge caves,
Scooped in the dark base of their aëry rocks
Mocking its moans, respond and roar for ever.            425
The meeting boughs and implicated leaves
Wove twilight o'er the Poet's path, as led
By love, or dream, or god, or mightier Death,
He sought in Nature's dearest haunt, some bank,
Her cradle, and his sepulchre. More dark            430
And dark the shades accumulate. The oak,
Expanding its immense and knotty arms,
Embraces the light beech. The pyramids
Of the tall cedar overarching, frame
Most solemn domes within, and far below,            435
Like clouds suspended in an emerald sky,
The ash and the acacia floating hang
Tremulous and pale. Like restless serpents, clothed
In rainbow and in fire, the parasites,
Starred with ten thousand blossoms, flow around            440
The gray trunks, and, as gamesome infants' eyes,
With gentle meanings, and most innocent wiles,
Fold their beams round the hearts of those that love,
These twine their tendrils with the wedded boughs
Uniting their close union; the woven leaves            445
Make net-work of the dark blue light of day,
And the night's noontide clearness, mutable
As shapes in the weird clouds. Soft mossy lawns
Beneath these canopies extend their swells,
Fragrant with perfumed herbs, and eyed with blooms            450
Minute yet beautiful. One darkest glen
Sends from its woods of musk-rose, twined with jasmine,
A soul-dissolving odour, to invite
To some more lovely mystery. Through the dell,
Silence and Twilight here, twin-sisters, keep            455
Their noonday watch, and sail among the shades,
Like vaporous shapes half seen; beyond, a well,
Dark, gleaming, and of most translucent wave,
Images all the woven boughs above,
And each depending leaf, and every speck            460

Of azure sky, darting between their chasms;
Nor aught else in the liquid mirror laves
Its portraiture, but some inconstant star
Between one foliaged lattice twinkling fair,
Or painted bird, sleeping beneath the moon,            465
Or gorgeous insect floating motionless,
Unconscious of the day, ere yet his wings
Have spread their glories to the gaze of noon.

Hither the Poet came.  His eyes beheld
Their own wan light through the reflected lines          470
Of his thin hair, distinct in the dark depth
Of that still fountain; as the human heart,
Gazing in dreams over the gloomy grave,
Sees its own treacherous likeness there.  He heard
The motion of the leaves, the grass that sprung          475
Startled and glanced and trembled even to feel
An unaccustomed presence, and the sound
Of the sweet brook that from the secret springs
Of that dark fountain rose.  A Spirit seemed
To stand beside him—clothed in no bright robes          480
Of shadowy silver or enshrining light,
Borrowed from aught the visible world affords
Of grace, or majesty, or mystery;—
But, undulating woods, and silent well,
And leaping rivulet, and evening gloom                   485
Now deepening the dark shades, for speech assuming,
Held commune with him, as if he and it
Were all that was,—only . . . when his regard
Was raised by intense pensiveness, . . . two eyes,
Two starry eyes, hung in the gloom of thought,           490
And seemed with their serene and azure smiles
To beckon him.
                    Obedient to the light
That shone within his soul, he went, pursuing
The windings of the dell.—The rivulet
Wanton and wild, through many a green ravine             495

Beneath the forest flowed.  Sometimes it fell
Among the moss with hollow harmony
Dark and profound.  Now on the polished stones
It danced; like childhood laughing as it went:
Then, through the plain in tranquil wanderings crept,  500
Reflecting every herb and drooping bud
That overhung its quietness.—'O stream!
Whose source is inaccessibly profound,
Whither do thy mysterious waters tend?
Thou imagest my life.  Thy darksome stillness,  505
Thy dazzling waves, thy loud and hollow gulfs,
Thy searchless fountain, and invisible course
Have each their type in me: and the wide sky,
And measureless ocean may declare as soon
What oozy cavern or what wandering cloud  510
Contains thy waters, as the universe
Tell where these living thoughts reside, when stretched
Upon thy flowers my bloodless limbs shall waste
I' the passing wind!'
                              Beside the grassy shore
Of the small stream he went; he did impress  515
On the green moss his tremulous step, that caught
Strong shuddering from his burning limbs.  As one
Roused by some joyous madness from the couch
Of fever, he did move; yet, not like him,
Forgetful of the grave, where, when the flame  520
Of his frail exultation shall be spent,
He must descend.  With rapid steps he went
Beneath the shade of trees, beside the flow
Of the wild babbling rivulet; and now
The forest's solemn canopies were changed  525
For the uniform and lightsome evening sky.
Gray rocks did peep from the spare moss, and stemmed
The struggling brook: tall spires of windlestrae
Threw their thin shadows down the rugged slope,
And nought but gnarled roots of ancient pines  530
Branchless and blasted, clenched with grasping roots
The unwilling soil.  A gradual change was here,

Yet ghastly. For, as fast years flow away,
The smooth brow gathers, and the hair grows thin
And white, and where irradiate dewy eyes          535
Had shone, gleam stony orbs:—so from his steps
Bright flowers departed, and the beautiful shade
Of the green groves, with all their odorous winds
And musical motions. Calm, he still pursued
The stream, that with a larger volume now         540
Rolled through the labyrinthine dell; and there
Fretted a path through its descending curves
With its wintry speed. On every side now rose
Rocks, which, in unimaginable forms,
Lifted their black and barren pinnacles           545
In the light of evening, and, its precipice
Obscuring the ravine, disclosed above,
Mid toppling stones, black gulfs and yawning caves,
Whose windings gave ten thousand various tongues
To the loud stream. Lo! where the pass expands    550
Its stony jaws, the abrupt mountain breaks,
And seems, with its accumulated crags,
To overhang the world: for wide expand
Beneath the wan stars and descending moon
Islanded seas, blue mountains, mighty streams,    555
Dim tracts and vast, robed in the lustrous gloom
Of leaden-coloured even, and fiery hills
Mingling their flames with twilight, on the verge
Of the remote horizon. The near scene,
In naked and severe simplicity,                   560
Made contrast with the universe. A pine,
Rock-rooted, stretched athwart the vacancy
Its swinging boughs, to each inconstant blast
Yielding one only response, at each pause
In most familiar cadence, with the howl           565
The thunder and the hiss of homeless streams
Mingling its solemn song, whilst the broad river,
Foaming and hurrying o'er its rugged path,
Fell into that immeasurable void
Scattering its waters to the passing winds.       570

Yet the gray precipice and solemn pine
And torrent, were not all;—one silent nook
Was there. Even on the edge of that vast mountain,
Upheld by knotty roots and fallen rocks,
It overlooked in its serenity                                      575
The dark earth, and the bending vault of stars.
It was a tranquil spot, that seemed to smile
Even in the lap of horror. Ivy clasped
The fissured stones with its entwining arms,
And did embower with leaves for ever green,               580
And berries dark, the smooth and even space
Of its inviolated floor, and here
The children of the autumnal whirlwind bore,
In wanton sport, those bright leaves, whose decay,
Red, yellow, or ethereally pale,                               585
Rivals the pride of summer. 'Tis the haunt
Of every gentle wind, whose breath can teach
The wilds to love tranquillity. One step,
One human step alone, has ever broken
The stillness of its solitude:—one voice                       590
Alone inspired its echoes;—even that voice
Which hither came, floating among the winds,
And led the loveliest among human forms
To make their wild haunts the depository
Of all the grace and beauty that endued                      595
Its motions, render up its majesty,
Scatter its music on the unfeeling storm,
And to the damp leaves and blue cavern mould,
Nurses of rainbow flowers and branching moss,
Commit the colours of that varying cheek,                    600
That snowy breast, those dark and drooping eyes.

The dim and hornèd moon hung low, and poured
A sea of lustre on the horizon's verge
That overflowed its mountains. Yellow mist
Filled the unbounded atmosphere, and drank                   605
Wan moonlight even to fulness: not a star
Shone, not a sound was heard; the very winds,

Danger's grim playmates, on that precipice
Slept, clasped in his embrace.—O, storm of death!
Whose sightless speed divides this sullen night:                610
And thou, colossal Skeleton, that, still
Guiding its irresistible career
In thy devastating omnipotence,
Art king of this frail world, from the red field
Of slaughter, from the reeking hospital,                        615
The patriot's sacred couch, the snowy bed
Of innocence, the scaffold and the throne,
A mighty voice invokes thee. Ruin calls
His brother Death. A rare and regal prey
He hath prepared, prowling around the world;                    620
Glutted with which thou mayst repose, and men
Go to their graves like flowers or creeping worms,
Nor ever more offer at thy dark shrine
The unheeded tribute of a broken heart.

When on the threshold of the green recess                       625
The wanderer's footsteps fell, he knew that death
Was on him. Yet a little, ere it fled,
Did he resign his high and holy soul
To images of the majestic past,
That paused within his passive being now,                       630
Like winds that bear sweet music, when they breathe
Through some dim latticed chamber. He did place
His pale lean hand upon the rugged trunk
Of the old pine. Upon an ivied stone
Reclined his languid head, his limbs did rest,                  635
Diffused and motionless, on the smooth brink
Of that obscurest chasm;—and thus he lay,
Surrendering to their final impulses
The hovering powers of life. Hope and despair,
The torturers, slept; no mortal pain or fear                    640
Marred his repose, the influxes of sense,
And his own being unalloyed by pain,
Yet feebler and more feeble, calmly fed
The stream of thought, till he lay breathing there

At peace, and faintly smiling:—his last sight          645
Was the great moon, which o'er the western line
Of the wide world her mighty horn suspended,
With whose dun beams inwoven darkness seemed
To mingle.  Now upon the jaggèd hills
It rests, and still as the divided frame          650
Of the vast meteor sunk, the Poet's blood,
That ever beat in mystic sympathy
With nature's ebb and flow, grew feebler still:
And when two lessening points of light alone
Gleamed through the darkness, the alternate gasp          655
Of his faint respiration scarce did stir
The stagnate night:—till the minutest ray
Was quenched, the pulse yet lingered in his heart.
It paused—it fluttered.  But when heaven remained
Utterly black, the murky shades involved          660
An image, silent, cold, and motionless,
As their own voiceless earth and vacant air.
Even as a vapour fed with golden beams
That ministered on sunlight, ere the west
Eclipses it, was now that wondrous frame—          665
No sense, no motion, no divinity—
A fragile lute, on whose harmonious strings
The breath of heaven did wander—a bright stream
Once fed with many-voicèd waves—a dream
Of youth, which night and time have quenched for ever,
Still, dark, and dry, and unremembered now.          671
    O, for Medea's wondrous alchemy,
Which wheresoe'er it fell made the earth gleam
With bright flowers, and the wintry boughs exhale
From vernal blooms fresh fragrance!  O, that God,          675
Profuse of poisons, would concede the chalice
Which but one living man has drained, who now,
Vessel of deathless wrath, a slave that feels
No proud exemption in the blighting curse
He bears, over the world wanders for ever,          680
Lone as incarnate death!  O, that the dream
Of dark magician in his visioned cave,

Raking the cinders of a crucible
For life and power, even when his feeble hand
Shakes in its last decay, were the true law          685
Of this so lovely world! But thou art fled
Like some frail exhalation; which the dawn
Robes in its golden beams,—ah! thou hast fled!
The brave, the gentle, and the beautiful,
The child of grace and genius. Heartless things     690
Are done and said i' the world, and many worms
And beasts and men live on, and mighty Earth
From sea and mountain, city and wilderness,
In vesper low or joyous orison,
Lifts still its solemn voice:—but thou art fled—    695
Thou canst no longer know or love the shapes
Of this phantasmal scene, who have to thee
Been purest ministers, who are, alas!
Now thou art not. Upon those pallid lips
So sweet even in their silence, on those eyes        700
That image sleep in death, upon that form
Yet safe from the worm's outrage, let no tear
Be shed—not even in thought. Nor, when those hues
Are gone, and those divinest lineaments,
Worn by the senseless wind, shall live alone         705
In the frail pauses of this simple strain,
Let not high verse, mourning the memory
Of that which is no more, or painting's woe
Or sculpture, speak in feeble imagery
Their own cold powers. Art and eloquence,            710
And all the shows o' the world are frail and vain
To weep a loss that turns their lights to shade.
It is a woe too 'deep for tears,' when all
Is reft at once, when some surpassing Spirit,
Whose light adorned the world around it, leaves      715
Those who remain behind, not sobs or groans,
The passionate tumult of a clinging hope;
But pale despair and cold tranquillity,
Nature's vast frame, the web of human things,
Birth and the grave, that are not as they were.      720

# DEDICATION TO
# THE REVOLT OF ISLAM

## TO MARY ———

### I

So now my summer task is ended, Mary,
    And I return to thee, mine own heart's home;
As to his Queen some victor Knight of Faëry,
    Earning bright spoils for her enchanted dome;
    Nor thou disdain, that ere my fame become      5
A star among the stars of mortal night,
    If it indeed may cleave its natal gloom,
Its doubtful promise thus I would unite
With thy belovèd name, thou Child of love and light.

### II

The toil which stole from thee so many an hour,      10
    Is ended,—and the fruit is at thy feet!
No longer where the woods to frame a bower
    With interlacèd branches mix and meet,
    Or where with sound like many voices sweet,
Waterfalls leap among wild islands green,      15
    Which framed for my lone boat a lone retreat
Of moss-grown trees and weeds, shall I be seen:
But beside thee, where still my heart has ever been.

### III

Thoughts of great deeds were mine, dear Friend, when first
    The clouds which wrap this world from youth did pass.      20
I do remember well the hour which burst

My spirit's sleep: a fresh May-dawn it was,
 When I walked forth upon the glittering grass,
And wept, I knew not why; until there rose
 From the near schoolroom, voices, that, alas!  25
Were but one echo from a world of woes—
The harsh and grating strife of tyrants and of foes.

### IV

And then I clasped my hands and looked around—
 —But none was near to mock my streaming eyes,
Which poured their warm drops on the sunny ground— 30
 So, without shame, I spake:—'I will be wise,
 And just, and free, and mild, if in me lies
Such power, for I grow weary to behold
 The selfish and the strong still tyrannise
Without reproach or check.' I then controlled  35
My tears, my heart grew calm, and I was meek and bold.

### V

And from that hour did I with earnest thought
 Heap knowledge from forbidden mines of lore,
Yet nothing that my tyrants knew or taught
 I cared to learn, but from that secret store  40
 Wrought linkèd armour for my soul, before
It might walk forth to war among mankind;
 Thus power and hope were strengthened more and more
Within me, till there came upon my mind
A sense of loneliness, a thirst with which I pined.  45

### VI

Alas, that love should be a blight and snare
 To those who seek all sympathies in one!—
Such once I sought in vain; then black despair,
 The shadow of a starless night, was thrown
 Over the world in which I moved alone:—  50

Yet never found I one not false to me,
  Hard hearts, and cold, like weights of icy stone
Which crushed and withered mine, that could not be
Aught but a lifeless clod, until revived by thee.

### VII

Thou Friend, whose presence on my wintry heart        55
  Fell, like bright Spring upon some herbless plain;
How beautiful and calm and free thou wert
  In thy young wisdom, when the mortal chain
  Of Custom thou didst burst and rend in twain,
And walked as free as light the clouds among,        60
  Which many an envious slave then breathed in vain
From his dim dungeon, and my spirit sprung
To meet thee from the woes which had begirt it long!

### VIII

No more alone through the world's wilderness,
  Although I trod the paths of high intent,        65
I journeyed now: no more companionless,
  Where solitude is like despair, I went.—
  There is the wisdom of a stern content
When Poverty can blight the just and good,
  When Infamy dares mock the innocent,        70
And cherished friends turn with the multitude
To trample: this was ours, and we unshaken stood!

### IX

Now has descended a serener hour,
  And with inconstant fortune, friends return;
Though suffering leaves the knowledge and the power        75
  Which says:—Let scorn be not repaid with scorn.
  And from thy side two gentle babes are born
To fill our home with smiles, and thus are we
  Most fortunate beneath life's beaming morn;

MARY SHELLEY

*From the painting by S. J. Stamp.  Now in the National Portrait Gallery, London.*

And these delights, and thou, have been to me                80
The parents of the Song I consecrate to thee.

### X

Is it, that now my inexperienced fingers
    But strike the prelude of a loftier strain?
Or, must the lyre on which my spirit lingers
    Soon pause in silence, ne'er to sound again,          85
    Though it might shake the Anarch Custom's reign,
And charm the minds of men to Truth's own sway
    Holier than was Amphion's?  I would fain
Reply in hope—but I am worn away,
And Death and Love are yet contending for their prey.     90

### XI

And what art thou?  I know, but dare not speak:
    Time may interpret to his silent years.
Yet in the paleness of thy thoughtful cheek,
    And in the light thine ample forehead wears,
    And in thy sweetest smiles, and in thy tears,          95
And in thy gentle speech, a prophecy
    Is whispered, to subdue my fondest fears:
And through thine eyes, even in thy soul I see
A lamp of vestal fire burning internally.

### XII

They say that thou wert lovely from thy birth,           100
    Of glorious parents, thou aspiring Child.
I wonder not—for One then left this earth
    Whose life was like a setting planet mild,
    Which clothed thee in the radiance undefiled
Of its departing glory; still her fame                    105
    Shines on thee, through the tempests dark and wild
Which shake these latter days; and thou canst claim
The shelter, from thy Sire, of an immortal name.

c

### XIII

One voice came forth from many a mighty spirit,
  Which was the echo of three thousand years;    110
And the tumultuous world stood mute to hear it,
  As some lone man who in a desert hears
  The music of his home:—unwonted fears
Fell on the pale oppressors of our race,
  And Faith, and Custom, and low-thoughted cares,    115
Like thunder-stricken dragons, for a space
Left the torn human heart, their food and dwelling-place.

### XIV

Truth's deathless voice pauses among mankind!
  If there must be no response to my cry—
If men must rise and stamp with fury blind    120
  On his pure name who loves them,—thou and I,
  Sweet friend! can look from our tranquillity
Like lamps into the world's tempestuous night,—
  Two tranquil stars, while clouds are passing by
Which wrap them from the foundering seaman's sight,    125
That burn from year to year with unextinguished light.

# FRAGMENTS
# FROM PRINCE ATHANASE

### I

'Twas at the season when the Earth upsprings
From slumber, as a spherèd angel's child,
Shadowing its eyes with green and golden wings,

Stands up before its mother bright and mild,
Of whose soft voice the air expectant seems—    5
So stood before the sun, which shone and smiled

To see it rise thus joyous from its dreams,
The fresh and radiant Earth.  The hoary grove
Waxed green—and flowers burst forth like starry beams;—

The grass in the warm sun did start and move,    10
And sea-buds burst under the waves serene:—
How many a one, though none be near to love,

Loves then the shade of his own soul, half seen
In any mirror—or the spring's young minions,
The wingèd leaves amid the copses green;—    15

How many a spirit then puts on the pinions
Of fancy, and outstrips the lagging blast,
And his own steps—and over wide dominions

Sweeps in his dream-drawn chariot, far and fast,
More fleet than storms—the wide world shrinks below,  20
When winter and despondency are past.

II

'Twas at this season that Prince Athanase
Passed the white Alps—those eagle-baffling mountains
Slept in their shrouds of snow;—beside the ways

The waterfalls were voiceless—for their fountains    25
Were changed to mines of sunless crystal now,
Or by the curdling winds—like brazen wings

Which clanged along the mountain's marble brow—
Warped into adamantine fretwork, hung
And filled with frozen light the chasm below.    30

III

THOU art the wine whose drunkenness is all
We can desire, O Love! and happy souls,
Ere from thy vine the leaves of autumn fall,

Catch thee, and feed from their o'erflowing bowls
Thousands who thirst for thine ambrosial dew;—                    35
Thou art the radiance which where ocean rolls

Investeth it; and when the heavens are blue
Thou fillest them; and when the earth is fair
The shadow of thy moving wings imbue

Its deserts and its mountains, till they wear             40
Beauty like some bright robe;—thou ever soarest
Among the towers of men, and as soft air

In spring, which moves the unawakened forest,
Clothing with leaves its branches bare and bleak,
Thou floatest among men; and aye implorest              45

That which from thee they should implore:—the weak
Alone kneel to thee, offering up the hearts
The strong have broken—yet where shall any seek

A garment whom thou clothest not?

# JULIAN AND MADDALO

## A CONVERSATION

### PREFACE

The meadows with fresh streams, the bees with thyme,
The goats with the green leaves of budding Spring,
Are saturated not—nor Love with tears.—VIRGIL's *Gallus*.

COUNT MADDALO is a Venetian nobleman of ancient
family and of great fortune, who, without mixing much in the
society of his countrymen, resides chiefly at his magnificent
palace in that city. He is a person of the most consummate
genius, and capable, if he would direct his energies to such
an end, of becoming the redeemer of his degraded country.
But it is his weakness to be proud: he derives, from a comparison of his own extraordinary mind with the dwarfish
intellects that surround him, an intense apprehension of the
nothingness of human life. His passions and his powers are
incomparably greater than those of other men; and, instead
of the latter having been employed in curbing the former,
they have mutually lent each other strength. His ambition
preys upon itself, for want of objects which it can consider
worthy of exertion. I say that Maddalo is proud, because I can
find no other word to express the concentered and impatient
feelings which consume him; but it is on his own hopes and
affections only that he seems to trample, for in social life no
human being can be more gentle, patient, and unassuming
than Maddalo. He is cheerful, frank, and witty. His more
serious conversation is a sort of intoxication; men are held by
it as by a spell. He has travelled much; and there is an in-
expressible charm in his relation of his adventures in different
countries.

Julian is an Englishman of good family, passionately
attached to those philosophical notions which assert the power

of man over his own mind, and the immense improvements
of which, by the extinction of certain moral superstitions,
human society may be yet susceptible. Without concealing
the evil in the world, he is for ever speculating how good may
be made superior. He is a complete infidel, and a scoffer at
all things reputed holy; and Maddalo takes a wicked pleasure
in drawing out his taunts against religion. What Maddalo
thinks on these matters is not exactly known. Julian, in spite
of his heterodox opinions, is conjectured by his friends to
possess some good qualities. How far this is possible the pious
reader will determine. Julian is rather serious.

Of the Maniac I can give no information. He seems, by his
own account, to have been disappointed in love. He was
evidently a very cultivated and amiable person when in his
right senses. His story, told at length, might be like many
other stories of the same kind: the unconnected exclamations
of his agony will perhaps be found a sufficient comment for
the text of every heart.

I RODE one evening with Count Maddalo
Upon the bank of land which breaks the flow
Of Adria towards Venice: a bare strand
Of hillocks, heaped from ever-shifting sand,
Matted with thistles and amphibious weeds,          5
Such as from earth's embrace the salt ooze breeds,
Is this; an uninhabited sea-side,
Which the lone fisher, when his nets are dried,
Abandons; and no other object breaks
The waste, but one dwarf tree and some few stakes   10
Broken and unrepaired, and the tide makes
A narrow space of level sand thereon,
Where 'twas our wont to ride while day went down.
This ride was my delight. I love all waste
And solitary places; where we taste                 15
The pleasure of believing what we see
Is boundless, as we wish our souls to be:
And such was this wide ocean, and this shore
More barren than its billows; and yet more

Than all, with a remembered friend I love          20
To ride as then I rode;—for the winds drove
The living spray along the sunny air
Into our faces; the blue heavens were bare,
Stripped to their depths by the awakening north;
And, from the waves, sound like delight broke forth   25
Harmonising with solitude, and sent
Into our hearts aëreal merriment.
So, as we rode, we talked; and the swift thought,
Winging itself with laughter, lingered not,
But flew from brain to brain,—such glee was ours,    30
Charged with light memories of remembered hours,
None slow enough for sadness: till we came
Homeward, which always makes the spirit tame.
This day had been cheerful but cold, and now
The sun was sinking, and the wind also.              35
Our talk grew somewhat serious, as may be
Talk interrupted with such raillery
As mocks itself, because it cannot scorn
The thoughts it would extinguish:—'twas forlorn,
Yet pleasing, such as once, so poets tell,            40
The devils held within the dales of Hell
Concerning God, freewill and destiny:
Of all that earth has been or yet may be,
All that vain men imagine or believe,
Or hope can paint or suffering may achieve,          45
We descanted, and I (for ever still
Is it not wise to make the best of ill?)
Argued against despondency, but pride
Made my companion take the darker side.
The sense that he was greater than his kind          50
Had struck, methinks, his eagle spirit blind
By gazing on its own exceeding light.
Meanwhile the sun paused ere it should alight,
Over the horizon of the mountains;—Oh,
How beautiful is sunset, when the glow               55
Of Heaven descends upon a land like thee,
Thou Paradise of exiles, Italy!

Thy mountains, seas, and vineyards, and the towers
Of cities they encircle!—it was ours
To stand on thee, beholding it: and then,                      60
Just where we had dismounted, the Count's men
Were waiting for us with the gondola.—
As those who pause on some delightful way
Though bent on pleasant pilgrimage, we stood
Looking upon the evening, and the flood                       65
Which lay between the city and the shore,
Paved with the image of the sky . . . the hoar
And aëry Alps towards the North appeared
Through mist, an heaven-sustaining bulwark reared
Between the East and West; and half the sky                   70
Was roofed with clouds of rich emblazonry
Dark purple at the zenith, which still grew
Down the steep West into a wondrous hue
Brighter than burning gold, even to the rent
Where the swift sun yet paused in his descent                 75
Among the many-folded hills: they were
Those famous Euganean hills, which bear,
As seen from Lido thro' the harbour piles,
The likeness of a clump of peakèd isles—
And then—as if the Earth and Sea had been                     80
Dissolved into one lake of fire, were seen
Those mountains towering as from waves of flame
Around the vaporous sun, from which there came
The inmost purple spirit of light, and made
Their very peaks transparent. 'Ere it fade,'                  85
Said my companion, 'I will show you soon
A better station'—so, o'er the lagune
We glided; and from that funereal bark
I leaned, and saw the city, and could mark
How from their many isles, in evening's gleam,               90
Its temples and its palaces did seem
Like fabrics of enchantment piled to Heaven.
I was about to speak, when—'We are even
Now at the point I meant,' said Maddalo,
And bade the gondolieri cease to row.                         95

'Look, Julian, on the west, and listen well
If you hear not a deep and heavy bell.'
I looked, and saw between us and the sun
A building on an island; such a one
As age to age might add, for uses vile,                    100
A windowless, deformed and dreary pile;
And on the top an open tower, where hung
A bell, which in the radiance swayed and swung;
We could just hear its hoarse and iron tongue:
The broad sun sunk behind it, and it tolled                105
In strong and black relief.—'What we behold
Shall be the madhouse and its belfry tower,'
Said Maddalo, 'and ever at this hour
Those who may cross the water, hear that bell
Which calls the maniacs, each one from his cell,          110
To vespers.'—'As much skill as need to pray
In thanks or hope for their dark lot have they
To their stern maker,' I replied. 'O ho!
You talk as in years past,' said Maddalo.
''Tis strange men change not. You were ever still          115
Among Christ's flock a perilous infidel,
A wolf for the meek lambs—if you can't swim
Beware of Providence.' I looked on him,
But the gay smile had faded in his eye.
'And such,'—he cried, 'is our mortality,                   120
And this must be the emblem and the sign
Of what should be eternal and divine!—
And like that black and dreary bell, the soul,
Hung in a heaven-illumined tower, must toll
Our thoughts and our desires to meet below                 125
Round the rent heart and pray—as madmen do
For what? they know not,—till the night of death
As sunset that strange vision, severeth
Our memory from itself, and us from all
We sought and yet were baffled.' I recall                  130
The sense of what he said, although I mar
The force of his expressions. The broad star
Of day meanwhile had sunk behind the hill,

And the black bell became invisible,
And the red tower looked gray, and all between          135
The churches, ships and palaces were seen
Huddled in gloom;—into the purple sea
The orange hues of heaven sunk silently.
We hardly spoke, and soon the gondola
Conveyed me to my lodging by the way.                   140
    The following morn was rainy, cold and dim:
Ere Maddalo arose, I called on him,
And whilst I waited with his child I played;
A lovelier toy sweet Nature never made,
A serious, subtle, wild, yet gentle being,              145
Graceful without design and unforeseeing,
With eyes—Oh speak not of her eyes!—which seem
Twin mirrors of Italian Heaven, yet gleam
With such deep meaning, as we never see
But in the human countenance: with me                   150
She was a special favourite: I had nursed
Her fine and feeble limbs when she came first
To this bleak world; and she yet seemed to know
On second sight her ancient playfellow,
Less changed than she was by six months or so;          155
For after her first shyness was worn out
We sate there, rolling billiard balls about,
When the Count entered. Salutations past—
'The word you spoke last night might well have cast
A darkness on my spirit—if man be                       160
The passive thing you say, I should not see
Much harm in the religions and old saws
(Tho' I may never own such leaden laws)
Which break a teachless nature to the yoke:
Mine is another faith'—thus much I spoke                165
And noting he replied not, added: 'See
This lovely child, blithe, innocent and free;
She spends a happy time with little care,
While we to such sick thoughts subjected are
As came on you last night—it is our will               170
That thus enchains us to permitted ill—

We might be otherwise—we might be all
We dream of happy, high, majestical.
Where is the love, beauty, and truth we seek
But in our mind? and if we were not weak                            175
Should we be less in deed than in desire?'
'Ay, if we were not weak—and we aspire
How vainly to be strong!' said Maddalo:
'You talk Utopia.' 'It remains to know,'
I then rejoined, 'and those who try may find                        180
How strong the chains are which our spirit bind;
Brittle perchance as straw . . . We are assured
Much may be conquered, much may be endured,
Of what degrades and crushes us. We know
That we have power over ourselves to do                             185
And suffer—what, we know not till we try;
But something nobler than to live and die—
So taught those kings of old philosophy
Who reigned, before Religion made men blind;
And those who suffer with their suffering kind                      190
Yet feel their faith, religion.' 'My dear friend,'
Said Maddalo, 'my judgement will not bend
To your opinion, though I think you might
Make such a system refutation-tight
As far as words go. I knew one like you                             195
Who to this city came some months ago,
With whom I argued in this sort, and he
Is now gone mad,—and so he answered me,—
Poor fellow! but if you would like to go
We'll visit him, and his wild talk will show                        200
How vain are such aspiring theories.'
'I hope to prove the induction otherwise,
And that a want of that true theory, still,
Which seeks a "soul of goodness" in things ill
Or in himself or others, has thus bowed                             205
His being—there are some by nature proud,
Who patient in all else demand but this—
To love and be beloved with gentleness;
And being scorned, what wonder if they die

Some living death? this is not destiny          210
But man's own wilful ill.'
                 As thus I spoke
Servants announced the gondola, and we
Through the fast-falling rain and high-wrought sea
Sailed to the island where the madhouse stands.
We disembarked. The clap of tortured hands,          215
Fierce yells and howlings and lamentings keen,
And laughter where complaint had merrier been,
Moans, shrieks, and curses, and blaspheming prayers
Accosted us. We climbed the oozy stairs
Into an old courtyard. I heard on high,          220
Then, fragments of most touching melody,
But looking up saw not the singer there—
Through the black bars in the tempestuous air
I saw, like weeds on a wrecked palace growing,
Long tangled locks flung wildly forth, and flowing,          225
Of those who on a sudden were beguiled
Into strange silence, and looked forth and smiled
Hearing sweet sounds.—Then I: 'Methinks there were
A cure of these with patience and kind care,
If music can thus move . . . but what is he          230
Whom we seek here?' 'Of his sad history
I know but this,' said Maddalo: 'he came
To Venice a dejected man, and fame
Said he was wealthy, or he had been so;
Some thought the loss of fortune wrought him woe;          235
But he was ever talking in such sort
As you do—far more sadly—he seemed hurt,
Even as a man with his peculiar wrong,
To hear but of the oppression of the strong,
Or those absurd deceits (I think with you          240
In some respects, you know) which carry through
The excellent impostors of this earth
When they outface detection—he had worth,
Poor fellow! but a humourist in his way'—
'Alas, what drove him mad?' 'I cannot say:          245
A lady came with him from France, and when

She left him and returned, he wandered then
About yon lonely isles of desert sand
Till he grew wild—he had no cash or land
Remaining,—the police had brought him here— 250
Some fancy took him and he would not bear
Removal; so I fitted up for him
Those rooms beside the sea, to please his whim,
And sent him busts and books and urns for flowers,
Which had adorned his life in happier hours, 255
And instruments of music—you may guess
A stranger could do little more or less
For one so gentle and unfortunate:
And those are his sweet strains which charm the
 weight
From madmen's chains, and make this Hell appear 260
A heaven of sacred silence, hushed to hear.'—
'Nay, this was kind of you—he had no claim,
As the world says'—'None—but the very same
Which I on all mankind were I as he
Fallen to such deep reverse;—his melody 265
Is interrupted—now we hear the din
Of madmen, shriek on shriek, again begin;
Let us now visit him; after this strain
He ever communes with himself again,
And sees nor hears not any.' Having said 270
These words we called the keeper, and he led
To an apartment opening on the sea—
There the poor wretch was sitting mournfully
Near a piano, his pale fingers twined
One with the other, and the ooze and wind 275
Rushed through an open casement, and did sway
His hair, and starred it with the brackish spray;
His head was leaning on a music book,
And he was muttering, and his lean limbs shook;
His lips were pressed against a folded leaf 280
In hue too beautiful for health, and grief
Smiled in their motions as they lay apart—
As one who wrought from his own fervid heart

The eloquence of passion, soon he raised
His sad meek face and eyes lustrous and glazed          285
And spoke—sometimes as one who wrote, and thought
His words might move some heart that heeded not,
If sent to distant lands: and then as one
Reproaching deeds never to be undone
With wondering self-compassion; then his speech          290
Was lost in grief, and then his words came each
Unmodulated, cold, expressionless,—
But that from one jarred accent you might guess
It was despair made them so uniform:
And all the while the loud and gusty storm          295
Hissed through the window, and we stood behind
Stealing his accents from the envious wind
Unseen.  I yet remember what he said
Distinctly: such impression his words made.


'Month after month,' he cried, 'to bear this load          300
And as a jade urged by the whip and goad
To drag life on, which like a heavy chain
Lengthens behind with many a link of pain!—
And not to speak my grief—O, not to dare
To give a human voice to my despair,          305
But live and move, and, wretched thing! smile on
As if I never went aside to groan,
And wear this mask of falsehood even to those
Who are most dear—not for my own repose—
Alas! no scorn or pain or hate could be          310
So heavy as that falsehood is to me—
But that I cannot bear more altered faces
Than needs must be, more changed and cold embraces,
More misery, disappointment, and mistrust
To own me for their father . . . Would the dust          315
Were covered in upon my body now!
That the life ceased to toil within my brow!
And then these thoughts would at the least be fled;
Let us not fear such pain can vex the dead.

'What Power delights to torture us? I know   320
That to myself I do not wholly owe
What now I suffer, though in part I may.
Alas! none strewed sweet flowers upon the way
Where wandering heedlessly, I met pale Pain
My shadow, which will leave me not again—   325
If I have erred, there was no joy in error,
But pain and insult and unrest and terror;
I have not as some do, bought penitence
With pleasure, and a dark yet sweet offence,
For then,—if love and tenderness and truth   330
Had overlived hope's momentary youth,
My creed should have redeemed me from repenting;
But loathèd scorn and outrage unrelenting
Met love excited by far other seeming
Until the end was gained . . . as one from dreaming   335
Of sweetest peace, I woke, and found my state
Such as it is.——
          'O Thou, my spirit's mate
Who, for thou art compassionate and wise,
Wouldst pity me from thy most gentle eyes
If this sad writing thou shouldst ever see—   340
My secret groans must be unheard by thee,
Thou wouldst weep tears bitter as blood to know
Thy lost friend's incommunicable woe.

'Ye few by whom my nature has been weighed
In friendship, let me not that name degrade   345
By placing on your hearts the secret load
Which crushes mine to dust. There is one road
To peace and that is truth, which follow ye!
Love sometimes leads astray to misery.
Yet think not though subdued—and I may well   350
Say that I am subdued—that the full Hell
Within me would infect the untainted breast
Of sacred nature with its own unrest;
As some perverted beings think to find
In scorn or hate a medicine for the mind   355

Which scorn or hate have wounded—O how vain!
The dagger heals not but may rend again . . .
Believe that I am ever still the same
In creed as in resolve, and what may tame
My heart, must leave the understanding free,          360
Or all would sink in this keen agony—
Nor dream that I will join the vulgar cry;
Or with my silence sanction tyranny;
Or seek a moment's shelter from my pain
In any madness which the world calls gain,          365
Ambition or revenge or thoughts as stern
As those which make me what I am; or turn
To avarice or misanthropy or lust . . .
Heap on me soon, O grave, thy welcome dust!
Till then the dungeon may demand its prey,          370
And Poverty and Shame may meet and say—
Halting beside me on the public way—
"That love-devoted youth is ours—let's sit
Beside him—he may live some six months yet."
Or the red scaffold, as our country bends,          375
May ask some willing victim, or ye friends
May fall under some sorrow which this heart
Or hand may share or vanquish or avert;
I am prepared—in truth with no proud joy—
To do or suffer aught, as when a boy          380
I did devote to justice and to love
My nature, worthless now! . . .
                              'I must remove
A veil from my pent mind. 'Tis torn aside!
O, pallid as Death's dedicated bride,
Thou mockery which art sitting by my side,          385
Am I not wan like thee? at the grave's call
I haste, invited to thy wedding-ball
To greet the ghastly paramour, for whom
Thou hast deserted me . . . and made the tomb
Thy bridal bed . . . But I beside your feet          390
Will lie and watch ye from my winding sheet—
Thus . . . wide awake tho' dead . . . yet stay, O stay!

Go not so soon—I know not what I say—
Hear but my reasons . . I am mad, I fear,
My fancy is o'erwrought . . thou art not here . . .  395
Pale art thou, 'tis most true . . but thou art gone,
Thy work is finished . . . I am left alone!—


'Nay, was it I who wooed thee to this breast
Which, like a serpent, thou envenomest
As in repayment of the warmth it lent?  400
Didst thou not seek me for thine own content?
Did not thy love awaken mine? I thought
That thou wert she who said, "You kiss me not
Ever, I fear you do not love me now"—
In truth I loved even to my overthrow  405
Her, who would fain forget these words: but they
Cling to her mind, and cannot pass away.


'You say that I am proud—that when I speak
My lip is tortured with the wrongs which break
The spirit it expresses . . . Never one  410
Humbled himself before, as I have done!
Even the instinctive worm on which we tread
Turns, though it wound not—then with prostrate head
Sinks in the dusk and writhes like me—and dies?
No: wears a living death of agonies!  415
As the slow shadows of the pointed grass
Mark the eternal periods, his pangs pass
Slow, ever-moving,—making moments be
As mine seem—each an immortality!


'That you had never seen me—never heard  420
My voice, and more than all had ne'er endured
The deep pollution of my loathed embrace—
That your eyes ne'er had lied love in my face—

That, like some maniac monk, I had torn out
The nerves of manhood by their bleeding root          425
With mine own quivering fingers, so that ne'er
Our hearts had for a moment mingled there
To disunite in horror—these were not
With thee, like some suppressed and hideous thought
Which flits athwart our musings, but can find          430
No rest within a pure and gentle mind . . .
Thou sealedst them with many a bare broad word,
And searedst my memory o'er them,—for I heard
And can forget not . . . they were ministered
One after one, those curses.  Mix them up          435
Like self-destroying poisons in one cup,
And they will make one blessing which thou ne'er
Didst imprecate for, on me,—death.

                              'It were
A cruel punishment for one most cruel,
If such can love, to make that love the fuel          440
Of the mind's hell; hate, scorn, remorse, despair:
But *me*—whose heart a stranger's tear might wear
As water-drops the sandy fountain-stone,
Who loved and pitied all things, and could moan
For woes which others hear not, and could see          445
The absent with the glance of phantasy,
And with the poor and trampled sit and weep,
Following the captive to his dungeon deep;
*Me*—who am as a nerve o'er which do creep
The else unfelt oppressions of this earth,          450
And was to thee the flame upon thy hearth,
When all beside was cold—that thou on me
Shouldst rain these plagues of blistering agony—
Such curses are from lips once eloquent
With love's too partial praise—let none relent          455
Who intend deeds too dreadful for a name
Henceforth, if an example for the same
They seek . . . for thou on me lookedst so, and so—

And didst speak thus . . and thus . . . I live to show
How much men bear and die not! 460

.        .        .        .        .

'Thou wilt tell,
With the grimace of hate, how horrible
It was to meet my love when thine grew less;
Thou wilt admire how I could e'er address
Such features to love's work . . . this taunt, though true, 
(For indeed Nature nor in form nor hue 465
Bestowed on me her choicest workmanship)
Shall not be thy defence . . . for since thy lip
Met mine first, years long past, since thine eye kindled
With soft fire under mine, I have not dwindled
Nor changed in mind or body, or in aught 470
But as love changes what it loveth not
After long years and many trials.

'How vain
Are words! I thought never to speak again,
Not even in secret,—not to my own heart—
But from my lips the unwilling accents start, 475
And from my pen the words flow as I write,
Dazzling my eyes with scalding tears . . . my sight
Is dim to see that charactered in vain
On this unfeeling leaf which burns the brain
And eats into it . . . blotting all things fair 480
And wise and good which time had written there.

'Those who inflict must suffer, for they see
The work of their own hearts, and this must be
Our chastisement or recompense—O child!
I would that thine were like to be more mild 485
For both our wretched sakes . . . for thine the most
Who feelest already all that thou hast lost
Without the power to wish it thine again;
And as slow years pass, a funereal train
Each with the ghost of some lost hope or friend 490

Following it like its shadow, wilt thou bend
No thought on my dead memory?

·         ·         ·         ·         ·

                              'Alas, love!
Fear me not . . . against thee I would not move
A finger in despite.  Do I not live
That thou mayst have less bitter cause to grieve?        495
I give thee tears for scorn and love for hate;
And that thy lot may be less desolate
Than his on whom thou tramplest, I refrain
From that sweet sleep which medicines all pain.
Then, when thou speakest of me, never say        500
"He could forgive not."  Here I cast away
All human passions, all revenge, all pride;
I think, speak, act no ill; I do but hide
Under these words, like embers, every spark
Of that which has consumed me—quick and dark        505
The grave is yawning . . . as its roof shall cover
My limbs with dust and worms under and over
So let Oblivion hide this grief . . . the air
Closes upon my accents, as despair
Upon my heart—let death upon despair!'        510

He ceased, and overcome leant back awhile,
Then rising, with a melancholy smile
Went to a sofa, and lay down, and slept
A heavy sleep, and in his dreams he wept
And muttered some familiar name, and we        515
Wept without shame in his society.
I think I never was impressed so much;
The man who were not, must have lacked a touch
Of human nature . . . then we lingered not,
Although our argument was quite forgot,        520
But calling the attendants, went to dine
At Maddalo's; yet neither cheer nor wine
Could give us spirits, for we talked of him

And nothing else, till daylight made stars dim;
And we agreed his was some dreadful ill 525
Wrought on him boldly, yet unspeakable,
By a dear friend; some deadly change in love
Of one vowed deeply which he dreamed not of;
For whose sake he, it seemed, had fixed a blot
Of falsehood on his mind which flourished not 530
But in the light of all-beholding truth;
And having stamped this canker on his youth
She had abandoned him—and how much more
Might be his woe, we guessed not—he had store
Of friends and fortune once, as we could guess 535
From his nice habits and his gentleness;
These were now lost . . . it were a grief indeed
If he had changed one unsustaining reed
For all that such a man might else adorn.
The colours of his mind seemed yet unworn; 540
For the wild language of his grief was high,
Such as in measure were called poetry;
And I remember one remark which then
Maddalo made. He said: 'Most wretched men
Are cradled into poetry by wrong, 545
They learn in suffering what they teach in song.'

If I had been an unconnected man
I, from this moment, should have formed some plan
Never to leave sweet Venice,—for to me
It was delight to ride by the lone sea; 550
And then, the town is silent—one may write
Or read in gondolas by day or night,
Having the little brazen lamp alight,
Unseen, uninterrupted; books are there,
Pictures, and casts from all those statues fair 555
Which were twin-born with poetry, and all
We seek in towns, with little to recall
Regrets for the green country. I might sit
In Maddalo's great palace, and his wit
And subtle talk would cheer the winter night 560

And make me know myself, and the firelight
Would flash upon our faces, till the day
Might dawn and make me wonder at my stay:
But I had friends in London too: the chief
Attraction here, was that I sought relief          565
From the deep tenderness that maniac wrought
Within me—'twas perhaps an idle thought—
But I imagined that if day by day
I watched him, and but seldom went away,
And studied all the beatings of his heart          570
With zeal, as men study some stubborn art
For their own good, and could by patience find
An entrance to the caverns of his mind,
I might reclaim him from his dark estate:
In friendships I had been most fortunate—          575
Yet never saw I one whom I would call
More willingly my friend; and this was all
Accomplished not; such dreams of baseless good
Oft come and go in crowds or solitude
And leave no trace—but what I now designed        580
Made for long years impression on my mind.
The following morning, urged by my affairs,
I left bright Venice.
                          After many years
And many changes I returned; the name
Of Venice, and its aspect, was the same;          585
But Maddalo was travelling far away
Among the mountains of Armenia.
His dog was dead. His child had now become
A woman; such as it has been my doom
To meet with few,—a wonder of this earth,         590
Where there is little of transcendent worth,—
Like one of Shakespeare's women: kindly she,
And, with a manner beyond courtesy,
Received her father's friend; and when I asked
Of the lorn maniac, she her memory tasked,        595
And told as she had heard the mournful tale:
'That the poor sufferer's health began to fail

Two years from my departure, but that then
The lady who had left him, came again.
Her mien had been imperious, but she now     600
Looked meek—perhaps remorse had brought her low.
Her coming made him better, and they stayed
Together at my father's—for I played,
As I remember, with the lady's shawl—
I might be six years old—but after all     605
She left him' . . . 'Why, her heart must have been tough:
How did it end?' 'And was not this enough?
They met—they parted'—'Child, is there no more?'
'Something within that interval which bore
The stamp of *why* they parted, *how* they met:     610
Yet if thine agèd eyes disdain to wet
Those wrinkled cheeks with youth's remembered tears,
Ask me no more, but let the silent years
Be closed and cered over their memory
As yon mute marble where their corpses lie.'     615
I urged and questioned still, she told me how
All happened—but the cold world shall not know.

# PROMETHEUS UNBOUND

## A LYRICAL DRAMA

### IN FOUR ACTS

AUDISNE HAEC AMPHIARAE, SUB TERRAM ABDITE?

## PREFACE

THE Greek tragic writers, in selecting as their subject any
portion of their national history or mythology, employed in
their treatment of it a certain arbitrary discretion. They by
no means conceived themselves bound to adhere to the

common interpretation or to imitate in story as in title their rivals and predecessors. Such a system would have amounted to a resignation of those claims to preference over their competitors which incited the composition. The Agamemnonian story was exhibited on the Athenian theatre with as many variations as dramas.

I have presumed to employ a similar licence. The *Prometheus Unbound* of Æschylus supposed the reconciliation of Jupiter with his victim as the price of the disclosure of the danger threatened to his empire by the consummation of his marriage with Thetis. Thetis, according to this view of the subject, was given in marriage to Peleus, and Prometheus, by the permission of Jupiter, delivered from his captivity by Hercules. Had I framed my story on this model, I should have done no more than have attempted to restore the lost drama of Æschylus; an ambition which, if my preference to this mode of treating the subject had incited me to cherish, the recollection of the high comparison such an attempt would challenge might well abate. But, in truth, I was averse from a catastrophe so feeble as that of reconciling the Champion with the Oppressor of mankind. The moral interest of the fable, which is so powerfully sustained by the sufferings and endurance of Prometheus, would be annihilated if we could conceive of him as unsaying his high language and quailing before his successful and perfidious adversary. The only imaginary being resembling in any degree Prometheus, is Satan; and Prometheus is, in my judgement, a more poetical character than Satan, because, in addition to courage, and majesty, and firm and patient opposition to omnipotent force, he is susceptible of being described as exempt from the taints of ambition, envy, revenge, and a desire for personal aggrandisement, which, in the Hero of *Paradise Lost*, interfere with the interest. The character of Satan engenders in the mind a pernicious casuistry which leads us to weigh his faults with his wrongs, and to excuse the former because the latter exceed all measure. In the minds of those who consider that magnificent fiction with a religious feeling it engenders something worse. But Prometheus is, as it were, the type of the highest perfection of moral and intellectual nature, impelled by the purest and the truest motives to the best and noblest ends.

This Poem was chiefly written upon the mountainous ruins of the Baths of Caracalla, among the flowery glades, and thickets of odoriferous blossoming trees, which are extended in ever winding labyrinths upon its immense platforms and dizzy arches suspended in the air. The bright blue sky of Rome, and the effect of the vigorous awakening spring in that divinest climate, and the new life with which it drenches the spirits even to intoxication, were the inspiration of this drama.

The imagery which I have employed will be found, in many instances, to have been drawn from the operations of the human mind, or from those external actions by which they are expressed. This is unusual in modern poetry, although Dante and Shakespeare are full of instances of the same kind: Dante indeed more than any other poet, and with greater success. But the Greek poets, as writers to whom no resource of awakening the sympathy of their contemporaries was unknown, were in the habitual use of this power; and it is the study of their works (since a higher merit would probably be denied me) to which I am willing that my readers should impute this singularity.

One word is due in candour to the degree in which the study of contemporary writings may have tinged my composition, for such has been a topic of censure with regard to poems far more popular, and indeed more deservedly popular, than mine. It is impossible that any one who inhabits the same age with such writers as those who stand in the foremost ranks of our own, can conscientiously assure himself that his language and tone of thought may not have been modified by the study of the productions of those extraordinary intellects. It is true, that, not the spirit of their genius, but the forms in which it has manifested itself, are due less to the peculiarities of their own minds than to the peculiarity of the moral and intellectual condition of the minds among which they have been produced. Thus a number of writers possess the form, whilst they want the spirit of those whom, it is alleged, they imitate; because the former is the endowment of the age in which they live,

and the latter must be the uncommunicated lightning of their
own mind.

The peculiar style of intense and comprehensive imagery
which distinguishes the modern literature of England, has not
been, as a general power, the product of the imitation of any
particular writer. The mass of capabilities remains at every
period materially the same; the circumstances which awaken
it to action perpetually change. If England were divided into
forty republics, each equal in population and extent to Athens,
there is no reason to suppose but that, under institutions not
more perfect than those of Athens, each would produce
philosophers and poets equal to those who (if we except
Shakespeare) have never been surpassed. We owe the great
writers of the golden age of our literature to that fervid
awakening of the public mind which shook to dust the oldest
and most oppressive form of the Christian religion. We owe
Milton to the progress and development of the same spirit:
the sacred Milton was, let it ever be remembered, a republican,
and a bold inquirer into morals and religion. The great
writers of our own age are, we have reason to suppose, the
companions and forerunners of some unimagined change in
our social condition or the opinions which cement it. The
cloud of mind is discharging its collected lightning, and the
equilibrium between institutions and opinions is now restoring,
or is about to be restored.

As to imitation, poetry is a mimetic art. It creates, but it
creates by combination and representation. Poetical abstrac-
tions are beautiful and new, not because the portions of which
they are composed had no previous existence in the mind of
man or in nature, but because the whole produced by their
combination has some intelligible and beautiful analogy with
those sources of emotion and thought, and with the contemporary condition of them: one great poet is a masterpiece of
nature which another not only ought to study but must study.
He might as wisely and as easily determine that his mind
should no longer be the mirror of all that is lovely in the
visible universe, as exclude from his contemplation the beautiful which exists in the writings of a great contemporary. The

pretence of doing it would be a presumption in any but the greatest; the effect, even in him, would be strained, unnatural, and ineffectual. A poet is the combined product of such internal powers as modify the nature of others; and of such external influences as excite and sustain these powers; he is not one, but both. Every man's mind is, in this respect, modified by all the objects of nature and art; by every word and every suggestion which he ever admitted to act upon his consciousness; it is the mirror upon which all forms are reflected, and in which they compose one form. Poets, not otherwise than philosophers, painters, sculptors, and musicians, are, in one sense, the creators, and, in another, the creations, of their age. From this subjection the loftiest do not escape. There is a similarity between Homer and Hesiod, between Æschylus and Euripides, between Virgil and Horace, between Dante and Petrarch, between Shakespeare and Fletcher, between Dryden and Pope; each has a generic resemblance under which their specific distinctions are arranged. If this similarity be the result of imitation, I am willing to confess that I have imitated.

Let this opportunity be conceded to me of acknowledging that I have, what a Scotch philosopher characteristically terms, 'a passion for reforming the world:' what passion incited him to write and publish his book, he omits to explain. For my part I had rather be damned with Plato and Lord Bacon, than go to Heaven with Paley and Malthus. But it is a mistake to suppose that I dedicate my poetical compositions solely to the direct enforcement of reform, or that I consider them in any degree as containing a reasoned system on the theory of human life. Didactic poetry is my abhorrence; nothing can be equally well expressed in prose that is not tedious and supererogatory in verse. My purpose has hitherto been simply to familiarise the highly refined imagination of the more select classes of poetical readers with beautiful idealisms of moral excellence; aware that until the mind can love, and admire, and trust, and hope, and endure, reasoned principles of moral conduct are seeds cast upon the highway of life which the unconscious passenger tramples into dust, although they would bear the harvest of his happiness. Should I live to accomplish what I purpose, that is, produce a systematical history of what appear to me to be the genuine elements of human society, let not the advocates of injustice and superstition flatter themselves that I should take Æschylus rather than Plato as my model.

The having spoken of myself with unaffected freedom will need little apology with the candid; and let the uncandid consider that they injure me less than their own hearts and minds by misrepresentation. Whatever talents a person may possess to amuse and instruct others, be they ever so inconsiderable, he is yet bound to exert them: if his attempt be ineffectual, let the punishment of an unaccomplished purpose have been sufficient; let none trouble themselves to heap the dust of oblivion upon his efforts; the pile they raise will betray his grave which might otherwise have been unknown.

## DRAMATIS PERSONÆ

| | | |
|---|---|---|
| PROMETHEUS. | ASIA | |
| DEMOGORGON. | PANTHEA | Oceanides. |
| JUPITER. | IONE | |
| THE EARTH. | HERCULES. | |
| OCEAN. | THE PHANTASM OF JUPITER. | |
| APOLLO. | THE SPIRIT OF THE EARTH. | |
| MERCURY. | THE SPIRIT OF THE MOON. | |
| | SPIRITS OF THE HOURS. | |

SPIRITS. ECHOES. FAUNS. FURIES.

## ACT I

SCENE.—*A Ravine of Icy Rocks in the Indian Caucasus.* PROMETHEUS *is discovered bound to the Precipice.* PANTHEA *and* IONE *are seated at his feet. Time, night. During the Scene, morning slowly breaks.*

*Prometheus.* Monarch of Gods and Dæmons, and all Spirits But One, who throng those bright and rolling worlds Which Thou and I alone of living things

Behold with sleepless eyes! regard this Earth
Made multitudinous with thy slaves, whom thou 5
Requitest for knee-worship, prayer, and praise,
And toil, and hecatombs of broken hearts,
With fear and self-contempt and barren hope.
Whilst me, who am thy foe, eyeless in hate,
Hast thou made reign and triumph, to thy scorn, 10
O'er mine own misery and thy vain revenge.
Three thousand years of sleep-unsheltered hours,
And moments aye divided by keen pangs
Till they seemed years, torture and solitude,
Scorn and despair,—these are mine empire:— 15
More glorious far than that which thou surveyest
From thine unenvied throne, O Mighty God!
Almighty, had I deigned to share the shame
Of thine ill tyranny, and hung not here
Nailed to this wall of eagle-baffling mountain, 20
Black, wintry, dead, unmeasured; without herb,
Insect, or beast, or shape or sound of life.
Ah me! alas, pain, pain ever, for ever!

No change, no pause, no hope! Yet I endure.
I ask the Earth, have not the mountains felt? 25
I ask yon Heaven, the all-beholding Sun,
Has it not seen? The Sea, in storm or calm,
Heaven's ever-changing Shadow, spread below,
Have its deaf waves not heard my agony?
Ah me! alas, pain, pain ever, for ever! 30

The crawling glaciers pierce me with the spears
Of their moon-freezing crystals, the bright chains
Eat with their burning cold into my bones.
Heaven's wingèd hound, polluting from thy lips
His beak in poison not his own, tears up 35
My heart; and shapeless sights come wandering by,
The ghastly people of the realm of dream,
Mocking me: and the Earthquake-fiends are charged
To wrench the rivets from my quivering wounds

When the rocks split and close again behind:          40
While from their loud abysses howling throng
The genii of the storm, urging the rage
Of whirlwind, and afflict me with keen hail.
And yet to me welcome is day and night,
Whether one breaks the hoar frost of the morn,          45
Or starry, dim, and slow, the other climbs
The leaden-coloured east; for then they lead
The wingless, crawling hours, one among whom
—As some dark Priest hales the reluctant victim—
Shall drag thee, cruel King, to kiss the blood          50
From these pale feet, which then might trample thee
If they disdained not such a prostrate slave.
Disdain! Ah no! I pity thee. What ruin
Will hunt thee undefended through the wide Heaven!
How will thy soul, cloven to its depth with terror,          55
Gape like a hell within! I speak in grief,
Not exultation, for I hate no more,
As then ere misery made me wise. The curse
Once breathed on thee I would recall. Ye Mountains,
Whose many-voicèd Echoes, through the mist          60
Of cataracts, flung the thunder of that spell!
Ye icy Springs, stagnant with wrinkling frost,
Which vibrated to hear me, and then crept
Shuddering through India! Thou serenest Air,
Through which the Sun walks burning without beams!          65
And ye swift Whirlwinds, who on poisèd wings
Hung mute and moveless o'er yon hushed abyss,
As thunder, louder than your own, made rock
The orbèd world! If then my words had power,
Though I am changed so that aught evil wish          70
Is dead within; although no memory be
Of what is hate, let them not lose it now!
What was that curse? for ye all heard me speak.

*First Voice ( from the Mountains).*
Thrice three hundred thousand years
O'er the Earthquake's couch we stood:          75

Oft, as men convulsed with fears,
    We trembled in our multitude.

*Second Voice (from the Springs).*
Thunderbolts had parched our water,
    We had been stained with bitter blood,
And had run mute, 'mid shrieks of slaughter,   80
    Thro' a city and a solitude.

*Third Voice (from the Air).*
I had clothed, since Earth uprose,
    Its wastes in colours not their own,
And oft had my serene repose
    Been cloven by many a rending groan.   85

*Fourth Voice (from the Whirlwinds).*
We had soared beneath these mountains
    Unresting ages; nor had thunder,
Nor yon volcano's flaming fountains,
    Nor any power above or under
    Ever made us mute with wonder.   90

*First Voice.*
But never bowed our snowy crest
As at the voice of thine unrest.

*Second Voice.*
Never such a sound before
To the Indian waves we bore.
A pilot asleep on the howling sea   95
Leaped up from the deck in agony,
And heard, and cried, 'Ah, woe is me!'
And died as mad as the wild waves be.

*Third Voice.*
By such dread words from Earth to Heaven
My still realm was never riven:   100
When its wound was closed, there stood
Darkness o'er the day like blood.

*Fourth Voice.*

And we shrank back: for dreams of ruin
To frozen caves our flight pursuing
Made us keep silence—thus—and thus—    105
Though silence is as hell to us.

*The Earth.*   The tongueless Caverns of the craggy hills
Cried, 'Misery!' then; the hollow Heaven replied,
'Misery!' And the Ocean's purple waves,
Climbing the land, howled to the lashing winds,    110
And the pale nations heard it, 'Misery!'
*Prometheus.*   I heard a sound of voices: not the voice
Which I gave forth.   Mother, thy sons and thou
Scorn him, without whose all-enduring will
Beneath the fierce omnipotence of Jove,    115
Both they and thou had vanished, like thin mist
Unrolled on the morning wind.  Know ye not me,
The Titan?  He who made his agony
The barrier to your else all-conquering foe?
Oh, rock-embosomed lawns, and snow-fed streams,    120
Now seen athwart frore vapours, deep below,
Through whose o'ershadowing woods I wandered once
With Asia, drinking life from her loved eyes;
Why scorns the spirit which informs ye, now
To commune with me? me alone, who checked,    125
As one who checks a fiend-drawn charioteer,
The falsehood and the force of him who reigns
Supreme, and with the groans of pining slaves
Fills your dim glens and liquid wildernesses:
Why answer ye not, still?  Brethren!
*The Earth.*                          They dare not.    130
*Prometheus.*   Who dares? for I would hear that curse again.
Ha, what an awful whisper rises up!
'Tis scarce like sound: it tingles through the frame
As lightning tingles, hovering ere it strike.
Speak, Spirit! from thine inorganic voice    135
I only know that thou art moving near
And love.  How cursed I him?

Oxford June 9th 1824.

UNIVERSITY COLLEGE, OXFORD

*The Earth.*                    How canst thou hear
Who knowest not the language of the dead?
  *Prometheus.*   Thou art a living spirit; speak as they.
  *The Earth.*   I dare not speak like life, lest Heaven's fell King
Should hear, and link me to some wheel of pain 141
More torturing than the one whereon I roll.
Subtle thou art and good, and though the Gods
Hear not this voice, yet thou art more than God,
Being wise and kind: earnestly hearken now. 145
  *Prometheus.*   Obscurely through my brain, like shadows dim,
Sweep awful thoughts, rapid and thick. I feel
Faint, like one mingled in entwining love;
Yet 'tis not pleasure.
  *The Earth.*                    No, thou canst not hear:
Thou art immortal, and this tongue is known 150
Only to those who die.
  *Prometheus.*                    And what art thou,
O, melancholy Voice?
  *The Earth.*                    I am the Earth,
Thy mother; she within whose stony veins,
To the last fibre of the loftiest tree
Whose thin leaves trembled in the frozen air, 155
Joy ran, as blood within a living frame,
When thou didst from her bosom, like a cloud
Of glory, arise, a spirit of keen joy!
And at thy voice her pining sons uplifted
Their prostrate brows from the polluting dust, 160
And our almighty Tyrant with fierce dread
Grew pale, until his thunder chained thee here.
Then, see those million worlds which burn and roll
Around us: their inhabitants beheld
My spherèd light wane in wide Heaven; the sea 165
Was lifted by strange tempest, and new fire
From earthquake-rifted mountains of bright snow
Shook its portentous hair beneath Heaven's frown;
Lightning and Inundation vexed the plains;
Blue thistles bloomed in cities; foodless toads 170
Within voluptuous chambers panting crawled:

D

When Plague had fallen on man, and beast, and worm,
And Famine; and black blight on herb and tree;
And in the corn, and vines, and meadow-grass,
Teemed ineradicable poisonous weeds                    175
Draining their growth, for my wan breast was dry
With grief; and the thin air, my breath, was stained
With the contagion of a mother's hate
Breathed on her child's destroyer; ay, I heard
Thy curse, the which, if thou rememberest not,          180
Yet my innumerable seas and streams,
Mountains, and caves, and winds, and yon wide air,
And the inarticulate people of the dead,
Preserve, a treasured spell. We meditate
In secret joy and hope those dreadful words,            185
But dare not speak them.

   *Prometheus.*                Venerable mother!
All else who live and suffer take from thee
Some comfort; flowers, and fruits, and happy sounds,
And love, though fleeting; these may not be mine.
But mine own words, I pray, deny me not.                190

   *The Earth.* They shall be told. Ere Babylon was dust,
The Magus Zoroaster, my dead child,
Met his own image walking in the garden.
That apparition, sole of men, he saw.
For know there are two worlds of life and death:        195
One that which thou beholdest; but the other
Is underneath the grave, where do inhabit
The shadows of all forms that think and live
Till death unite them and they part no more;
Dreams and the light imaginings of men,                 200
And all that faith creates or love desires,
Terrible, strange, sublime and beauteous shapes.
There thou art, and dost hang, a writhing shade,
'Mid whirlwind-peopled mountains; all the gods
Are there, and all the powers of nameless worlds,       205
Vast, sceptred phantoms; heroes, men, and beasts;
And Demogorgon, a tremendous gloom;
And he, the supreme Tyrant, on his throne

Of burning gold. Son, one of these shall utter
The curse which all remember. Call at will                    210
Thine own ghost, or the ghost of Jupiter,
Hades or Typhon, or what mightier Gods
From all-prolific Evil, since thy ruin
Have sprung, and trampled on my prostrate sons,
Ask, and they must reply: so the revenge            215
Of the Supreme may sweep through vacant shades,
As rainy wind through the abandoned gate
Of a fallen palace.

    *Prometheus.*          Mother, let not aught
Of that which may be evil, pass again
My lips, or those of aught resembling me.            220
Phantasm of Jupiter, arise, appear!

*Ione.*

    My wings are folded o'er mine ears:
        My wings are crossèd o'er mine eyes:
    Yet through their silver shade appears,
        And through their lulling plumes arise,            225
    A Shape, a throng of sounds;
        May it be no ill to thee
    O thou of many wounds!
Near whom for our sweet sister's sake,
Ever thus we watch and wake.            230

*Panthea.*

    The sound is of whirlwind underground,
        Earthquake, and fire, and mountains cloven;
    The shape is awful like the sound,
        Clothed in dark purple, star-inwoven.
    A sceptre of pale gold            235
        To stay steps proud, o'er the slow cloud
    His veinèd hand doth hold.
Cruel he looks, but calm and strong,
Like one who does, not suffers wrong.

*Phantasm of Jupiter.* Why have the secret powers of this
strange world            240

Driven me, a frail and empty phantom, hither
On direst storms? What unaccustomed sounds
Are hovering on my lips, unlike the voice
With which our pallid race hold ghastly talk
In darkness? And, proud sufferer, who art thou?        245

*Prometheus.*   Tremendous Image, as thou art must be
He whom thou shadowest forth. I am his foe,
The Titan. Speak the words which I would hear,
Although no thought inform thine empty voice.

*The Earth.*   Listen! And though your echoes must be mute,
Gray mountains, and old woods, and haunted springs,        251
Prophetic caves, and isle-surrounding streams,
Rejoice to hear what yet ye cannot speak.

*Phantasm.*   A spirit seizes me and speaks within:
It tears me as fire tears a thunder-cloud.        255

*Panthea.*   See, how he lifts his mighty looks, the Heaven
Darkens above.

*Ione.*                     He speaks! O shelter me!

*Prometheus.*   I see the curse on gestures proud and cold,
And looks of firm defiance, and calm hate,
And such despair as mocks itself with smiles,        260
Written as on a scroll: yet speak: Oh, speak!


*Phantasm.*

Fiend, I defy thee! with a calm, fixed mind,
     All that thou canst inflict I bid thee do;
Foul Tyrant both of Gods and Human-kind,
     One only being shalt thou not subdue.        265
Rain then thy plagues upon me here,
Ghastly disease, and frenzying fear;
And let alternate frost and fire
Eat into me, and be thine ire
Lightning, and cutting hail, and legioned forms        270
Of furies, driving by upon the wounding storms.


Ay, do thy worst. Thou art omnipotent.
     O'er all things but thyself I gave thee power,

And my own will.  Be thy swift mischiefs sent
   To blast mankind, from yon ethereal tower.    275
Let thy malignant spirit move
In darkness over those I love:
On me and mine I imprecate
The utmost torture of thy hate;
And thus devote to sleepless agony,    280
This undeclining head while thou must reign on high.

But thou, who art the God and Lord: O, thou,
   Who fillest with thy soul this world of woe,
To whom all things of Earth and Heaven do bow
   In fear and worship: all-prevailing foe!    285
I curse thee! let a sufferer's curse
Clasp thee, his torturer, like remorse;
Till thine Infinity shall be
A robe of envenomed agony;
And thine Omnipotence a crown of pain,    290
To cling like burning gold round thy dissolving brain.

Heap on thy soul, by virtue of this Curse,
   Ill deeds, then be thou damned, beholding good,
Both infinite as is the universe,
   And thou, and thy self-torturing solitude.    295
An awful image of calm power
Though now thou sittest, let the hour
Come, when thou must appear to be
That which thou art internally;
And after many a false and fruitless crime    300
Scorn track thy lagging fall through boundless space
    and time.

*Prometheus.*   Were these my words, O Parent?
*The Earth.*                        They were thine.
*Prometheus.*   It doth repent me: words are quick and vain;
Grief for awhile is blind, and so was mine.
I wish no living thing to suffer pain.    305

*The Earth.*

Misery, Oh misery to me,
That Jove at length should vanquish thee.
Wail, howl aloud, Land and Sea,
The Earth's rent heart shall answer ye.
Howl, Spirits of the living and the dead,          310
Your refuge, your defence lies fallen and vanquishèd.

*First Echo.*

Lies fallen and vanquishèd!

*Second Echo.*

Fallen and vanquishèd!

*Ione.*

Fear not: 'tis but some passing spasm,
    The Titan is unvanquished still.          315
But see, where through the azure chasm
    Of yon forked and snowy hill
Trampling the slant winds on high
    With golden-sandalled feet, that glow
Under plumes of purple dye,          320
Like rose-ensanguined ivory,
    A Shape comes now,
Stretching on high from his right hand
A serpent-cinctured wand.

*Panthea.*    'Tis Jove's world-wandering herald, Mercury.    325

*Ione.*

And who are those with hydra tresses
    And iron wings that climb the wind,
Whom the frowning God represses
    Like vapours steaming up behind,
Clanging loud, an endless crowd—          330

*Panthea.*

These are Jove's tempest-walking hounds,
Whom he gluts with groans and blood,

When charioted on sulphurous cloud
  He bursts Heaven's bounds.

*Ione.*

Are they now led, from the thin dead        335
On new pangs to be fed?

*Panthea.*

The Titan looks as ever, firm, not proud.

*First Fury.*  Ha! I scent life!
*Second Fury.*              Let me but look into his eyes!
*Third Fury.*  The hope of torturing him smells like a heap
Of corpses, to a death-bird after battle.          340
*First Fury.*  Darest thou delay, O Herald! take cheer, Hounds
Of Hell: what if the Son of Maia soon
Should make us food and sport—who can please long
The Omnipotent?
*Mercury.*          Back to your towers of iron,
And gnash, beside the streams of fire and wail,      345
Your foodless teeth.  Geryon, arise! and Gorgon,
Chimæra, and thou Sphinx, subtlest of fiends
Who ministered to Thebes Heaven's poisoned wine,
Unnatural love, and more unnatural hate:
These shall perform your task.
*First Fury.*              Oh, mercy! mercy!      350
We die with our desire: drive us not back!
*Mercury.*  Crouch then in silence.

                         Awful Sufferer!
To thee unwilling, most unwillingly
I come, by the great Father's will driven down,
To execute a doom of new revenge.              355
Alas! I pity thee, and hate myself
That I can do no more: aye from thy sight
Returning, for a season, Heaven seems Hell,
So thy worn form pursues me night and day,
Smiling reproach.  Wise art thou, firm and good,    360
But vainly wouldst stand forth alone in strife
Against the Omnipotent; as yon clear lamps

That measure and divide the weary years
From which there is no refuge, long have taught
And long must teach.  Even now thy Torturer arms      365
With the strange might of unimagined pains
The powers who scheme slow agonies in Hell,
And my commission is to lead them here,
Or what more subtle, foul, or savage fiends
People the abyss, and leave them to their task.      370
Be it not so! there is a secret known
To thee, and to none else of living things,
Which may transfer the sceptre of wide Heaven,
The fear of which perplexes the Supreme:
Clothe it in words, and bid it clasp his throne      375
In intercession; bend thy soul in prayer,
And like a suppliant in some gorgeous fane,
Let the will kneel within thy haughty heart:
For benefits and meek submission tame
The fiercest and the mightiest.

    *Prometheus.*              Evil minds      380
Change good to their own nature. I gave all
He has; and in return he chains me here
Years, ages, night and day: whether the Sun
Split my parched skin, or in the moony night
The crystal-wingèd snow cling round my hair:      385
Whilst my belovèd race is trampled down
By his thought-executing ministers.
Such is the tyrant's recompense: 'tis just:
He who is evil can receive no good;
And for a world bestowed, or a friend lost,      390
He can feel hate, fear, shame; not gratitude:
He but requites me for his own misdeed.
Kindness to such is keen reproach, which breaks
With bitter stings the light sleep of Revenge.
Submission, thou dost know I cannot try:      395
For what submission but that fatal word,
The death-seal of mankind's captivity,
Like the Sicilian's hair-suspended sword,
Which trembles o'er his crown, would he accept,

Or could I yield? Which yet I will not yield. 400
Let others flatter Crime, where it sits throned
In brief Omnipotence: secure are they:
For Justice, when triumphant, will weep down
Pity, not punishment, on her own wrongs,
Too much avenged by those who err. I wait, 405
Enduring thus, the retributive hour
Which since we spake is even nearer now.
But hark, the hell-hounds clamour: fear delay:
Behold! Heaven lowers under thy Father's frown.
 *Mercury.* Oh, that we might be spared: I to inflict 410
And thou to suffer! Once more answer me:
Thou knowest not the period of Jove's power?
 *Prometheus.* I know but this, that it must come.
 *Mercury.*        Alas!
Thou canst not count thy years to come of pain?
 *Prometheus.* They last while Jove must reign: nor more,
   nor less 415
Do I desire or fear.
 *Mercury.*    Yet pause, and plunge
Into Eternity, where recorded time,
Even all that we imagine, age on age,
Seems but a point, and the reluctant mind
Flags wearily in its unending flight, 420
Till it sink, dizzy, blind, lost, shelterless;
Perchance it has not numbered the slow years
Which thou must spend in torture, unreprieved?
 *Prometheus.* Perchance no thought can count them, yet they
   pass.
 *Mercury.* If thou might'st dwell among the Gods the while
Lapped in voluptuous joy?
 *Prometheus.*    I would not quit 426
This bleak ravine, these unrepentant pains.
 *Mercury.* Alas! I wonder at, yet pity thee.
 *Prometheus.* Pity the self-despising slaves of Heaven,
Not me, within whose mind sits peace serene, 430
As light in the sun, throned: how vain is talk!
Call up the fiends.

*Ione.*                    O, sister, look! White fire
Has cloven to the roots yon huge snow-loaded cedar;
How fearfully God's thunder howls behind!

*Mercury.*    I must obey his words and thine: alas!          435
Most heavily remorse hangs at my heart!

*Panthea.*    See where the child of Heaven, with wingèd feet,
Runs down the slanted sunlight of the dawn.

*Ione.*    Dear sister, close thy plumes over thine eyes
Lest thou behold and die: they come: they come          440
Blackening the birth of day with countless wings,
And hollow underneath, like death.

*First Fury.*                              Prometheus!

*Second Fury.*    Immortal Titan!

*Third Fury.*                    Champion of Heaven's slaves!

*Prometheus.*    He whom some dreadful voice invokes is here,
Prometheus, the chained Titan. Horrible forms,          445
What and who are ye? Never yet there came
Phantasms so foul through monster-teeming Hell
From the all-miscreative brain of Jove;
Whilst I behold such execrable shapes,
Methinks I grow like what I contemplate,          450
And laugh and stare in loathsome sympathy.

*First Fury.*    We are the ministers of pain, and fear,
And disappointment, and mistrust, and hate,
And clinging crime; and as lean dogs pursue
Through wood and lake some struck and sobbing fawn,          455
We track all things that weep, and bleed, and live,
When the great King betrays them to our will.

*Prometheus.*    Oh! many fearful natures in one name,
I know ye; and these lakes and echoes know
The darkness and the clangour of your wings.          460
But why more hideous than your loathèd selves
Gather ye up in legions from the deep?

*Second Fury.*    We knew not that: Sisters, rejoice, rejoice!

*Prometheus.*    Can aught exult in its deformity?

*Second Fury.*    The beauty of delight makes lovers glad,          465
Gazing on one another: so are we.
As from the rose which the pale priestess kneels

To gather for her festal crown of flowers
The aëreal crimson falls, flushing her cheek,
So from our victim's destined agony       470
The shade which is our form invests us round,
Else we are shapeless as our mother Night.

*Prometheus.* I laugh your power, and his who sent you here,
To lowest scorn. Pour forth the cup of pain.

*First Fury.* Thou thinkest we will rend thee bone from bone,
And nerve from nerve, working like fire within?    476

*Prometheus.* Pain is my element, as hate is thine;
Ye rend me now; I care not.

*Second Fury.*           Dost imagine
We will but laugh into thy lidless eyes?

*Prometheus.* I weigh not what ye do, but what ye suffer, 480
Being evil. Cruel was the power which called
You, or aught else so wretched, into light.

*Third Fury.* Thou think'st we will live through thee, one by one,
Like animal life, and though we can obscure not
The soul which burns within, that we will dwell    485
Beside it, like a vain loud multitude
Vexing the self-content of wisest men:
That we will be dread thought beneath thy brain,
And foul desire round thine astonished heart,
And blood within thy labyrinthine veins    490
Crawling like agony?

*Prometheus.*         Why, ye are thus now;
Yet am I king over myself, and rule
The torturing and conflicting throngs within,
As Jove rules you when Hell grows mutinous.

### Chorus of Furies.

From the ends of the earth, from the ends of the earth, 495
Where the night has its grave and the morning its birth,
               Come, come, come!
Oh, ye who shake hills with the scream of your mirth,
When cities sink howling in ruin; and ye
Who with wingless footsteps trample the sea,    500
And close upon Shipwreck and Famine's track,

Sit chattering with joy on the foodless wreck;
                Come, come, come!
        Leave the bed, low, cold, and red,
        Strewed beneath a nation dead;                505
        Leave the hatred, as in ashes
        Fire is left for future burning:
        It will burst in bloodier flashes
        When ye stir it, soon returning:
        Leave the self-contempt implanted        510
        In young spirits, sense-enchanted,
            Misery's yet unkindled fuel:
        Leave Hell's secrets half unchanted
            To the maniac dreamer; cruel
        More than ye can be with hate        515
            Is he with fear.
                Come, come, come!
    We are steaming up from Hell's wide gate
    And we burthen the blast of the atmosphere,
    But vainly we toil till ye come here.        520

*Ione.*    Sister, I hear the thunder of new wings.
*Panthea.*    These solid mountains quiver with the sound
Even as the tremulous air: their shadows make
The space within my plumes more black than night.

#### First Fury.

    Your call was as a wingèd car        525
    Driven on whirlwinds fast and far;
    It rapt us from red gulfs of war.

#### Second Fury.

    From wide cities, famine-wasted;

#### Third Fury.

    Groans half heard, and blood untasted;

#### Fourth Fury.

    Kingly conclaves stern and cold,        530
    Where blood with gold is bought and sold;

*Fifth Fury.*

From the furnace, white and hot,
In which—

*A Fury.*

  Speak not: whisper not:
I know all that ye would tell,
But to speak might break the spell   535
Which must bend the Invincible,
 The stern of thought;
He yet defies the deepest power of Hell.


*A Fury.*

Tear the veil!

*Another Fury.*
  It is torn.


*Chorus.*
     The pale stars of the morn
Shine on a misery, dire to be borne.   540
Dost thou faint, mighty Titan? We laugh thee to scorn.
Dost thou boast the clear knowledge thou waken'dst for man?
Then was kindled within him a thirst which outran
Those perishing waters; a thirst of fierce fever,
Hope, love, doubt, desire, which consume him for ever. 545
 One came forth of gentle worth
  Smiling on the sanguine earth;
 His words outlived him, like swift poison
  Withering up truth, peace, and pity.
 Look! where round the wide horizon  550
  Many a million-peopled city
 Vomits smoke in the bright air.
 Mark that outcry of despair!
 'Tis his mild and gentle ghost
  Wailing for the faith he kindled:  555
 Look again, the flames almost
  To a glow-worm's lamp have dwindled:

The survivors round the embers
   Gather in dread.

               Joy, joy, joy!          560
Past ages crowd on thee, but each one remembers.
And the future is dark, and the present is spread
Like a pillow of thorns for thy slumberless head.

*Semichorus I.*

   Drops of bloody agony flow
   From his white and quivering brow.          565
   Grant a little respite now:
   See a disenchanted nation
   Springs like day from desolation;
   To Truth its state is dedicate,
   And Freedom leads it forth, her mate;          570
   A legioned band of linkèd brothers
   Whom Love calls children—

*Semichorus II.*

              'Tis another's:
   See how kindred murder kin:
   'Tis the vintage-time for death and sin:
   Blood, like new wine, bubbles within:          575
     Till Despair smothers
   The struggling world, which slaves and tyrants win.

               [*All the* FURIES *vanish except one.*

*Ione.*   Hark, sister! what a low yet dreadful groan
Quite unsuppressed is tearing up the heart
Of the good Titan, as storms tear the deep,          580
And beasts hear the sea moan in inland caves.
Darest thou observe how the fiends torture him?
   *Panthea.*   Alas! I looked forth twice, but will no more.
   *Ione.*   What didst thou see?
   *Panthea.*          A woful sight: a youth
With patient looks nailed to a crucifix.          585
   *Ione.*   What next?

*Panthea*.                    The heaven around, the earth below
Was peopled with thick shapes of human death,
All horrible, and wrought by human hands,
And some appeared the work of human hearts.
For men were slowly killed by frowns and smiles:          590
And other sights too foul to speak and live
Were wandering by. Let us not tempt worse fear
By looking forth: those groans are grief enough.

*Fury*. Behold an emblem: those who do endure
Deep wrongs for man, and scorn, and chains, but heap     595
Thousandfold torment on themselves and him.

*Prometheus*. Remit the anguish of that lighted stare;
Close those wan lips; let that thorn-wounded brow
Stream not with blood; it mingles with thy tears!
Fix, fix those tortured orbs in peace and death,          600
So thy sick throes shake not that crucifix,
So those pale fingers play not with thy gore.
O, horrible! Thy name I will not speak,
It hath become a curse. I see, I see
The wise, the mild, the lofty, and the just,              605
Whom thy slaves hate for being like to thee,
Some hunted by foul lies from their heart's home,
An early-chosen, late-lamented home;
As hooded ounces cling to the driven hind;
Some linked to corpses in unwholesome cells:              610
Some—Hear I not the multitude laugh loud?—
Impaled in lingering fire: and mighty realms
Float by my feet, like sea-uprooted isles,
Whose sons are kneaded down in common blood
By the red light of their own burning homes.              615

*Fury*. Blood thou canst see, and fire; and canst hear groans;
Worse things, unheard, unseen, remain behind.

*Prometheus*. Worse?

*Fury*.                    In each human heart terror survives
The ravin it has gorged: the loftiest fear
All that they would disdain to think were true:           620
Hypocrisy and custom make their minds
The fanes of many a worship, now outworn.

They dare not devise good for man's estate,
And yet they know not that they do not dare.
The good want power, but to weep barren tears.   625
The powerful goodness want: worse need for them.
The wise want love; and those who love want wisdom;
And all best things are thus confused to ill.
Many are strong and rich, and would be just,
But live among their suffering fellow-men   630
As if none felt: they know not what they do.

   *Prometheus.* Thy words are like a cloud of wingèd snakes;
And yet I pity those they torture not.

    *Fury.* Thou pitiest them? I speak no more!   [*Vanishes.*
    *Prometheus.*                                 Ah woe!
Ah woe! Alas! pain, pain ever, for ever!   635
I close my tearless eyes, but see more clear
Thy works within my woe-illumèd mind,
Thou subtle tyrant! Peace is in the grave.
The grave hides all things beautiful and good:
I am a God and cannot find it there,   640
Nor would I seek it: for, though dread revenge,
This is defeat, fierce king, not victory.
The sights with which thou torturest gird my soul
With new endurance, till the hour arrives
When they shall be no types of things which are.   645

   *Panthea.* Alas! what sawest thou more?
   *Prometheus.*                  There are two woes:
To speak, and to behold; thou spare me one.
Names are there, Nature's sacred watchwords, they
Were borne aloft in bright emblazonry;
The nations thronged around, and cried aloud,   650
As with one voice, Truth, liberty, and love!
Suddenly fierce confusion fell from heaven
Among them: there was strife, deceit, and fear:
Tyrants rushed in, and did divide the spoil.
This was the shadow of the truth I saw.   655

   *The Earth.* I felt thy torture, son; with such mixed joy
As pain and virtue give. To cheer thy state
I bid ascend those subtle and fair spirits,

Whose homes are the dim caves of human thought,
And who inhabit, as birds wing the wind,                     660
Its world-surrounding aether: they behold
Beyond that twilight realm, as in a glass,
The future: may they speak comfort to thee!

   *Panthea.*   Look, sister, where a troop of spirits gather,
Like flocks of clouds in spring's delightful weather,       665
Thronging in the blue air!

   *Ione.*                And see! more come,
Like fountain-vapours when the winds are dumb,
That climb up the ravine in scattered lines.
And, hark! is it the music of the pines?
Is it the lake? Is it the waterfall?                         670

   *Panthea.*   'Tis something sadder, sweeter far than all.

### Chorus of Spirits.

From unremembered ages we
Gentle guides and guardians be
Of heaven-oppressed mortality;
And we breathe, and sicken not,                              675
The atmosphere of human thought:
Be it dim, and dank, and gray,
Like a storm-extinguished day,
Travelled o'er by dying gleams;
  Be it bright as all between                               680
Cloudless skies and windless streams,
  Silent, liquid, and serene;
As the birds within the wind,
  As the fish within the wave,
As the thoughts of man's own mind                           685
  Float through all above the grave;
We make there our liquid lair,
Voyaging cloudlike and unpent
Through the boundless element:
Thence we bear the prophecy                                  690
Which begins and ends in thee!

   *Ione.*   More yet come, one by one: the air around them
Looks radiant as the air around a star.

*First Spirit.*

On a battle-trumpet's blast
I fled hither, fast, fast, fast,                            695
'Mid the darkness upward cast.
From the dust of creeds outworn,
From the tyrant's banner torn,
Gathering 'round me, onward borne,
There was mingled many a cry—                              700
Freedom! Hope! Death! Victory!
Till they faded through the sky;
And one sound, above, around,
One sound beneath, around, above,
Was moving; 'twas the soul of Love;                        705
'Twas the hope, the prophecy,
Which begins and ends in thee.

*Second Spirit.*

A rainbow's arch stood on the sea,
Which rocked beneath, immovably;
And the triumphant storm did flee,                         710
Like a conqueror, swift and proud,
Between, with many a captive cloud,
A shapeless, dark and rapid crowd,
Each by lightning riven in half:
I heard the thunder hoarsely laugh:                        715
Mighty fleets were strewn like chaff
And spread beneath a hell of death
O'er the white waters. I alit
On a great ship lightning-split,
And speeded hither on the sigh                             720
Of one who gave an enemy
His plank, then plunged aside to die.

*Third Spirit.*

I sate beside a sage's bed,
And the lamp was burning red
Near the book where he had fed,                            725

When a Dream with plumes of flame,
To his pillow hovering came,
And I knew it was the same
Which had kindled long ago
Pity, eloquence, and woe;      730
And the world awhile below
Wore the shade, its lustre made.
It has borne me here as fleet
As Desire's lightning feet:
I must ride it back ere morrow,      735
Or the sage will wake in sorrow.

### Fourth Spirit.

On a poet's lips I slept
Dreaming like a love-adept
In the sound his breathing kept;
Nor seeks nor finds he mortal blisses,      740
But feeds on the aëreal kisses
Of shapes that haunt thought's wildernesses.
He will watch from dawn to gloom
The lake-reflected sun illume
The yellow bees in the ivy-bloom,      745
Nor heed nor see, what things they be;
But from these create he can
Forms more real than living man,
Nurslings of immortality!
One of these awakened me,      750
And I sped to succour thee.

### Ione.

Behold'st thou not two shapes from the east and west
Come, as two doves to one belovèd nest,
Twin nurslings of the all-sustaining air
On swift still wings glide down the atmosphere?      755
And, hark! their sweet, sad voices! 'tis despair
Mingled with love and then dissolved in sound.

*Panthea.*   Canst thou speak, sister? all my words are drowned.

*Ione.*   Their beauty gives me voice.  See how they float
On their sustaining wings of skiey grain,                              760
Orange and azure deepening into gold:
Their soft smiles light the air like a star's fire.


### Chorus of Spirits.

Hast thou beheld the form of Love?


### Fifth Spirit.

As over wide dominions
 I sped, like some swift cloud that wings the wide air's wilder-
  nesses,
That planet-crested shape swept by on lightning-braide d
 pinions,
 Scattering the liquid joy of life from his ambrosial tresses:
His footsteps paved the world with light; but as I passed 'twas
 fading,
 And hollow Ruin yawned behind: great sages bound in
  madness,
And headless patriots, and pale youths who perished, un-
 upbraiding,
 Gleamed in the night.  I wandered o'er, till thou, O King of
  sadness,
 Turned by thy smile the worst I saw to recollected gladness.


### Sixth Spirit.

Ah, sister!  Desolation is a delicate thing:                          772
 It walks not on the earth, it floats not on the air,
But treads with silent footstep, and fans with silent wing
 The tender hopes which in their hearts the best and gentlest
  bear;                                                          775
Who, soothed to false repose by the fanning plumes above
 And the music-stirring motion of its soft and busy feet,
Dream visions of aëreal joy, and call the monster, Love,
 And wake, and find the shadow Pain, as he whom now we
  greet.

*Chorus.*

Though Ruin now Love's shadow be,                780
Following him, destroyingly,
   On Death's white and wingèd steed,
Which the fleetest cannot flee,
   Trampling down both flower and weed,
Man and beast, and foul and fair,                785
Like a tempest through the air;
Thou shalt quell this horseman grim,
Woundless though in heart or limb.

*Prometheus.*   Spirits! how know ye this shall be?

*Chorus.*

In the atmosphere we breathe,                790
As buds grow red when the snow-storms flee,
   From Spring gathering up beneath,
Whose mild winds shake the elder brake,
And the wandering herdsmen know
That the white-thorn soon will blow:                795
   Wisdom, Justice, Love, and Peace,
   When they struggle to increase,
     Are to us as soft winds be
     To shepherd boys, the prophecy
     Which begins and ends in thee.                800

*Ione.*   Where are the Spirits fled?
  *Panthea.*                                  Only a sense
Remains of them, like the omnipotence
Of music, when the inspired voice and lute
Languish, ere yet the responses are mute,
Which through the deep and labyrinthine soul,                805
Like echoes through long caverns, wind and roll.
  *Prometheus.*   How fair these airborn shapes! and yet I feel
Most vain all hope but love; and thou art fair,
Asia! who, when my being overflowed,
Wert like a golden chalice to bright wine                810
Which else had sunk into the thirsty dust.

All things are still: alas! how heavily
This quiet morning weighs upon my heart;
Though I should dream I could even sleep with grief
If slumber were denied not. I would fain      815
Be what it is my destiny to be,
The saviour and the strength of suffering man,
Or sink into the original gulf of things:
There is no agony, and no solace left;
Earth can console, Heaven can torment no more.      820
    *Panthea.*   Hast thou forgotten one who watches thee
The cold dark night, and never sleeps but when
The shadow of thy spirit falls on her?
    *Prometheus.*   I said all hope was vain but love: thou lovest.
    *Panthea.*   Deeply in truth; but the eastern star looks white,
And Asia waits in that far Indian vale,      826
The scene of her sad exile; rugged once
And desolate and frozen, like this ravine;
But now invested with fair flowers and herbs,
And haunted by sweet airs and sounds, which flow      830
Among the woods and waters, from the aether
Of her transforming presence, which would fade
If it were mingled not with thine. Farewell!

END OF THE FIRST ACT.

## ACT II

SCENE I.—*Morning. A lovely Vale in the Indian Caucasus.*
    *Asia alone.*

    *Asia.*   From all the blasts of heaven thou hast descended:
Yes, like a spirit, like a thought, which makes
Unwonted tears throng to the horny eyes,
And beatings haunt the desolated heart,
Which should have learnt repose: thou hast descended      5
Cradled in tempests; thou dost wake, O Spring!
O child of many winds! As suddenly
Thou comest as the memory of a dream,

Which now is sad because it hath been sweet;
Like genius, or like joy which riseth up      10
As from the earth, clothing with golden clouds
The desert of our life.
This is the season, this the day, the hour;
At sunrise thou shouldst come, sweet sister mine,
Too long desired, too long delaying, come!      15
How like death-worms the wingless moments crawl!
The point of one white star is quivering still
Deep in the orange light of widening morn
Beyond the purple mountains: through a chasm
Of wind-divided mist the darker lake      20
Reflects it: now it wanes: it gleams again
As the waves fade, and as the burning threads
Of woven cloud unravel in pale air:
'Tis lost! and through yon peaks of cloud-like snow
The roseate sunlight quivers: hear I not      25
The Æolian music of her sea-green plumes
Winnowing the crimson dawn?      [PANTHEA *enters*.
               I feel, I see
Those eyes which burn through smiles that fade in tears,
Like stars half quenched in mists of silver dew.
Belovèd and most beautiful, who wearest      30
The shadow of that soul by which I live,
How late thou art! the spherèd sun had climbed
The sea; my heart was sick with hope, before
The printless air felt thy belated plumes.
   *Panthea*.    Pardon, great Sister! but my wings were faint
With the delight of a remembered dream,      36
As are the noontide plumes of summer winds
Satiate with sweet flowers. I was wont to sleep
Peacefully, and awake refreshed and calm
Before the sacred Titan's fall, and thy      40
Unhappy love, had made, through use and pity,
Both love and woe familiar to my heart
As they had grown to thine: erewhile I slept
Under the glaucous caverns of old Ocean
Within dim bowers of green and purple moss,      45

Our young Ione's soft and milky arms
Locked then, as now, behind my dark, moist hair,
While my shut eyes and cheek were pressed within
The folded depth of her life-breathing bosom:
But not as now, since I am made the wind           50
Which fails beneath the music that I bear
Of thy most wordless converse; since dissolved
Into the sense with which love talks, my rest
Was troubled and yet sweet; my waking hours
Too full of care and pain.

  *Asia.*       Lift up thine eyes,           55
And let me read thy dream.

  *Panthea.*       As I have said
With our sea-sister at his feet I slept.
The mountain mists, condensing at our voice
Under the moon, had spread their snowy flakes,
From the keen ice shielding our linkèd sleep.      60
Then two dreams came. One, I remember not.
But in the other his pale wound-worn limbs
Fell from Prometheus, and the azure night
Grew radiant with the glory of that form
Which lives unchanged within, and his voice fell    65
Like music which makes giddy the dim brain,
Faint with intoxication of keen joy:
'Sister of her whose footsteps pave the world
With loveliness—more fair than aught but her,
Whose shadow thou art—lift thine eyes on me.'       70
I lifted them: the overpowering light
Of that immortal shape was shadowed o'er
By love; which, from his soft and flowing limbs,
And passion-parted lips, and keen, faint eyes,
Steamed forth like vaporous fire; an atmosphere     75
Which wrapped me in its all-dissolving power,
As the warm æther of the morning sun
Wraps ere it drinks some cloud of wandering dew.
I saw not, heard not, moved not, only felt
His presence flow and mingle through my blood       80
Till it became his life, and his grew mine,

And I was thus absorbed, until it passed,
And like the vapours when the sun sinks down,
Gathering again in drops upon the pines,
And tremulous as they, in the deep night          85
My being was condensed; and as the rays
Of thought were slowly gathered, I could hear
His voice, whose accents lingered ere they died
Like footsteps of weak melody: thy name
Among the many sounds alone I heard              90
Of what might be articulate; though still
I listened through the night when sound was none.
Ione wakened then, and said to me:
'Canst thou divine what troubles me to-night?
I always knew what I desired before,             95
Nor ever found delight to wish in vain.
But now I cannot tell thee what I seek;
I know not; something sweet, since it is sweet
Even to desire; it is thy sport, false sister;
Thou hast discovered some enchantment old,       100
Whose spells have stolen my spirit as I slept
And mingled it with thine: for when just now
We kissed, I felt within thy parted lips
The sweet air that sustained me, and the warmth
Of the life-blood, for loss of which I faint,   105
Quivered between our intertwining arms.'
I answered not, for the Eastern star grew pale,
But fled to thee.

   *Asia.*           Thou speakest, but thy words
Are as the air: I feel them not: Oh, lift
Thine eyes, that I may read his written soul!    110

   *Panthea.*   I lift them though they droop beneath the load
Of that they would express: what canst thou see
But thine own fairest shadow imaged there?

   *Asia.*   Thine eyes are like the deep, blue, boundless heaven
Contracted to two circles underneath             115
Their long, fine lashes; dark, far, measureless,
Orb within orb, and line through line inwoven.

   *Panthea.*   Why lookest thou as if a spirit passed?

*Asia.*    There is a change: beyond their inmost depth
I see a shade, a shape: 'tis He, arrayed                    120
In the soft light of his own smiles, which spread
Like radiance from the cloud-surrounded morn.
Prometheus, it is thine! depart not yet!
Say not those smiles that we shall meet again
Within that bright pavilion which their beams        125
Shall build o'er the waste world? The dream is told.
What shape is that between us? Its rude hair
Roughens the wind that lifts it, its regard
Is wild and quick, yet 'tis a thing of air,
For through its gray robe gleams the golden dew        130
Whose stars the noon has quenched not.
    *Dream.*                                    Follow! Follow!
    *Panthea.*    It is mine other dream.
    *Asia.*                                    It disappears.
    *Panthea.*    It passes now into my mind. Methought
As we sate here, the flower-infolding buds
Burst on yon lightning-blasted almond-tree,            135
When swift from the white Scythian wilderness
A wind swept forth wrinkling the Earth with frost:
I looked, and all the blossoms were blown down;
But on each leaf was stamped, as the blue bells
Of Hyacinth tell Apollo's written grief,                140
O, FOLLOW, FOLLOW!
    *Asia.*                        As you speak, your words
Fill, pause by pause, my own forgotten sleep
With shapes. Methought among these lawns together
We wandered, underneath the young gray dawn,
And multitudes of dense white fleecy clouds            145
Were wandering in thick flocks along the mountains
Shepherded by the slow, unwilling wind;
And the white dew on the new-bladed grass,
Just piercing the dark earth, hung silently;
And there was more which I remember not:                150
But on the shadows of the morning clouds,
Athwart the purple mountain slope, was written
FOLLOW, O, FOLLOW! as they vanished by;

And on each herb, from which Heaven's dew had fallen,
The like was stamped, as with a withering fire;                    155
A wind arose among the pines; it shook
The clinging music from their boughs, and then
Low, sweet, faint sounds, like the farewell of ghosts,
Were heard: O, FOLLOW, FOLLOW, FOLLOW ME!
And then I said: 'Panthea, look on me.'                            160
But in the depth of those belovèd eyes
Still I saw, FOLLOW, FOLLOW!
  *Echo.*       Follow, follow!
  *Panthea.* The crags, this clear spring morning, mock our voices
As they were spirit-tongued.
  *Asia.*      It is some being
Around the crags. What fine clear sounds! O, list!                 165

     *Echoes (unseen).*
    Echoes we: listen!
    We cannot stay:
    As dew-stars glisten
     Then fade away—
      Child of Ocean!                 170

 *Asia.* Hark! Spirits speak. The liquid responses
Of their aëreal tongues yet sound.
  *Panthea.*    I hear.
       *Echoes.*
   O, follow, follow,
    As our voice recedeth
   Through the caverns hollow,                        175
    Where the forest spreadeth;
     (*More distant.*)
    O, follow, follow!
   Through the caverns hollow,
  As the song floats thou pursue,
  Where the wild bee never flew,                            180
  Through the noontide darkness deep,
  By the odour-breathing sleep
  Of faint night flowers, and the waves
  At the fountain-lighted caves,

>     While our music, wild and sweet,          185
>        Mocks thy gently falling feet,
>                Child of Ocean!

*Asia.*    Shall we pursue the sound?  It grows more faint
And distant.
    *Panthea.*    List! the strain floats nearer now.

#### Echoes.

>        In the world unknown          190
>           Sleeps a voice unspoken;
>        By thy step alone
>           Can its rest be broken;
>                Child of Ocean!

*Asia.*    How the notes sink upon the ebbing wind!          195

#### Echoes.

>        O, follow, follow!
>           Through the caverns hollow,
>     As the song floats thou pursue,
>     By the woodland noontide dew;
>     By the forest, lakes, and fountains,          200
>     Through the many-folded mountains;
>     To the rents, and gulfs, and chasms,
>     Where the Earth reposed from spasms,
>     On the day when He and thou
>     Parted, to commingle now;          205
>                Child of Ocean!

*Asia.*    Come, sweet Panthea, link thy hand in mine,
And follow, ere the voices fade away.

SCENE II.—*A Forest, intermingled with Rocks and Caverns.* ASIA
   *and* PANTHEA *pass into it.  Two young Fauns are sitting on
   a Rock listening.*

#### Semichorus I. of Spirits.

>     The path through which that lovely twain
>        Have passed, by cedar, pine, and yew,

And each dark tree that ever grew,
Is curtained out from Heaven's wide blue;
Nor sun, nor moon, nor wind, nor rain,                5
    Can pierce its interwoven bowers,
  Nor aught, save where some cloud of dew,
Drifted along the earth-creeping breeze,
Between the trunks of the hoar trees,
    Hangs each a pearl in the pale flowers          10
  Of the green laurel, blown anew;
And bends, and then fades silently,
One frail and fair anemone:
Or when some star of many a one
That climbs and wanders through steep night,          15
Has found the cleft through which alone
Beams fall from high those depths upon
Ere it is borne away, away,
By the swift Heavens that cannot stay,
It scatters drops of golden light,                    20
Like lines of rain that ne'er unite:
And the gloom divine is all around,
And underneath is the mossy ground.

### Semichorus II.

There the voluptuous nightingales,
  Are awake through all the broad noonday.        25
When one with bliss or sadness fails,
    And through the windless ivy-boughs,
  Sick with sweet love, droops dying away
On its mate's music-panting bosom;
Another from the swinging blossom,                    30
    Watching to catch the languid close
Of the last strain, then lifts on high
The wings of the weak melody,
'Till some new strain of feeling bear
  The song, and all the woods are mute;           35
When there is heard through the dim air
The rush of wings, and rising there
    Like many a lake-surrounded flute,

Sounds overflow the listener's brain
So sweet, that joy is almost pain.                    40

*Semichorus I.*

There those enchanted eddies play
  Of echoes, music-tongued, which draw,
  By Demogorgon's mighty law,
  With melting rapture, or sweet awe,
All spirits on that secret way;                       45
  As inland boats are driven to Ocean
Down streams made strong with mountain-thaw:
    And first there comes a gentle sound
    To those in talk or slumber bound,
  And wakes the destined soft emotion,—             50
Attracts, impels them; those who saw
  Say from the breathing earth behind
  There steams a plume-uplifting wind
Which drives them on their path, while they
  Believe their own swift wings and feet            55
The sweet desires within obey:
And so they float upon their way,
Until, still sweet, but loud and strong,
The storm of sound is driven along,
  Sucked up and hurrying: as they fleet            60
  Behind, its gathering billows meet
And to the fatal mountain bear
Like clouds amid the yielding air.

*First Faun.*   Canst thou imagine where those spirits live
Which make such delicate music in the woods?          65
We haunt within the least frequented caves
And closest coverts, and we know these wilds,
Yet never meet them, though we hear them oft:
Where may they hide themselves?
  *Second Faun.*                    'Tis hard to tell:
I have heard those more skilled in spirits say,       70
The bubbles, which the enchantment of the sun
Sucks from the pale faint water-flowers that pave

The oozy bottom of clear lakes and pools,
Are the pavilions where such dwell and float
Under the green and golden atmosphere 75
Which noontide kindles through the woven leaves;
And when these burst, and the thin fiery air,
The which they breathed within those lucent domes,
Ascends to flow like meteors through the night,
They ride on them, and rein their headlong speed, 80
And bow their burning crests, and glide in fire
Under the waters of the earth again.

*First Faun.* If such live thus, have others other lives,
Under pink blossoms or within the bells
Of meadow flowers, or folded violets deep, 85
Or on their dying odours, when they die,
Or in the sunlight of the spherèd dew?

*Second Faun.* Ay, many more which we may well divine.
But, should we stay to speak, noontide would come,
And thwart Silenus find his goats undrawn, 90
And grudge to sing those wise and lovely songs
Of Fate, and Chance, and God, and Chaos old,
And Love, and the chained Titan's woful doom,
And how he shall be loosed, and make the earth
One brotherhood: delightful strains which cheer 95
Our solitary twilights, and which charm
To silence the unenvying nightingales.

SCENE III.—*A Pinnacle of Rock among Mountains.*
ASIA *and* PANTHEA.

*Panthea.* Hither the sound has borne us—to the realm
Of Demogorgon, and the mighty portal,
Like a volcano's meteor-breathing chasm,
Whence the oracular vapour is hurled up
Which lonely men drink wandering in their youth, 5
And call truth, virtue, love, genius, or joy,
That maddening wine of life, whose dregs they drain
To deep intoxication; and uplift,
Like Mænads who cry loud, Evoe! Evoe!

The voice which is contagion to the world.                        10
   *Asia.*  Fit throne for such a Power! Magnificent!
How glorious art thou, Earth! And if thou be
The shadow of some spirit lovelier still,
Though evil stain its work, and it should be
Like its creation, weak yet beautiful,                            15
I could fall down and worship that and thee.
Even now my heart adoreth: Wonderful!
Look, sister, ere the vapour dim thy brain:
Beneath is a wide plain of billowy mist,
As a lake, paving in the morning sky,                             20
With azure waves which burst in silver light,
Some Indian vale. Behold it, rolling on
Under the curdling winds, and islanding
The peak whereon we stand, midway, around,
Encinctured by the dark and blooming forests,                     25
Dim twilight-lawns, and stream-illumined caves,
And wind-enchanted shapes of wandering mist;
And far on high the keen sky-cleaving mountains
From icy spires of sun-like radiance fling
The dawn, as lifted Ocean's dazzling spray,                       30
From some Atlantic islet scattered up,
Spangles the wind with lamp-like water-drops.
The vale is girdled with their walls, a howl
Of cataracts from their thaw-cloven ravines,
Satiates the listening wind, continuous, vast,                    35
Awful as silence. Hark! the rushing snow!
The sun-awakened avalanche! whose mass,
Thrice sifted by the storm, had gathered there
Flake after flake, in heaven-defying minds
As thought by thought is piled, till some great truth            40
Is loosened, and the nations echo round,
Shaken to their roots, as do the mountains now.
   *Panthea.*  Look how the gusty sea of mist is breaking
In crimson foam, even at our feet! it rises
As Ocean at the enchantment of the moon                          45
Round foodless men wrecked on some oozy isle.
   *Asia.*  The fragments of the cloud are scattered up;

The wind that lifts them disentwines my hair;
Its billows now sweep o'er mine eyes; my brain
Grows dizzy; see'st thou shapes within the mist? 50
   *Panthea.* A countenance with beckoning smiles: there burns
An azure fire within its golden locks!
Another and another: hark! they speak!


### Song of Spirits.

To the deep, to the deep,
            Down, down! 55
Through the shade of sleep,
Through the cloudy strife
Of Death and of Life;
Through the veil and the bar
Of things which seem and are 60
Even to the steps of the remotest throne,
            Down, down!


While the sound whirls around,
            Down, down!
As the fawn draws the hound, 65
As the lightning the vapour,
As a weak moth the taper;
Death, despair; love, sorrow;
Time both; to-day, to-morrow;
As steel obeys the spirit of the stone, 70
            Down, down!


Through the gray, void abysm,
            Down, down!
Where the air is no prism,
And the moon and stars are not, 75
And the cavern-crags wear not
The radiance of Heaven,
Nor the gloom to Earth given,
Where there is One pervading, One alone,
            Down, down! 80

E

In the depth of the deep,
   Down, down!
Like veiled lightning asleep,
Like the spark nursed in embers,
The last look Love remembers,   85
Like a diamond, which shines
On the dark wealth of mines,
A spell is treasured but for thee alone.
   Down, down!

We have bound thee, we guide thee;   90
   Down, down!
With the bright form beside thee;
Resist not the weakness,
Such strength is in meekness
That the Eternal, the Immortal,   95
Must unloose through life's portal
The snake-like Doom coiled underneath his throne
   By that alone.

SCENE IV.—*The Cave of Demogorgon.* ASIA *and* PANTHEA.

*Panthea.* What veilèd form sits on that ebon throne?
*Asia.* The veil has fallen.
*Panthea.*     I see a mighty darkness
Filling the seat of power, and rays of gloom
Dart round, as light from the meridian sun.
—Ungazed upon and shapeless; neither limb,   5
Nor form, nor outline; yet we feel it is
A living Spirit.
*Demogorgon.* Ask what thou wouldst know.
*Asia.* What canst thou tell?
*Demogorgon.*    All things thou dar'st demand.
*Asia.* Who made the living world?
*Demogorgon.*     God.
*Asia.*        Who made all
That it contains? thought, passion, reason, will,   10
Imagination?
*Demogorgon.* God: Almighty God.

*Asia.* Who made that sense which, when the winds of Spring
In rarest visitation, or the voice
Of one belovèd heard in youth alone,
Fills the faint eyes with falling tears which dim          15
The radiant looks of unbewailing flowers,
And leaves this peopled earth a solitude
When it returns no more?

*Demogorgon.*                    Merciful God.

*Asia.*    And who made terror, madness, crime, remorse,
Which from the links of the great chain of things,          20
To every thought within the mind of man
Sway and drag heavily, and each one reels
Under the load towards the pit of death;
Abandoned hope, and love that turns to hate;
And self-contempt, bitterer to drink than blood;          25
Pain, whose unheeded and familiar speech
Is howling, and keen shrieks, day after day;
And Hell, or the sharp fear of Hell?

*Demogorgon.*                    He reigns.

*Asia.*    Utter his name: a world pining in pain
Asks but his name: curses shall drag him down.          30

*Demogorgon.*    He reigns.

*Asia.*                    I feel, I know it: who?

*Demogorgon.*                                        He reigns.

*Asia.*    Who reigns? There was the Heaven and Earth at
    first,
And Light and Love; then Saturn, from whose throne
Time fell, an envious shadow: such the state
Of the earth's primal spirits beneath his sway,          35
As the calm joy of flowers and living leaves
Before the wind or sun has withered them
And semivital worms; but he refused
The birthright of their being, knowledge, power,
The skill which wields the elements, the thought          40
Which pierces this dim universe like light,
Self-empire, and the majesty of love;
For thirst of which they fainted. Then Prometheus
Gave wisdom, which is strength, to Jupiter,

And with this law alone, 'Let man be free,'          45
Clothed him with the dominion of wide Heaven.
To know nor faith, nor love, nor law; to be
Omnipotent but friendless is to reign;
And Jove now reigned; for on the race of man
First famine, and then toil, and then disease,          50
Strife, wounds, and ghastly death unseen before,
Fell; and the unseasonable seasons drove
With alternating shafts of frost and fire,
Their shelterless, pale tribes to mountain caves:
And in their desert hearts fierce wants he sent,          55
And mad disquietudes, and shadows idle
Of unreal good, which levied mutual war,
So ruining the lair wherein they raged.
Prometheus saw, and waked the legioned hopes
Which sleep within folded Elysian flowers,          60
Nepenthe, Moly, Amaranth, fadeless blooms,
That they might hide with thin and rainbow wings
The shape of Death; and Love he sent to bind
The disunited tendrils of that vine
Which bears the wine of life, the human heart;          65
And he tamed fire which, like some beast of prey,
Most terrible, but lovely, played beneath
The frown of man; and tortured to his will
Iron and gold, the slaves and signs of power,
And gems and poisons, and all subtlest forms          70
Hidden beneath the mountains and the waves.
He gave man speech, and speech created thought,
Which is the measure of the universe;
And Science struck the thrones of earth and heaven,
Which shook, but fell not; and the harmonious mind          75
Poured itself forth in all-prophetic song;
And music lifted up the listening spirit
Until it walked, exempt from mortal care,
Godlike, o'er the clear billows of sweet sound;
And human hands first mimicked and then mocked,          80
With moulded limbs more lovely than its own,
The human form, till marble grew divine;

And mothers, gazing, drank the love men see
Reflected in their race, behold, and perish.
He told the hidden power of herbs and springs,          85
And Disease drank and slept. Death grew like sleep.
He taught the implicated orbits woven
Of the wide-wandering stars; and how the sun
Changes his lair, and by what secret spell
The pale moon is transformed, when her broad eye          90
Gazes not on the interlunar sea:
He taught to rule, as life directs the limbs,
The tempest-wingèd chariots of the Ocean,
And the Celt knew the Indian. Cities then
Were built, and through their snow-like columns flowed          95
The warm winds, and the azure aether shone,
And the blue sea and shadowy hills were seen.
Such, the alleviations of his state,
Prometheus gave to man, for which he hangs
Withering in destined pain: but who rains down          100
Evil, the immedicable plague, which, while
Man looks on his creation like a God
And sees that it is glorious, drives him on,
The wreck of his own will, the scorn of earth,
The outcast, the abandoned, the alone?          105
Not Jove: while yet his frown shook Heaven, ay, when
His adversary from adamantine chains
Cursed him, he trembled like a slave. Declare
Who is his master? Is he too a slave?
    *Demogorgon.* All spirits are enslaved which serve things evil:
Thou knowest if Jupiter be such or no.          111
    *Asia.*   Whom calledst thou God?
    *Demogorgon.*                      I spoke but as ye speak,
For Jove is the supreme of living things.
    *Asia.*   Who is the master of the slave?
    *Demogorgon.*                      If the abysm
Could vomit forth its secrets. . . . But a voice          115
Is wanting, the deep truth is imageless;
For what would it avail to bid thee gaze
On the revolving world? What to bid speak

Fate, Time, Occasion, Chance, and Change? To these
All things are subject but eternal Love.                              120
  *Asia.*   So much I asked before, and my heart gave
The response thou hast given; and of such truths
Each to itself must be the oracle.
One more demand; and do thou answer me
As mine own soul would answer, did it know                125
That which I ask. Prometheus shall arise
Henceforth the sun of this rejoicing world:
When shall the destined hour arrive?
  *Demogorgon.*                              Behold!
  *Asia.*   The rocks are cloven, and through the purple night
I see cars drawn by rainbow-wingèd steeds               130
Which trample the dim winds: in each there stands
A wild-eyed charioteer urging their flight.
Some look behind, as fiends pursued them there,
And yet I see no shapes but the keen stars:
Others, with burning eyes, lean forth, and drink        135
With eager lips the wind of their own speed,
As if the thing they loved fled on before,
And now, even now, they clasped it. Their bright locks
Stream like a comet's flashing hair: they all
Sweep onward.
  *Demogorgon.*   These are the immortal Hours,         140
Of whom thou didst demand. One waits for thee.
  *Asia.*   A spirit with a dreadful countenance
Checks its dark chariot by the craggy gulf.
Unlike thy brethren, ghastly charioteer,
Who art thou? Whither wouldst thou bear me? Speak!     145
  *Spirit.*   I am the shadow of a destiny
More dread than is my aspect: ere yon planet
Has set, the darkness which ascends with me
Shall wrap in lasting night heaven's kingless throne.
  *Asia.*   What meanest thou?
  *Panthea.*                     That terrible shadow floats
Up from its throne, as may the lurid smoke               151
Of earthquake-ruined cities o'er the sea.
Lo! it ascends the car; the coursers fly

Terrified: watch its path among the stars
Blackening the night!

   *Asia.*               Thus I am answered: strange!     155
   *Panthea.*    See, near the verge, another chariot stays;
An ivory shell inlaid with crimson fire,
Which comes and goes within its sculptured rim
Of delicate strange tracery; the young spirit
That guides it has the dove-like eyes of hope;     160
How its soft smiles attract the soul! as light
Lures wingèd insects through the lampless air.

*Spirit.*

My coursers are fed with the lightning,
   They drink of the whirlwind's stream,
And when the red morning is bright'ning     165
   They bathe in the fresh sunbeam;
   They have strength for their swiftness I deem,
Then ascend with me, daughter of Ocean.

I desire: and their speed makes night kindle;
   I fear: they outstrip the Typhoon;     170
Ere the cloud piled on Atlas can dwindle
   We encircle the earth and the moon:
   We shall rest from long labours at noon:
Then ascend with me, daughter of Ocean.

SCENE V.—*The Car pauses within a Cloud on the top of a snowy
   Mountain.* ASIA, PANTHEA, *and the* SPIRIT OF THE HOUR.

*Spirit.*

On the brink of the night and the morning
   My coursers are wont to respire;
But the Earth has just whispered a warning
   That their flight must be swifter than fire:
   They shall drink the hot speed of desire!     5

   *Asia.*    Thou breathest on their nostrils, but my breath
Would give them swifter speed.

*Spirit.*                              Alas! it could not.

*Panthea.*   Oh Spirit! pause, and tell whence is the light
Which fills this cloud? the sun is yet unrisen.

*Spirit.*   The sun will rise not until noon. Apollo          10
Is held in heaven by wonder; and the light
Which fills this vapour, as the aëreal hue
Of fountain-gazing roses fills the water,
Flows from thy mighty sister.

*Panthea.*                              Yes, I feel—

*Asia.*   What is it with thee, sister? Thou art pale.          15

*Panthea.*   How thou art changed! I dare not look on thee;
I feel but see thee not. I scarce endure
The radiance of thy beauty. Some good change
Is working in the elements, which suffer
Thy presence thus unveiled. The Nereids tell          20
That on the day when the clear hyaline
Was cloven at thine uprise, and thou didst stand
Within a veinèd shell, which floated on
Over the calm floor of the crystal sea,
Among the Ægean isles, and by the shores          25
Which bear thy name; love, like the atmosphere
Of the sun's fire filling the living world,
Burst from thee, and illumined earth and heaven
And the deep ocean and the sunless caves
And all that dwells within them; till grief cast          30
Eclipse upon the soul from which it came:
Such art thou now; nor is it I alone,
Thy sister, thy companion, thine own chosen one,
But the whole world which seeks thy sympathy.
Hearest thou not sounds i' the air which speak the love          35
Of all articulate beings? Feelest thou not
The inanimate winds enamoured of thee? List!          [*Music.*

*Asia.*   Thy words are sweeter than aught else but his
Whose echoes they are: yet all love is sweet,
Given or returned. Common as light is love,          40
And its familiar voice wearies not ever.
Like the wide heaven, the all-sustaining air,
It makes the reptile equal to the God:

They who inspire it most are fortunate,
As I am now; but those who feel it most                    45
Are happier still, after long sufferings,
As I shall soon become.

    *Panthea.*           List! Spirits speak.

          *Voice in the Air, singing.*

  Life of Life! thy lips enkindle
    With their love the breath between them;
  And thy smiles before they dwindle                    50
    Make the cold air fire; then screen them
  In those looks, where whoso gazes
  Faints, entangled in their mazes.

  Child of Light! thy limbs are burning
    Through the vest which seems to hide them;    55
  As the radiant lines of morning
    Through the clouds ere they divide them;
  And this atmosphere divinest
  Shrouds thee wheresoe'er thou shinest.

  Fair are others; none beholds thee,                  60
    But thy voice sounds low and tender
  Like the fairest, for it folds thee
    From the sight, that liquid splendour,
  And all feel, yet see thee never,
  As I feel now, lost for ever!                          65

  Lamp of Earth! where'er thou movest
    Its dim shapes are clad with brightness,
  And the souls of whom thou lovest
    Walk upon the winds with lightness,
  Till they fail, as I am failing,                       70
  Dizzy, lost, yet unbewailing!

             *Asia.*

  My soul is an enchanted boat,
  Which, like a sleeping swan, doth float
Upon the silver waves of thy sweet singing;
  And thine doth like an angel sit                       75

  Beside a helm conducting it,
Whilst all the winds with melody are ringing.
  It seems to float ever, for ever,
  Upon that many-winding river,
  Between mountains, woods, abysses,          80
  A paradise of wildernesses!
Till, like one in slumber bound,
Borne to the ocean, I float down, around,
Into a sea profound, of ever-spreading sound:

  Meanwhile thy spirit lifts its pinions          85
  In music's most serene dominions;
Catching the winds that fan that happy heaven.
  And we sail on, away, afar,
  Without a course, without a star,
But, by the instinct of sweet music driven;          90
  Till through Elysian garden islets
  By thee, most beautiful of pilots,
  Where never mortal pinnace glided,
  The boat of my desire is guided:
Realms where the air we breathe is love,          95
Which in the winds on the waves doth move,
Harmonizing this earth with what we feel above.

  We have passed Age's icy caves,
  And Manhood's dark and tossing waves,
And Youth's smooth ocean, smiling to betray:          100
  Beyond the glassy gulfs we flee
  Of shadow-peopled Infancy,
Through Death and Birth, to a diviner day;
  A paradise of vaulted bowers,
  Lit by downward-gazing flowers,          105
  And watery paths that wind between
  Wildernesses calm and green,
Peopled by shapes too bright to see,
And rest, having beheld; somewhat like thee;
Which walk upon the sea, and chant melodiously!          110

END OF THE SECOND ACT.

# ACT III

SCENE I.—*Heaven.* JUPITER *on his Throne;* THETIS *and the
          other Deities assembled.*

*Jupiter.*   Ye congregated powers of heaven, who share
The glory and the strength of him ye serve,
Rejoice! henceforth I am omnipotent.
All else had been subdued to me; alone
The soul of man, like unextinguished fire,                    5
Yet burns towards heaven with fierce reproach, and doubt,
And lamentation, and reluctant prayer,
Hurling up insurrection, which might make
Our antique empire insecure, though built
On eldest faith, and hell's coeval, fear;                    10
And though my curses through the pendulous air,
Like snow on herbless peaks, fall flake by flake,
And cling to it; though under my wrath's night
It climbs the crags of life, step after step,
Which wound it, as ice wounds unsandalled feet,              15
It yet remains supreme o'er misery,
Aspiring, unrepressed, yet soon to fall:
Even now have I begotten a strange wonder,
That fatal child, the terror of the earth,
Who waits but till the destined hour arrive,                 20
Bearing from Demogorgon's vacant throne
The dreadful might of ever-living limbs
Which clothed that awful spirit unbeheld,
To redescend, and trample out the spark.
Pour forth heaven's wine, Idæan Ganymede,                    25
And let it fill the Dædal cups like fire,
And from the flower-inwoven soil divine
Ye all-triumphant harmonies arise,
As dew from earth under the twilight stars:
Drink! be the nectar circling through your veins            30
The soul of joy, ye ever-living Gods,
Till exultation burst in one wide voice
Like music from Elysian winds.

And thou
Ascend beside me, veilèd in the light
Of the desire which makes thee one with me,                    35
Thetis, bright image of eternity!
When thou didst cry, 'Insufferable might!
God! Spare me! I sustain not the quick flames,
The penetrating presence; all my being,
Like him whom the Numidian seps did thaw          40
Into a dew with poison, is dissolved,
Sinking through its foundations:' even then
Two mighty spirits, mingling, made a third
Mightier than either, which, unbodied now,
Between us floats, felt, although unbeheld,                     45
Waiting the incarnation, which ascends,
(Hear ye the thunder of the fiery wheels
Griding the winds?) from Demogorgon's throne.
Victory! victory! Feel'st thou not, O world,
The earthquake of his chariot thundering up           50
Olympus?

> [*The Car of the* Hour *arrives.* Demogorgon *descends,*
> *and moves towards the Throne of* Jupiter.

Awful shape, what art thou? Speak!
*Demogorgon.*    Eternity. Demand no direr name.
Descend, and follow me down the abyss.
I am thy child, as thou wert Saturn's child;
Mightier than thee: and we must dwell together           55
Henceforth in darkness. Lift thy lightnings not.
The tyranny of heaven none may retain,
Or reassume, or hold, succeeding thee:
Yet if thou wilt, as 'tis the destiny
Of trodden worms to writhe till they are dead,          60
Put forth thy might.
*Jupiter.*              Detested prodigy!
Even thus beneath the deep Titanian prisons
I trample thee! thou lingerest?
                              Mercy! mercy!
No pity, no release, no respite! Oh,

That thou wouldst make mine enemy my judge,                    65
Even where he hangs, seared by my long revenge,
On Caucasus! he would not doom me thus.
Gentle, and just, and dreadless, is he not
The monarch of the world? What then art thou?
No refuge! no appeal!

      Sink with me then,                    70
We two will sink on the wide waves of ruin,
Even as a vulture and a snake outspent
Drop, twisted in inextricable fight,
Into a shoreless sea. Let hell unlock
Its mounded oceans of tempestuous fire,                        75
And whelm on them into the bottomless void
This desolated world, and thee, and me,
The conqueror and the conquered, and the wreck
Of that for which they combated.

        Ai! Ai!

The elements obey me not. I sink                               80
Dizzily down, ever, for ever, down.
And, like a cloud, mine enemy above
Darkens my fall with victory! Ai, Ai!

SCENE II.—*The Mouth of a great River in the Island Atlantis.*
  OCEAN *is discovered reclining near the Shore;* APOLLO *stands*
  *beside him.*

 *Ocean.* He fell, thou sayest, beneath his conqueror's frown?
 *Apollo.* Ay, when the strife was ended which made dim
The orb I rule, and shook the solid stars,
The terrors of his eye illumined heaven
With sanguine light, through the thick ragged skirts           5
Of the victorious darkness, as he fell:
Like the last glare of day's red agony,
Which, from a rent among the fiery clouds,
Burns far along the tempest-wrinkled deep.
 *Ocean.* He sunk to the abyss? To the dark void?         10
 *Apollo.* An eagle so caught in some bursting cloud
On Caucasus, his thunder-baffled wings

Entangled in the whirlwind, and his eyes
Which gazed on the undazzling sun, now blinded
By the white lightning, while the ponderous hail          15
Beats on his struggling form, which sinks at length
Prone, and the aëreal ice clings over it.

   *Ocean.*   Henceforth the fields of heaven-reflecting sea
Which are my realm, will heave, unstained with blood,
Beneath the uplifting winds, like plains of corn          20
Swayed by the summer air; my streams will flow
Round many-peopled continents, and round
Fortunate isles; and from their glassy thrones
Blue Proteus and his humld nymphs shall mark
The shadow of fair ships, as mortals see          25
The floating bark of the light-laden moon
With that white star, its sightless pilot's crest,
Borne down the rapid sunset's ebbing sea;
Tracking their path no more by blood and groans,
And desolation, and the mingled voice          30
Of slavery and command; but by the light
Of wave-reflected flowers, and floating odours,
And music soft, and mild, free, gentle voices,
And sweetest music, such as spirits love.

   *Apollo.*   And I shall gaze not on the deeds which make          35
My mind obscure with sorrow, as eclipse
Darkens the sphere I guide; but list, I hear
The small, clear, silver lute of the young Spirit
That sits i' the morning star.

   *Ocean.*               Thou must away;
Thy steeds will pause at even, till when farewell:          40
The loud deep calls me home even now to feed it
With azure calm out of the emerald urns
Which stand for ever full beside my throne.
Behold the Nereids under the green sea,
Their wavering limbs borne on the wind-like stream,          45
Their white arms lifted o'er their streaming hair
With garlands pied and starry sea-flower crowns,
Hastening to grace their mighty sister's joy.

                          *[A sound of waves is heard.*

It is the unpastured sea hungering for calm.
Peace, monster; I come now. Farewell.

   *Apollo.*                                   Farewell.   50

Scene III.—*Caucasus*. Prometheus, Hercules, Ione, The
    Earth, Spirits, Asia, *and* Panthea, *borne in the Car with
    the* Spirit of the Hour. Hercules *unbinds* Prometheus,
    *who descends.*

  *Hercules.*    Most glorious among Spirits, thus doth strength
To wisdom, courage, and long-suffering love,
And thee, who art the form they animate,
Minister like a slave.

   *Prometheus.*         Thy gentle words
Are sweeter even than freedom long desired      5
And long delayed.

               Asia, thou light of life,
Shadow of beauty unbeheld: and ye,
Fair sister nymphs, who made long years of pain
Sweet to remember, through your love and care:
Henceforth we will not part. There is a cave,     10
All overgrown with trailing odorous plants,
Which curtain out the day with leaves and flowers,
And paved with veinèd emerald, and a fountain
Leaps in the midst with an awakening sound.
From its curved roof the mountain's frozen tears     15
Like snow, or silver, or long diamond spires,
Hang downward, raining forth a doubtful light:
And there is heard the ever-moving air,
Whispering without from tree to tree, and birds,
And bees; and all around are mossy seats,     20
And the rough walls are clothed with long soft grass;
A simple dwelling, which shall be our own;
Where we will sit and talk of time and change,
As the world ebbs and flows, ourselves unchanged.
What can hide man from mutability?     25
And if ye sigh, then I will smile; and thou,
Ione, shalt chant fragments of sea-music,
Until I weep, when ye shall smile away

The tears she brought, which yet were sweet to shed.
We will entangle buds and flowers and beams     30
Which twinkle on the fountain's brim, and make
Strange combinations out of common things,
Like human babes in their brief innocence;
And we will search, with looks and words of love,
For hidden thoughts, each lovelier than the last,     35
Our unexhausted spirits; and like lutes
Touched by the skill of the enamoured wind,
Weave harmonies divine, yet ever new,
From difference sweet where discord cannot be;
And hither come, sped on the charmèd winds,     40
Which meet from all the points of heaven, as bees
From every flower aëreal Enna feeds,
At their known island-homes in Himera,
The echoes of the human world, which tell
Of the low voice of love, almost unheard,     45
And dove-eyed pity's murmured pain, and music,
Itself the echo of the heart, and all
That tempers or improves man's life, now free;
And lovely apparitions,—dim at first,
Then radiant, as the mind, arising bright     50
From the embrace of beauty (whence the forms
Of which these are the phantoms) casts on them
The gathered rays which are reality—
Shall visit us, the progeny immortal
Of Painting, Sculpture, and rapt Poesy,     55
And arts, though unimagined, yet to be.
The wandering voices and the shadows these
Of all that man becomes, the mediators
Of that best worship love, by him and us
Given and returned; swift shapes and sounds, which grow     60
More fair and soft as man grows wise and kind,
And, veil by veil, evil and error fall:
Such virtue has the cave and place around.

[*Turning to the* SPIRIT OF THE HOUR.

For thee, fair Spirit, one toil remains. Ione,
Give her that curvèd shell, which Proteus old     65

Made Asia's nuptial boon, breathing within it
A voice to be accomplished, and which thou
Didst hide in grass under the hollow rock.

 *Ione.* Thou most desired Hour, more loved and lovely
Than all thy sisters, this is the mystic shell;  70
See the pale azure fading into silver
Lining it with a soft yet glowing light:
Looks it not like lulled music sleeping there?

 *Spirit.* It seems in truth the fairest shell of Ocean:
Its sound must be at once both sweet and strange.  75

 *Prometheus.* Go, borne over the cities of mankind
On whirlwind-footed coursers: once again
Outspeed the sun around the orbèd world;
And as thy chariot cleaves the kindling air,
Thou breathe into the many-folded shell,  80
Loosening its mighty music; it shall be
As thunder mingled with clear echoes: then
Return; and thou shalt dwell beside our cave.
And thou, O Mother Earth!—

 *The Earth.*     I hear, I feel;
Thy lips are on me, and thy touch runs down  85
Even to the adamantine central gloom
Along these marble nerves; 'tis life, 'tis joy,
And through my withered, old, and icy frame
The warmth of an immortal youth shoots down
Circling. Henceforth the many children fair  90
Folded in my sustaining arms; all plants,
And creeping forms, and insects rainbow-winged,
And birds, and beasts, and fish, and human shapes,
Which drew disease and pain from my wan bosom,
Draining the poison of despair, shall take  95
And interchange sweet nutriment; to me
Shall they become like sister-antelopes
By one fair dam, snow-white and swift as wind,
Nursed among lilies near a brimming stream.
The dew-mists of my sunless sleep shall float  100
Under the stars like balm: night-folded flowers
Shall suck unwithering hues in their repose:

And men and beasts in happy dreams shall gather
Strength for the coming day, and all its joy:
And death shall be the last embrace of her          105
Who takes the life she gave, even as a mother
Folding her child, says, 'Leave me not again.'

    *Asia.*  Oh, mother! wherefore speak the name of death?
Cease they to love, and move, and breathe, and speak,
Who die?

    *The Earth.*  It would avail not to reply:          110
Thou art immortal, and this tongue is known
But to the uncommunicating dead.
Death is the veil which those who live call life:
They sleep, and it is lifted: and meanwhile
In mild variety the seasons mild                    115
With rainbow-skirted showers, and odorous winds,
And long blue meteors cleansing the dull night,
And the life-kindling shafts of the keen sun's
All-piercing bow, and the dew-mingled rain
Of the calm moonbeams, a soft influence mild,       120
Shall clothe the forests and the fields, ay, even
The crag-built deserts of the barren deep,
With ever-living leaves, and fruits, and flowers.
And thou! There is a cavern where my spirit
Was panted forth in anguish whilst thy pain         125
Made my heart mad, and those who did inhale it
Became mad too, and built a temple there,
And spoke, and were oracular, and lured
The erring nations round to mutual war,
And faithless faith, such as Jove kept with thee;   130
Which breath now rises, as amongst tall weeds
A violet's exhalation, and it fills
With a serener light and crimson air
Intense, yet soft, the rocks and woods around;
It feeds the quick growth of the serpent vine,      135
And the dark linkèd ivy tangling wild,
And budding, blown, or odour-faded blooms
Which star the winds with points of coloured light,
As they rain through them, and bright golden globes

Of fruit, suspended in their own green heaven, 140
And through their veinèd leaves and amber stems,
The flowers whose purple and translucid bowls
Stand ever mantling aëreal dew,
The drink of spirits: and it circles round,
Like the soft waving wings of noonday dreams, 145
Inspiring calm and happy thoughts, like mine,
Now thou art thus restored. This cave is thine.
Arise! Appear!

        *A* SPIRIT *rises in the likeness of a winged child.*
        This is my torch-bearer;
Who let his lamp out in old time with gazing
On eyes from which he kindled it anew 150
With love, which is as fire, sweet daughter mine,
For such is that within thine own. Run, wayward,
And guide this company beyond the peak
Of Bacchic Nysa, Mænad-haunted mountain,
And beyond Indus and its tribute rivers, 155
Trampling the torrent streams and glassy lakes
With feet unwet, unwearied, undelaying,
And up the green ravine, across the vale,
Beside the windless and crystalline pool,
Where ever lies, on unerasing waves, 160
The image of a temple, built above,
Distinct with column, arch and architrave,
And palm-like capital, and over-wrought,
And populous most with living imagery,
Praxitelean shapes, whose marble smiles 165
Fill the hushed air with everlasting love.
It is deserted now, but once it bore
Thy name, Prometheus; there the emulous youths
Bore to thy honour through the divine gloom
The lamp which was thine emblem; even as those 170
Who bear the untransmitted torch of hope
Into the grave, across the night of life,
As thou hast borne it most triumphantly
To this far goal of Time. Depart, farewell.
Beside that temple is the destined cave. 175

SCENE IV.—*A Forest. In the Background a Cave.* PROMETHEUS,
   ASIA, PANTHEA, IONE, *and the* SPIRIT OF THE EARTH.

*Ione.*     Sister, it is not earthly: how it glides
Under the leaves! how on its head there burns
A light, like a green star, whose emerald beams
Are twined with its fair hair! how, as it moves,
The splendour drops in flakes upon the grass!          5
Knowest thou it?
   *Panthea.*          It is the delicate spirit
That guides the earth through heaven. From afar
The populous constellations call that light
The loveliest of the planets; and sometimes
It floats along the spray of the salt sea,              10
Or makes its chariot of a foggy cloud,
Or walks through fields or cities while men sleep,
Or o'er the mountain tops, or down the rivers,
Or through the green waste wilderness, as now,
Wondering at all it sees. Before Jove reigned          15
It loved our sister Asia, and it came
Each leisure hour to drink the liquid light
Out of her eyes, for which it said it thirsted
As one bit by a dipsas, and with her
It made its childish confidence, and told her          20
All it had known or seen, for it saw much,
Yet idly reasoned what it saw; and called her—
For whence it sprung it knew not, nor do I—
Mother, dear mother.
   *The Spirit of the Earth* (*running to Asia*). Mother, dearest
         mother;
May I then talk with thee as I was wont?               25
May I then hide my eyes in thy soft arms,
After thy looks have made them tired of joy?
May I then play beside thee the long noons,
When work is none in the bright silent air?
   *Asia.* I love thee, gentlest being, and henceforth    30
Can cherish thee unenvied: speak, I pray:
Thy simple talk once solaced, now delights.

*Spirit of the Earth.* Mother, I am grown wiser, though a child
Cannot be wise like thee, within this day;
And happier too; happier and wiser both.          35
Thou knowest that toads, and snakes, and loathly worms,
And venomous and malicious beasts, and boughs
That bore ill berries in the woods, were ever
An hindrance to my walks o'er the green world:
And that, among the haunts of humankind,          40
Hard-featured men, or with proud, angry looks,
Or cold, staid gait, or false and hollow smiles,
Or the dull sneer of self-loved ignorance,
Or other such foul masks, with which ill thoughts
Hide that fair being whom we spirits call man;          45
And women too, ugliest of all things evil,
(Though fair, even in a world where thou art fair,
When good and kind, free and sincere like thee),
When false or frowning made me sick at heart
To pass them, though they slept, and I unseen.          50
Well, my path lately lay through a great city
Into the woody hills surrounding it:
A sentinel was sleeping at the gate:
When there was heard a sound, so loud, it shook
The towers amid the moonlight, yet more sweet          55
Than any voice but thine, sweetest of all;
A long, long sound, as it would never end:
And all the inhabitants leaped suddenly
Out of their rest, and gathered in the streets,
Looking in wonder up to Heaven, while yet          60
The music pealed along. I hid myself
Within a fountain in the public square,
Where I lay like a reflex of the moon
Seen in a wave under green leaves; and soon
Those ugly human shapes and visages          65
Of which I spoke as having wrought me pain,
Passed floating through the air, and fading still
Into the winds that scattered them; and those
From whom they passed seemed mild and lovely forms
After some foul disguise had fallen, and all          70

Were somewhat changed, and after brief surprise
And greetings of delighted wonder, all
Went to their sleep again: and when the dawn
Came, wouldst thou think that toads, and snakes, and efts,
Could e'er be beautiful? yet so they were,                    75
And that with little change of shape or hue:
All things had put their evil nature off:
I cannot tell my joy, when o'er a lake
Upon a drooping bough with nightshade twined,
I saw two azure halcyons clinging downward              80
And thinning one bright bunch of amber berries,
With quick long beaks, and in the deep there lay
Those lovely forms imaged as in a sky;
So, with my thoughts full of these happy changes,
We meet again, the happiest change of all.                85
    *Asia.*   And never will we part, till thy chaste sister
Who guides the frozen and inconstant moon
Will look on thy more warm and equal light
Till her heart thaw like flakes of April snow
And love thee.
    *Spirit of the Earth.*   What; as Asia loves Prometheus?   90
    *Asia.*   Peace, wanton, thou art yet not old enough.
Think ye by gazing on each other's eyes
To multiply your lovely selves, and fill
With spherèd fires the interlunar air?
    *Spirit of the Earth.* Nay, mother, while my sister trims
      her lamp                                                          95
'Tis hard I should go darkling.
    *Asia.*                                   Listen; look!
                      [*The* SPIRIT OF THE HOUR *enters.*
    *Prometheus.*   We feel what thou hast heard and seen: yet
      speak.
    *Spirit of the Hour.*        Soon as the sound had ceased whose
      thunder filled
The abysses of the sky and the wide earth,
There was a change: the impalpable thin air              100
And the all-circling sunlight were transformed,
As if the sense of love dissolved in them

Had folded itself round the spherèd world.
My vision then grew clear, and I could see
Into the mysteries of the universe:                    105
Dizzy as with delight I floated down,
Winnowing the lightsome air with languid plumes,
My coursers sought their birthplace in the sun,
Where they henceforth will live exempt from toil,
Pasturing flowers of vegetable fire;                   110
And where my moonlike car will stand within
A temple, gazed upon by Phidian forms
Of thee, and Asia, and the Earth, and me,
And you fair nymphs looking the love we feel,—
In memory of the tidings it has borne,—                115
Beneath a dome fretted with graven flowers,
Poised on twelve columns of resplendent stone,
And open to the bright and liquid sky.
Yoked to it by an amphisbaenic snake
The likeness of those wingèd steeds will mock          120
The flight from which they find repose. Alas,
Whither has wandered now my partial tongue
When all remains untold which ye would hear?
As I have said, I floated to the earth:
It was, as it is still, the pain of bliss               125
To move, to breathe, to be; I wandering went
Among the haunts and dwellings of mankind,
And first was disappointed not to see
Such mighty change as I had felt within
Expressed in outward things; but soon I looked,         130
And behold, thrones were kingless, and men walked
One with the other even as spirits do,
None fawned, none trampled; hate, disdain, or fear,
Self-love or self-contempt, on human brows
No more inscribed, as o'er the gate of hell,            135
'All hope abandon ye who enter here;'
None frowned, none trembled, none with eager fear
Gazed on another's eye of cold command,
Until the subject of a tyrant's will
Became, worse fate, the abject of his own,              140

Which spurred him, like an outspent horse, to death.
None wrought his lips in truth-entangling lines
Which smiled the lie his tongue disdained to speak;
None, with firm sneer, trod out in his own heart
The sparks of love and hope till there remained          145
Those bitter ashes, a soul self-consumed,
And the wretch crept a vampire among men,
Infecting all with his own hideous ill;
None talked that common, false, cold, hollow talk
Which makes the heart deny the *yes* it breathes,        150
Yet question that unmeant hypocrisy
With such a self-mistrust as has no name.
And women, too, frank, beautiful, and kind
As the free heaven which rains fresh light and dew
On the wide earth, past; gentle radiant forms,           155
From custom's evil taint exempt and pure;
Speaking the wisdom once they could not think,
Looking emotions once they feared to feel,
And changed to all which once they dared not be,
Yet being now, made earth like heaven; nor pride,        160
Nor jealousy, nor envy, nor ill shame,
The bitterest of those drops of treasured gall,
Spoilt the sweet taste of the nepenthe, love.

Thrones, altars, judgement-seats, and prisons; wherein,
And beside which, by wretched men were borne             165
Sceptres, tiaras, swords, and chains, and tomes
Of reasoned wrong, glozed on by ignorance,
Were like those monstrous and barbaric shapes,
The ghosts of a no-more-remembered fame,
Which, from their unworn obelisks, look forth            170
In triumph o'er the palaces and tombs
Of those who were their conquerors: mouldering round,
These imaged to the pride of kings and priests
A dark yet mighty faith, a power as wide
As is the world it wasted, and are now                   175
But an astonishment; even so the tools
And emblems of its last captivity,

Amid the dwellings of the peopled earth,
Stand, not o'erthrown, but unregarded now.
And those foul shapes, abhorred by god and man,—        180
Which, under many a name and many a form
Strange, savage, ghastly, dark and execrable,
Were Jupiter, the tyrant of the world;
And which the nations, panic-stricken, served
With blood, and hearts broken by long hope, and love    185
Dragged to his altars soiled and garlandless,
And slain among men's unreclaiming tears,
Flattering the thing they feared, which fear was hate,—
Frown, mouldering fast, o'er their abandoned shrines:
The painted veil, by those who were, called life,        190
Which mimicked, as with colours idly spread,
All men believed and hoped, is torn aside;
The loathsome mask has fallen, the man remains
Sceptreless, free, uncircumscribed, but man
Equal, unclassed, tribeless, and nationless,             195
Exempt from awe, worship, degree, the king
Over himself; just, gentle, wise: but man
Passionless?——no, yet free from guilt or pain,
Which were, for his will made or suffered them,
Nor yet exempt, though ruling them like slaves,          200
From chance, and death, and mutability,
The clogs of that which else might oversoar
The loftiest star of unascended heaven,
Pinnacled dim in the intense inane.

END OF THE THIRD ACT.

# ACT IV

SCENE.—*A Part of the Forest near the Cave of* PROMETHEUS.
PANTHEA *and* IONE *are sleeping: they awaken gradually during
the first Song.*

*Voice of the unseen Spirits.*

The pale stars are gone!
For the sun, their swift shepherd,

To their folds them compelling,
In the depths of the dawn,
Hastes, in meteor-eclipsing array, and they flee    5
Beyond his blue dwelling,
As fawns flee the leopard.
But where are ye?

*A Train of dark Forms and Shadows passes by confusedly,*
*singing.*

Here, oh, here:
We bear the bier    10
Of the Father of many a cancelled year!
Spectres we
Of the dead Hours be,
We bear Time to his tomb in eternity.

Strew, oh strew    15
Hair, not yew!
Wet the dusty pall with tears, not dew!
Be the faded flowers
Of Death's bare bowers
Spread on the corpse of the King of Hours!    20

Haste, oh, haste!
As shades are chased,
Trembling, by day, from heaven's blue waste.
We melt away,
Like dissolving spray,    25
From the children of a diviner day,
With the lullaby
Of winds that die
On the bosom of their own harmony!

*Ione.*

What dark forms were they?    30

*Panthea.*

The past Hours weak and gray,
With the spoil which their toil

Raked together
From the conquest but One could foil.

*Ione.*

Have they passed?

*Panthea.*

They have passed;                    35
They outspeeded the blast,
While 'tis said, they are fled:

*Ione.*

Whither, oh, whither?

*Panthea.*

To the dark, to the past, to the dead.

*Voice of the unseen Spirits.*

Bright clouds float in heaven,                    40
Dew-stars gleam on earth,
Waves assemble on ocean,
They are gathered and driven
By the storm of delight, by the panic of glee!
They shake with emotion,                    45
They dance in their mirth.
But where are ye?

The pine boughs are singing
Old songs with new gladness,
The billows and fountains                    50
Fresh music are flinging,
Like the notes of a spirit from land and from sea;
The storms mock the mountains
With the thunder of gladness.
But where are ye?                    55

*Ione.*   What charioteers are these?
*Panthea.*                    Where are their chariots?

*Semichorus of Hours.*

The voice of the Spirits of Air and of Earth
    Have drawn back the figured curtain of sleep
Which covered our being and darkened our birth
    In the deep.

*A Voice.*

In the deep?

*Semichorus II.*

Oh, below the deep.   60

*Semichorus I.*

An hundred ages we had been kept
    Cradled in visions of hate and care,
And each one who waked as his brother slept,
    Found the truth—

*Semichorus II.*

Worse than his visions were!

*Semichorus I.*

We have heard the lute of Hope in sleep;   65
    We have known the voice of Love in dreams;
We have felt the wand of Power, and leap—

*Semichorus II.*

As the billows leap in the morning beams!

*Chorus.*

Weave the dance on the floor of the breeze,
    Pierce with song heaven's silent light,   70
Enchant the day that too swiftly flees,
    To check its flight ere the cave of Night.

Once the hungry Hours were hounds
    Which chased the day like a bleeding deer,
And it limped and stumbled with many wounds   75
    Through the nightly dells of the desert year.

But now, oh weave the mystic measure
　Of music, and dance, and shapes of light,
Let the Hours, and the spirits of might and pleasure,
　Like the clouds and sunbeams, unite.

*A Voice.*

Unite! 80

*Panthea.*　See, where the Spirits of the human mind
Wrapped in sweet sounds, as in bright veils, approach.

*Chorus of Spirits.*

We join the throng
Of the dance and the song,
By the whirlwind of gladness borne along; 85
As the flying-fish leap
From the Indian deep,
And mix with the sea-birds, half asleep.

*Chorus of Hours.*

Whence come ye, so wild and so fleet,
For sandals of lightning are on your feet, 90
And your wings are soft and swift as thought,
And your eyes are as love which is veilèd not?

*Chorus of Spirits.*

We come from the mind
Of human kind
Which was late so dusk, and obscene, and blind, 95
Now 'tis an ocean
Of clear emotion,
A heaven of serene and mighty motion

From that deep abyss
Of wonder and bliss, 100
Whose caverns are crystal palaces;
From those skiey towers
Where Thought's crowned powers
Sit watching your dance, ye happy Hours!

From the dim recesses                                    105
Of woven caresses,
Where lovers catch ye by your loose tresses;
From the azure isles,
Where sweet Wisdom smiles,
Delaying your ships with her siren wiles.                 110

From the temples high
Of Man's ear and eye,
Roofed over Sculpture and Poesy;
From the murmurings
Of the unsealed springs                                   115
Where Science bedews her Dædal wings.

Years after years,
Through blood, and tears,
And a thick hell of hatreds, and hopes, and fears;
We waded and flew,                                        120
And the islets were few
Where the bud-blighted flowers of happiness grew.

Our feet now, every palm,
Are sandalled with calm,
And the dew of our wings is a rain of balm;               125
And, beyond our eyes,
The human love lies
Which makes all it gazes on Paradise.

*Chorus of Spirits and Hours.*

Then weave the web of the mystic measure;
From the depths of the sky and the ends of the earth,
Come, swift Spirits of might and of pleasure,            131
Fill the dance and the music of mirth,
As the waves of a thousand streams rush by
To an ocean of splendour and harmony!

*Chorus of Spirits.*

Our spoil is won,                                         135
Our task is done,

We are free to dive, or soar, or run;
  Beyond and around,
  Or within the bound
Which clips the world with darkness round.        140

  We'll pass the eyes
  Of the starry skies
Into the hoar deep to colonize:
  Death, Chaos, and Night,
  From the sound of our flight,        145
Shall flee, like mist from a tempest's might.

  And Earth, Air, and Light,
  And the Spirit of Might,
Which drives round the stars in their fiery flight;
  And Love, Thought, and Breath,        150
  The powers that quell Death,
Wherever we soar shall assemble beneath.

  And our singing shall build
  In the void's loose field
A world for the Spirit of Wisdom to wield;        155
  We will take our plan
  From the new world of man,
And our work shall be called the Promethean.

*Chorus of Hours.*

Break the dance, and scatter the song;
  Let some depart, and some remain.        160

*Semichorus I.*

We, beyond heaven, are driven along:

*Semichorus II.*

Us the enchantments of earth retain:

*Semichorus I.*

Ceaseless, and rapid, and fierce, and free,
With the Spirits which build a new earth and sea,
And a heaven where yet heaven could never be.        165

*Semichorus II.*

Solemn, and slow, and serene, and bright,
Leading the Day and outspeeding the Night,
With the powers of a world of perfect light.

*Semichorus I.*

We whirl, singing loud, round the gathering sphere,
Till the trees, and the beasts, and the clouds appear  170
From its chaos made calm by love, not fear.

*Semichorus II.*

We encircle the ocean and mountains of earth,
And the happy forms of its death and birth
Change to the music of our sweet mirth.

*Chorus of Hours and Spirits.*

Break the dance, and scatter the song,                        175
   Let some depart, and some remain,
Wherever we fly we lead along
In leashes, like starbeams, soft yet strong,
   The clouds that are heavy with love's sweet rain.

*Panthea.*   Ha! they are gone!
*Ione.*              Yet feel you no delight    180
From the past sweetness?
*Panthea.*          As the bare green hill
When some soft cloud vanishes into rain,
Laughs with a thousand drops of sunny water
To the unpavilioned sky!
*Ione.*          Even whilst we speak
New notes arise. What is that awful sound?                    185
  *Panthea.*   'Tis the deep music of the rolling world
Kindling within the strings of the waved air
Æolian modulations.
  *Ione.*          Listen too,
How every pause is filled with under-notes,
Clear, silver, icy, keen, awakening tones,                    190

SHELLEY

*From the painting by Amelia Curran. Now in the National Portrait Gallery, London.*

Which pierce the sense, and live within the soul,
As the sharp stars pierce winter's crystal air
And gaze upon themselves within the sea.
    *Panthea.*  But see where through two openings in the forest
Which hanging branches overcanopy,           195
And where two runnels of a rivulet,
Between the close moss violet-inwoven,
Have made their path of melody, like sisters
Who part with sighs that they may meet in smiles,
Turning their dear disunion to an isle          200
Of lovely grief, a wood of sweet sad thoughts;
Two visions of strange radiance float upon
The ocean-like enchantment of strong sound,
Which flows intenser, keener, deeper yet
Under the ground and through the windless air.    205
    *Ione.*  I see a chariot like that thinnest boat,
In which the Mother of the Months is borne
By ebbing light into her western cave,
When she upsprings from interlunar dreams;
O'er which is curved an orblike canopy         210
Of gentle darkness, and the hills and woods,
Distinctly seen through that dusk aery veil,
Regard like shapes in an enchanter's glass;
Its wheels are solid clouds, azure and gold,
Such as the genii of the thunderstorm         215
Pile on the floor of the illumined sea
When the sun rushes under it; they roll
And move and grow as with an inward wind;
Within it sits a wingèd infant, white
Its countenance, like the whiteness of bright snow,    220
Its plumes are as feathers of sunny frost,
Its limbs gleam white, through the wind-flowing folds
Of its white robe, woof of ethereal pearl.
Its hair is white, the brightness of white light
Scattered in strings; yet its two eyes are heavens    225
Of liquid darkness, which the Deity
Within seems pouring, as a storm is poured
From jaggèd clouds, out of their arrowy lashes,

F

Tempering the cold and radiant air around,
With fire that is not brightness; in its hand          230
It sways a quivering moonbeam, from whose point
A guiding power directs the chariot's prow
Over its wheelèd clouds, which as they roll
Over the grass, and flowers, and waves, wake sounds,
Sweet as a singing rain of silver dew.               235
    *Panthea.*    And from the other opening in the wood
Rushes, with loud and whirlwind harmony,
A sphere, which is as many thousand spheres,
Solid as crystal, yet through all its mass
Flow, as through empty space, music and light:       240
Ten thousand orbs involving and involved,
Purple and azure, white, and green, and golden,
Sphere within sphere; and every space between
Peopled with unimaginable shapes,
Such as ghosts dream dwell in the lampless deep,     245
Yet each inter-transpicuous, and they whirl
Over each other with a thousand motions,
Upon a thousand sightless axles spinning,
And with the force of self-destroying swiftness,
Intensely, slowly, solemnly roll on,                 250
Kindling with mingled sounds, and many tones,
Intelligible words and music wild.
With mighty whirl and multitudinous orb
Grinds the bright brook into an azure mist
Of elemental subtlety, like light;                   255
And the wild odour of the forest flowers,
The music of the living grass and air,
The emerald light of leaf-entangled beams
Round its intense yet self-conflicting speed,
Seem kneaded into one aëreal mass                    260
Which drowns the sense. Within the orb itself,
Pillowed upon its alabaster arms,
Like to a child o'erwearied with sweet toil,
On its own folded wings, and wavy hair,
The Spirit of the Earth is laid asleep,              265
And you can see its little lips are moving,

Amid the changing light of their own smiles,
Like one who talks of what he loves in dream.
*Ione.*   'Tis only mocking the orb's harmony.
*Panthea.*   And from a star upon its forehead, shoot,        270
Like swords of azure fire, or golden spears
With tyrant-quelling myrtle overtwined,
Embleming heaven and earth united now,
Vast beams like spokes of some invisible wheel
Which whirl as the orb whirls, swifter than thought,        275
Filling the abyss with sun-like lightenings,
And perpendicular now, and now transverse,
Pierce the dark soil, and as they pierce and pass,
Make bare the secrets of the earth's deep heart;
Infinite mine of adamant and gold,        280
Valueless stones, and unimagined gems,
And caverns on crystalline columns poised
With vegetable silver overspread;
Wells of unfathomed fire, and water springs
Whence the great sea, even as a child is fed,        285
Whose vapours clothe earth's monarch mountain-tops
With kingly, ermine snow.  The beams flash on
And make appear the melancholy ruins
Of cancelled cycles; anchors, beaks of ships;
Planks turned to marble; quivers, helms, and spears,        290
And gorgon-headed targes, and the wheels
Of scythèd chariots, and the emblazonry
Of trophies, standards, and armorial beasts,
Round which death laughed, sepulchred emblems
Of dead destruction, ruin within ruin!        295
The wrecks beside of many a city vast,
Whose population which the earth grew over
Was mortal, but not human; see, they lie,
Their monstrous works, and uncouth skeletons,
Their statues, homes and fanes; prodigious shapes        300
Huddled in gray annihilation, split,
Jammed in the hard, black deep; and over these,
The anatomies of unknown wingèd things,
And fishes which were isles of living scale,

And serpents, bony chains, twisted around                305
The iron crags, or within heaps of dust
To which the tortuous strength of their last pangs
Had crushed the iron crags; and over these
The jaggèd alligator, and the might
Of earth-convulsing behemoth, which once              310
Were monarch beasts, and on the slimy shores,
And weed-overgrown continents of earth,
Increased and multiplied like summer worms
On an abandoned corpse, till the blue globe
Wrapped deluge round it like a cloak, and they       315
Yelled, gasped, and were abolished; or some God
Whose throne was in a comet, passed, and cried,
'Be not!' And like my words they were no more.

### The Earth.

The joy, the triumph, the delight, the madness!
The boundless, overflowing, bursting gladness,       320
The vaporous exultation not to be confined!
Ha! ha! the animation of delight
Which wraps me, like an atmosphere of light,
And bears me as a cloud is borne by its own wind.

### The Moon.

Brother mine, calm wanderer,                          325
Happy globe of land and air,
Some Spirit is darted like a beam from thee,
Which penetrates my frozen frame,
And passes with the warmth of flame,
With love, and odour, and deep melody                330
Through me, through me!

### The Earth.

Ha! ha! the caverns of my hollow mountains,
My cloven fire-crags, sound-exulting fountains
Laugh with a vast and inextinguishable laughter.
The oceans, and the deserts, and the abysses,        335
And the deep air's unmeasured wildernesses,
Answer from all their clouds and billows, echoing after.

They cry aloud as I do.  Sceptred curse,
Who all our green and azure universe
Threatenedst to muffle round with black destruction, sending
A solid cloud to rain hot thunderstones,                341
And splinter and knead down my children's bones,
All I bring forth, to one void mass battering and blending,—

Until each crag-like tower, and storied column,
Palace, and obelisk, and temple solemn,                 345
My imperial mountains crowned with cloud, and snow, and fire;
My sea-like forests, every blade and blossom
Which finds a grave or cradle in my bosom,
Were stamped by thy strong hate into a lifeless mire:

How art thou sunk, withdrawn, covered, drunk up      350
By thirsty nothing, as the brackish cup
Drained by a desert-troop, a little drop for all;
And from beneath, around, within, above,
Filling thy void annihilation, love
Burst in like light on caves cloven by the thunder-ball.    355

### The Moon.

The snow upon my lifeless mountains
Is loosened into living fountains,
My solid oceans flow, and sing, and shine:
A spirit from my heart bursts forth,
It clothes with unexpected birth                       360
My cold bare bosom: Oh! it must be thine
On mine, on mine!

Gazing on thee I feel, I know
Green stalks burst forth, and bright flowers grow,
And living shapes upon my bosom move:                  365
Music is in the sea and air,
Wingèd clouds soar here and there,
Dark with the rain new buds are dreaming of:
'Tis love, all love!

*The Earth.*

It interpenetrates my granite mass,                                    370
  Through tangled roots and trodden clay doth pass
Into the utmost leaves and delicatest flowers;
  Upon the winds, among the clouds 'tis spread,
  It wakes a life in the forgotten dead,
They breathe a spirit up from their obscurest bowers.    375


  And like a storm bursting its cloudy prison
  With thunder, and with whirlwind, has arisen
Out of the lampless caves of unimagined being:
  With earthquake shock and swiftness making shiver
  Thought's stagnant chaos, unremoved for ever,          380
Till hate, and fear, and pain, light-vanquished shadows,
  fleeing,


  Leave Man, who was a many-sided mirror,
  Which could distort to many a shape of error,
This true fair world of things, a sea reflecting love;
  Which over all his kind, as the sun's heaven          385
  Gliding o'er ocean, smooth, serene, and even,
Darting from starry depths radiance and light, doth move:


  Leave Man, even as a leprous child is left,
  Who follows a sick beast to some warm cleft
Of rocks, through which the might of healing springs is poured;
  Then when it wanders home with rosy smile,           391
  Unconscious, and its mother fears awhile
It is a spirit, then, weeps on her child restored.


  Man, oh, not men! a chain of linkèd thought,
  Of love and might to be divided not,                  395
Compelling the elements with adamantine stress;
  As the sun rules, even with a tyrant's gaze,
  The unquiet republic of the maze
Of planets, struggling fierce towards heaven's free wilderness.

Man, one harmonious soul of many a soul,    400
  Whose nature is its own divine control,
Where all things flow to all, as rivers to the sea;
    Familiar acts are beautiful through love;
    Labour, and pain, and grief, in life's green grove
Sport like tame beasts, none knew how gentle they could be!

His will, with all mean passions, bad delights,    406
  And selfish cares, its trembling satellites,
A spirit ill to guide, but mighty to obey,
    Is as a tempest-wingèd ship, whose helm
    Love rules, through waves which dare not overwhelm,    410
Forcing life's wildest shores to own its sovereign sway.

All things confess his strength.  Through the cold mass
  Of marble and of colour his dreams pass;
Bright threads whence mothers weave the robes their children
    wear;
    Language is a perpetual Orphic song,    415
    Which rules with Dædal harmony a throng
Of thoughts and forms, which else senseless and shapeless were.

The lightning is his slave; heaven's utmost deep
  Gives up her stars, and like a flock of sheep
They pass before his eye, are numbered, and roll on!    420
    The tempest is his steed, he strides the air;
    And the abyss shouts from her depth laid bare,
Heaven, hast thou secrets?  Man unveils me; I have none.

### The Moon.

The shadow of white death has passed
  From my path in heaven at last,    425
A clinging shroud of solid frost and sleep;
    And through my newly-woven bowers,
    Wander happy paramours,
Less mighty, but as mild as those who keep
      Thy vales more deep.    430

### The Earth.

As the dissolving warmth of dawn may fold
  A half unfrozen dew-globe, green, and gold,
And crystalline, till it becomes a wingèd mist,
  And wanders up the vault of the blue day,
  Outlives the moon, and on the sun's last ray     435
Hangs o'er the sea, a fleece of fire and amethyst.

### The Moon.

Thou art folded, thou art lying
  In the light which is undying
Of thine own joy, and heaven's smile divine;
  All suns and constellations shower     440
  On thee a light, a life, a power
Which doth array thy sphere; thou pourest thine
     On mine, on mine!

### The Earth.

I spin beneath my pyramid of night,
  Which points into the heavens dreaming delight,     445
Murmuring victorious joy in my enchanted sleep;
  As a youth lulled in love-dreams faintly sighing,
  Under the shadow of his beauty lying,
Which round his rest a watch of light and warmth doth keep.

### The Moon.

  As in the soft and sweet eclipse,     450
  When soul meets soul on lovers' lips,
High hearts are calm, and brightest eyes are dull;
  So when thy shadow falls on me,
  Then am I mute and still, by thee
Covered; of thy love, Orb most beautiful,     455
    Full, oh, too full!
  Thou art speeding round the sun
  Brightest world of many a one;
  Green and azure sphere which shinest
  With a light which is divinest     460
  Among all the lamps of Heaven

To whom life and light is given;
I, thy crystal paramour
Borne beside thee by a power
Like the polar Paradise,                               465
Magnet-like of lovers' eyes;
I, a most enamoured maiden
Whose weak brain is overladen
With the pleasure of her love,
Maniac-like around thee move                           470
Gazing, an insatiate bride,
On thy form from every side
Like a Mænad, round the cup
Which Agave lifted up
In the weird Cadmæan forest.                           475
Brother, wheresoe'er thou soarest
I must hurry, whirl and follow
Through the heavens wide and hollow,
Sheltered by the warm embrace
Of thy soul from hungry space,                         480
Drinking from thy sense and sight
Beauty, majesty, and might,
As a lover or a chameleon
Grows like what it looks upon,
As a violet's gentle eye                               485
Gazes on the azure sky
Until its hue grows like what it beholds,
As a gray and watery mist
Glows like solid amethyst
Athwart the western mountain it enfolds,               490
When the sunset sleeps
      Upon its snow—

### The Earth.

And the weak day weeps
      That it should be so.
Oh, gentle Moon, the voice of thy delight              495
Falls on me like thy clear and tender light
Soothing the seaman, borne the summer night,

 Through isles for ever calm;
  Oh, gentle Moon, thy crystal accents pierce
  The caverns of my pride's deep universe,     500
  Charming the tiger joy, whose tramplings fierce
   Made wounds which need thy balm.
 *Panthea.* I rise as from a bath of sparkling water,
A bath of azure light, among dark rocks,
Out of the stream of sound.
 *Ione.*       Ah me! sweet sister,    505
The stream of sound has ebbed away from us,
And you pretend to rise out of its wave,
Because your words fall like the clear, soft dew
Shaken from a bathing wood-nymph's limbs and hair.
 *Panthea.* Peace! peace! A mighty Power, which is as
  darkness,              510
Is rising out of Earth, and from the sky
Is showered like night, and from within the air
Bursts, like eclipse which had been gathered up
Into the pores of sunlight: the bright visions,
Wherein the singing spirits rode and shone,    515
Gleam like pale meteors through a watery night.
 *Ione.* There is a sense of words upon mine ear.
 *Panthea.* An universal sound like words: Oh, list!

### *Demogorgon.*

Thou, Earth, calm empire of a happy soul,
 Sphere of divinest shapes and harmonies,    520
Beautiful orb! gathering as thou dost roll
 The love which paves thy path along the skies:

### *The Earth.*

I hear: I am as a drop of dew that dies.

### *Demogorgon.*

Thou, Moon, which gazest on the nightly Earth
 With wonder, as it gazes upon thee;     525
Whilst each to men, and beasts, and the swift birth
 Of birds, is beauty, love, calm, harmony:

*The Moon.*

I hear: I am a leaf shaken by thee!

*Demogorgon.*

Ye Kings of suns and stars, Dæmons and Gods,
  Aetherial Dominations, who possess                    530
Elysian, windless, fortunate abodes
  Beyond Heaven's constellated wilderness:

*A Voice from above.*

Our great Republic hears, we are blest, and bless.

*Demogorgon.*

Ye happy Dead, whom beams of brightest verse
  Are clouds to hide, not colours to portray,          535
Whether your nature is that universe
  Which once ye saw and suffered—

*A Voice from beneath.*

                              Or as they
Whom we have left, we change and pass away.

*Demogorgon.*

Ye elemental Genii, who have homes
  From man's high mind even to the central stone        540
Of sullen lead; from Heaven's star-fretted domes
  To the dull weed some sea-worm battens on:

*A confused Voice.*

We hear: thy words waken Oblivion.

*Demogorgon.*

Spirits, whose homes are flesh: ye beasts and birds,
  Ye worms, and fish; ye living leaves and buds;        545
Lightning and wind; and ye untameable herds,
  Meteors and mists, which throng air's solitudes:

*A Voice.*

Thy voice to us is wind among still woods.

*Demogorgon.*

Man, who wert once a despot and a slave;
   A dupe and a deceiver; a decay;         550
A traveller from the cradle to the grave
   Through the dim night of this immortal day:

*All.*

Speak: thy strong words may never pass away.

*Demogorgon.*

This is the day, which down the void abysm
At the Earth-born's spell yawns for Heaven's despotism,
   And Conquest is dragged captive through the deep:
Love, from its awful throne of patient power
In the wise heart, from the last giddy hour
   Of dread endurance, from the slippery, steep,
And narrow verge of crag-like agony, springs      560
And folds over the world its healing wings.

Gentleness, Virtue, Wisdom, and Endurance,
These are the seals of that most firm assurance
   Which bars the pit over Destruction's strength;
And if, with infirm hand, Eternity,      565
Mother of many acts and hours, should free
   The serpent that would clasp her with his length;
These are the spells by which to reassume
An empire o'er the disentangled doom.

To suffer woes which Hope thinks infinite;      570
To forgive wrongs darker than death or night;
   To defy Power, which seems omnipotent;
To love, and bear; to hope till Hope creates
From its own wreck the thing it contemplates;
   Neither to change, nor falter, nor repent;     575
This, like thy glory, Titan, is to be
Good, great and joyous, beautiful and free;
This is alone Life, Joy, Empire, and Victory.

# THE CENCI

## A TRAGEDY IN FIVE ACTS

### DEDICATION TO LEIGH HUNT, ESQ.

MY DEAR FRIEND—I inscribe with your name, from a distant country, and after an absence whose months have seemed years, this the latest of my literary efforts.

Those writings which I have hitherto published, have been little else than visions which impersonate my own apprehensions of the beautiful and the just. I can also perceive in them the literary defects incidental to youth and impatience; they are dreams of what ought to be, or may be. The drama which I now present to you is a sad reality. I lay aside the presumptuous attitude of an instructor, and am content to paint, with such colours as my own heart furnishes, that which has been.

Had I known a person more highly endowed than yourself with all that it becomes a man to possess, I had solicited for this work the ornament of his name. One more gentle, honourable, innocent and brave; one of more exalted toleration for all who do and think evil, and yet himself more free from evil; one who knows better how to receive, and how to confer a benefit, though he must ever confer far more than he can receive; one of simpler, and, in the highest sense of the word, of purer life and manners I never knew: and I had already been fortunate in friendships when your name was added to the list.

In that patient and irreconcilable enmity with domestic and political tyranny and imposture which the tenor of your life has illustrated, and which, had I health and talents, should illustrate mine, let us, comforting each other in our task, live and die.

All happiness attend you! Your affectionate friend,

PERCY B. SHELLEY.
ROME, *May* 29, 1819.

## PREFACE

A MANUSCRIPT was communicated to me during my travels in Italy, which was copied from the archives of the Cenci Palace at Rome, and contains a detailed account of the horrors which ended in the extinction of one of the noblest and richest families of that city during the Pontificate of Clement VIII, in the year 1599. The story is, that an old man having spent his life in debauchery and wickedness, conceived at length an implacable hatred towards his children; which showed itself towards one daughter under the form of an incestuous passion, aggravated by every circumstance of cruelty and violence. This daughter, after long and vain attempts to escape from what she considered a perpetual contamination both of body and mind, at length plotted with her mother-in-law and brother to murder their common tyrant. The young maiden, who was urged to this tremendous deed by an impulse which overpowered its horror, was evidently a most gentle and amiable being, a creature formed to adorn and be admired, and thus violently thwarted from her nature by the necessity of circumstance and opinion. The deed was quickly discovered, and, in spite of the most earnest prayers made to the Pope by the highest persons in Rome, the criminals were put to death. The old man had during his life repeatedly bought his pardon from the Pope for capital crimes of the most enormous and unspeakable kind, at the price of a hundred thousand crowns; the death therefore of his victims can scarcely be accounted for by the love of justice. The Pope, among other motives for severity, probably felt that whoever killed the Count Cenci deprived his treasury of a certain and copious source of revenue.[1] Such a story, if told so as to present to the reader all the feelings of those who once acted

[1] The Papal Government formerly took the most extraordinary precautions against the publicity of facts which offer so tragical a demonstration of its own wickedness and weakness; so that the communication of the MS. had become, until very lately, a matter of some difficulty.

it, their hopes and fears, their confidences and misgivings, their various interests, passions, and opinions, acting upon and with each other, yet all conspiring to one tremendous end, would be as a light to make apparent some of the most dark and secret caverns of the human heart.

On my arrival at Rome I found that the story of the Cenci was a subject not to be mentioned in Italian society without awakening a deep and breathless interest; and that the feelings of the company never failed to incline to a romantic pity for the wrongs, and a passionate exculpation of the horrible deed to which they urged her, who has been mingled two centuries with the common dust. All ranks of people knew the outlines of this history, and participated in the overwhelming interest which it seems to have the magic of exciting in the human heart. I had a copy of Guido's picture of Beatrice which is preserved in the Colonna Palace, and my servant instantly recognized it as the portrait of *La Cenci*.

This national and universal interest which the story produces and has produced for two centuries and among all ranks of people in a great City, where the imagination is kept for ever active and awake, first suggested to me the conception of its fitness for a dramatic purpose. In fact it is a tragedy which has already received, from its capacity of awakening and sustaining the sympathy of men, approbation and success. Nothing remained as I imagined, but to clothe it to the apprehensions of my countrymen in such language and action as would bring it home to their hearts. The deepest and the sublimest tragic compositions, *King Lear* and the two plays in which the tale of Œdipus is told, were stories which already existed in tradition, as matters of popular belief and interest, before Shakespeare and Sophocles made them familiar to the sympathy of all succeeding generations of mankind.

This story of the Cenci is indeed eminently fearful and monstrous: anything like a dry exhibition of it on the stage would be insupportable. The person who would treat such a subject must increase the ideal, and diminish the actual horror of the events, so that the pleasure which arises from the poetry which exists in these tempestuous sufferings and crimes may mitigate the pain of the contemplation of the moral deformity from which they spring. There must also be nothing attempted to make the exhibition subservient to what is vulgarly termed a moral purpose. The highest moral purpose aimed at in the highest species of the drama, is the teaching the human heart, through its sympathies and anti-pathies, the knowledge of itself; in proportion to the pos-session of which knowledge, every human being is wise, just, sincere, tolerant and kind. If dogmas can do more, it is well: but a drama is no fit place for the enforcement of them. Un-doubtedly, no person can be truly dishonoured by the act of another; and the fit return to make to the most enormous injuries is kindness and forbearance, and a resolution to con-vert the injurer from his dark passions by peace and love. Revenge, retaliation, atonement, are pernicious mistakes. If Beatrice had thought in this manner she would have been wiser and better; but she would never have been a tragic character: the few whom such an exhibition would have interested, could never have been sufficiently interested for a dramatic purpose, from the want of finding sympathy in their interest among the mass who surround them. It is in the rest-less and anatomizing casuistry with which men seek the justi-fication of Beatrice, yet feel that she has done what needs justification; it is in the superstitious horror with which they contemplate alike her wrongs and their revenge, that the dramatic character of what she did and suffered, consists.

I have endeavoured as nearly as possible to represent the characters as they probably were, and have sought to avoid the error of making them actuated by my own conceptions of right or wrong, false or true: thus under a thin veil converting names and actions of the sixteenth century into cold imperson-ations of my own mind. They are represented as Catholics, and as Catholics deeply tinged with religion. To a Protestant apprehension there will appear something unnatural in the earnest and perpetual sentiment of the relations between God and men which pervade the tragedy of the Cenci. It will especially be startled at the combination of an undoubting persuasion of the truth of the popular religion with a cool and determined perseverance in enormous guilt. But religion in Italy is not, as in Protestant countries, a cloak to be worn on particular days; or a passport which those who do not wish to be railed at carry with them to exhibit; or a gloomy passion for penetrating the impenetrable mysteries of our being, which terrifies its possessor at the darkness of the abyss to the brink of which it has conducted him. Religion coexists, as it were, in the mind of an Italian Catholic, with a faith in that of which all men have the most certain knowledge. It is interwoven with the whole fabric of life. It is adoration, faith, submission, penitence, blind admiration; not a rule for moral conduct. It has no necessary connection with any one virtue. The most atrocious villain may be rigidly devout, and without any shock to established faith, confess himself to be so. Religion pervades intensely the whole frame of society, and is, according to the temper of the mind which it inhabits, a passion, a persuasion, an excuse, a refuge; never a check. Cenci himself built a chapel in the court of his Palace, and dedicated it to St. Thomas the Apostle, and established masses for the peace of his soul. Thus in the first scene of the fourth act Lucretia's design in exposing herself to the consequences of an expostulation with Cenci after having administered the opiate, was to induce him by a feigned tale to confess himself before death; this being esteemed by Catholics as essential to salvation; and she only relinquishes her purpose when she perceives that her perseverance would expose Beatrice to new outrages.

I have avoided with great care in writing this play the introduction of what is commonly called mere poetry, and I imagine there will scarcely be found a detached simile or a single isolated description, unless Beatrice's description of the chasm appointed for her father's murder should be judged to be of that nature.[1]

In a dramatic composition the imagery and the passion should interpenetrate one another, the former being reserved

[1] An idea in this speech was suggested by a most sublime passage in *El Purgatorio de San Patricio* of Calderon; the only plagiarism which I have intentionally committed in the whole piece.

simply for the full development and illustration of the latter. Imagination is as the immortal God which should assume flesh for the redemption of mortal passion. It is thus that the most remote and the most familiar imagery may alike be fit for dramatic purposes when employed in the illustration of strong feeling, which raises what is low, and levels to the apprehension that which is lofty, casting over all the shadow of its own greatness. In other respects, I have written more carelessly; that is, without an over-fastidious and learned choice of words. In this respect I entirely agree with those modern critics who assert that in order to move men to true sympathy we must use the familiar language of men, and that our great ancestors the ancient English poets are the writers, a study of whom might incite us to do that for our own age which they have done for theirs. But it must be the real language of men in general and not that of any particular class to whose society the writer happens to belong. So much for what I have attempted; I need not be assured that success is a very different matter; particularly for one whose attention has but newly been awakened to the study of dramatic literature.

I endeavoured whilst at Rome to observe such monuments of this story as might be accessible to a stranger. The portrait of Beatrice at the Colonna Palace is admirable as a work of art: it was taken by Guido during her confinement in prison. But it is most interesting as a just representation of one of the loveliest specimens of the workmanship of Nature. There is a fixed and pale composure upon the features: she seems sad and stricken down in spirit, yet the despair thus expressed is lightened by the patience of gentleness. Her head is bound with folds of white drapery from which the yellow strings of her golden hair escape, and fall about her neck. The moulding of her face is exquisitely delicate; the eyebrows are distinct and arched: the lips have that permanent meaning of imagination and sensibility which suffering has not repressed and which it seems as if death scarcely could extinguish. Her forehead is large and clear; her eyes, which we are told were remarkable for their vivacity, are swollen with weeping and lustreless, but beautifully tender and serene. In the whole mien there is a simplicity and dignity which, united with her exquisite loveliness and deep sorrow, are inexpressibly pathetic. Beatrice Cenci appears to have been one of those rare persons in whom energy and gentleness dwell together without destroying one another: her nature was simple and profound. The crimes and miseries in which she was an actor and a sufferer are as the mask and the mantle in which circumstances clothed her for her impersonation on the scene of the world.

The Cenci Palace is of great extent; and though in part modernized, there yet remains a vast and gloomy pile of feudal architecture in the same state as during the dreadful scenes which are the subject of this tragedy. The Palace is situated in an obscure corner of Rome, near the quarter of the Jews, and from the upper windows you see the immense ruins of Mount Palatine half hidden under their profuse overgrowth of trees. There is a court in one part of the Palace (perhaps that in which Cenci built the Chapel to St. Thomas), supported by granite columns and adorned with antique friezes of fine workmanship, and built up, according to the ancient Italian fashion, with balcony over balcony of open-work. One of the gates of the Palace formed of immense stones and leading through a passage, dark and lofty and opening into gloomy subterranean chambers, struck me particularly.

Of the Castle of Petrella, I could obtain no further information than that which is to be found in the manuscript.

## DRAMATIS PERSONÆ

Count Francesco Cenci.

Giacomo, ⎫
Bernardo, ⎭ *his Sons.*

Cardinal Camillo.

Orsino, *a Prelate.*

Savella, *the Pope's Legate.*

Olimpio, ⎫
Marzio, ⎭ *Assassins.*

Andrea, *Servant to Cenci.*

Nobles, Judges, Guards, Servants.

Lucretia, *Wife of* Cenci, *and Step-mother of his children.*
Beatrice, *his Daughter.*

The Scene lies principally in Rome, but changes during the Fourth Act to Petrella, a castle among the Apulian Apennines.

Time.   During the Pontificate of Clement VIII.

## ACT I

### Scene I.—*An Apartment in the Cenci Palace.*

*Enter* Count Cenci, *and* Cardinal Camillo.

*Camillo.*   That matter of the murder is hushed up
If you consent to yield his Holiness
Your fief that lies beyond the Pincian gate.—
It needed all my interest in the conclave
To bend him to this point: he said that you      5
Bought perilous impunity with your gold;
That crimes like yours if once or twice compounded
Enriched the Church, and respited from hell
An erring soul which might repent and live:—
But that the glory and the interest      10
Of the high throne he fills, little consist
With making it a daily mart of guilt
As manifold and hideous as the deeds
Which you scarce hide from men's revolted eyes.

*Cenci.*   The third of my possessions—let it go!                15
Ay, I once heard the nephew of the Pope
Had sent his architect to view the ground,
Meaning to build a villa on my vines
The next time I compounded with his uncle:
I little thought he should outwit me so!                          20
Henceforth no witness—not the lamp—shall see
That which the vassal threatened to divulge
Whose throat is choked with dust for his reward.
The deed he saw could not have rated higher
Than his most worthless life:—it angers me!                       25
Respited me from Hell!—So may the Devil
Respite their souls from Heaven.  No doubt Pope Clement,
And his most charitable nephews, pray
That the Apostle Peter and the Saints
Will grant for their sake that I long enjoy                       30
Strength, wealth, and pride, and lust, and length of days
Wherein to act the deeds which are the stewards
Of their revenue.—But much yet remains
To which they show no title.
      *Camillo.*                    Oh, Count Cenci!
So much that thou mightst honourably live                         35
And reconcile thyself with thine own heart
And with thy God, and with the offended world.
How hideously look deeds of lust and blood
Through those snow white and venerable hairs!—
Your children should be sitting round you now,                    40
But that you fear to read upon their looks
The shame and misery you have written there.
Where is your wife?  Where is your gentle daughter?
Methinks her sweet looks, which make all things else
Beauteous and glad, might kill the fiend within you.              45
Why is she barred from all society
But her own strange and uncomplaining wrongs?
Talk with me, Count,—you know I mean you well.
I stood beside your dark and fiery youth
Watching its bold and bad career, as men                          50
Watch meteors, but it vanished not—I marked

Your desperate and remorseless manhood; now
Do I behold you in dishonoured age
Charged with a thousand unrepented crimes.
Yet I have ever hoped you would amend,                          55
And in that hope have saved your life three times.

   *Cenci.* For which Aldobrandino owes you now
My fief beyond the Pincian.—Cardinal,
One thing, I pray you, recollect henceforth,
And so we shall converse with less restraint.                   60
A man you knew spoke of my wife and daughter—
He was accustomed to frequent my house;
So the next day *his* wife and daughter came
And asked if I had seen him; and I smiled:
I think they never saw him any more.                            65

   *Camillo.* Thou execrable man, beware!—

   *Cenci.*                                   Of thee?
Nay this is idle:—We should know each other.
As to my character for what men call crime
Seeing I please my senses as I list,
And vindicate that right with force or guile,                   70
It is a public matter, and I care not
If I discuss it with you. I may speak
Alike to you and my own conscious heart—
For you give out that you have half reformed me,
Therefore strong vanity will keep you silent                    75
If fear should not; both will, I do not doubt.
All men delight in sensual luxury,
All men enjoy revenge; and most exult
Over the tortures they can never feel—
Flattering their secret peace with others' pain.                80
But I delight in nothing else. I love
The sight of agony, and the sense of joy,
When this shall be another's, and that mine.
And I have no remorse and little fear,
Which are, I think, the checks of other men.                    85
This mood has grown upon me, until now
Any design my captious fancy makes
The picture of its wish, and it forms none

But such as men like you would start to know,
Is as my natural food and rest debarred          90
Until it be accomplished.
   *Camillo.*             Art thou not
Most miserable?
   *Cenci.*        Why, miserable?—
No.—I am what your theologians call
Hardened;—which they must be in impudence,
So to revile a man's peculiar taste.          95
True, I was happier than I am, while yet
Manhood remained to act the thing I thought;
While lust was sweeter than revenge; and now
Invention palls:—Ay, we must all grow old—
And but that there yet remains a deed to act          100
Whose horror might make sharp an appetite
Duller than mine—I'd do—I know not what.
When I was young I thought of nothing else
But pleasure; and I fed on honey sweets:
Men, by St. Thomas! cannot live like bees,          105
And I grew tired:—yet, till I killed a foe,
And heard his groans, and heard his children's groans,
Knew I not what delight was else on earth,
Which now delights me little. I the rather
Look on such pangs as terror ill conceals,          110
The dry fixed eyeball; the pale quivering lip,
Which tell me that the spirit weeps within
Tears bitterer than the bloody sweat of Christ.
I rarely kill the body, which preserves,
Like a strong prison, the soul within my power,          115
Wherein I feed it with the breath of fear
For hourly pain.
   *Camillo.*         Hell's most abandoned fiend
Did never, in the drunkenness of guilt,
Speak to his heart as now you speak to me;
I thank my God that I believe you not.          120
              *Enter* ANDREA.
   *Andrea.* My Lord, a gentleman from Salamanca
Would speak with you.

*Cenci.*                    Bid him attend me in
The grand saloon.                         [*Exit* ANDREA.
    *Camillo.*              Farewell; and I will pray
Almighty God that thy false, impious words
Tempt not his spirit to abandon thee.     [*Exit* CAMILLO.
    *Cenci.*  The third of my possessions! I must use          126
Close husbandry, or gold, the old man's sword,
Falls from my withered hand. But yesterday
There came an order from the Pope to make
Fourfold provision for my cursèd sons;                          130
Whom I had sent from Rome to Salamanca,
Hoping some accident might cut them off;
And meaning if I could to starve them there.
I pray thee, God, send some quick death upon them!
Bernardo and my wife could not be worse                        135
If dead and damned:—then, as to Beatrice—
                    [*Looking around him suspiciously.*
I think they cannot hear me at that door;
What if they should? And yet I need not speak
Though the heart triumphs with itself in words.
O, thou most silent air, that shalt not hear                   140
What now I think! Thou, pavement, which I tread
Towards her chamber,—let your echoes talk
Of my imperious step scorning surprise,
But not of my intent!—Andrea!

*Enter* ANDREA.

*Andrea.*                              My lord?
    *Cenci.*  Bid Beatrice attend me in her chamber            145
This evening:—no, at midnight and alone.        [*Exeunt.*


SCENE II.—*A Garden of the Cenci Palace. Enter*
BEATRICE *and* ORSINO, *as in conversation.*

*Beatrice.*  Pervert not truth,
Orsino. You remember where we held
That conversation;—nay, we see the spot
Even from this cypress;—two long years are past
Since, on an April midnight, underneath            5

The moonlight ruins of mount Palatine,
I did confess to you my secret mind.
   *Orsino.*   You said you loved me then.
   *Beatrice.*               You are a Priest,
Speak to me not of love.
   *Orsino.*            I may obtain
The dispensation of the Pope to marry.                          10
Because I am a Priest do you believe
Your image, as the hunter some struck deer,
Follows me not whether I wake or sleep?
   *Beatrice.*   As I have said, speak to me not of love;
Had you a dispensation I have not;                              15
Nor will I leave this home of misery
Whilst my poor Bernard, and that gentle lady
To whom I owe life, and these virtuous thoughts,
Must suffer what I still have strength to share.
Alas, Orsino! All the love that once                           20
I felt for you, is turned to bitter pain.
Ours was a youthful contract, which you first
Broke, by assuming vows no Pope will loose.
And thus I love you still, but holily,
Even as a sister or a spirit might;                            25
And so I swear a cold fidelity.
And it is well perhaps we shall not marry.
You have a sly, equivocating vein
That suits me not.—Ah, wretched that I am!
Where shall I turn? Even now you look on me                    30
As you were not my friend, and as if you
Discovered that I thought so, with false smiles
Making my true suspicion seem your wrong.
Ah, no! forgive me; sorrow makes me seem
Sterner than else my nature might have been;                   35
I have a weight of melancholy thoughts,
And they forbode,—but what can they forbode
Worse than I now endure?
   *Orsino.*              All will be well.
Is the petition yet prepared? You know
My zeal for all you wish, sweet Beatrice;                      40

Doubt not but I will use my utmost skill
So that the Pope attend to your complaint.

*Beatrice.* Your zeal for all I wish;—Ah me, you are cold!
Your utmost skill . . . speak but one word . . . (*aside*) Alas!
Weak and deserted creature that I am,               45
Here I stand bickering with my only friend!  [*To* ORSINO.
This night my father gives a sumptuous feast,
Orsino; he has heard some happy news
From Salamanca, from my brothers there,
And with this outward show of love he mocks        50
His inward hate. 'Tis bold hypocrisy,
For he would gladlier celebrate their deaths,
Which I have heard him pray for on his knees:
Great God! that such a father should be mine!
But there is mighty preparation made,              55
And all our kin, the Cenci, will be there,
And all the chief nobility of Rome.
And he has bidden me and my pale Mother
Attire ourselves in festival array.
Poor lady! She expects some happy change          60
In his dark spirit from this act; I none.
At supper I will give you the petition:
Till when—farewell.

*Orsino.* Farewell. (*Exit* BEATRICE.)  I know the Pope
Will ne'er absolve me from my priestly vow
But by absolving me from the revenue              65
Of many a wealthy see; and, Beatrice,
I think to win thee at an easier rate.
Nor shall he read her eloquent petition:
He might bestow her on some poor relation
Of his sixth cousin, as he did her sister,         70
And I should be debarred from all access.
Then as to what she suffers from her father,
In all this there is much exaggeration:—
Old men are testy and will have their way;
A man may stab his enemy, or his vassal,           75
And live a free life as to wine or women,
And with a peevish temper may return

To a dull home, and rate his wife and children;
Daughters and wives call this foul tyranny.
I shall be well content if on my conscience                 80
There rest no heavier sin than what they suffer
From the devices of my love—a net
From which she shall escape not. Yet I fear
Her subtle mind, her awe-inspiring gaze,
Whose beams anatomize me nerve by nerve                     85
And lay me bare, and make me blush to see
My hidden thoughts.—Ah, no! A friendless girl
Who clings to me, as to her only hope:—
I were a fool, not less than if a panther
Were panic-stricken by the antelope's eye,                  90
If she escape me.                                    [Exit.

SCENE III.—*A Magnificent Hall in the Cenci Palace. A Banquet.*

   *Enter* CENCI, LUCRETIA, BEATRICE, ORSINO, CAMILLO,
   NOBLES.

  *Cenci.*  Welcome, my friends and kinsmen; welcome ye,
Princes and Cardinals, pillars of the church,
Whose presence honours our festivity.
I have too long lived like an anchorite,
And in my absence from your merry meetings               5
An evil word is gone abroad of me;
But I do hope that you, my noble friends,
When you have shared the entertainment here,
And heard the pious cause for which 'tis given,
And we have pledged a health or two together,            10
Will think me flesh and blood as well as you;
Sinful indeed, for Adam made all so,
But tender-hearted, meek and pitiful.

  *First Guest.*  In truth, my Lord, you seem too light of heart,
Too sprightly and companionable a man,                   15
To act the deeds that rumour pins on you.
(*To his Companion.*)  I never saw such blithe and open cheer
In any eye!

*Second Guest.*   Some most desired event,
In which we all demand a common joy,
Has brought us hither; let us hear it, Count.          20
*Cenci.*   It is indeed a most desired event.
If, when a parent from a parent's heart
Lifts from this earth to the great Father of all
A prayer, both when he lays him down to sleep,
And when he rises up from dreaming it;          25
One supplication, one desire, one hope,
That he would grant a wish for his two sons,
Even all that he demands in their regard—
And suddenly beyond his dearest hope
It is accomplished, he should then rejoice,          30
And call his friends and kinsmen to a feast,
And task their love to grace his merriment,—
Then honour me thus far—for I am he.
   *Beatrice (to* LUCRETIA). Great God! How horrible! Some
        dreadful ill
Must have befallen my brothers.
   *Lucretia.*                    Fear not, Child,          35
He speaks too frankly.
   *Beatrice.*                Ah! My blood runs cold.
I fear that wicked laughter round his eye,
Which wrinkles up the skin even to the hair.
   *Cenci.*   Here are the letters brought from Salamanca;
Beatrice, read them to your mother. God!          40
I thank thee! In one night didst thou perform,
By ways inscrutable, the thing I sought.
My disobedient and rebellious sons
Are dead!—Why, dead!—What means this change of cheer?
You hear me not, I tell you they are dead;          45
And they will need no food or raiment more:
The tapers that did light them the dark way
Are their last cost. The Pope, I think, will not
Expect I should maintain them in their coffins.
Rejoice with me—my heart is wondrous glad.          50

[LUCRETIA *sinks, half fainting;* BEATRICE *supports her.*

*Beatrice.*   It is not true!—Dear lady, pray look up.
Had it been true, there is a God in Heaven,
He would not live to boast of such a boon.
Unnatural man, thou knowest that it is false.
  *Cenci.*   Ay, as the word of God; whom here I call          55
To witness that I speak the sober truth;—
And whose most favouring Providence was shown
Even in the manner of their deaths.  For Rocco
Was kneeling at the mass, with sixteen others,
When the church fell and crushed him to a mummy,          60
The rest escaped unhurt.  Cristofano
Was stabbed in error by a jealous man,
Whilst she he loved was sleeping with his rival;
All in the self-same hour of the same night;
Which shows that Heaven has special care of me.          65
I beg those friends who love me, that they mark
The day a feast upon their calendars.
It was the twenty-seventh of December:
Ay, read the letters if you doubt my oath.

[*The Assembly appears confused; several of the guests rise.*

*First Guest.*   Oh, horrible!  I will depart—
*Second Guest.*                              And I.—
*Third Guest.*                                    No, stay!  70
I do believe it is some jest; though faith!
'Tis mocking us somewhat too solemnly.
I think his son has married the Infanta,
Or found a mine of gold in El Dorado;
'Tis but to season some such news; stay, stay!          75
I see 'tis only raillery by his smile.
  *Cenci* (*filling a bowl of wine, and lifting it up*).   Oh, thou bright
          wine whose purple splendour leaps
And bubbles gaily in this golden bowl
Under the lamplight, as my spirits do,
To hear the death of my accursèd sons!          80
Could I believe thou wert their mingled blood,
Then would I taste thee like a sacrament,
And pledge with thee the mighty Devil in Hell,

Who, if a father's curses, as men say,
Climb with swift wings after their children's souls,          85
And drag them from the very throne of Heaven,
Now triumphs in my triumph!—But thou art
Superfluous; I have drunken deep of joy,
And I will taste no other wine to-night.
Here, Andrea! Bear the bowl around.

 *A Guest (rising).*     Thou wretch!          90
Will none among this noble company
Check the abandoned villain?

 *Camillo.*     For God's sake
Let me dismiss the guests! You are insane,
Some ill will come of this.

 *Second Guest.*   Seize, silence him!

 *First Guest.* I will!

 *Third Guest.*  And I!

*Cenci (addressing those who rise with a threatening gesture).*

 Who moves? Who speaks?

      *(turning to the Company)*

         'tis nothing,          95
Enjoy yourselves.—Beware! For my revenge
Is as the sealed commission of a king
That kills, and none dare name the murderer.

 [*The Banquet is broken up; several of the Guests are departing.*

 *Beatrice.* I do entreat you, go not, noble guests;
What, although tyranny and impious hate          100
Stand sheltered by a father's hoary hair?
What, if 'tis he who clothed us in these limbs
Who tortures them, and triumphs? What, if we,
The desolate and the dead, were his own flesh,
His children and his wife, whom he is bound          105
To love and shelter? Shall we therefore find
No refuge in this merciless wide world?
O think what deep wrongs must have blotted out
First love, then reverence in a child's prone mind,

Till it thus vanquish shame and fear! O think!   110
I have borne much, and kissed the sacred hand
Which crushed us to the earth, and thought its stroke
Was perhaps some paternal chastisement!
Have excused much, doubted; and when no doubt
Remained, have sought by patience, love, and tears   115
To soften him, and when this could not be
I have knelt down through the long sleepless nights
And lifted up to God, the Father of all,
Passionate prayers: and when these were not heard
I have still borne,—until I meet you here,   120
Princes and kinsmen, at this hideous feast
Given at my brothers' deaths. Two yet remain,
His wife remains and I, whom if ye save not,
Ye may soon share such merriment again
As fathers make over their children's graves.   125
O Prince Colonna, thou art our near kinsman,
Cardinal, thou art the Pope's chamberlain,
Camillo, thou art chief justiciary,
Take us away!

   *Cenci.* (*He has been conversing with* CAMILLO *during the first
part of* BEATRICE'S *speech; he hears the conclusion, and now
advances.*)        I hope my good friends here
Will think of their own daughters—or perhaps   130
Of their own throats—before they lend an ear
To this wild girl.

   *Beatrice* (*not noticing the words of Cenci*). Dare no one look
        on me?
None answer? Can one tyrant overbear
The sense of many best and wisest men?
Or is it that I sue not in some form   135
Of scrupulous law, that ye deny my suit?
O God! That I were buried with my brothers!
And that the flowers of this departed spring
Were fading on my grave! And that my father
Were celebrating now one feast for all!   140

   *Camillo.* A bitter wish for one so young and gentle;
Can we do nothing?

*Colonna.*                Nothing that I see.
Count Cenci were a dangerous enemy:
Yet I would second any one.
    *A Cardinal.*                And I.
    *Cenci.*   Retire to your chamber, insolent girl!        145
    *Beatrice.*   Retire thou, impious man! Ay, hide thyself
Where never eye can look upon thee more!
Wouldst thou have honour and obedience
Who art a torturer? Father, never dream
Though thou mayst overbear this company,        150
But ill must come of ill.—Frown not on me!
Haste, hide thyself, lest with avenging looks
My brothers' ghosts should hunt thee from thy seat!
Cover thy face from every living eye,
And start if thou but hear a human step:        155
Seek out some dark and silent corner, there,
Bow thy white head before offended God,
And we will kneel around, and fervently
Pray that he pity both ourselves and thee.
    *Cenci.*   My friends, I do lament this insane girl        160
Has spoilt the mirth of our festivity.
Good night, farewell; I will not make you longer
Spectators of our dull domestic quarrels.
Another time.—                *[Exeunt all but* CENCI *and* BEATRICE.
            My brain is swimming round;
Give me a bowl of wine!                *[To* BEATRICE.
                Thou painted viper!        165
Beast that thou art! Fair and yet terrible!
I know a charm shall make thee meek and tame,
Now get thee from my sight!                *[Exit* BEATRICE.
                Here, Andrea,
Fill up this goblet with Greek wine. I said
I would not drink this evening; but I must;        170
For, strange to say, I feel my spirits fail
With thinking what I have decreed to do.—
                *[Drinking the wine.*
Be thou the resolution of quick youth
Within my veins, and manhood's purpose stern,

SHELLEY IN ROME

From the painting by Joseph Severn

And age's firm, cold, subtle villainy;                                    175
As if thou wert indeed my children's blood
Which I did thirst to drink! The charm works well;
It must be done; it shall be done, I swear!                         [*Exit*.

END OF THE FIRST ACT.


## ACT II

SCENE I.—*An Apartment in the Cenci Palace.   Enter*
LUCRETIA *and* BERNARDO.

*Lucretia.*   Weep not, my gentle boy; he struck but me
Who have borne deeper wrongs.  In truth, if he
Had killed me, he had done a kinder deed.
O God, Almighty, do Thou look upon us,
We have no other friend but only Thee!                                    5
Yet weep not; though I love you as my own,
I am not your true mother.
    *Bernardo.*                           O more, more,
Than ever mother was to any child,
That have you been to me!  Had he not been
My father, do you think that I should weep!               10
    *Lucretia.*   Alas! Poor boy, what else couldst thou have done?

*Enter* BEATRICE.

*Beatrice* (*in a hurried voice*).   Did he pass this way?  Have
        you seen him, brother?
Ah, no! that is his step upon the stairs;
'Tis nearer now; his hand is on the door;
Mother, if I to thee have ever been                                       15
A duteous child, now save me!  Thou, great God,
Whose image upon earth a father is,
Dost Thou indeed abandon me?  He comes;
The door is opening now; I see his face;
He frowns on others, but he smiles on me,                          20
Even as he did after the feast last night.

G

*Enter a Servant.*

Almighty God, how merciful Thou art!
'Tis but Orsino's servant.—Well, what news?

*Servant.* My master bids me say, the Holy Father
Has sent back your petition thus unopened.    [*Giving a paper.*
And he demands at what hour 'twere secure                    26
To visit you again?

*Lucretia.*            At the Ave Mary.        [*Exit Servant.*
So, daughter, our last hope has failed; Ah me!
How pale you look; you tremble, and you stand
Wrapped in some fixed and fearful meditation,               30
As if one thought were over strong for you:
Your eyes have a chill glare; O, dearest child!
Are you gone mad? If not, pray speak to me.

*Beatrice.* You see I am not mad: I speak to you.

*Lucretia.* You talked of something that your father did   35
After that dreadful feast? Could it be worse
Than when he smiled, and cried, 'My sons are dead!'
And every one looked in his neighbour's face
To see if others were as white as he?
At the first word he spoke I felt the blood                 40
Rush to my heart, and fell into a trance;
And when it passed I sat all weak and wild;
Whilst you alone stood up, and with strong words
Checked his unnatural pride; and I could see
The devil was rebuked that lives in him                     45
Until this hour thus have you ever stood
Between us and your father's moody wrath
Like a protecting presence: your firm mind
Has been our only refuge and defence:
What can have thus subdued it? What can now                 50
Have given you that cold melancholy look,
Succeeding to your unaccustomed fear?

*Beatrice.* What is it that you say? I was just thinking
'Twere better not to struggle any more.
Men, like my father, have been dark and bloody,            55
Yet never—Oh! Before worse comes of it
'Twere wise to die: it ends in that at last.

*Lucretia.* Oh, talk not so, dear child! Tell me at once
What did your father do or say to you?
He stayed not after that accursèd feast                          60
One moment in your chamber.—Speak to me.

*Bernardo.* Oh, sister, sister, prithee, speak to us!

*Beatrice (speaking very slowly with a forced calmness).* It was
    one word, Mother, one little word;
One look, one smile. (*Wildly.*) Oh! He has trampled me
Under his feet, and made the blood stream down            65
My pallid cheeks. And he has given us all
Ditch-water, and the fever-stricken flesh
Of buffaloes, and bade us eat or starve,
And we have eaten.—He has made me look
On my beloved Bernardo, when the rust                      70
Of heavy chains has gangrened his sweet limbs,
And I have never yet despaired—but now!
What could I say?                          [*Recovering herself.*
    Ah, no! 'tis nothing new.
The sufferings we all share have made me wild:
He only struck and cursed me as he passed;                 75
He said, he looked, he did;—nothing at all
Beyond his wont, yet it disordered me.
Alas! I am forgetful of my duty,
I should preserve my senses for your sake.

*Lucretia.* Nay, Beatrice; have courage, my sweet girl,    80
If any one despairs it should be I
Who loved him once, and now must live with him
Till God in pity call for him or me.
For you may, like your sister, find some husband,
And smile, years hence, with children round your knees;   85
Whilst I, then dead, and all this hideous coil
Shall be remembered only as a dream.

*Beatrice.* Talk not to me, dear lady, of a husband.
Did you not nurse me when my mother died?
Did you not shield me and that dearest boy?                90
And had we any other friend but you
In infancy, with gentle words and looks,
To win our father not to murder us?

And shall I now desert you? May the ghost
Of my dead Mother plead against my soul                    95
If I abandon her who filled the place
She left, with more, even, than a mother's love!
 *Bernardo.* And I am of my sister's mind. Indeed
I would not leave you in this wretchedness,
Even though the Pope should make me free to live      100
In some blithe place, like others of my age,
With sports, and delicate food, and the fresh air.
Oh, never think that I will leave you, Mother!
 *Lucretia.* My dear, dear children!

*Enter* CENCI, *suddenly.*

 *Cenci.*         What, Beatrice here!
Come hither!    [*She shrinks back, and covers her face.*
      Nay, hide not your face, 'tis fair;      105
Look up! Why, yesternight you dared to look
With disobedient insolence upon me,
Bending a stern and an inquiring brow
On what I meant; whilst I then sought to hide
That which I came to tell you—but in vain.                110
 *Beatrice* (*wildly, staggering towards the door*). O that the
   earth would gape! Hide me, O God!
 *Cenci.* Then it was I whose inarticulate words
Fell from my lips, and who with tottering steps
Fled from your presence, as you now from mine.
Stay, I command you—from this day and hour               115
Never again, I think, with fearless eye,
And brow superior, and unaltered cheek,
And that lip made for tenderness or scorn,
Shalt thou strike dumb the meanest of mankind;
Me least of all. Now get thee to thy chamber!             120
Thou too, loathed image of thy cursèd mother,

[*To* BERNARDO.

Thy milky, meek face makes me sick with hate!

[*Exeunt* BEATRICE *and* BERNARDO.

*(Aside.)* So much has passed between us as must make
Me bold, her fearful.—'Tis an awful thing
To touch such mischief as I now conceive:                    125
So men sit shivering on the dewy bank,
And try the chill stream with their feet; once in . . .
How the delighted spirit pants for joy!

   *Lucretia (advancing timidly towards him).* O husband! Pray
      forgive poor Beatrice.
She meant not any ill.

   *Cenci.*           Nor you perhaps?                    130
Nor that young imp, whom you have taught by rote
Parricide with his alphabet? Nor Giacomo?
Nor those two most unnatural sons, who stirred
Enmity up against me with the Pope?
Whom in one night merciful God cut off:                      135
Innocent lambs! They thought not any ill.
You were not here conspiring? You said nothing
Of how I might be dungeoned as a madman;
Or be condemned to death for some offence,
And you would be the witnesses?—This failing,             140
How just it were to hire assassins, or
Put sudden poison in my evening drink?
Or smother me when overcome by wine?
Seeing we had no other judge but God,
And He had sentenced me, and there were none             145
But you to be the executioners
Of His decree enregistered in Heaven?
Oh, no! You said not this?

   *Lucretia.*        So help me God,
I never thought the things you charge me with!

   *Cenci.* If you dare speak that wicked lie again            150
I'll kill you. What! It was not by your counsel
That Beatrice disturbed the feast last night?
You did not hope to stir some enemies
Against me, and escape, and laugh to scorn
What every nerve of you now trembles at?                    155
You judged that men were bolder than they are;
Few dare to stand between their grave and me.

*Lucretia.*   Look not so dreadfully! By my salvation
I knew not aught that Beatrice designed;
Nor do I think she designed any thing                         160
Until she heard you talk of her dead brothers.
   *Cenci.*   Blaspheming liar! You are damned for this!
But I will take you where you may persuade
The stones you tread on to deliver you:
For men shall there be none but those who dare               165
All things—not question that which I command.
On Wednesday next I shall set out: you know
That savage rock, the Castle of Petrella:
'Tis safely walled, and moated round about:
Its dungeons underground, and its thick towers               170
Never told tales; though they have heard and seen
What might make dumb things speak.—Why do you linger?
Make speediest preparation for the journey! [*Exit* LUCRETIA.
The all-beholding sun yet shines; I hear
A busy stir of men about the streets;                        175
I see the bright sky through the window panes:
It is a garish, broad, and peering day;
Loud, light, suspicious, full of eyes and ears,
And every little corner, nook, and hole
Is penetrated with the insolent light.                       180
Come darkness! Yet, what is the day to me?
And wherefore should I wish for night, who do
A deed which shall confound both night and day?
'Tis she shall grope through a bewildering mist
Of horror: if there be a sun in heaven                       185
She shall not dare to look upon its beams;
Nor feel its warmth. Let her then wish for night;
The act I think shall soon extinguish all
For me: I bear a darker deadlier gloom
Than the earth's shade, or interlunar air,                   190
Or constellations quenched in murkiest cloud,
In which I walk secure and unbeheld
Towards my purpose.—Would that it were done!          [*Exit.*

Scene II.—*A Chamber in the Vatican. Enter* Camillo
*and* Giacomo, *in conversation.*

*Camillo.*    There is an obsolete and doubtful law
By which you might obtain a bare provision
Of food and clothing—
*Giacomo.*                        Nothing more? Alas!
Bare must be the provision which strict law
Awards, and agèd, sullen avarice pays.                      5
Why did my father not apprentice me
To some mechanic trade? I should have then
Been trained in no highborn necessities
Which I could meet not by my daily toil.
The eldest son of a rich nobleman                           10
Is heir to all his incapacities;
He has wide wants, and narrow powers. If you,
Cardinal Camillo, were reduced at once
From thrice-driven beds of down, and delicate food,
An hundred servants, and six palaces,                       15
To that which nature doth indeed require?—
*Camillo.*    Nay, there is reason in your plea; 'twere hard.
*Giacomo.*    'Tis hard for a firm man to bear: but I
Have a dear wife, a lady of high birth,
Whose dowry in ill hour I lent my father                    20
Without a bond or witness to the deed:
And children, who inherit her fine senses,
The fairest creatures in this breathing world;
And she and they reproach me not. Cardinal,
Do you not think the Pope would interpose                   25
And stretch authority beyond the law?
*Camillo.*    Though your peculiar case is hard, I know
The Pope will not divert the course of law.
After that impious feast the other night
I spoke with him, and urged him then to check              30
Your father's cruel hand; he frowned and said,
'Children are disobedient, and they sting
Their fathers' hearts to madness and despair,
Requiting years of care with contumely.

I pity the Count Cenci from my heart;                        35
His outraged love perhaps awakened hate,
And thus he is exasperated to ill.
In the great war between the old and young
I, who have white hairs and a tottering body,
Will keep at least blameless neutrality.'                    40

*Enter* ORSINO.

You, my good Lord Orsino, heard those words.
   *Orsino.*   What words?
   *Giacomo.*                    Alas, repeat them not again!
There then is no redress for me, at least
None but that which I may achieve myself,
Since I am driven to the brink.—But, say,                    45
My innocent sister and my only brother
Are dying underneath my father's eye.
The memorable torturers of this land,
Galeaz Visconti, Borgia, Ezzelin,
Never inflicted on the meanest slave                         50
What these endure; shall they have no protection?
   *Camillo.*   Why, if they would petition to the Pope
I see not how he could refuse it—yet
He holds it of most dangerous example
In aught to weaken the paternal power,                       55
Being, as 'twere, the shadow of his own.
I pray you now excuse me. I have business
That will not bear delay.              [*Exit* CAMILLO.
   *Giacomo.*                    But you, Orsino,
Have the petition: wherefore not present it?
   *Orsino.*   I have presented it, and backed it with     60
My earnest prayers, and urgent interest;
It was returned unanswered. I doubt not
But that the strange and execrable deeds
Alleged in it—in truth they might well baffle
Any belief—have turned the Pope's displeasure               65
Upon the accusers from the criminal:
So I should guess from what Camillo said.
   *Giacomo.*   My friend, that palace-walking devil Gold

Has whispered silence to his Holiness:
And we are left, as scorpions ringed with fire.                    70
What should we do but strike ourselves to death?
For he who is our murderous persecutor
Is shielded by a father's holy name,
Or I would—                                        [*Stops abruptly.*
   *Orsino.*     What? Fear not to speak your thought.
Words are but holy as the deeds they cover:                    75
A priest who has forsworn the God he serves;
A judge who makes Truth weep at his decree;
A friend who should weave counsel, as I now,
But as the mantle of some selfish guile;
A father who is all a tyrant seems,                    80
Were the profaner for his sacred name.
   *Giacomo.*   Ask me not what I think; the unwilling brain
Feigns often what it would not; and we trust
Imagination with such phantasies
As the tongue dares not fashion into words,                    85
Which have no words, their horror makes them dim
To the mind's eye.—My heart denies itself
To think what you demand.
   *Orsino.*            But a friend's bosom
Is as the inmost cave of our own mind
Where we sit shut from the wide gaze of day,                    90
And from the all-communicating air.
You look what I suspected—
   *Giacomo.*         Spare me now!
I am as one lost in a midnight wood,
Who dares not ask some harmless passenger
The path across the wilderness, lest he,                    95
As my thoughts are, should be—a murderer.
I know you are my friend, and all I dare
Speak to my soul that will I trust with thee.
But now my heart is heavy, and would take
Lone counsel from a night of sleepless care.                    100
Pardon me, that I say farewell—farewell!
I would that to my own suspected self
I could address a word so full of peace.

*Orsino.*    Farewell!—Be your thoughts better or more bold.

[*Exit* GIACOMO.

I had disposed the Cardinal Camillo                    105
To feed his hope with cold encouragement:
It fortunately serves my close designs
That 'tis a trick of this same family
To analyse their own and other minds.
Such self-anatomy shall teach the will                 110
Dangerous secrets: for it tempts our powers,
Knowing what must be thought, and may be done,
Into the depth of darkest purposes:
So Cenci fell into the pit; even I,
Since Beatrice unveiled me to myself,                  115
And made me shrink from what I cannot shun,
Show a poor figure to my own esteem,
To which I grow half reconciled. I'll do
As little mischief as I can; that thought
Shall fee the accuser conscience.

(*After a pause.*)            Now what harm         120
If Cenci should be murdered?—Yet, if murdered,
Wherefore by me? And what if I could take
The profit, yet omit the sin and peril
In such an action? Of all earthly things
I fear a man whose blows outspeed his words;          125
And such is Cenci: and while Cenci lives
His daughter's dowry were a secret grave
If a priest wins her.—Oh, fair Beatrice!
Would that I loved thee not, or loving thee
Could but despise danger and gold and all             130
That frowns between my wish and its effect,
Or smiles beyond it! There is no escape . . .
Her bright form kneels beside me at the altar,
And follows me to the resort of men,
And fills my slumber with tumultuous dreams,          135
So when I wake my blood seems liquid fire;
And if I strike my damp and dizzy head
My hot palm scorches it: her very name,
But spoken by a stranger, makes my heart

Sicken and pant; and thus unprofitably 140
I clasp the phantom of unfelt delights
Till weak imagination half possesses
The self-created shadow. Yet much longer
Will I not nurse this life of feverous hours:
From the unravelled hopes of Giacomo. 145
I must work out my own dear purposes.
I see, as from a tower, the end of all:
Her father dead; her brother bound to me
By a dark secret, surer than the grave;
Her mother scared and unexpostulating 150
From the dread manner of her wish achieved:
And she!—Once more take courage, my faint heart;
What dares a friendless maiden matched with thee?
I have such foresight as assures success:
Some unbeheld divinity doth ever, 155
When dread events are near, stir up men's minds
To black suggestions; and he prospers best,
Not who becomes the instrument of ill,
But who can flatter the dark spirit, that makes
Its empire and its prey of other hearts 160
Till it become his slave . . . as I will do. [*Exit.*

END OF THE SECOND ACT.


ACT III

SCENE I.—*An Apartment in the Cenci Palace.* LUCRETIA,
*to her enter* BEATRICE.

*Beatrice.* (*She enters staggering, and speaks wildly.*) Reach me
that handkerchief!—My brain is hurt;
My eyes are full of blood; just wipe them for me . . .
I see but indistinctly . . .
*Lucretia.* My sweet child,
You have no wound; 'tis only a cold dew
That starts from your dear brow . . . Alas! Alas! 5
What has befallen?

*Beatrice.*          How comes this hair undone?
Its wandering strings must be what blind me so,
And yet I tied it fast.—O, horrible!
The pavement sinks under my feet! The walls
Spin round! I see a woman weeping there,          10
And standing calm and motionless, whilst I
Slide giddily as the world reels. . . . My God!
The beautiful blue heaven is flecked with blood!
The sunshine on the floor is black! The air
Is changed to vapours such as the dead breathe          15
In charnel pits! Pah! I am choked! There creeps
A clinging, black, contaminating mist
About me . . . 'tis substantial, heavy, thick,
I cannot pluck it from me, for it glues
My fingers and my limbs to one another,          20
And eats into my sinews, and dissolves
My flesh to a pollution, poisoning
The subtle, pure, and inmost spirit of life!
My God! I never knew what the mad felt
Before; for I am mad beyond all doubt!          25
(*More wildly.*) No, I am dead! These putrefying limbs
Shut round and sepulchre the panting soul
Which would burst forth into the wandering air! (*A pause.*)
What hideous thought was that I had even now?
'Tis gone; and yet its burthen remains here          30
O'er these dull eyes . . . upon this weary heart!
O, world! O, life! O, day! O, misery!
     *Lucretia.* What ails thee, my poor child? She answers not:
Her spirit apprehends the sense of pain,
But not its cause; suffering has dried away          35
The source from which it sprung . . .
     *Beatrice* (*franticly*).          Like Parricide . . .
Misery has killed its father: yet its father
Never like mine . . . O, God! What thing am I?
     *Lucretia.* My dearest child, what has your father done?
     *Beatrice* (*doubtfully*). Who art thou, questioner? I have no
          father.          40
(*Aside.*) She is the madhouse nurse who tends on me,

It is a piteous office.     [*To* LUCRETIA, *in a slow, subdued voice.*
                    Do you know
I thought I was that wretched Beatrice
Men speak of, whom her father sometimes hales
From hall to hall by the entangled hair;                    45
At others, pens up naked in damp cells
Where scaly reptiles crawl, and starves her there,
Till she will eat strange flesh. This woful story
So did I overact in my sick dreams,
That I imagined . . . no, it cannot be!                    50
Horrible things have been in this wide world,
Prodigious mixtures, and confusions strange
Of good and ill; and worse have been conceived
Than ever there was found a heart to do.
But never fancy imaged such a deed                    55
As . . .                    [*Pauses, suddenly recollecting herself.*
          Who art thou? Swear to me, ere I die
With fearful expectation, that indeed
Thou art not what thou seemest . . . Mother!
    *Lucretia.*                                        Oh!
My sweet child, know you . . .
    *Beatrice.*                    Yet speak it not:
For then if this be truth, that other too                    60
Must be a truth, a firm enduring truth,
Linked with each lasting circumstance of life,
Never to change, never to pass away.
Why so it is. This is the Cenci Palace;
Thou art Lucretia; I am Beatrice.                    65
I have talked some wild words, but will no more.
Mother, come near me: from this point of time,
I am . . .                    [*Her voice dies away faintly.*
    *Lucretia.* Alas! What has befallen thee, child?
What has thy father done?
    *Beatrice.*                    What have I done?
Am I not innocent? Is it my crime                    70
That one with white hair, and imperious brow,
Who tortured me from my forgotten years,
As parents only dare, should call himself

My father, yet should be!—Oh, what am I?
What name, what place, what memory shall be mine?    75
What retrospects, outliving even despair?
  *Lucretia.*  He is a violent tyrant, surely, child:
We know that death alone can make us free;
His death or ours.  But what can he have done
Of deadlier outrage or worse injury?    80
Thou art unlike thyself; thine eyes shoot forth
A wandering and strange spirit.  Speak to me,
Unlock those pallid hands whose fingers twine
With one another.
  *Beatrice.*                    'Tis the restless life
Tortured within them.  If I try to speak    85
I shall go mad.  Ay, something must be done;
What, yet I know not . . . something which shall make
The thing that I have suffered but a shadow
In the dread lightning which avenges it;
Brief, rapid, irreversible, destroying    90
The consequence of what it cannot cure.
Some such thing is to be endured or done:
When I know what, I shall be still and calm,
And never anything will move me more.
But now!—O blood, which art my father's blood,    95
Circling through these contaminated veins,
If thou, poured forth on the polluted earth,
Could wash away the crime, and punishment
By which I suffer . . . no, that cannot be!
Many might doubt there were a God above    100
Who sees and permits evil, and so die:
That faith no agony shall obscure in me.
  *Lucretia.*  It must indeed have been some bitter wrong;
Yet what, I dare not guess.  Oh, my lost child,
Hide not in proud impenetrable grief    105
Thy sufferings from my fear.
  *Beatrice.*                    I hide them not.
What are the words which you would have me speak?
I, who can feign no image in my mind
Of that which has transformed me: I, whose thought

Is like a ghost shrouded and folded up 110
In its own formless horror: of all words,
That minister to mortal intercourse,
Which wouldst thou hear? For there is none to tell
My misery: if another ever knew
Aught like to it, she died as I will die, 115
And left it, as I must, without a name.
Death! Death! Our law and our religion call thee
A punishment and a reward . . . Oh, which
Have I deserved?
    *Lucretia.*        The peace of innocence;
Till in your season you be called to heaven. 120
Whate'er you may have suffered, you have done
No evil. Death must be the punishment
Of crime, or the reward of trampling down
The thorns which God has strewed upon the path
Which leads to immortality.
    *Beatrice.*          Ay, death . . . 125
The punishment of crime. I pray thee, God,
Let me not be bewildered while I judge.
If I must live day after day, and keep
These limbs, the unworthy temple of Thy spirit,
As a foul den from which what Thou abhorrest 130
May mock Thee, unavenged . . . it shall not be!
Self-murder . . . no, that might be no escape,
For Thy decree yawns like a Hell between
Our will and it:—O! In this mortal world
There is no vindication and no law 135
Which can adjudge and execute the doom
Of that through which I suffer.

*Enter* ORSINO.

(*She approaches him solemnly.*)    Welcome, Friend!
I have to tell you that, since last we met,
I have endured a wrong so great and strange,
That neither life nor death can give me rest. 140
Ask me not what it is, for there are deeds
Which have no form, sufferings which have no tongue.

*Orsino.*   And what is he who has thus injured you?
*Beatrice.*   The man they call my father: a dread name.
*Orsino.*   It cannot be . . .
*Beatrice.*                What it can be, or not,                145
Forbear to think. It is, and it has been;
Advise me how it shall not be again.
I thought to die; but a religious awe
Restrains me, and the dread lest death itself
Might be no refuge from the consciousness                150
Of what is yet unexpiated. Oh, speak!
*Orsino.*   Accuse him of the deed, and let the law
Avenge thee.
*Beatrice.*       Oh, ice-hearted counsellor!
If I could find a word that might make known
The crime of my destroyer; and that done,`              155
My tongue should like a knife tear out the secret
Which cankers my heart's core; ay, lay all bare
So that my unpolluted fame should be
With vilest gossips a stale mouthèd story;
A mock, a byword, an astonishment:—                     160
If this were done, which never shall be done,
Think of the offender's gold, his dreaded hate,
And the strange horror of the accuser's tale,
Baffling belief, and overpowering speech;
Scarce whispered, unimaginable, wrapped                 165
In hideous hints . . . Oh, most assured redress!
*Orsino.*   You will endure it then?
*Beatrice.*                Endure?—Orsino,
It seems your counsel is small profit.

[*Turns from him, and speaks half to herself.*

                Ay,
All must be suddenly resolved and done.
What is this undistinguishable mist                     170
Of thoughts, which rise, like shadow after shadow,
Darkening each other?
*Orsino.*              Should the offender live?
Triumph in his misdeed? and make, by use,

His crime, whate'er it is, dreadful no doubt,
Thine element; until thou mayst become          175
Utterly lost; subdued even to the hue
Of that which thou permittest?
   *Beatrice (to herself).*          Mighty death!
Thou double-visaged shadow? Only judge!
Rightfullest arbiter!          [*She retires absorbed in thought.*
   *Lucretia.*          If the lightning
Of God has e'er descended to avenge . . .          180
   *Orsino.*   Blaspheme not! His high Providence commits
Its glory on this earth, and their own wrongs
Into the hands of men; if they neglect
To punish crime . . .
   *Lucretia.*          But if one, like this wretch,
Should mock, with gold, opinion, law, and power?          185
If there be no appeal to that which makes
The guiltiest tremble? If because our wrongs,
For that they are unnatural, strange, and monstrous,
Exceed all measure of belief? O God!
If, for the very reasons which should make          190
Redress most swift and sure, our injurer triumphs?
And we, the victims, bear worse punishment
Than that appointed for their torturer?
   *Orsino.*          Think not
But that there is redress where there is wrong,
So we be bold enough to seize it.
   *Lucretia.*          How?          195
If there were any way to make all sure,
I know not . . . but I think it might be good
To . . .
   *Orsino.* Why, his late outrage to Beatrice;
For it is such, as I but faintly guess,
As makes remorse dishonour, and leaves her          200
Only one duty, how she may avenge:
You, but one refuge from ills ill endured;
Me, but one counsel . . .
   *Lucretia.*          For we cannot hope
That aid, or retribution, or resource

Will arise thence, where every other one          205
Might find them with less need.          [BEATRICE *advances*.
  *Orsino*.                              Then . . .
  *Beatrice*.                                        Peace, Orsino!
And, honoured Lady, while I speak, I pray,
That you put off, as garments overworn,
Forbearance and respect, remorse and fear,
And all the fit restraints of daily life,          210
Which have been borne from childhood, but which now
Would be a mockery to my holier plea.
As I have said, I have endured a wrong,
Which, though it be expressionless, is such
As asks atonement; both for what is past,          215
And lest I be reserved, day after day,
To load with crimes an overburthened soul,
And be . . . what ye can dream not. I have prayed
To God, and I have talked with my own heart,
And have unravelled my entangled will,          220
And have at length determined what is right.
Art thou my friend, Orsino? False or true?
Pledge thy salvation ere I speak.
  *Orsino*.                              I swear
To dedicate my cunning, and my strength,
My silence, and whatever else is mine,          225
To thy commands.
  *Lucretia*.          You think we should devise
His death?
  *Beatrice*.          And execute what is devised,
And suddenly. We must be brief and bold.
  *Orsino*.          And yet most cautious.
  *Lucretia*.                    For the jealous laws
Would punish us with death and infamy          230
For that which it became themselves to do.
  *Beatrice*.          Be cautious as ye may, but prompt. Orsino,
What are the means?
  *Orsino*.                    I know two dull, fierce outlaws,
Who think man's spirit as a worm's, and they
Would trample out, for any slight caprice,          235

The meanest or the noblest life. This mood
Is marketable here in Rome. They sell
What we now want.

    *Lucretia.*            To-morrow before dawn,
Cenci will take us to that lonely rock,
Petrella, in the Apulian Apennines.          240
If he arrive there . . .

    *Beatrice.*          He must not arrive.

    *Orsino.*  Will it be dark before you reach the tower?

    *Lucretia.*  The sun will scarce be set.

    *Beatrice.*              But I remember
Two miles on this side of the fort, the road
Crosses a deep ravine; 'tis rough and narrow,    245
And winds with short turns down the precipice;
And in its depth there is a mighty rock,
Which has, from unimaginable years,
Sustained itself with terror and with toil
Over a gulf, and with the agony          250
With which it clings seems slowly coming down;
Even as a wretched soul hour after hour,
Clings to the mass of life; yet clinging, leans;
And leaning, makes more dark the dread abyss
In which it fears to fall: beneath this crag    255
Huge as despair, as if in weariness,
The melancholy mountain yawns . . . below,
You hear but see not an impetuous torrent
Raging among the caverns, and a bridge
Crosses the chasm; and high above there grow,    260
With intersecting trunks, from crag to crag,
Cedars, and yews, and pines; whose tangled hair
Is matted in one solid roof of shade
By the dark ivy's twine. At noonday here
'Tis twilight, and at sunset blackest night.    265

    *Orsino.*  Before you reach that bridge make some excuse
For spurring on your mules, or loitering
Until . . .

    *Beatrice.*  What sound is that?

    *Lucretia.*  Hark! No, it cannot be a servant's step

It must be Cenci, unexpectedly
Returned . . . Make some excuse for being here.
   *Beatrice.* (*To* ORSINO, *as she goes out.*) That step we hear approach must never pass
     The bridge of which we spoke.

                    [*Exeunt* LUCRETIA *and* BEATRICE.
   *Orsino.*                            What shall I do?
Cenci must find me here, and I must bear
The imperious inquisition of his looks                    275
As to what brought me hither: let me mask
Mine own in some inane and vacant smile.

       *Enter* GIACOMO, *in a hurried manner.*

How! Have you ventured hither? Know you then
That Cenci is from home?
   *Giacomo.*                    I sought him here;
And now must wait till he returns.
   *Orsino.*                            Great God!                    280
Weigh you the danger of this rashness?
   *Giacomo.*                                Ay!
Does my destroyer know his danger? We
Are now no more, as once, parent and child,
But man to man; the oppressor to the oppressed;
The slanderer to the slandered; foe to foe:                    285
He has cast Nature off, which was his shield,
And Nature casts him off, who is her shame;
And I spurn both. Is it a father's throat
Which I will shake, and say, I ask not gold;
I ask not happy years; nor memories                    290
Of tranquil childhood; nor home-sheltered love;
Though all these hast thou torn from me, and more;
But only my fair fame; only one hoard
Of peace, which I thought hidden from thy hate,
Under the penury heaped on me by thee,                    295
Or I will . . . God can understand and pardon,
Why should I speak with man?
   *Orsino.*                            Be calm, dear friend.
   *Giacomo.* Well, I will calmly tell you what he did.
This old Francesco Cenci, as you know,

Borrowed the dowry of my wife from me,                    300
And then denied the loan; and left me so
In poverty, the which I sought to mend
By holding a poor office in the state.
It had been promised to me, and already
I bought new clothing for my raggèd babes,                    305
And my wife smiled; and my heart knew repose.
When Cenci's intercession, as I found,
Conferred this office on a wretch, whom thus
He paid for vilest service.  I returned
With this ill news, and we sate sad together                    310
Solacing our despondency with tears
Of such affection and unbroken faith
As temper life's worst bitterness; when he,
As he is wont, came to upbraid and curse,
Mocking our poverty, and telling us                    315
Such was God's scourge for disobedient sons.
And then, that I might strike him dumb with shame,
I spoke of my wife's dowry; but he coined
A brief yet specious tale, how I had wasted
The sum in secret riot; and he saw                    320
My wife was touched, and he went smiling forth.
And when I knew the impression he had made,
And felt my wife insult with silent scorn
My ardent truth, and look averse and cold,
I went forth too: but soon returned again;                    325
Yet not so soon but that my wife had taught
My children her harsh thoughts, and they all cried,
'Give us clothes, father!  Give us better food!
What you in one night squander were enough
For months!'  I looked, and saw that home was hell.                    330
And to that hell will I return no more
Until mine enemy has rendered up
Atonement, or, as he gave life to me
I will, reversing Nature's law . . .
  *Orsino.*                              Trust me,
The compensation which thou seekest here                    335
Will be denied.

    *Giacomo.*          Then . . . Are you not my friend?
Did you not hint at the alternative,
Upon the brink of which you see I stand,
The other day when we conversed together?
My wrongs were then less. That word parricide,    340
Although I am resolved, haunts me like fear.
    *Orsino.*   It must be fear itself, for the bare word
Is hollow mockery. Mark, how wisest God
Draws to one point the threads of a just doom,
So sanctifying it: what you devise    345
Is, as it were, accomplished.
    *Giacomo.*              Is he dead?
    *Orsino.*   His grave is ready. Know that since we met
Cenci has done an outrage to his daughter.
    *Giacomo.*  What outrage?
    *Orsino.*            That she speaks not, but you may
Conceive such half conjectures as I do,    350
From her fixed paleness, and the lofty grief
Of her stern brow bent on the idle air,
And her severe unmodulated voice,
Drowning both tenderness and dread; and last
From this; that whilst her step-mother and I,    355
Bewildered in our horror, talked together
With obscure hints; both self-misunderstood
And darkly guessing, stumbling, in our talk,
Over the truth, and yet to its revenge,
She interrupted us, and with a look    360
Which told before she spoke it, he must die: . . .
    *Giacomo.*  It is enough. My doubts are well appeased;
There is a higher reason for the act
Than mine; there is a holier judge than me,
A more unblamed avenger. Beatrice,    365
Who in the gentleness of thy sweet youth
Hast never trodden on a worm, or bruised
A living flower, but thou hast pitied it
With needless tears! Fair sister, thou in whom
Men wondered how such loveliness and wisdom    370
Did not destroy each other! Is there made

Ravage of thee? O, heart, I ask no more
Justification! Shall I wait, Orsino,
Till he return, and stab him at the door?

   *Orsino.* Not so; some accident might interpose 375
To rescue him from what is now most sure;
And you are unprovided where to fly,
How to excuse or to conceal. Nay, listen:
All is contrived; success is so assured
That . . .

              *Enter* BEATRICE.

   *Beatrice.* 'Tis my brother's voice! You know me not? 380
   *Giacomo.* My sister, my lost sister!
   *Beatrice.*              Lost indeed!
I see Orsino has talked with you, and
That you conjecture things too horrible
To speak, yet far less than the truth. Now, stay not,
He might return: yet kiss me; I shall know 385
That then thou hast consented to his death.
Farewell, farewell! Let piety to God,
Brotherly love, justice and clemency,
And all things that make tender hardest hearts
Make thine hard, brother. Answer not . . . farewell. 390
                      [*Exeunt severally.*

SCENE II.—*A mean Apartment in* GIACOMO'S *House.*
GIACOMO *alone.*

   *Giacomo.* 'Tis midnight, and Orsino comes not yet.
            [*Thunder, and the sound of a storm.*
What! can the everlasting elements
Feel with a worm like man? If so, the shaft
Of mercy-wingèd lightning would not fall
On stones and trees, My wife and children sleep: 5
They are now living in unmeaning dreams:
But I must wake, still doubting if that deed
Be just which is most necessary. O,
Thou unreplenished lamp! whose narrow fire
Is shaken by the wind, and on whose edge 10

Devouring darkness hovers! Thou small flame,
Which, as a dying pulse rises and falls,
Still flickerest up and down, how very soon,
Did I not feed thee, wouldst thou fail and be
As thou hadst never been! So wastes and sinks          15
Even now, perhaps, the life that kindled mine:
But that no power can fill with vital oil
That broken lamp of flesh. Ha! 'tis the blood
Which fed these veins that ebbs till all is cold:
It is the form that moulded mine that sinks            20
Into the white and yellow spasms of death:
It is the soul by which mine was arrayed
In God's immortal likeness which now stands
Naked before Heaven's judgement seat!          [*A bell strikes.*
                              One! Two!
The hours crawl on; and when my hairs are white,       25
My son will then perhaps be waiting thus,
Tortured between just hate and vain remorse;
Chiding the tardy messenger of news
Like those which I expect. I almost wish
He be not dead, although my wrongs are great;          30
Yet . . . 'tis Orsino's step . . .

*Enter* ORSINO.

                                   Speak!
    *Orsino.*                              I am come
To say he has escaped.
    *Giacomo.*                  Escaped!
    *Orsino.*                          And safe
Within Petrella. He passed by the spot
Appointed for the deed an hour too soon.
    *Giacomo.*   Are we the fools of such contingencies?   35
And do we waste in blind misgivings thus
The hours when we should act? Then wind and thunder,
Which seemed to howl his knell, is the loud laughter
With which Heaven mocks our weakness! I henceforth
Will ne'er repent of aught designed or done            40
But my repentance.

*Orsino.*                 See, the lamp is out.

*Giacomo.*   If no remorse is ours when the dim air
Has drank this innocent flame, why should we quail
When Cenci's life, that light by which ill spirits
See the worst deeds they prompt, shall sink for ever?                45
No, I am hardened.

*Orsino.*                 Why, what need of this?
Who feared the pale intrusion of remorse
In a just deed? Although our first plan failed,
Doubt not but he will soon be laid to rest.
But light the lamp; let us not talk i' the dark.                50

*Giacomo (lighting the lamp).* And yet once quenched I cannot
     thus relume
My father's life: do you not think his ghost
Might plead that argument with God?

*Orsino.*                             Once gone
You cannot now recall your sister's peace;
Your own extinguished years of youth and hope;                55
Nor your wife's bitter words; nor all the taunts
Which, from the prosperous, weak misfortune takes;
Nor your dead mother; nor . . .

*Giacomo.*                 O, speak no more!
I am resolved, although this very hand
Must quench the life that animated it.                60

*Orsino.*   There is no need of that. Listen: you know
Olimpio, the castellan of Petrella
In old Colonna's time; him whom your father
Degraded from his post? And Marzio,
That desperate wretch, whom he deprived last year                65
Of a reward of blood, well earned and due?

*Giacomo.*   I knew Olimpio; and they say he hated
Old Cenci so, that in his silent rage
His lips grew white only to see him pass.
Of Marzio I know nothing.

*Orsino.*                 Marzio's hate                70
Matches Olimpio's. I have sent these men,
But in your name, and as at your request,
To talk with Beatrice and Lucretia.

*Giacomo.*   Only to talk?

*Orsino.*                    The moments which even now
Pass onward to to-morrow's midnight hour                    75
May memorize their flight with death: ere then
They must have talked, and may perhaps have done,
And made an end . . .

*Giacomo.*                    Listen! What sound is that?

*Orsino.*  The house-dog moans, and the beams crack: nought
    else.

*Giacomo.*   It is my wife complaining in her sleep:          80
I doubt not she is saying bitter things
Of me; and all my children round her dreaming
That I deny them sustenance.

*Orsino.*                    Whilst he
Who truly took it from them, and who fills
Their hungry rest with bitterness, now sleeps                85
Lapped in bad pleasures, and triumphantly
Mocks thee in visions of successful hate
Too like the truth of day.

*Giacomo.*                    If e'er he wakes
Again, I will not trust to hireling hands . . .

*Orsino.*  Why, that were well. I must be gone; good-night.
When next we meet—may all be done!

*Giacomo.*                              And all            91
Forgotten: Oh, that I had never been!        [*Exeunt.*

END OF THE THIRD ACT.

## ACT IV

SCENE I.—*An Apartment in the Castle of Petrella.*

*Enter* CENCI.

*Cenci.*   She comes not; yet I left her even now
Vanquished and faint. She knows the penalty
Of her delay: yet what if threats are vain?
Am I not now within Petrella's moat?
Or fear I still the eyes and ears of Rome?                    5

Might I not drag her by the golden hair?
Stamp on her? Keep her sleepless till her brain
Be overworn? Tame her with chains and famine?
Less would suffice. Yet so to leave undone
What I most seek! No, 'tis her stubborn will                    10
Which by its own consent shall stoop as low
As that which drags it down.

*Enter* LUCRETIA.

                              Thou loathèd wretch!
Hide thee from my abhorrence: fly, begone!
Yet stay! Bid Beatrice come hither.
    *Lucretia.*                          Oh,
Husband! I pray for thine own wretched sake                    15
Heed what thou dost. A man who walks like thee
Through crimes, and through the danger of his crimes,
Each hour may stumble o'er a sudden grave.
And thou art old; thy hairs are hoary gray;
As thou wouldst save thyself from death and hell,                    20
Pity thy daughter; give her to some friend
In marriage: so that she may tempt thee not
To hatred, or worse thoughts, if worse there be.
    *Cenci.* What! like her sister who has found a home
To mock my hate from with prosperity?                    25
Strange ruin shall destroy both her and thee
And all that yet remain. My death may be
Rapid, her destiny outspeeds it. Go,
Bid her come hither, and before my mood
Be changed, lest I should drag her by the hair.                    30
    *Lucretia.* She sent me to thee, husband. At thy presence
She fell, as thou dost know, into a trance;
And in that trance she heard a voice which said,
'Cenci must die! Let him confess himself!
Even now the accusing Angel waits to hear                    35
If God, to punish his enormous crimes,
Harden his dying heart!'
    *Cenci.*                    Why—such things are . . .
No doubt divine revelings may be made.

'Tis plain I have been favoured from above,
For when I cursed my sons they died.—Ay . . . so . . .          40
As to the right or wrong, that's talk . . . repentance . . .
Repentance is an easy moment's work
And more depends on God than me. Well . . . well . . .
I must give up the greater point, which was
To poison and corrupt her soul.
                    [*A pause;* LUCRETIA *approaches anxiously, and
                          then shrinks back as he speaks.*
                              One, two;          45
Ay . . . Rocco and Cristofano my curse
Strangled: and Giacomo, I think, will find
Life a worse Hell than that beyond the grave:
Beatrice shall, if there be skill in hate,
Die in despair, blaspheming: to Bernardo,          50
He is so innocent, I will bequeath
The memory of these deeds, and make his youth
The sepulchre of hope, where evil thoughts
Shall grow like weeds on a neglected tomb.
When all is done, out in the wide Campagna,          55
I will pile up my silver and my gold;
My costly robes, paintings and tapestries;
My parchments and all records of my wealth,
And make a bonfire in my joy, and leave
Of my possessions nothing but my name;          60
Which shall be an inheritance to strip
Its wearer bare as infamy. That done,
My soul, which is a scourge, will I resign
Into the hands of him who wielded it;
Be it for its own punishment or theirs,          65
He will not ask it of me till the lash
Be broken in its last and deepest wound;
Until its hate be all inflicted. Yet,
Lest death outspeed my purpose, let me make
Short work and sure . . .                    [*Going.*
    *Lucretia.* (*Stops him.*)   Oh, stay! It was a feint:          70
She had no vision, and she heard no voice.
I said it but to awe thee.

*Cenci.*                    That is well.
Vile palterer with the sacred truth of God,
Be thy soul choked with that blaspheming lie!
For Beatrice worse terrors are in store                    75
To bend her to my will.
    *Lucretia.*                    Oh! to what will?
What cruel sufferings more than she has known
Canst thou inflict?
    *Cenci.*                    Andrea! Go call my daughter,
And if she comes not tell her that I come.
What sufferings? I will drag her, step by step,                    80
Through infamies unheard of among men:
She shall stand shelterless in the broad noon
Of public scorn, for acts blazoned abroad,
One among which shall be . . . What? Canst thou guess?
She shall become (for what she most abhors                    85
Shall have a fascination to entrap
Her loathing will) to her own conscious self
All she appears to others; and when dead,
As she shall die unshrived and unforgiven,
A rebel to her father and her God,                    90
Her corpse shall be abandoned to the hounds;
Her name shall be the terror of the earth;
Her spirit shall approach the throne of God
Plague-spotted with my curses. I will make
Body and soul a monstrous lump of ruin.                    95

*Enter* ANDREA.

    *Andrea.* The Lady Beatrice . . .
    *Cenci.*                    Speak, pale slave! What
Said she?
    *Andrea.* My Lord, 'twas what she looked; she said:
'Go tell my father that I see the gulf
Of Hell between us two, which he may pass,
I will not.'                    [*Exit* ANDREA.
    *Cenci.* Go thou quick, Lucretia,                    100
Tell her to come; yet let her understand
Her coming is consent: and say, moreover,

That if she come not I will curse her.          [*Exit* LUCRETIA.
                              Ha!
With what but with a father's curse doth God
Panic-strike armèd victory, and make pale          105
Cities in their prosperity?  The world's Father
Must grant a parent's prayer against his child,
Be he who asks even what men call me.
Will not the deaths of her rebellious brothers
Awe her before I speak?  For I on them          110
Did imprecate quick ruin, and it came.
                    *Enter* LUCRETIA.
Well; what?  Speak, wretch!
    *Lucretia.*                    She said, 'I cannot come;
Go tell my father that I see a torrent
Of his own blood raging between us.'
      *Cenci* (*kneeling*).                    God!
Hear me!  If this most specious mass of flesh,          115
Which Thou hast made my daughter; this my blood,
This particle of my divided being;
Or rather, this my bane and my disease,
Whose sight infects and poisons me; this devil
Which sprung from me as from a hell, was meant          120
To aught good use; if her bright loveliness
Was kindled to illumine this dark world;
If nursed by Thy selectest dew of love
Such virtues blossom in her as should make
The peace of life, I pray Thee for my sake,          125
As Thou the common God and Father art
Of her, and me, and all; reverse that doom!
Earth, in the name of God, let her food be
Poison, until she be encrusted round
With leprous stains!  Heaven, rain upon her head          130
The blistering drops of the Maremma's dew,
Till she be speckled like a toad; parch up
Those love-enkindled lips, warp those fine limbs
To loathèd lameness!  All-beholding sun,
Strike in thine envy those life-darting eyes          135
With thine own blinding beams!

*Lucretia.*                              Peace! Peace!
For thine own sake unsay those dreadful words.
When high God grants He punishes such prayers.

*Cenci* (*leaping up, and throwing his right hand towards Heaven*).

  He does His will, I mine! This in addition,
That if she have a child . . .
 *Lucretia.*     Horrible thought!   140
 *Cenci.* That if she ever have a child; and thou,
Quick Nature! I adjure thee by thy God,
That thou be fruitful in her, and increase
And multiply, fulfilling his command,
And my deep imprecation! May it be   145
A hideous likeness of herself, that as
From a distorting mirror, she may see
Her image mixed with what she most abhors,
Smiling upon her from her nursing breast.
And that the child may from its infancy   150
Grow, day by day, more wicked and deformed,
Turning her mother's love to misery:
And that both she and it may live until
It shall repay her care and pain with hate,
Or what may else be more unnatural.   155
So he may hunt her through the clamorous scoffs
Of the loud world to a dishonoured grave.
Shall I revoke this curse? Go, bid her come,
Before my words are chronicled in Heaven.  [*Exit* LUCRETIA.
I do not feel as if I were a man,   160
But like a fiend appointed to chastise
The offences of some unremembered world.
My blood is running up and down my veins;
A fearful pleasure makes it prick and tingle:
I feel a giddy sickness of strange awe;   165
My heart is beating with an expectation
Of horrid joy.
      *Enter* LUCRETIA.

What? Speak!

*Lucretia.*                    She bids thee curse;
And if thy curses, as they cannot do,
Could kill her soul . . .
   *Cenci.*                She would not come. 'Tis well,
I can do both: first take what I demand,                170
And then extort concession. To thy chamber!
Fly ere I spurn thee: and beware this night
That thou cross not my footsteps. It were safer
To come between the tiger and his prey.      [*Exit* LUCRETIA.
It must be late; mine eyes grow weary dim                175
With unaccustomed heaviness of sleep.
Conscience! Oh, thou most insolent of lies!
They say that sleep, that healing dew of Heaven,
Steeps not in balm the foldings of the brain
Which thinks thee an impostor. I will go                180
First to belie thee with an hour of rest,
Which will be deep and calm, I feel: and then . . .
O, multitudinous Hell, the fiends will shake
Thine arches with the laughter of their joy!
There shall be lamentation heard in Heaven                185
As o'er an angel fallen; and upon Earth
All good shall droop and sicken, and ill things
Shall with a spirit of unnatural life
Stir and be quickened . . . even as I am now.        [*Exit.*

SCENE II.—*Before the Castle of Petrella. Enter* BEATRICE *and*
LUCRETIA *above on the Ramparts.*

*Beatrice.* They come not yet.
   *Lucretia.*                'Tis scarce midnight.
   *Beatrice.*                How slow
Behind the course of thought, even sick with speed,
Lags leaden-footed time!
   *Lucretia.*            The minutes pass . . .
If he should wake before the deed is done?
   *Beatrice.* O, mother! He must never wake again.                5
What thou hast said persuades me that our act
Will but dislodge a spirit of deep hell
Out of a human form.

*Lucretia.*                    'Tis true he spoke
Of death and judgement with strange confidence
For one so wicked; as a man believing                    10
In God, yet recking not of good or ill.
And yet to die without confession! . . .

*Beatrice.*                    Oh!
Believe that Heaven is merciful and just,
And will not add our dread necessity
To the amount of his offences.

*Enter* OLIMPIO *and* MARZIO, *below.*

*Lucretia.*                    See,                    15
They come.

*Beatrice.*    All mortal things must hasten thus
To their dark end. Let us go down.

                    [*Exeunt* LUCRETIA *and* BEATRICE *from above.*

*Olimpio.*    How feel you to this work?

*Marzio.*                    As one who thinks
A thousand crowns excellent market price
For an old murderer's life. Your cheeks are pale.                    20

*Olimpio.*    It is the white reflection of your own,
Which you call pale.

*Marzio.*                    Is that their natural hue?

*Olimpio.*    Or 'tis my hate and the deferred desire
To wreak it, which extinguishes their blood.

*Marzio.*    You are inclined then to this business?

*Olimpio.*                    Ay.                    25
If one should bribe me with a thousand crowns
To kill a serpent which had stung my child,
I could not be more willing.

*Enter* BEATRICE *and* LUCRETIA, *below.*

                    Noble ladies!

*Beatrice.*    Are ye resolved?

*Olimpio.*                    Is he asleep?

*Marzio.*                    Is all
Quiet?

*Lucretia.*    I mixed an opiate with his drink:                    30
He sleeps so soundly . . .

H

*Beatrice.*                    That his death will be
But as a change of sin-chastising dreams,
A dark continuance of the Hell within him,
Which God extinguish! But ye are resolved?
Ye know it is a high and holy deed?                          35
    *Olimpio.*  We are resolved.
    *Marzio.*                    As to the how this act
Be warranted, it rests with you.
    *Beatrice.*                    Well, follow!
    *Olimpio.*  Hush! Hark! What noise is that?
    *Marzio.*        •          Ha! some one comes!
    *Beatrice.*  Ye conscience-stricken cravens, rock to rest
Your baby hearts. It is the iron gate,                       40
Which ye left open, swinging to the wind,
That enters whistling as in scorn. Come, follow!
And be your steps like mine, light, quick and bold.  [*Exeunt.*


SCENE III.—*An Apartment in the Castle. Enter* BEATRICE *and*
LUCRETIA.

    *Lucretia.*  They are about it now.
    *Beatrice.*                    Nay, it is done.
    *Lucretia.*  I have not heard him groan.
    *Beatrice.*                    He will not groan.
    *Lucretia.*  What sound is that?
    *Beatrice.*                    List! 'tis the tread of feet
About his bed.
    *Lucretia.*      My God!
If he be now a cold stiff corpse . . .
    *Beatrice.*                    O, fear not                5
What may be done, but what is left undone:
The act seals all.
                    *Enter* OLIMPIO *and* MARZIO.
                    Is it accomplished?
    *Marzio.*                    What?
    *Olimpio.*  Did you not call?
    *Beatrice.*          When?
    *Olimpio.*                    Now.

*Beatrice.* I ask if all is over?

*Olimpio.* We dare not kill an old and sleeping man;
His thin gray hair, his stern and reverend brow,     10
His veinèd hands crossed on his heaving breast,
And the calm innocent sleep in which he lay,
Quelled me. Indeed, indeed, I cannot do it.

*Marzio.* But I was bolder; for I chid Olimpio,
And bade him bear his wrongs to his own grave     15
And leave me the reward. And now my knife
Touched the loose wrinkled throat, when the old man
Stirred in his sleep, and said, 'God! hear, O, hear,
A father's curse! What, art Thou not our Father?'
And then he laughed. I knew it was the ghost     20
Of my dead father speaking through his lips,
And could not kill him.

*Beatrice.* Miserable slaves!
Where, if ye dare not kill a sleeping man,
Found ye the boldness to return to me
With such a deed undone? Base palterers!     25
Cowards and traitors! Why, the very conscience
Which ye would sell for gold and for revenge
Is an equivocation: it sleeps over
A thousand daily acts disgracing men;
And when a deed where mercy insults Heaven . . .     30
Why do I talk?

    [*Snatching a dagger from one of them and raising it.*
    Hadst thou a tongue to say,
'She murdered her own father!'—I must do it!
But never dream ye shall outlive him long!

*Olimpio.* Stop, for God's sake!

*Marzio.* I will go back and kill him.

*Olimpio.* Give me the weapon, we must do thy will.     35

*Beatrice.* Take it! Depart! Return!

    [*Exeunt* OLIMPIO *and* MARZIO.
    How pale thou art!
We do but that which 'twere a deadly crime
To leave undone.

*Lucretia.* Would it were done!

*Beatrice.*                                    Even whilst
That doubt is passing through your mind, the world
Is conscious of a change.  Darkness and Hell                40
Have swallowed up the vapour they sent forth
To blacken the sweet light of life.  My breath
Comes, methinks, lighter, and the jellied blood
Runs freely through my veins.  Hark!

*Enter* OLIMPIO *and* MARZIO.

                                    He is . . .
*Olimpio.*                                    Dead!
*Marzio.*  We strangled him that there might be no blood;  45
And then we threw his heavy corpse i' the garden
Under the balcony; 'twill seem it fell.
    *Beatrice* (*giving them a bag of coin*).  Here, take this gold, and
        hasten to your homes.
And, Marzio, because thou wast only awed
By that which made me tremble, wear thou this!            50
                                    [*Clothes him in a rich mantle.*

It was the mantle which my grandfather
Wore in his high prosperity, and men
Envied his state: so may they envy thine.
Thou wert a weapon in the hand of God
To a just use.  Live long and thrive! And, mark,         55
If thou hast crimes, repent: this deed is none.
                                    [*A horn is sounded.*

    *Lucretia.*  Hark, 'tis the castle horn; my God! it sounds
Like the last trump.
    *Beatrice.*                Some tedious guest is coming.
    *Lucretia.*  The drawbridge is let down; there is a tramp
Of horses in the court; fly, hide yourselves!            60
                                    [*Exeunt* OLIMPIO *and* MARZIO.

    *Beatrice.*  Let us retire to counterfeit deep rest;
I scarcely need to counterfeit it now:
The spirit which doth reign within these limbs
Seems strangely undisturbed.  I could even sleep         64
Fearless and calm: all ill is surely past.               [*Exeunt.*

SCENE IV.—*Another Apartment in the Castle. Enter on one side the*
    LEGATE SAVELLA, *introduced by a Servant, and on the other*
    LUCRETIA *and* BERNARDO.

*Savella.*    Lady, my duty to his Holiness
Be my excuse that thus unseasonably
I break upon your rest. I must speak with
Count Cenci; doth he sleep?
    *Lucretia (in a hurried and confused manner).* I think he sleeps;
Yet wake him not, I pray, spare me awhile,                    5
He is a wicked and a wrathful man;
Should he be roused out of his sleep to-night,
Which is, I know, a hell of angry dreams,
It were not well; indeed it were not well.
Wait till day break . . . *(aside)* O, I am deadly sick!          10
    *Savella.* I grieve thus to distress you, but the Count
Must answer charges of the gravest import,
And suddenly; such my commission is.
    *Lucretia (with increased agitation).* I dare not rouse him: I
        know none who dare . . .
'Twere perilous; . . . you might as safely waken                15
A serpent; or a corpse in which some fiend
Were laid to sleep.
    *Savella.*            Lady, my moments here
Are counted. I must rouse him from his sleep,
Since none else dare.
    *Lucretia (aside).*        O, terror! O, despair!
*(To* BERNARDO.*)* Bernardo, conduct you the Lord Legate to    20
Your father's chamber.        [*Exeunt* SAVELLA *and* BERNARDO.

*Enter* BEATRICE.

*Beatrice.*                'Tis a messenger
Come to arrest the culprit who now stands
Before the throne of unappealable God.
Both Earth and Heaven, consenting arbiters,
Acquit our deed.
    *Lucretia.*        Oh, agony of fear!                        25
Would that he yet might live! Even now I heard

The Legate's followers whisper as they passed
They had a warrant for his instant death.
All was prepared by unforbidden means
Which we must pay so dearly, having done.                    30
Even now they search the tower, and find the body;
Now they suspect the truth; now they consult
Before they come to tax us with the fact;
O, horrible, 'tis all discovered!
 *Beatrice.*       Mother,
What is done wisely, is done well. Be bold                    35
As thou art just. 'Tis like a truant child
To fear that others know what thou hast done,
Even from thine own strong consciousness, and thus
Write on unsteady eyes and altered cheeks
All thou wouldst hide. Be faithful to thyself,                40
And fear no other witness but thy fear.
For if, as cannot be, some circumstance
Should rise in accusation, we can blind
Suspicion with such cheap astonishment,
Or overbear it with such guiltless pride,                    45
As murderers cannot feign. The deed is done,
And what may follow now regards not me.
I am as universal as the light;
Free as the earth-surrounding air; as firm
As the world's centre. Consequence, to me,                    50
Is as the wind which strikes the solid rock
But shakes it not.     *[A cry within and tumult.*
 *Voices.*   Murder! Murder! Murder!

   *Enter* BERNARDO *and* SAVELLA.

 *Savella* (*to his followers*). Go search the castle round; sound
  the alarm;
Look to the gates that none escape!
 *Beatrice.*      What now?
 *Bernardo.* I know not what to say . . . my father's dead. 55
 *Beatrice.* How; dead! he only sleeps; you mistake, brother.
His sleep is very calm, very like death;
'Tis wonderful how well a tyrant sleeps.

He is not dead?

 *Bernardo.*   Dead; murdered.

 *Lucretia (with extreme agitation).*  Oh no, no,

He is not murdered though he may be dead;   60

I have alone the keys of those apartments.

 *Savella.* Ha! Is it so?

 *Beatrice.*     My Lord, I pray excuse us;

We will retire; my mother is not well:

She seems quite overcome with this strange horror.

        [*Exeunt* LUCRETIA *and* BEATRICE.

 *Savella.* Can you suspect who may have murdered him? 65

 *Bernardo.* I know not what to think.

 *Savella.*      Can you name any

Who had an interest in his death?

 *Bernardo.*     Alas!

I can name none who had not, and those most

Who most lament that such a deed is done;

My mother, and my sister, and myself.    70

 *Savella.* 'Tis strange! There were clear marks of violence.

I found the old man's body in the moonlight

Hanging beneath the window of his chamber,

Among the branches of a pine: he could not

Have fallen there, for all his limbs lay heaped  75

And effortless; 'tis true there was no blood . . .

Favour me, Sir; it much imports your house

That all should be made clear; to tell the ladies

That I request their presence.    [*Exit* BERNARDO.

   *Enter* GUARDS *bringing in* MARZIO.

 *Guard.*      We have one.

 *Officer.* My Lord, we found this ruffian and another 80

Lurking among the rocks; there is no doubt

But that they are the murderers of Count Cenci:

Each had a bag of coin; this fellow wore

A gold-inwoven robe, which shining bright

Under the dark rocks to the glimmering moon  85

Betrayed them to our notice: the other fell

Desperately fighting.

*Savella.*                    What does he confess?

*Officer.*    He keeps firm silence; but these lines found on him
May speak.

*Savella.*    Their language is at least sincere.        [*Reads.*

'*To the Lady Beatrice.*                                        90

'*That the atonement of what my nature sickens to conjecture may
soon arrive, I send thee, at thy brother's desire, those who will speak
and do more than I dare write.* . . . .

                            '*Thy devoted servant, Orsino.*'

*Enter* LUCRETIA, BEATRICE, *and* BERNARDO.

Knowest thou this writing, Lady?

*Beatrice.*                    No.

*Savella.*                        Nor thou?        95

*Lucretia.*  (*Her conduct throughout the scene is marked by extreme
            agitation.*)  Where was it found?  What is it?  It should be
Orsino's hand!  It speaks of that strange horror
Which never yet found utterance, but which made
Between that hapless child and her dead father
A gulf of obscure hatred.

*Savella.*                    Is it so?        100
Is it true, Lady, that thy father did
Such outrages as to awaken in thee
Unfilial hate?

*Beatrice.*    Not hate, 'twas more than hate:
This is most true, yet wherefore question me?

*Savella.*    There is a deed demanding question done;        105
Thou hast a secret which will answer not.

*Beatrice.*  What sayest?  My Lord, your words are bold and
            rash.

*Savella.*    I do arrest all present in the name
Of the Pope's Holiness.  You must to Rome.

*Lucretia.*  O, not to Rome!  Indeed we are not guilty.  110

*Beatrice.*  Guilty!  Who dares talk of guilt?  My Lord,
I am more innocent of parricide
Than is a child born fatherless . . . Dear mother,
Your gentleness and patience are no shield

For this keen-judging world, this two-edged lie,                          115
Which seems, but is not. What! will human laws,
Rather will ye who are their ministers,
Bar all access to retribution first,
And then, when Heaven doth interpose to do
What ye neglect, arming familiar things                                   120
To the redress of an unwonted crime,
Make ye the victims who demanded it
Culprits? 'Tis ye are culprits! That poor wretch
Who stands so pale, and trembling, and amazed,
If it be true he murdered Cenci, was                                      125
A sword in the right hand of justest God.
Wherefore should I have wielded it? Unless
The crimes which mortal tongue dare never name
God therefore scruples to avenge.

    *Savella.*                    You own
That you desired his death?

    *Beatrice.*                         It would have been        130
A crime no less than his, if for one moment
That fierce desire had faded in my heart.
'Tis true I did believe, and hope, and pray,
Ay, I even knew . . . for God is wise and just,
That some strange sudden death hung over him.                            135
'Tis true that this did happen, and most true
There was no other rest for me on earth,
No other hope in Heaven . . . now what of this?

    *Savella.* Strange thoughts beget strange deeds; and here are
        both:
I judge thee not.

    *Beatrice.*            And yet, if you arrest me,        140
You are the judge and executioner
Of that which is the life of life: the breath
Of accusation kills an innocent name,
And leaves for lame acquittal the poor life
Which is a mask without it. 'Tis most false        145
That I am guilty of foul parricide;
Although I must rejoice, for justest cause,
That other hands have sent my father's soul

To ask the mercy he denied to me.
Now leave us free; stain not a noble house                    150
With vague surmises of rejected crime;
Add to our sufferings and your own neglect
No heavier sum: let them have been enough:
Leave us the wreck we have.
    *Savella.*                                I dare not, Lady.
I pray that you prepare yourselves for Rome:                   155
There the Pope's further pleasure will be known.
    *Lucretia.*  O, not to Rome! O, take us not to Rome!
    *Beatrice.*  Why not to Rome, dear mother?  There as here
Our innocence is as an armèd heel
To trample accusation.  God is there                           160
As here, and with His shadow ever clothes
The innocent, the injured and the weak;
And such are we.  Cheer up, dear Lady, lean
On me; collect your wandering thoughts.  My Lord,
As soon as you have taken some refreshment,                    165
And had all such examinations made
Upon the spot, as may be necessary
To the full understanding of this matter,
We shall be ready.  Mother; will you come?
    *Lucretia.*  Ha! they will bind us to the rack, and wrest   170
Self-accusation from our agony!
Will Giacomo be there?  Orsino?  Marzio?
All present; all confronted; all demanding
Each from the other's countenance the thing
Which is in every heart!  O, misery!                           175
                        *[She faints, and is borne out.*
    *Savella.*    She faints: an ill appearance this.
    *Beatrice.*                                My Lord,
She knows not yet the uses of the world.
She fears that power is as a beast which grasps
And loosens not: a snake whose look transmutes
All things to guilt which is its nutriment.                    180
She cannot know how well the supine slaves
Of blind authority read the truth of things
When written on a brow of guilelessness:

She sees not yet triumphant Innocence
Stand at the judgement-seat of mortal man, 185
A judge and an accuser of the wrong
Which drags it there. Prepare yourself, my Lord;
Our suite will join yours in the court below. [*Exeunt.*

END OF THE FOURTH ACT.


# ACT V

Scene I.—*An Apartment in* Orsino's *Palace. Enter* Orsino *and*
Giacomo.

*Giacomo.* Do evil deeds thus quickly come to end?
O, that the vain remorse which must chastise
Crimes done, had but as loud a voice to warn
As its keen sting is mortal to avenge!
O, that the hour when present had cast off 5
The mantle of its mystery, and shown
The ghastly form with which it now returns
When its scared game is roused, cheering the hounds
Of conscience to their prey! Alas! Alas!
It was a wicked thought, a piteous deed, 10
To kill an old and hoary-headed father.
*Orsino.* It has turned out unluckily, in truth.
*Giacomo.* To violate the sacred doors of sleep;
To cheat kind Nature of the placid death
Which she prepares for overwearied age; 15
To drag from Heaven an unrepentant soul
Which might have quenched in reconciling prayers
A life of burning crimes . . .
*Orsino.*                  You cannot say
I urged you to the deed.
*Giacomo.*                  O, had I never
Found in thy smooth and ready countenance 20
The mirror of my darkest thoughts; hadst thou
Never with hints and questions made me look

Upon the monster of my thought, until
It grew familiar to desire . . .
   *Orsino*.            'Tis thus
Men cast the blame of their unprosperous acts     25
Upon the abettors of their own resolve;
Or anything but their weak, guilty selves.
And yet, confess the truth, it is the peril
In which you stand that gives you this pale sickness
Of penitence; confess 'tis fear disguised     30
From its own shame that takes the mantle now
Of thin remorse. What if we yet were safe?
   *Giacomo*.   How can that be? Already Beatrice,
Lucretia and the murderer are in prison.
I doubt not officers are, whilst we speak,     35
Sent to arrest us.
   *Orsino*.        I have all prepared
For instant flight. We can escape even now,
So we take fleet occasion by the hair.
   *Giacomo*.   Rather expire in tortures, as I may.
What! will you cast by self-accusing flight     40
Assured conviction upon Beatrice?
She, who alone in this unnatural work,
Stands like God's angel ministered upon
By fiends; avenging such a nameless wrong
As turns black parricide to piety;     45
Whilst we for basest ends . . . I fear, Orsino,
While I consider all your words and looks,
Comparing them with your proposal now,
That you must be a villain. For what end
Could you engage in such a perilous crime,     50
Training me on with hints, and signs, and smiles,
Even to this gulf? Thou art no liar? No,
Thou art a lie! Traitor and murderer!
Coward and slave! But, no, defend thyself;     [*Drawing*.
Let the sword speak what the indignant tongue     55
Disdains to brand thee with.
   *Orsino*.           Put up your weapon.
Is it the desperation of your fear

Makes you thus rash and sudden with a friend,
Now ruined for your sake? If honest anger
Have moved you, know, that what I just proposed    60
Was but to try you. As for me, I think,
Thankless affection led me to this point,
From which, if my firm temper could repent,
I cannot now recede. Even whilst we speak
The ministers of justice wait below:    65
They grant me these brief moments. Now if you
Have any word of melancholy comfort
To speak to your pale wife, 'twere best to pass
Out at the postern, and avoid them so.

    *Giacomo.* O, generous friend! How canst thou pardon me?
Would that my life could purchase thine!

    *Orsino.*                 That wish    71
Now comes a day too late. Haste; fare thee well!
Hear'st thou not steps along the corridor?    [*Exit* GIACOMO.
I'm sorry for it; but the guards are waiting
At his own gate, and such was my contrivance    75
That I might rid me both of him and them.
I thought to act a solemn comedy
Upon the painted scene of this new world,
And to attain my own peculiar ends
By some such plot of mingled good and ill    80
As others weave; but there arose a Power
Which grasped and snapped the threads of my device
And turned it to a net of ruin . . . Ha!    [*A shout is heard.*
Is that my name I hear proclaimed abroad?
But I will pass, wrapped in a vile disguise;    85
Rags on my back, and a false innocence
Upon my face, through the misdeeming crowd
Which judges by what seems. 'Tis easy then
For a new name and for a country new,
And a new life, fashioned on old desires,    90
To change the honours of abandoned Rome.
And these must be the masks of that within,
Which must remain unaltered . . . Oh, I fear
That what is past will never let me rest!

Why, when none else is conscious, but myself,                    95
Of my misdeeds, should my own heart's contempt
Trouble me?  Have I not the power to fly
My own reproaches?  Shall I be the slave
Of . . . what?  A word? which those of this false world
Employ against each other, not themselves;                    100
As men wear daggers not for self-offence.
But if I am mistaken, where shall I
Find the disguise to hide me from myself,
As now I skulk from every other eye?                    [*Exit.*

SCENE II.—*A Hall of Justice.* CAMILLO, JUDGES, *&c., are
discovered seated;* MARZIO *is led in.*

*First Judge.*   Accused, do you persist in your denial?
I ask you, are you innocent, or guilty?
I demand who were the participators
In your offence?  Speak truth and the whole truth.
*Marzio.*   My God!  I did not kill him; I know nothing;   5
Olimpio sold the robe to me from which
You would infer my guilt.
*Second Judge.*                    Away with him!
*First Judge.*  Dare you, with lips yet white from the rack's kiss
Speak false?  Is it so soft a questioner,
That you would bandy lover's talk with it                    10
Till it wind out your life and soul?  Away!
*Marzio.*   Spare me!  O, spare!  I will confess.
*First Judge.*                                        Then speak.
*Marzio.*   I strangled him in his sleep.
*First Judge.*                                        Who urged you to it?
*Marzio.*   His own son Giacomo, and the young prelate
Orsino sent me to Petrella; there                    15
The ladies Beatrice and Lucretia
Tempted me with a thousand crowns, and I
And my companion forthwith murdered him.
Now let me die.
*First Judge.*   This sounds as bad as truth.  Guards, there,
Lead forth the prisoner!

*Enter* LUCRETIA, BEATRICE, *and* GIACOMO, *guarded.*

Look upon this man;                    20
When did you see him last?
 *Beatrice.*    We never saw him.
 *Marzio.* You know me too well, Lady Beatrice.
 *Beatrice.* I know thee! How? where? when?
 *Marzio.*    You know 'twas I
Whom you did urge with menaces and bribes
To kill your father. When the thing was done    25
You clothed me in a robe of woven gold
And bade me thrive: how I have thriven, you see.
You, my Lord Giacomo, Lady Lucretia,
You know that what I speak is true.

    [BEATRICE *advances towards him; he covers*
     *his face, and shrinks back.*

Oh, dart
The terrible resentment of those eyes        30
On the dead earth! Turn them away from me!
They wound: 'twas torture forced the truth. My Lords,
Having said this let me be led to death.
 *Beatrice.* Poor wretch, I pity thee: yet stay awhile.
 *Camillo.* Guards, lead him not away.
 *Beatrice.*    Cardinal Camillo,  35
You have a good repute for gentleness
And wisdom: can it be that you sit here
To countenance a wicked farce like this?
When some obscure and trembling slave is dragged
From sufferings which might shake the sternest heart    40
And bade to answer, not as he believes,
But as those may suspect or do desire
Whose questions thence suggest their own reply:
And that in peril of such hideous torments
As merciful God spares even the damned. Speak now    45
The thing you surely know, which is that you,
If your fine frame were stretched upon that wheel,

And you were told: 'Confess that you did poison
Your little nephew; that fair blue-eyed child
Who was the lodestar of your life:'—and though          50
All see, since his most swift and piteous death,
That day and night, and heaven and earth, and time,
And all the things hoped for or done therein
Are changed to you, through your exceeding grief,
Yet you would say, 'I confess anything:'                55
And beg from your tormentors, like that slave,
The refuge of dishonourable death.
I pray thee, Cardinal, that thou assert
My innocence.

   *Camillo* (*much moved*).   What shall we think, my Lords?
Shame on these tears! I thought the heart was frozen    60
Which is their fountain. I would pledge my soul
That she is guiltless.

   *Judge.*                 Yet she must be tortured.

   *Camillo.*   I would as soon have tortured mine own nephew
(If he now lived he would be just her age;
His hair, too, was her colour, and his eyes             65
Like hers in shape, but blue and not so deep)
As that most perfect image of God's love
That ever came sorrowing upon the earth.
She is as pure as speechless infancy!

   *Judge.*   Well, be her purity on your head, my Lord,    70
If you forbid the rack. His Holiness
Enjoined us to pursue this monstrous crime
By the severest forms of law; nay even
To stretch a point against the criminals.
The prisoners stand accused of parricide               75
Upon such evidence as justifies
Torture.

   *Beatrice.*   What evidence? This man's?

   *Judge.*                         Even so.

   *Beatrice* (*to* MARZIO).   Come near. And who art thou thus
      chosen forth
Out of the multitude of living men
To kill the innocent?

*Marzio.*                I am Marzio, 80
Thy father's vassal.

*Beatrice.*              Fix thine eyes on mine;
Answer to what I ask.                [*Turning to the* JUDGES.
                    I prithee mark
His countenance: unlike bold calumny
Which sometimes dares not speak the thing it looks,
He dares not look the thing he speaks, but bends 85
His gaze on the blind earth.
(*To* MARZIO.)        .        What! wilt thou say
That I did murder my own father?

*Marzio.*                          Oh!
Spare me! My brain swims round . . . I cannot speak . . .
It was that horrid torture forced the truth.
Take me away! Let her not look on me! 90
I am a guilty miserable wretch;
I have said all I know; now, let me die!

*Beatrice.* My Lords, if by my nature I had been
So stern, as to have planned the crime alleged,
Which your suspicions dictate to this slave, 95
And the rack makes him utter, do you think
I should have left this two-edged instrument
Of my misdeed; this man, this bloody knife
With my own name engraven on the heft,
Lying unsheathed amid a world of foes, 100
For my own death? That with such horrible need
For deepest silence, I should have neglected
So trivial a precaution, as the making
His tomb the keeper of a secret written
On a thief's memory? What is his poor life? 105
What are a thousand lives? A parricide
Had trampled them like dust; and, see, he lives!
(*Turning to* MARZIO.) And thou . . .

*Marzio.*                Oh, spare me! Speak to me no more!
That stern yet piteous look, those solemn tones,
Wound worse than torture.
    (*To the* JUDGES.)        I have told it all; 110
For pity's sake lead me away to death.

*Camillo.*   Guards, lead him nearer the Lady Beatrice,
He shrinks from her regard like autumn's leaf
From the keen breath of the serenest north.

  *Beatrice.*   O thou who tremblest on the giddy verge    115
Of life and death, pause ere thou answerest me;
So mayst thou answer God with less dismay:
What evil have we done thee? I, alas!
Have lived but on this earth a few sad years,
And so my lot was ordered, that a father    120
First turned the moments of awakening life
To drops, each poisoning youth's sweet hope; and then
Stabbed with one blow my everlasting soul;
And my untainted fame; and even that peace
Which sleeps within the core of the heart's heart;    125
But the wound was not mortal; so my hate
Became the only worship I could lift
To our great father, who in pity and love,
Armed thee, as thou dost say, to cut him off;
And thus his wrong becomes my accusation;    130
And art thou the accuser? If thou hopest
Mercy in heaven, show justice upon earth:
Worse than a bloody hand is a hard heart.
If thou hast done murders, made thy life's path
Over the trampled laws of God and man,    135
Rush not before thy Judge, and say: 'My maker,
I have done this and more; for there was one
Who was most pure and innocent on earth;
And because she endured what never any
Guilty or innocent endured before:    140
Because her wrongs could not be told, not thought;
Because thy hand at length did rescue her;
I with my words killed her and all her kin.'
Think, I adjure you, what it is to slay
The reverence living in the minds of men    145
Towards our ancient house, and stainless fame!
Think what it is to strangle infant pity,
Cradled in the belief of guileless looks,
Till it become a crime to suffer. Think

What 'tis to blot with infamy and blood 150
All that which shows like innocence, and is,
Hear me, great God! I swear, most innocent,
So that the world lose all discrimination
Between the sly, fierce, wild regard of guilt,
And that which now compels thee to reply 155
To what I ask: Am I, or am I not
A parricide?
    *Marzio.*       Thou art not!
    *Judge.*               What is this?
    *Marzio.*   I here declare those whom I did accuse
Are innocent. 'Tis I alone am guilty.
    *Judge.*   Drag him away to torments; let them be 160
Subtle and long drawn out, to tear the folds
Of the heart's inmost cell. Unbind him not
Till he confess.
    *Marzio.*      Torture me as ye will:
A keener pang has wrung a higher truth
From my last breath. She is most innocent! 165
Bloodhounds, not men, glut yourselves well with me;
I will not give you that fine piece of nature
To rend and ruin.           [*Exit* MARZIO, *guarded.*
    *Camillo.*     What say ye now, my Lords?
    *Judge.*   Let tortures strain the truth till it be white
As snow thrice sifted by the frozen wind. 170
    *Camillo.*   Yet stained with blood.
    *Judge* (*to* BEATRICE).       Know you this paper, Lady?
    *Beatrice.*   Entrap me not with questions. Who stands here
As my accuser? Ha! wilt thou be he,
Who art my judge? Accuser, witness, judge,
What, all in one? Here is Orsino's name; 175
Where is Orsino? Let his eye meet mine.
What means this scrawl? Alas! ye know not what,
And therefore on the chance that it may be
Some evil, will ye kill us?

*Enter an Officer.*

*Officer.*                Marzio's dead.

   *Judge.*   What did he say?

   *Officer.*                    Nothing. As soon as we   180
Had bound him on the wheel, he smiled on us,
As one who baffles a deep adversary;
And holding his breath, died.

   *Judge.*              There remains nothing
But to apply the question to those prisoners,
Who yet remain stubborn.

   *Camillo.*            I overrule   185
Further proceedings, and in the behalf
Of these most innocent and noble persons
Will use my interest with the Holy Father.

   *Judge.*   Let the Pope's pleasure then be done. Meanwhile
Conduct these culprits each to separate cells;   190
And be the engines ready: for this night
If the Pope's resolution be as grave,
Pious, and just as once, I'll wring the truth
Out of those nerves and sinews, groan by groan.   *[Exeunt.*

SCENE III.—*The Cell of a Prison.* BEATRICE *is discovered
asleep on a couch. Enter* BERNARDO.

   *Bernardo.*   How gently slumber rests upon her face,
Like the last thoughts of some day sweetly spent
Closing in night and dreams, and so prolonged.
After such torments as she bore last night,
How light and soft her breathing comes. Ay me!   5
Methinks that I shall never sleep again.
But I must shake the heavenly dew of rest
From this sweet folded flower, thus . . . wake! awake!
What, sister, canst thou sleep?

   *Beatrice (awaking).*         I was just dreaming
That we were all in Paradise. Thou knowest   10
This cell seems like a kind of Paradise
After our father's presence.

   *Bernardo.*           Dear, dear sister,
Would that thy dream were not a dream! O God!
How shall I tell?

*Beatrice.*        What wouldst thou tell, sweet brother?

*Bernardo.*   Look not so calm and happy, or even whilst   15
I stand considering what I have to say
My heart will break.

*Beatrice.*            See now, thou mak'st me weep:
How very friendless thou wouldst be, dear child,
If I were dead. Say what thou hast to say.

*Bernardo.*   They have confessed; they could endure no more
The tortures . . .

*Beatrice.*            Ha! What was there to confess?   21
They must have told some weak and wicked lie
To flatter their tormentors. Have they said
That they were guilty? O white innocence,
That thou shouldst wear the mask of guilt to hide   25
Thine awful and serenest countenance
From those who know thee not!

*Enter* JUDGE *with* LUCRETIA *and* GIACOMO, *guarded.*

                    Ignoble hearts!
For some brief spasms of pain, which are at least
As mortal as the limbs through which they pass,
Are centuries of high splendour laid in dust?   30
And that eternal honour which should live
Sunlike, above the reek of mortal fame,
Changed to a mockery and a byword? What!
Will you give up these bodies to be dragged
At horses' heels, so that our hair should sweep   35
The footsteps of the vain and senseless crowd,
Who, that they may make our calamity
Their worship and their spectacle, will leave
The churches and the theatres as void
As their own hearts? Shall the light multitude   40
Fling, at their choice, curses or faded pity,
Sad funeral flowers to deck a living corpse,
Upon us as we pass to pass away,
And leave . . . what memory of our having been?
Infamy, blood, terror, despair? O thou,   45
Who wert a mother to the parentless,

Kill not thy child! Let not her wrongs kill thee!
Brother, lie down with me upon the rack,
And let us each be silent as a corpse;
It soon will be as soft as any grave.                          50
'Tis but the falsehood it can wring from fear
Makes the rack cruel.

 *Giacomo*.    They will tear the truth
Even from thee at last, those cruel pains:
For pity's sake say thou art guilty now.

 *Lucretia*. Oh, speak the truth! Let us all quickly die; 55
And after death, God is our judge, not they;
He will have mercy on us.

 *Bernardo*.    If indeed
It can be true, say so, dear sister mine;
And then the Pope will surely pardon you,
And all be well.

 *Judge*.   Confess, or I will warp 60
Your limbs with such keen tortures . . .

 *Beatrice*.      Tortures! Turn
The rack henceforth into a spinning-wheel! .
Torture your dog, that he may tell when last
He lapped the blood his master shed . . . not me!
My pangs are of the mind, and of the heart, 65
And of the soul; ay, of the inmost soul,
Which weeps within tears as of burning gall
To see, in this ill world where none are true,
My kindred false to their deserted selves.
And with considering all the wretched life 70
Which I have lived, and its now wretched end,
And the small justice shown by Heaven and Earth
To me or mine; and what a tyrant thou art,
And what slaves these; and what a world we make,
The oppressor and the oppressed . . . such pangs compel 75
My answer. What is it thou wouldst with me?

 *Judge*. Art thou not guilty of thy father's death?

 *Beatrice*. Or wilt thou rather tax high-judging God
That He permitted such an act as that
Which I have suffered, and which He beheld; 80

Made it unutterable, and took from it
All refuge, all revenge, all consequence,
But that which thou hast called my father's death?
Which is or is not what men call a crime,
Which either I have done, or have not done;　85
Say what ye will. I shall deny no more.
If ye desire it thus, thus let it be,
And so an end of all. Now do your will;
No other pains shall force another word.

   *Judge.*　　She is convicted, but has not confessed.　90
Be it enough. Until their final sentence
Let none have converse with them. You, young Lord,
Linger not here!

   *Beatrice.*　　　　Oh, tear him not away!

   *Judge.* Guards, do your duty.

   *Bernardo (embracing* BEATRICE). Oh! would ye divide
Body from soul?

   *Officer.*　　　　That is the headsman's business.　95

     [*Exeunt all but* LUCRETIA, BEATRICE, *and* GIACOMO.

   *Giacomo.* Have I confessed? Is it all over now?
No hope! No refuge! O weak, wicked tongue
Which hast destroyed me, would that thou hadst been
Cut out and thrown to dogs first! To have killed
My father first, and then betrayed my sister;　100
Ay, thee! the one thing innocent and pure
In this black guilty world, to that which I
So well deserve! My wife! my little ones!
Destitute, helpless, and I . . . Father! God!
Canst Thou forgive even the unforgiving,　105
When their full hearts break thus, thus! . . .

     [*Covers his face and weeps.*

   *Lucretia.*　　　　　　O my child!
To what a dreadful end are we all come!
Why did I yield? Why did I not sustain
Those torments? Oh, that I were all dissolved
Into these fast and unavailing tears,　110
Which flow and feel not!

*Beatrice.*                    What 'twas weak to do,
'Tis weaker to lament, once being done;
Take cheer! The God who knew my wrong, and made
Our speedy act the angel of His wrath,
Seems, and but seems, to have abandoned us.                    115
Let us not think that we shall die for this.
Brother, sit near me; give me your firm hand,
You had a manly heart. Bear up! Bear up!
O dearest Lady, put your gentle head
Upon my lap, and try to sleep awhile:                    120
Your eyes look pale, hollow and overworn,
With heaviness of watching and slow grief.
Come, I will sing you some low, sleepy tune,
Not cheerful, nor yet sad; some dull old thing,
Some outworn and unused monotony,                    125
Such as our country gossips sing and spin,
Till they almost forget they live: lie down!
So, that will do. Have I forgot the words?
Faith! They are sadder than I thought they were.


SONG

False friend, wilt thou smile or weep                    130
When my life is laid asleep?
Little cares for a smile or a tear,
The clay-cold corpse upon the bier!
        Farewell! Heigho!
        What is this whispers low?                    135
There is a snake in thy smile, my dear;
And bitter poison within thy tear.
Sweet sleep, were death like to thee,
Or if thou couldst mortal be,
I would close these eyes of pain;                    140
When to wake? Never again.
        O World! Farewell!
        Listen to the passing bell!
It says, thou and I must part,                    144
With a light and a heavy heart.    [*The scene closes.*

SCENE IV.—*A Hall of the Prison. Enter* CAMILLO *and*
BERNARDO.

*Camillo.*   The Pope is stern; not to be moved or bent.
He looked as calm and keen as is the engine
Which tortures and which kills, exempt itself
From aught that it inflicts; a marble form,
A rite, a law, a custom: not a man.                    5
He frowned, as if to frown had been the trick
Of his machinery, on the advocates
Presenting the defences, which he tore
And threw behind, muttering with hoarse, harsh voice:
'Which among ye defended their old father               10
Killed in his sleep?' Then to another: 'Thou
Dost this in virtue of thy place; 'tis well.'
He turned to me then, looking deprecation,
And said these three words, coldly: 'They must die.'
    *Bernardo.*   And yet you left him not?
    *Camillo.*                                I urged him still;
Pleading, as I could guess, the devilish wrong           16
Which prompted your unnatural parent's death.
And he replied: 'Paolo Santa Croce
Murdered his mother yester evening,
And he is fled. Parricide grows so rife                  20
That soon, for some just cause no doubt, the young
Will strangle us all, dozing in our chairs.
Authority, and power, and hoary hair
Are grown crimes capital. You are my nephew,
You come to ask their pardon; stay a moment;            25
Here is their sentence; never see me more
Till, to the letter, it be all fulfilled.'
    *Bernardo.*   O God, not so! I did believe indeed
That all you said was but sad preparation
For happy news. Oh, there are words and looks           30
To bend the sternest purpose! Once I knew them,
Now I forget them at my dearest need.
What think you if I seek him out, and bathe
His feet and robe with hot and bitter tears?

Importune him with prayers, vexing his brain                    35
With my perpetual cries, until in rage
He strike me with his pastoral cross, and trample
Upon my prostrate head, so that my blood
May stain the senseless dust on which he treads,
And remorse waken mercy?  I will do it!                         40
Oh, wait till I return!                          [*Rushes out.*

    *Camillo.*          Alas! poor boy!
A wreck-devoted seaman thus might pray
To the deaf sea.

    *Enter* LUCRETIA, BEATRICE, *and* GIACOMO, *guarded.*

    *Beatrice.*       I hardly dare to fear
That thou bring'st other news than a just pardon.
    *Camillo.*   May God in heaven be less inexorable      45
To the Pope's prayers, than he has been to mine.
Here is the sentence and the warrant.
    *Beatrice* (*wildly*).          O
My God!  Can it be possible I have
To die so suddenly?  So young to go
Under the obscure, cold, rotting, wormy ground!                50
To be nailed down into a narrow place;
To see no more sweet sunshine; hear no more
Blithe voice of living thing; muse not again
Upon familiar thoughts, sad, yet thus lost—
How fearful! to be nothing!  Or to be . . .                    55
What?  Oh, where am I?  Let me not go mad!
Sweet Heaven, forgive weak thoughts!  If there should be
No God, no Heaven, no Earth in the void world;
The wide, gray, lampless, deep, unpeopled world!
If all things then should be . . . my father's spirit,         60
His eye, his voice, his touch surrounding me;
The atmosphere and breath of my dead life!
If sometimes, as a shape more like himself,
Even the form which tortured me on earth,
Masked in gray hairs and wrinkles, he should come              65
And wind me in his hellish arms, and fix
His eyes on mine, and drag me down, down, down!

For was he not alone omnipotent
On Earth, and ever present?  Even though dead,
Does not his spirit live in all that breathe,                    70
And work for me and mine still the same ruin,
Scorn, pain, despair?  Who ever yet returned
To teach the laws of Death's untrodden realm?
Unjust perhaps as those which drive us now,
Oh, whither, whither?
 *Lucretia.*     Trust in God's sweet love,       75
The tender promises of Christ: ere night,
Think, we shall be in Paradise.
 *Beatrice.*      'Tis past!
Whatever comes my heart shall sink no more.
And yet, I know not why, your words strike chill:
How tedious, false and cold seem all things.  I              80
Have met with much injustice in this world;
No difference has been made by God or man,
Or any power moulding my wretched lot,
'Twixt good or evil, as regarded me.
I am cut off from the only world I know,                       85
From light, and life, and love, in youth's sweet prime.
You do well telling me to trust in God,
I hope I do trust in Him.  In whom else
Can any trust?  And yet my heart is cold.
   [*During the latter speeches* GIACOMO *has retired conversing
    with* CAMILLO, *who now goes out;* GIACOMO *advances.*
 *Giacomo.* Know you not, Mother . . . Sister, know you not?
Bernardo even now is gone to implore                           91
The Pope to grant our pardon.
 *Lucretia.*    Child, perhaps
It will be granted.  We may all then live
To make these woes a tale for distant years:
Oh, what a thought!  It gushes to my heart                     95
Like the warm blood.
 *Beatrice.*   Yet both will soon be cold.
Oh, trample out that thought!  Worse than despair,
Worse than the bitterness of death, is hope:
It is the only ill which can find place

Upon the giddy, sharp and narrow hour                    100
Tottering beneath us. Plead with the swift frost
That it should spare the eldest flower of spring:
Plead with awakening earthquake, o'er whose couch
Even now a city stands, strong, fair, and free;
Now stench and blackness yawn, like death. Oh, plead    105
With famine, or wind-walking Pestilence,
Blind lightning, or the deaf sea, not with man!
Cruel, cold, formal man; righteous in words,
In deeds a Cain. No, Mother, we must die:
Since such is the reward of innocent lives;             110
Such the alleviation of worst wrongs.
And whilst our murderers live, and hard, cold men,
Smiling and slow, walk through a world of tears
To death as to life's sleep; 'twere just the grave
Were some strange joy for us. Come, obscure Death,      115
And wind me in thine all-embracing arms!
Like a fond mother hide me in thy bosom,
And rock me to the sleep from which none wake.
Live ye, who live, subject to one another
As we were once, who now . . .

BERNARDO *rushes in.*

*Bernardo.*                          Oh, horrible!       120
That tears, that looks, that hope poured forth in prayer,
Even till the heart is vacant and despairs,
Should all be vain! The ministers of death
Are waiting round the doors. I thought I saw
Blood on the face of one . . . What if 'twere fancy?    125
Soon the heart's blood of all I love on earth
Will sprinkle him, and he will wipe it off
As if 'twere only rain. O life! O world!
Cover me! let me be no more! To see
That perfect mirror of pure innocence                   130
Wherein I gazed, and grew happy and good,
Shivered to dust! To see thee, Beatrice,
Who made all lovely thou didst look upon . . .
Thee, light of life . . . dead, dark! while I say, sister,

To hear I have no sister; and thou, Mother, 135
Whose love was as a bond to all our loves . . .
Dead! The sweet bond broken!

*Enter* CAMILLO *and Guards.*

They come! Let me
Kiss those warm lips before their crimson leaves
Are blighted . . . white . . . cold. Say farewell, before
Death chokes that gentle voice! Oh, let me hear 140
You speak!
  *Beatrice.*   Farewell, my tender brother. Think
Of our sad fate with gentleness, as now:
And let mild, pitying thoughts lighten for thee
Thy sorrow's load. Err not in harsh despair,
But tears and patience. One thing more, my child: 145
For thine own sake be constant to the love
Thou bearest us; and to the faith that I,
Though wrapped in a strange cloud of crime and shame,
Lived ever holy and unstained. And though
Ill tongues shall wound me, and our common name 150
Be as a mark stamped on thine innocent brow
For men to point at as they pass, do thou
Forbear, and never think a thought unkind
Of those, who perhaps love thee in their graves.
So mayest thou die as I do; fear and pain 155
Being subdued. Farewell! Farewell! Farewell!
  *Bernardo.* I cannot say, farewell!
  *Camillo.*                     Oh, Lady Beatrice!
  *Beatrice.*   Give yourself no unnecessary pain,
My dear Lord Cardinal. Here, Mother, tie
My girdle for me, and bind up this hair 160
In any simple knot; ay, that does well.
And yours I see is coming down. How often
Have we done this for one another; now
We shall not do it any more. My Lord,
We are quite ready. Well, 'tis very well. 165

THE END.

# THE MASK OF ANARCHY

## WRITTEN ON THE OCCASION OF THE MASSACRE AT MANCHESTER

### I

As I lay asleep in Italy
There came a voice from over the Sea,
And with great power it forth led me
To walk in the visions of Poesy.

### II

I met Murder on the way—                    5
He had a mask like Castlereagh—
Very smooth he looked, yet grim;
Seven blood-hounds followed him:

### III

All were fat; and well they might
Be in admirable plight,                      10
For one by one, and two by two,
He tossed them human hearts to chew
Which from his wide cloak he drew.

### IV

Next came Fraud, and he had on,
Like Eldon, an ermined gown;                 15
His big tears, for he wept well,
Turned to mill-stones as they fell.

### V

And the little children, who
Round his feet played to and fro,
Thinking every tear a gem,                    20
Had their brains knocked out by them.

### VI

Clothed with the Bible, as with light,
And the shadows of the night,
Like Sidmouth, next, Hypocrisy
On a crocodile rode by.                          25

### VII

And many more Destructions played
In this ghastly masquerade,
All disguised, even to the eyes,
Like Bishops, lawyers, peers, or spies.

### VIII

Last came Anarchy: he rode                        30
On a white horse, splashed with blood;
He was pale even to the lips,
Like Death in the Apocalypse.

### IX

And he wore a kingly crown;
And in his grasp a sceptre shone;                 35
On his brow this mark I saw—
'I AM GOD, AND KING, AND LAW!'

### X

With a pace stately and fast,
Over English land he passed,
Trampling to a mire of blood                      40
The adoring multitude.

### XI

And a mighty troop around,
With their trampling shook the ground,
Waving each a bloody sword,
For the service of their Lord.                     45

### XII

And with glorious triumph, they
Rode through England proud and gay,
Drunk as with intoxication
Of the wine of desolation.

### XIII

O'er fields and towns, from sea to sea,          50
Passed the Pageant swift and free,
Tearing up, and trampling down;
Till they came to London town.

### XIV

And each dweller, panic-stricken,
Felt his heart with terror sicken          55
Hearing the tempestuous cry
Of the triumph of Anarchy.

### XV

For with pomp to meet him came,
Clothed in arms like blood and flame,
The hired murderers, who did sing          60
'Thou art God, and Law, and King.

### XVI

'We have waited, weak and lone
For thy coming, Mighty One!
Our purses are empty, our swords are cold,
Give us glory, and blood, and gold.'          65

### XVII

Lawyers and priests, a motley crowd,
To the earth their pale brows bowed;
Like a bad prayer not over loud,
Whispering—'Thou art Law and God.'—

WILLIAM GODWIN

*From the painting by James Northcote. Now in the National Portrait Gallery, London.*

### XVIII

Then all cried with one accord,                    70
'Thou art King, and God, and Lord;
Anarchy, to thee we bow,
Be thy name made holy now!'

### XIX

And Anarchy, the Skeleton,
Bowed and grinned to every one,                   75
As well as if his education
Had cost ten millions to the nation.

### XX

For he knew the Palaces
Of our Kings were rightly his;
His the sceptre, crown, and globe,                 80
And the gold-inwoven robe.

### XXI

So he sent his slaves before
To seize upon the Bank and Tower,
And was proceeding with intent
To meet his pensioned Parliament                   85

### XXII

When one fled past, a maniac maid,
And her name was Hope, she said:
But she looked more like Despair,
And she cried out in the air:

### XXIII

'My father Time is weak and gray                   90
With waiting for a better day;
See how idiot-like he stands,
Fumbling with his palsied hands!

I

### XXIV

'He has had child after child,
And the dust of death is piled                    95
Over every one but me—
Misery, oh, Misery!'

### XXV

Then she lay down in the street,
Right before the horses' feet,
Expecting, with a patient eye,                    100
Murder, Fraud, and Anarchy.

### XXVI

When between her and her foes
A mist, a light, an image rose,
Small at first, and weak, and frail
Like the vapour of a vale:                        105

### XXVII

Till as clouds grow on the blast,
Like tower-crowned giants striding fast,
And glare with lightnings as they fly,
And speak in thunder to the sky,

### XXVIII

It grew—a Shape arrayed in mail                   110
Brighter than the viper's scale,
And upborne on wings whose grain
Was as the light of sunny rain.

### XXIX

On its helm, seen far away,
A planet, like the Morning's, lay;                115
And those plumes its light rained through
Like a shower of crimson dew.

### XXX

With step as soft as wind it passed
O'er the heads of men—so fast
That they knew the presence there,                    120
And looked,—but all was empty air.

### XXXI

As flowers beneath May's footstep waken,
As stars from Night's loose hair are shaken,
As waves arise when loud winds call,
Thoughts sprung where'er that step did fall.     125

### XXXII

And the prostrate multitude
Looked—and ankle-deep in blood,
Hope, that maiden most serene,
Was walking with a quiet mien:

### XXXIII

And Anarchy, the ghastly birth,                       130
Lay dead earth upon the earth;
The Horse of Death tameless as wind
Fled, and with his hoofs did grind
To dust the murderers thronged behind.

### XXXIV

A rushing light of clouds and splendour,         135
A sense awakening and yet tender
Was heard and felt—and at its close
These words of joy and fear arose

### XXXV

As if their own indignant Earth
Which gave the sons of England birth               140
Had felt their blood upon her brow,
And shuddering with a mother's throe

### XXXVI

Had turnèd every drop of blood
By which her face had been bedewed
To an accent unwithstood,—          145
As if her heart had cried aloud:

### XXXVII

'Men of England, heirs of Glory,
Heroes of unwritten story,
Nurslings of one mighty Mother,
Hopes of her, and one another;          150

### XXXVIII

'Rise like Lions after slumber
In unvanquishable number,
Shake your chains to earth like dew
Which in sleep had fallen on you—
Ye are many—they are few.          155

### XXXIX

'What is Freedom?—ye can tell
That which slavery is, too well—
For its very name has grown
To an echo of your own.

### XL

''Tis to work and have such pay          160
As just keeps life from day to day
In your limbs, as in a cell
For the tyrants' use to dwell,

### XLI

'So that ye for them are made
Loom, and plough, and sword, and spade,          165
With or without your own will bent
To their defence and nourishment.

### XLII

''Tis to see your children weak
With their mothers pine and peak,
When the winter winds are bleak,—          170
They are dying whilst I speak.

### XLIII

''Tis to hunger for such diet
As the rich man in his riot
Casts to the fat dogs that lie
Surfeiting beneath his eye;                175

### XLIV

''Tis to let the Ghost of Gold
Take from Toil a thousandfold
More than e'er its substance could
In the tyrannies of old.

### XLV

'Paper coin—that forgery                   180
Of the title-deeds, which ye
Hold to something of the worth
Of the inheritance of Earth.

### XLVI

''Tis to be a slave in soul
And to hold no strong control               185
Over your own wills, but be
All that others make of ye.

### XLVII

'And at length when ye complain
With a murmur weak and vain
'Tis to see the Tyrant's crew               190
Ride over your wives and you—
Blood is on the grass like dew.

### XLVIII

'Then it is to feel revenge
Fiercely thirsting to exchange
Blood for blood—and wrong for wrong—    195
Do not thus when ye are strong.

### XLIX

'Birds find rest, in narrow nest
When weary of their wingèd quest;
Beasts find fare, in woody lair
When storm and snow are in the air.    200

### L

'Asses, swine, have litter spread
And with fitting food are fed;
All things have a home but one—
Thou, Oh, Englishman, hast none!

### LI

'This is Slavery—savage men,    205
Or wild beasts within a den
Would endure not as ye do—
But such ills they never knew.

### LII

'What art thou, Freedom? O! could slaves
Answer from their living graves    210
This demand—tyrants would flee
Like a dream's dim imagery:

### LIII

'Thou art not, as impostors say,
A shadow soon to pass away,
A superstition, and a name    215
Echoing from the cave of Fame.

### LIV

'For the labourer thou art bread,
And a comely table spread
From his daily labour come
In a neat and happy home.                    220

### LV

'Thou art clothes, and fire, and food
For the trampled multitude—
No—in countries that are free
Such starvation cannot be
As in England now we see.                    225

### LVI

'To the rich thou art a check,
When his foot is on the neck
Of his victim, thou dost make
That he treads upon a snake.

### LVII

'Thou art Justice—ne'er for gold          230
May thy righteous laws be sold
As laws are in England—thou
Shield'st alike the high and low.

### LVIII

'Thou art Wisdom—Freemen never
Dream that God will damn for ever          235
All who think those things untrue
Of which Priests make such ado.

### LIX

'Thou art Peace—never by thee
Would blood and treasure wasted be
As tyrants wasted them, when all          240
Leagued to quench thy flame in Gaul.

### LX

'What if English toil and blood
Was poured forth, even as a flood?
It availed, Oh, Liberty,
To dim, but not extinguish thee.                     245

### LXI

'Thou art Love—the rich have kissed
Thy feet, and like him following Christ,
Give their substance to the free
And through the rough world follow thee,

### LXII

'Or turn their wealth to arms, and make     250
War for thy belovèd sake
On wealth, and war, and fraud—whence they
Drew the power which is their prey.

### LXIII

'Science, Poetry, and Thought
Are thy lamps; they make the lot             255
Of the dwellers in a cot
So serene, they curse it not.

### LXIV

'Spirit, Patience, Gentleness,
All that can adorn and bless
Art thou—let deeds, not words, express       260
Thine exceeding loveliness.

### LXV

'Let a great Assembly be
Of the fearless and the free
On some spot of English ground
Where the plains stretch wide around.         265

### LXVI

'Let the blue sky overhead,
The green earth on which ye tread,
All that must eternal be
Witness the solemnity.

### LXVII

'From the corners uttermost                                    270
Of the bounds of English coast;
From every hut, village, and town
Where those who live and suffer moan
For others' misery or their own,

### LXVIII

'From the workhouse and the prison                             275
Where pale as corpses newly risen,
Women, children, young and old
Groan for pain, and weep for cold—

### LXIX

'From the haunts of daily life
Where is waged the daily strife                                280
With common wants and common cares
Which sows the human heart with tares—

### LXX

'Lastly from the palaces
Where the murmur of distress
Echoes, like the distant sound                                 285
Of a wind alive around

### LXXI

'Those prison halls of wealth and fashion,
Where some few feel such compassion
For those who groan, and toil, and wail
As must make their brethren pale—                              290

### LXXII

'Ye who suffer woes untold,
Or to feel, or to behold
Your lost country bought and sold
With a price of blood and gold—

### LXXIII

'Let a vast assembly be,                         295
And with great solemnity
Declare with measured words that ye
Are, as God has made ye, free—

### LXXIV

'Be your strong and simple words
Keen to wound as sharpened swords,        300
And wide as targes let them be,
With their shade to cover ye.

### LXXV

'Let the tyrants pour around
With a quick and startling sound,
Like the loosening of a sea,                      305
Troops of armed emblazonry.

### LXXVI

'Let the charged artillery drive
Till the dead air seems alive
With the clash of clanging wheels,
And the tramp of horses' heels.                 310

### LXXVII

'Let the fixèd bayonet
Gleam with sharp desire to wet
Its bright point in English blood
Looking keen as one for food.

### LXXVIII

'Let the horsemen's scimitars          315
Wheel and flash, like sphereless stars
Thirsting to eclipse their burning
In a sea of death and mourning.

### LXXIX

'Stand ye calm and resolute,
Like a forest close and mute,          320
With folded arms and looks which are
Weapons of unvanquished war,

### LXXX

'And let Panic, who outspeeds
The career of armèd steeds
Pass, a disregarded shade          325
Through your phalanx undismayed.

### LXXXI

'Let the laws of your own land,
Good or ill, between ye stand
Hand to hand, and foot to foot,
Arbiters of the dispute,          330

### LXXXII

'The old laws of England—they
Whose reverend heads with age are gray,
Children of a wiser day;
And whose solemn voice must be
Thine own echo—Liberty!          335

### LXXXIII

'On those who first should violate
Such sacred heralds in their state
Rest the blood that must ensue,
And it will not rest on you.

### LXXXIV

'And if then the tyrants dare                340
Let them ride among you there,
Slash, and stab, and maim, and hew,—
What they like, that let them do.

### LXXXV

'With folded arms and steady eyes,
And little fear, and less surprise,          345
Look upon them as they slay
Till their rage has died away.

### LXXXVI

'Then they will return with shame
To the place from which they came,
And the blood thus shed will speak          350
In hot blushes on their cheek.

### LXXXVII

'Every woman in the land
Will point at them as they stand—
They will hardly dare to greet
Their acquaintance in the street.           355

### LXXXVIII

'And the bold, true warriors
Who have hugged Danger in wars
Will turn to those who would be free,
Ashamed of such base company.

### LXXXIX

'And that slaughter to the Nation           360
Shall steam up like inspiration,
Eloquent, oracular;
A volcano heard afar.

### XC

'And these words shall then become
Like Oppression's thundered doom          365
Ringing through each heart and brain,
Heard again—again—again—

### XCI

'Rise like Lions after slumber
In unvanquishable number—
Shake your chains to earth like dew          370
Which in sleep had fallen on you—
Ye are many—they are few.'

# FROM PETER BELL THE THIRD

## HELL

### I

HELL is a city much like London—
    A populous and a smoky city;
There are all sorts of people undone,
And there is little or no fun done;
    Small justice shown, and still less pity.          5

### II

There is a Castles, and a Canning,
    A Cobbett, and a Castlereagh;
All sorts of caitiff corpses planning
All sorts of cozening for trepanning
    Corpses less corrupt than they.          10

### III

There is a * * * , who has lost
   His wits, or sold them, none knows which;
He walks about a double ghost,
And though as thin as Fraud almost—
   Ever grows more grim and rich.          15

### IV

There is a Chancery Court; a King;
   A manufacturing mob; a set
Of thieves who by themselves are sent
Similar thieves to represent;
   An army; and a public debt.          20

### V

Which last is a scheme of paper money,
   And means—being interpreted—
'Bees, keep your wax—give us the honey,
And we will plant, while skies are sunny,
   Flowers, which in winter serve instead.'     25

### VI

There is a great talk of revolution—
   And a great chance of despotism—
German soldiers—camps—confusion—
Tumults—lotteries—rage—delusion—
   Gin—suicide—and methodism;        30

### VII

Taxes too, on wine and bread,
   And meat, and beer, and tea, and cheese,
From which those patriots pure are fed,
Who gorge before they reel to bed
   The tenfold essence of all these.       35

### VIII

There are mincing women, mewing,
   (Like cats, who *amant miserè*[1],)
Of their own virtue, and pursuing
Their gentler sisters to that ruin,
   Without which—what were chastity?[2]     40

### IX

Lawyers—judges—old hobnobbers
   Are there—bailiffs—chancellors—
Bishops—great and little robbers—
Rhymesters—pamphleteers—stockjobbers—
   Men of glory in the wars,—     45

### X

Things whose trade is, over ladies
   To lean, and flirt, and stare, and simper,
Till all that is divine in woman
Grows cruel, courteous, smooth, inhuman,
   Crucified 'twixt a smile and whimper.     50

### XI

Trusting, toiling, wailing, moiling,
   Frowning, preaching—such a riot!
Each with never-ceasing labour,
Whilst he thinks he cheats his neighbour,
   Cheating his own heart of quiet.     55

[1] One of the attributes in Linnaeus's description of the Cat. To a similar cause the caterwauling of more than one species of this genus is to be referred;—except, indeed, that the poor quadruped is compelled to quarrel with its own pleasures, whilst the biped is supposed only to quarrel with those of others.—[SHELLEY'S NOTE.]

[2] What would this husk and excuse for a virtue be without its kernel prostitution, or the kernel prostitution without this husk of a virtue? I wonder the women of the town do not form an association, like the Society for the Suppression of Vice, for the support of what may be called the 'King, Church, and Constitution' of their order. But this subject is almost too horrible for a joke.—[SHELLEY'S NOTE.]

### XII

And all these meet at levees;—
   Dinners convivial and political;—
Suppers of epic poets;—teas,
Where small talk dies in agonies;—
   Breakfasts professional and critical;     60

### XIII

Lunches and snacks so aldermanic
   That one would furnish forth ten dinners,
Where reigns a Cretan-tonguèd panic,
Lest news Russ, Dutch, or Alemannic
   Should make some losers, and some winners;— 65

### XIV

At conversazioni—balls—
   Conventicles—and drawing-rooms—
Courts of law—committees—calls
Of a morning—clubs—book-stalls—
   Churches—masquerades—and tombs.     70

### XV

And this is Hell—and in this smother
   All are damnable and damned;
Each one damning, damns the other;
They are damned by one another,
   By none other are they damned.     75

### XVI

'Tis a lie to say, 'God damns[1]!'
   Where was Heaven's Attorney General
When they first gave out such flams?
Let there be an end of shams,
   They are mines of poisonous mineral.    80

[1] This libel on our national oath, and this accusation of all our country-men of being in the daily practice of solemnly asseverating the most enormous falsehood, I fear deserves the notice of a more active Attorney General than that here alluded to.—[SHELLEY'S NOTE.]

### XVII

Statesmen damn themselves to be
 Cursed; and lawyers damn their souls
To the auction of a fee;
Churchmen damn themselves to see
 God's sweet love in burning coals.                85

### XVIII

The rich are damned, beyond all cure,
 To taunt, and starve, and trample on
The weak and wretched; and the poor
Damn their broken hearts to endure
 Stripe on stripe, with groan on groan.           90

### XIX

Sometimes the poor are damned indeed
 To take,—not means for being blessed,—
But Cobbett's snuff, revenge; that weed
From which the worms that it doth feed
 Squeeze less than they before possessed.          95

### XX

And some few, like we know who,
 Damned—but God alone knows why—
To believe their minds are given
To make this ugly Hell a Heaven;
 In which faith they live and die.                100

### XXI

Thus, as in a town, plague-stricken,
 Each man be he sound or no
Must indifferently sicken;
As when day begins to thicken,
 None knows a pigeon from a crow,—                105

### XXII

So good and bad, sane and mad,
  The oppressor and the oppressed;
Those who weep to see what others
Smile to inflict upon their brothers;
  Lovers, haters, worst and best;          110

### XXIII

All are damned—they breathe an air,
  Thick, infected, joy-dispelling:
Each pursues what seems most fair,
Mining like moles, through mind, and there
Scoop palace-caverns vast, where Care      115
  In thronèd state is ever dwelling.

## COLERIDGE AND WORDSWORTH

### I

AMONG the guests who often stayed
  Till the Devil's petits-soupers,
A man there came, fair as a maid,
And Peter noted what he said,             120
  Standing behind his master's chair.

### II

He was a mighty poet—and
  A subtle-souled psychologist;
All things he seemed to understand,
Of old or new—of sea or land—            125
  But his own mind—which was a mist.

### III

This was a man who might have turned
  Hell into Heaven—and so in gladness
A Heaven unto himself have earned;
But he in shadows undiscerned            130
  Trusted,—and damned himself to madness.

IV

He spoke of poetry, and how
   'Divine it was—a light—a love—
A spirit which like wind doth blow
As it listeth, to and fro;            135
   A dew rained down from God above;


V

'A power which comes and goes like dream,
   And which none can ever trace—
Heaven's light on earth—Truth's brightest beam.'
And when he ceased there lay the gleam   140
   Of those words upon his face.


VI

Now Peter, when he heard such talk,
   Would, heedless of a broken pate,
Stand like a man asleep, or balk
Some wishing guest of knife or fork,    145
   Or drop and break his master's plate.


VII

At night he oft would start and wake
   Like a lover, and began
In a wild measure songs to make
On moor, and glen, and rocky lake,    150
   And on the heart of man—


VIII

And on the universal sky—
   And the wide earth's bosom green,—
And the sweet, strange mystery
Of what beyond these things may lie,   155
   And yet remain unseen.

### IX

For in his thought he visited
　　The spots in which, ere dead and damned,
He his wayward life had led;
Yet knew not whence the thoughts were fed　160
　　Which thus his fancy crammed.


### X

And these obscure remembrances
　　Stirred such harmony in Peter,
That, whensoever he should please,
He could speak of rocks and trees　165
　　In poetic metre.


### XI

For though it was without a sense
　　Of memory, yet he remembered well
Many a ditch and quick-set fence;
Of lakes he had intelligence,　170
　　He knew something of heath and fell.


### XII

He had also dim recollections
　　Of pedlars tramping on their rounds;
Milk-pans and pails; and odd collections
Of saws, and proverbs; and reflections　175
　　Old parsons make in burying-grounds.


### XIII

But Peter's verse was clear, and came
　　Announcing from the frozen hearth
Of a cold age, that none might tame
The soul of that diviner flame　180
　　It augured to the Earth:

XIV

Like gentle rains, on the dry plains,
  Making that green which late was gray,
Or like the sudden moon, that stains
Some gloomy chamber's window-panes          185
  With a broad light like day.

XV

For language was in Peter's hand
  Like clay while he was yet a potter;
And he made songs for all the land,
Sweet both to feel and understand,          190
  As pipkins late to mountain Cotter.

XVI

And Mr.——, the bookseller,
  Gave twenty pounds for some;—then scorning
A footman's yellow coat to wear,
Peter, too proud of heart, I fear,          195
  Instantly gave the Devil warning.

XVII

Whereat the Devil took offence,
  And swore in his soul a great oath then,
'That for his damned impertinence
He'd bring him to a proper sense            200
  Of what was due to gentlemen!'

# LETTER TO MARIA GISBORNE

LEGHORN, *July* 1, 1820.

THE spider spreads her webs, whether she be
In poet's tower, cellar, or barn, or tree;
The silk-worm in the dark green mulberry leaves
His winding sheet and cradle ever weaves;
So I, a thing whom moralists call worm,     5
Sit spinning still round this decaying form,
From the fine threads of rare and subtle thought—
No net of words in garish colours wrought
To catch the idle buzzers of the day—
But a soft cell, where when that fades away,     10
Memory may clothe in wings my living name
And feed it with the asphodels of fame,
Which in those hearts which must remember me
Grow, making love an immortality.

Whoever should behold me now, I wist,     15
Would think I were a mighty mechanist,
Bent with sublime Archimedean art
To breathe a soul into the iron heart
Of some machine portentous, or strange gin,
Which by the force of figured spells might win     20
Its way over the sea, and sport therein;
For round the walls are hung dread engines, such
As Vulcan never wrought for Jove to clutch
Ixion or the Titan:—or the quick
Wit of that man of God, St. Dominic,     25
To convince Atheist, Turk, or Heretic,
Or those in philanthropic council met,
Who thought to pay some interest for the debt
They owed to Jesus Christ for their salvation,

By giving a faint foretaste of damnation
To Shakespeare, Sidney, Spenser, and the rest
Who made our land an island of the blest,
When lamp-like Spain, who now relumes her fire
On Freedom's hearth, grew dim with Empire:—
With thumbscrews, wheels, with tooth and spike and jag,
Which fishers found under the utmost crag      36
Of Cornwall and the storm-encompassed isles,
Where to the sky the rude sea rarely smiles
Unless in treacherous wrath, as on the morn
When the exulting elements in scorn,      40
Satiated with destroyed destruction, lay
Sleeping in beauty on their mangled prey,
As panthers sleep;—and other strange and dread
Magical forms the brick floor overspread,—
Proteus transformed to metal did not make      45
More figures, or more strange; nor did he take
Such shapes of unintelligible brass,
Or heap himself in such a horrid mass
Of tin and iron not to be understood;
And forms of unimaginable wood,      50
To puzzle Tubal Cain and all his brood:
Great screws, and cones, and wheels, and grooved blocks,
The elements of what will stand the shocks
Of wave and wind and time.—Upon the table
More knacks and quips there be than I am able      55
To catalogize in this verse of mine:—
A pretty bowl of wood—not full of wine,
But quicksilver; that dew which the gnomes drink
When at their subterranean toil they swink,
Pledging the demons of the earthquake, who      60
Reply to them in lava—cry halloo!
And call out to the cities o'er their head,—
Roofs, towers, and shrines, the dying and the dead,
Crash through the chinks of earth—and then all quaff
Another rouse, and hold their sides and laugh.      65
This quicksilver no gnome has drunk—within
The walnut bowl it lies, veinèd and thin,

In colour like the wake of light that stains
The Tuscan deep, when from the moist moon rains
The inmost shower of its white fire—the breeze          70
Is still—blue Heaven smiles over the pale seas.
And in this bowl of quicksilver—for I
Yield to the impulse of an infancy
Outlasting manhood—I have made to float
A rude idealism of a paper boat:—                       75
A hollow screw with cogs—Henry will know
The thing I mean and laugh at me,—if so
He fears not I should do more mischief.—Next
Lie bills and calculations much perplexed,
With steam-boats, frigates, and machinery quaint        80
Traced over them in blue and yellow paint.
Then comes a range of mathematical
Instruments, for plans nautical and statical;
A heap of rosin, a queer broken glass
With ink in it;—a china cup that was                     85
What it will never be again, I think,—
A thing from which sweet lips were wont to drink
The liquor doctors rail at—and which I
Will quaff in spite of them—and when we die
We'll toss up who died first of drinking tea,           90
And cry out,—'Heads or tails?' where'er we be.
Near that a dusty paint-box, some odd hooks,
A half-burnt match, an ivory block, three books,
Where conic sections, spherics, logarithms,
To great Laplace, from Saunderson and Sims,             95
Lie heaped in their harmonious disarray
Of figures,—disentangle them who may.
Baron de Tott's Memoirs beside them lie,
And some odd volumes of old chemistry.
Near those a most inexplicable thing,                   100
With lead in the middle—I'm conjecturing
How to make Henry understand; but no—
I'll leave, as Spenser says, with many mo,
This secret in the pregnant womb of time,
Too vast a matter for so weak a rhyme.                  105

And here like some weird Archimage sit I,
Plotting dark spells, and devilish enginery,
The self-impelling steam-wheels of the mind
Which pump up oaths from clergymen, and grind
The gentle spirit of our meek reviews                    110
Into a powdery foam of salt abuse,
Ruffling the ocean of their self-content;—
I sit—and smile or sigh as is my bent,
But not for them—Libeccio rushes round
With an inconstant and an idle sound,                     115
I heed him more than them—the thunder-smoke
Is gathering on the mountains, like a cloak
Folded athwart their shoulders broad and bare;
The ripe corn under the undulating air
Undulates like an ocean;—and the vines                    120
Are trembling wide in all their trellised lines—
The murmur of the awakening sea doth fill
The empty pauses of the blast;—the hill
Looks hoary through the white electric rain,
And from the glens beyond, in sullen strain,              125
The interrupted thunder howls; above
One chasm of Heaven smiles, like the eye of Love
On the unquiet world;—while such things are,
How could one worth your friendship heed the war
Of worms? the shriek of the world's carrion jays,         130
Their censure, or their wonder, or their praise?

You are not here! the quaint witch Memory sees,
In vacant chairs, your absent images,
And points where once you sat, and now should be
But are not.—I demand if ever we                          135
Shall meet as then we met;—and she replies,
Veiling in awe her second-sighted eyes:
'I know the past alone—but summon home
My sister Hope,—she speaks of all to come.'
But I, an old diviner, who knew well                      140
Every false verse of that sweet oracle,
Turned to the sad enchantress once again,

And sought a respite from my gentle pain,
In citing every passage o'er and o'er
Of our communion—how on the sea-shore          145
We watched the ocean and the sky together,
Under the roof of blue Italian weather;
How I ran home through last year's thunder-storm,
And felt the transverse lightning linger warm
Upon my cheek—and how we often made          150
Feasts for each other, where good will outweighed
The frugal luxury of our country cheer,
As well it might, were it less firm and clear
Than ours must ever be;—and how we spun
A shroud of talk to hide us from the sun          155
Of this familiar life, which seems to be
But is not:—or is but quaint mockery
Of all we would believe, and sadly blame
The jarring and inexplicable frame
Of this wrong world:—and then anatomize          160
The purposes and thoughts of men whose eyes
Were closed in distant years;—or widely guess
The issue of the earth's great business,
When we shall be as we no longer are—
Like babbling gossips safe, who hear the war          165
Of winds, and sigh, but tremble not;—or how
You listened to some interrupted flow
Of visionary rhyme,—in joy and pain
Struck from the inmost fountains of my brain,
With little skill perhaps;—or how we sought          170
Those deepest wells of passion or of thought
Wrought by wise poets in the waste of years,
Staining their sacred waters with our tears;
Quenching a thirst ever to be renewed!
Or how I, wisest lady! then endued          175
The language of a land which now is free,
And, winged with thoughts of truth and majesty,
Flits round the tyrant's sceptre like a cloud,
And bursts the peopled prisons, and cries aloud,
'My name is Legion!'—that majestic tongue          180

Which Calderon over the desert flung
Of ages and of nations; and which found
An echo in our hearts, and with the sound
Startled oblivion;—thou wert then to me
As is a nurse—when inarticulately                    185
A child would talk as its grown parents do.
If living winds the rapid clouds pursue,
If hawks chase doves through the aethereal way,
Huntsmen the innocent deer, and beasts their prey,
Why should not we rouse with the spirit's blast       190
Out of the forest of the pathless past
These recollected pleasures?
                            You are now
In London, that great sea, whose ebb and flow
At once is deaf and loud, and on the shore
Vomits its wrecks, and still howls on for more.       195
Yet in its depth what treasures! You will see
That which was Godwin,—greater none than he
Though fallen—and fallen on evil times—to stand
Among the spirits of our age and land,
Before the dread tribunal of *to come*                200
The foremost,—while Rebuke cowers pale and dumb.
You will see Coleridge—he who sits obscure
In the exceeding lustre and the pure
Intense irradiation of a mind,
Which, with its own internal lightning blind,         205
Flags wearily through darkness and despair—
A cloud-encircled meteor of the air,
A hooded eagle among blinking owls.—
You will see Hunt—one of those happy souls
Which are the salt of the earth, and without whom     210
This world would smell like what it is—a tomb;
Who is, what others seem; his room no doubt
Is still adorned with many a cast from Shout,
With graceful flowers tastefully placed about;
And coronals of bay from ribbons hung,                215
And brighter wreaths in neat disorder flung;
The gifts of the most learned among some dozens

Of female friends, sisters-in-law, and cousins.
And there is he with his eternal puns,
Which beat the dullest brain for smiles, like duns    220
Thundering for money at a poet's door;
Alas! it is no use to say, 'I'm poor!'
Or oft in graver mood, when he will look
Things wiser than were ever read in book,
Except in Shakespeare's wisest tenderness.—    225
You will see Hogg,—and I cannot express
His virtues,—though I know that they are great,
Because he locks, then barricades the gate
Within which they inhabit;—of his wit
And wisdom, you'll cry out when you are bit.    230
He is a pearl within an oyster shell,
One of the richest of the deep;—and there
Is English Peacock, with his mountain Fair,
Turned into a Flamingo;—that shy bird
That gleams i' the Indian air—have you not heard    235
When a man marries, dies, or turns Hindoo,
His best friends hear no more of him?—but you
Will see him, and will like him too, I hope,
With the milk-white Snowdonian Antelope
Matched with this cameleopard—his fine wit    240
Makes such a wound, the knife is lost in it;
A strain too learnèd for a shallow age,
Too wise for selfish bigots; let his page,
Which charms the chosen spirits of the time,
Fold itself up for the serener clime    245
Of years to come, and find its recompense
In that just expectation.—Wit and sense,
Virtue and human knowledge; all that might
Make this dull world a business of delight,
Are all combined in Horace Smith.—And these,    250
With some exceptions, which I need not tease
Your patience by descanting on,—are all
You and I know in London.
                                        I recall
My thoughts, and bid you look upon the night.

As water does a sponge, so the moonlight 255
Fills the void, hollow, universal air—
What see you?—unpavilioned Heaven is fair,
Whether the moon, into her chamber gone,
Leaves midnight to the golden stars, or wan
Climbs with diminished beams the azure steep; 260
Or whether clouds sail o'er the inverse deep,
Piloted by the many-wandering blast,
And the rare stars rush through them dim and fast:—
All this is beautiful in every land.—
But what see you beside?—a shabby stand 265
Of Hackney coaches—a brick house or wall
Fencing some lonely court, white with the scrawl
Of our unhappy politics;—or worse—
A wretched woman reeling by, whose curse
Mixed with the watchman's, partner of her trade, 270
You must accept in place of serenade—
Or yellow-haired Pollonia murmuring
To Henry, some unutterable thing.
I see a chaos of green leaves and fruit
Built round dark caverns, even to the root 275
Of the living stems that feed them—in whose bowers
There sleep in their dark dew the folded flowers;
Beyond, the surface of the unsickled corn
Trembles not in the slumbering air, and borne
In circles quaint, and ever-changing dance, 280
Like wingèd stars the fire-flies flash and glance,
Pale in the open moonshine, but each one
Under the dark trees seems a little sun,
A meteor tamed; a fixed star gone astray
From the silver regions of the milky way;— 285
Afar the Contadino's song is heard,
Rude, but made sweet by distance—and a bird
Which cannot be the Nightingale, and yet
I know none else that sings so sweet as it
At this late hour;—and then all is still— 290
Now—Italy or London, which you will!

Next winter you must pass with me; I'll have
My house by that time turned into a grave
Of dead despondence and low-thoughted care,
And all the dreams which our tormentors are;                    295
Oh! that Hunt, Hogg, Peacock, and Smith were there,
With everything belonging to them fair!—
We will have books, Spanish, Italian, Greek;
And ask one week to make another week
As like his father, as I'm unlike mine,                         300
Which is not his fault, as you may divine.
Though we eat little flesh and drink no wine,
Yet let's be merry: we'll have tea and toast;
Custards for supper, and an endless host
Of syllabubs and jellies and mince-pies,                        305
And other such lady-like luxuries,—
Feasting on which we will philosophize!
And we'll have fires out of the Grand Duke's wood,
To thaw the six weeks' winter in our blood,
And then we'll talk;—what shall we talk about?                  310
Oh! there are themes enough for many a bout
Of thought-entangled descant;—as to nerves—
With cones and parallelograms and curves
I've sworn to strangle them if once they dare
To bother me—when you are with me there.                        315
And they shall never more sip laudanum,
From Helicon or Himeros[1];—well, come,
And in despite of God and of the devil,
We'll make our friendly philosophic revel
Outlast the leafless time; till buds and flowers                320
Warn the obscure inevitable hours,
Sweet meeting by sad parting to renew;—
'To-morrow to fresh woods and pastures new.'

[1] Ἵμερος, from which the river Himera was named, is, with some slight
shade of difference, a synonym of Love.—[SHELLEY'S NOTE.]

# THE WITCH OF ATLAS

## TO MARY

(ON HER OBJECTING TO THE FOLLOWING POEM, UPON THE
SCORE OF ITS CONTAINING NO HUMAN INTEREST)

I

How, my dear Mary,—are you critic-bitten
  (For vipers kill, though dead) by some review,
That you condemn these verses I have written,
  Because they tell no story, false or true?
What, though no mice are caught by a young kitten,     5
  May it not leap and play as grown cats do,
Till its claws come? Prithee, for this one time,
Content thee with a visionary rhyme.

II

What hand would crush the silken-wingèd fly,
  The youngest of inconstant April's minions,     10
Because it cannot climb the purest sky,
  Where the swan sings, amid the sun's dominions?
Not thine. Thou knowest 'tis its doom to die,
  When Day shall hide within her twilight pinions
The lucent eyes, and the eternal smile,     15
Serene as thine, which lent it life awhile.

III

To thy fair feet a wingèd Vision came,
  Whose date should have been longer than a day,
And o'er thy head did beat its wings for fame,
  And in thy sight its fading plumes display;     20
The watery bow burned in the evening flame.
  But the shower fell, the swift Sun went his way—
And that is dead.—O, let me not believe
That anything of mine is fit to live!

### IV

Wordsworth informs us he was nineteen years    25
   Considering and retouching Peter Bell;
Watering his laurels with the killing tears
   Of slow, dull care, so that their roots to Hell
Might pierce, and their wide branches blot the spheres
   Of Heaven, with dewy leaves and flowers; this well    30
May be, for Heaven and Earth conspire to foil
The over-busy gardener's blundering toil.

### V

My witch indeed is not so sweet a creature
   As Ruth or Lucy, whom his graceful praise
Clothes for our grandsons—but she matches Peter,    35
   Though he took nineteen years, and she three days
In dressing.  Light the vest of flowing metre
   She wears; he, proud as dandy with his stays,
Has hung upon his wiry limbs a dress
Like King Lear's 'looped and windowed raggedness.'    40

### VI

If you strip Peter, you will see a fellow
   Scorched by Hell's hyperequatorial climate
Into a kind of a sulphureous yellow:
   A lean mark, hardly fit to fling a rhyme at;
In shape a Scaramouch, in hue Othello.    45
   If you unveil my Witch, no priest nor primate
Can shrive you of that sin,—if sin there be
In love, when it becomes idolatry.


## THE WITCH OF ATLAS

### I

BEFORE those cruel Twins, whom at one birth
   Incestuous Change bore to her father Time,
Error and Truth, had hunted from the Earth    50
   All those bright natures which adorned its prime,

CASA MAGNI

And left us nothing to believe in, worth
　　The pains of putting into learnèd rhyme,
A lady-witch there lived on Atlas' mountain          55
Within a cavern, by a secret fountain.


II

Her mother was one of the Atlantides:
　　The all-beholding Sun had ne'er beholden
In his wide voyage o'er continents and seas
　　So fair a creature, as she lay enfolden          60
In the warm shadow of her loveliness;—
　　He kissed her with his beams, and made all golden
The chamber of gray rock in which she lay—
She, in that dream of joy, dissolved away.


III

'Tis said, she first was changed into a vapour,     65
　　And then into a cloud, such clouds as flit,
Like splendour-wingèd moths about a taper,
　　Round the red west when the sun dies in it:
And then into a meteor, such as caper
　　On hill-tops when the moon is in a fit:          70
Then, into one of those mysterious stars
Which hide themselves between the Earth and Mars.


IV

Ten times the Mother of the Months had bent
　　Her bow beside the folding-star, and bidden
With that bright sign the billows to indent         75
　　The sea-deserted sand—like children chidden,
At her command they ever came and went—
　　Since in that cave a dewy splendour hidden
Took shape and motion: with the living form
Of this embodied Power, the cave grew warm.         80

K

V

A lovely lady garmented in light
    From her own beauty—deep her eyes, as are
Two openings of unfathomable night
    Seen through a Temple's cloven roof—her hair
Dark—the dim brain whirls dizzy with delight,          85
    Picturing her form; her soft smiles shone afar,
And her low voice was heard like love, and drew
All living things towards this wonder new.

VI

And first the spotted cameleopard came,
    And then the wise and fearless elephant;          90
Then the sly serpent, in the golden flame
    Of his own volumes intervolved;—all gaunt
And sanguine beasts her gentle looks made tame,
    They drank before her at her sacred fount;
And every beast of beating heart grew bold,          95
Such gentleness and power even to behold.

VII

The brinded lioness led forth her young,
    That she might teach them how they should forego
Their inborn thirst of death; the pard unstrung
    His sinews at her feet, and sought to know          100
With looks whose motions spoke without a tongue
    How he might be as gentle as the doe.
The magic circle of her voice and eyes
All savage natures did imparadise.

VIII

And old Silenus, shaking a green stick          105
    Of lilies, and the wood-gods in a crew
Came, blithe, as in the olive copses thick
    Cicadae are, drunk with the noonday dew:
And Dryope and Faunus followed quick,
    Teasing the God to sing them something new;          110
Till in this cave they found the lady lone,
Sitting upon a seat of emerald stone.

IX

And universal Pan, 'tis said, was there,
  And though none saw him,—through the adamant
Of the deep mountains, through the trackless air,     115
  And through those living spirits, like a want,
He passed out of his everlasting lair
  Where the quick heart of the great world doth pant,
And felt that wondrous lady all alone,—
And she felt him, upon her emerald throne.     120

X

And every nymph of stream and spreading tree,
  And every shepherdess of Ocean's flocks,
Who drives her white waves over the green sea,
  And Ocean with the brine on his gray locks,
And quaint Priapus with his company,     125
  All came, much wondering how the enwombèd rocks
Could have brought forth so beautiful a birth;—
Her love subdued their wonder and their mirth.

XI

The herdsmen and the mountain maidens came,
  And the rude kings of pastoral Garamant—     130
Their spirits shook within them, as a flame
  Stirred by the air under a cavern gaunt:
Pigmies, and Polyphemes, by many a name,
  Centaurs, and Satyrs, and such shapes as haunt
Wet clefts,—and lumps neither alive nor dead,     135
Dog-headed, bosom-eyed, and bird-footed.

XII

For she was beautiful—her beauty made
  The bright world dim, and everything beside
Seemed like the fleeting image of a shade:
  No thought of living spirit could abide,     140
Which to her looks had ever been betrayed,
  On any object in the world so wide,
On any hope within the circling skies,
But on her form, and in her inmost eyes.

### XIII

Which when the lady knew, she took her spindle　　145
　　And twined three threads of fleecy mist, and three
Long lines of light, such as the dawn may kindle
　　The clouds and waves and mountains with; and she
As many star-beams, ere their lamps could dwindle
　　In the belated moon, wound skilfully;　　150
And with these threads a subtle veil she wove—
A shadow for the splendour of her love.

### XIV

The deep recesses of her odorous dwelling
　　Were stored with magic treasures—sounds of air,
Which had the power all spirits of compelling,　　155
　　Folded in cells of crystal silence there;
Such as we hear in youth, and think the feeling
　　Will never die—yet ere we are aware,
The feeling and the sound are fled and gone,
And the regret they leave remains alone.　　160

### XV

And there lay Visions swift, and sweet, and quaint,
　　Each in its thin sheath, like a chrysalis;
Some eager to burst forth, some weak and faint
　　With the soft burthen of intensest bliss
It was its work to bear to many a saint　　165
　　Whose heart adores the shrine which holiest is,
Even Love's:—and others white, green, gray, and black,
And of all shapes—and each was at her beck.

### XVI

And odours in a kind of aviary
　　Of ever-blooming Eden-trees she kept,　　170
Clipped in a floating net, a love-sick Fairy
　　Had woven from dew-beams while the moon yet slept;
As bats at the wired window of a dairy,
　　They beat their vans; and each was an adept,
When loosed and missioned, making wings of winds,　　175
To stir sweet thoughts or sad, in destined minds.

XVII

And liquors clear and sweet, whose healthful might
  Could medicine the sick soul to happy sleep,
And change eternal death into a night
  Of glorious dreams—or if eyes needs must weep,       180
Could make their tears all wonder and delight,
  She in her crystal vials did closely keep:
If men could drink of those clear vials, 'tis said
The living were not envied of the dead.

XVIII

Her cave was stored with scrolls of strange device,    185
  The works of some Saturnian Archimage,
Which taught the expiations at whose price
  Men from the Gods might win that happy age
Too lightly lost, redeeming native vice;
  And which might quench the Earth-consuming rage   190
Of gold and blood—till men should live and move
Harmonious as the sacred stars above;

XIX

And how all things that seem untameable,
  Not to be checked and not to be confined,
Obey the spells of Wisdom's wizard skill;              195
  Time, earth, and fire—the ocean and the wind,
And all their shapes—and man's imperial will;
  And other scrolls whose writings did unbind
The inmost lore of Love—let the profane
Tremble to ask what secrets they contain.              200

XX

And wondrous works of substances unknown,
  To which the enchantment of her father's power
Had changed those ragged blocks of savage stone,
  Were heaped in the recesses of her bower;
Carved lamps and chalices, and vials which shone       205
  In their own golden beams—each like a flower,
Out of whose depth a fire-fly shakes his light
Under a cypress in a starless night.

### XXI

At first she lived alone in this wild home,
    And her own thoughts were each a minister,    210
Clothing themselves, or with the ocean foam,
    Or with the wind, or with the speed of fire,
To work whatever purposes might come
    Into her mind; such power her mighty Sire
Had girt them with, whether to fly or run,    215
Through all the regions which he shines upon.

### XXII

The Ocean-nymphs and Hamadryades,
    Oreads and Naiads, with long weedy locks,
Offered to do her bidding through the seas,
    Under the earth, and in the hollow rocks,    220
And far beneath the matted roots of trees,
    And in the gnarlèd heart of stubborn oaks,
So they might live for ever in the light
Of her sweet presence—each a satellite.

### XXIII

'This may not be,' the wizard maid replied;    225
    'The fountains where the Naiades bedew
Their shining hair, at length are drained and dried;
    The solid oaks forget their strength, and strew
Their latest leaf upon the mountains wide;
    The boundless ocean like a drop of dew    230
Will be consumed—the stubborn centre must
Be scattered, like a cloud of summer dust.

### XXIV

'And ye with them will perish, one by one;—
    If I must sigh to think that this shall be,
If I must weep when the surviving Sun    235
    Shall smile on your decay—oh, ask not me
To love you till your little race is run;
    I cannot die as ye must—over me
Your leaves shall glance—the streams in which ye dwell
Shall be my paths henceforth, and so—farewell!'—    240

XXV

She spoke and wept:—the dark and azure well
  Sparkled beneath the shower of her bright tears,
And every little circlet where they fell
  Flung to the cavern-roof inconstant spheres
And intertangled lines of light:—a knell          245
  Of sobbing voices came upon her ears
From those departing Forms, o'er the serene
Of the white streams and of the forest green.

XXVI

All day the wizard lady sate aloof,
  Spelling out scrolls of dread antiquity,          250
Under the cavern's fountain-lighted roof;
  Or broidering the pictured poesy
Of some high tale upon her growing woof,
  Which the sweet splendour of her smiles could dye
In hues outshining heaven—and ever she          255
Added some grace to the wrought poesy.

XXVII

While on her hearth lay blazing many a piece
  Of sandal wood, rare gums, and cinnamon;
Men scarcely know how beautiful fire is—
  Each flame of it is as a precious stone          260
Dissolved in ever-moving light, and this
  Belongs to each and all who gaze upon.
The Witch beheld it not, for in her hand
She held a woof that dimmed the burning brand.

XXVIII

This lady never slept, but lay in trance          265
  All night within the fountain—as in sleep.
Its emerald crags glowed in her beauty's glance;
  Through the green splendour of the water deep
She saw the constellations reel and dance
  Like fire-flies—and withal did ever keep          270
The tenour of her contemplations calm,
With open eyes, closed feet, and folded palm.

### XXIX

And when the whirlwinds and the clouds descended
  From the white pinnacles of that cold hill,
She passed at dewfall to a space extended,      275
  Where in a lawn of flowering asphodel
Amid a wood of pines and cedars blended,
  There yawned an inextinguishable well
Of crimson fire—full even to the brim,
And overflowing all the margin trim.           280

### XXX

Within the which she lay when the fierce war
  Of wintry winds shook that innocuous liquor
In many a mimic moon and bearded star
  O'er woods and lawns;—the serpent heard it flicker
In sleep, and dreaming still, he crept afar—    285
  And when the windless snow descended thicker
Than autumn leaves, she watched it as it came
Melt on the surface of the level flame.

### XXXI

She had a boat, which some say Vulcan wrought
  For Venus, as the chariot of her star;       290
But it was found too feeble to be fraught
  With all the ardours in that sphere which are,
And so she sold it, and Apollo bought
  And gave it to this daughter: from a car
Changed to the fairest and the lightest boat   295
Which ever upon mortal stream did float.

### XXXII

And others say, that, when but three hours old,
  The first-born Love out of his cradle lept,
And clove dun Chaos with his wings of gold,
  And like a horticultural adept,              300
Stole a strange seed, and wrapped it up in mould,
  And sowed it in his mother's star, and kept
Watering it all the summer with sweet dew,
And with his wings fanning it as it grew.

### XXXIII

The plant grew strong and green, the snowy flower          305
   Fell, and the long and gourd-like fruit began
To turn the light and dew by inward power
   To its own substance; woven tracery ran
Of light firm texture, ribbed and branching, o'er
   The solid rind, like a leaf's veinèd fan—          310
Of which Love scooped this boat—and with soft motion
Piloted it round the circumfluous ocean.

### XXXIV

This boat she moored upon her fount, and lit
   A living spirit within all its frame,
Breathing the soul of swiftness into it.          315
   Couched on the fountain like a panther tame,
One of the twain at Evan's feet that sit—
   Or as on Vesta's sceptre a swift flame—
Or on blind Homer's heart a wingèd thought—
In joyous expectation lay the boat.          320

### XXXV

Then by strange art she kneaded fire and snow
   Together, tempering the repugnant mass
With liquid love—all things together grow
   Through which the harmony of love can pass;
And a fair Shape out of her hands did flow—          325
   A living Image, which did far surpass
In beauty that bright shape of vital stone
Which drew the heart out of Pygmalion.

### XXXVI

A sexless thing it was, and in its growth
   It seemed to have developed no defect          330
Of either sex, yet all the grace of both,—
   In gentleness and strength its limbs were decked;
The bosom swelled lightly with its full youth,
   The countenance was such as might select
Some artist that his skill should never die,          335
Imaging forth such perfect purity.

### XXXVII

From its smooth shoulders hung two rapid wings,
    Fit to have borne it to the seventh sphere,
Tipped with the speed of liquid lightenings,
    Dyed in the ardours of the atmosphere:                340
She led her creature to the boiling springs
    Where the light boat was moored, and said: 'Sit here!'
And pointed to the prow, and took her seat
Beside the rudder, with opposing feet.

### XXXVIII

And down the streams which clove those mountains vast,
    Around their inland islets, and amid                346
The panther-peopled forests, whose shade cast
    Darkness and odours, and a pleasure hid
In melancholy gloom, the pinnace passed;
    By many a star-surrounded pyramid                350
Of icy crag cleaving the purple sky,
And caverns yawning round unfathomably.

### XXXIX

The silver noon into that winding dell,
    With slanted gleam athwart the forest tops,
Tempered like golden evening, feebly fell;                355
    A green and glowing light, like that which drops
From folded lilies in which glow-worms dwell,
    When Earth over her face Night's mantle wraps;
Between the severed mountains lay on high,
Over the stream, a narrow rift of sky.                360

### XL

And ever as she went, the Image lay
    With folded wings and unawakened eyes;
And o'er its gentle countenance did play
    The busy dreams, as thick as summer flies,
Chasing the rapid smiles that would not stay,                365
    And drinking the warm tears, and the sweet sighs
Inhaling, which, with busy murmur vain,
They had aroused from that full heart and brain.

XLI

And ever down the prone vale, like a cloud
  Upon a stream of wind, the pinnace went:     370
Now lingering on the pools, in which abode
  The calm and darkness of the deep content
In which they paused; now o'er the shallow road
  Of white and dancing waters, all besprent
With sand and polished pebbles:—mortal boat     375
In such a shallow rapid could not float.

XLII

And down the earthquaking cataracts which shiver
  Their snow-like waters into golden air,
Or under chasms unfathomable ever
  Sepulchre them, till in their rage they tear     380
A subterranean portal for the river,
  It fled—the circling sunbows did upbear
Its fall down the hoar precipice of spray,
Lighting it far upon its lampless way.

XLIII

And when the wizard lady would ascend     385
  The labyrinths of some many-winding vale,
Which to the inmost mountain upward tend—
  She called 'Hermaphroditus!'—and the pale
And heavy hue which slumber could extend
  Over its lips and eyes, as on the gale     390
A rapid shadow from a slope of grass,
Into the darkness of the stream did pass.

XLIV

And it unfurled its heaven-coloured pinions,
  With stars of fire spotting the stream below;
And from above into the Sun's dominions     395
  Flinging a glory, like the golden glow
In which Spring clothes her emerald-wingèd minions,
  All interwoven with fine feathery snow
And moonlit splendour of intensest rime,
With which frost paints the pines in winter time.     400

XLV

And then it winnowed the Elysian air
    Which ever hung about that lady bright,
With its aethereal vans—and speeding there,
    Like a star up the torrent of the night,
Or a swift eagle in the morning glare          405
    Breasting the whirlwind with impetuous flight,
The pinnace, oared by those enchanted wings,
Clove the fierce streams towards their upper springs.

XLVI

The water flashed, like sunlight by the prow
    Of a noon-wandering meteor flung to Heaven;   410
The still air seemed as if its waves did flow
    In tempest down the mountains; loosely driven
The lady's radiant hair streamed to and fro:
    Beneath, the billows having vainly striven
Indignant and impetuous, roared to feel          415
The swift and steady motion of the keel.

XLVII

Or, when the weary moon was in the wane,
    Or in the noon of interlunar night,
The lady-witch in visions could not chain
    Her spirit; but sailed forth under the light   420
Of shooting stars, and bade extend amain
    Its storm-outspeeding wings, the Hermaphrodite;
She to the Austral waters took her way,
Beyond the fabulous Thamondocana,—

XLVIII

Where, like a meadow which no scythe has shaven,   425
    Which rain could never bend, or whirl-blast shake,
With the Antarctic constellations paven,
    Canopus and his crew, lay the Austral lake—
There she would build herself a windless haven
    Out of the clouds whose moving turrets make    430
The bastions of the storm, when through the sky
The spirits of the tempest thundered by:

### XLIX

A haven beneath whose translucent floor
    The tremulous stars sparkled unfathomably,
And around which the solid vapours hoar,            435
    Based on the level waters, to the sky
Lifted their dreadful crags, and like a shore
    Of wintry mountains, inaccessibly
Hemmed in with rifts and precipices gray,
And hanging crags, many a cove and bay.            440

### L

And whilst the outer lake beneath the lash
    Of the wind's scourge, foamed like a wounded thing,
And the incessant hail with stony clash
    Ploughed up the waters, and the flagging wing
Of the roused cormorant in the lightning flash     445
    Looked like the wreck of some wind-wandering
Fragment of inky thunder-smoke—this haven
Was as a gem to copy Heaven engraven,—

### LI

On which that lady played her many pranks,
    Circling the image of a shooting star,          450
Even as a tiger on Hydaspes' banks
    Outspeeds the antelopes which speediest are,
In her light boat; and many quips and cranks
    She played upon the water, till the car
Of the late moon, like a sick matron wan,          455
To journey from the misty east began.

### LII

And then she called out of the hollow turrets
    Of those high clouds, white, golden and vermilion,
The armies of her ministering spirits—
    In mighty legions, million after million,        460
They came, each troop emblazoning its merits
    On meteor flags; and many a proud pavilion
Of the intertexture of the atmosphere
They pitched upon the plain of the calm mere.

### LIII

They framed the imperial tent of their great Queen    465
   Of woven exhalations, underlaid
With lambent lightning-fire, as may be seen
   A dome of thin and open ivory inlaid
With crimson silk—cressets from the serene
   Hung there, and on the water for her tread    470
A tapestry of fleece-like mist was strewn,
Dyed in the beams of the ascending moon.

### LIV

And on a throne o'erlaid with starlight, caught
   Upon those wandering isles of aëry dew,
Which highest shoals of mountain shipwreck not,    475
   She sate, and heard all that had happened new
Between the earth and moon, since they had brought
   The last intelligence—and now she grew
Pale as that moon, lost in the watery night—
And now she wept, and now she laughed outright.    480

### LV

These were tame pleasures; she would often climb
   The steepest ladder of the crudded rack
Up to some beakèd cape of cloud sublime,
   And like Arion on the dolphin's back
Ride singing through the shoreless air;—oft-time    485
   Following the serpent lightning's winding-track,
She ran upon the platforms of the wind,
And laughed to hear the fire-balls roar behind.

### LVI

And sometimes to those streams of upper air
   Which whirl the earth in its diurnal round,    490
She would ascend, and win the spirits there
   To let her join their chorus. Mortals found
That on those days the sky was calm and fair,
   And mystic snatches of harmonious sound
Wandered upon the earth where'er she passed,    495
And happy thoughts of hope, too sweet to last.

LVII

But her choice sport was, in the hours of sleep,
  To glide adown old Nilus, where he threads
Egypt and Aethiopia, from the steep
  Of utmost Axumè, until he spreads,                    500
Like a calm flock of silver-fleecèd sheep,
  His waters on the plain: and crested heads
Of cities and proud temples gleam amid,
And many a vapour-belted pyramid.

LVIII

By Moeris and the Mareotid lakes,                       505
  Strewn with faint blooms like bridal chamber floors,
Where naked boys bridling tame water-snakes,
  Or charioteering ghastly alligators,
Had left on the sweet waters mighty wakes
  Of those huge forms—within the brazen doors           510
Of the great Labyrinth slept both boy and beast,
Tired with the pomp of their Osirian feast.

LIX

And where within the surface of the river
  The shadows of the massy temples lie,
And never are erased—but tremble ever                   515
  Like things which every cloud can doom to die,
Through lotus-paven canals, and wheresoever
  The works of man pierced that serenest sky
With tombs, and towers, and fanes, 'twas her delight
To wander in the shadow of the night.                   520

LX

With motion like the spirit of that wind
  Whose soft step deepens slumber, her light feet
Passed through the peopled haunts of humankind,
  Scattering sweet visions from her presence sweet,
Through fane, and palace-court, and labyrinth mined     525
  With many a dark and subterranean street
Under the Nile, through chambers high and deep
She passed, observing mortals in their sleep.

### LXI

A pleasure sweet doubtless it was to see
　　Mortals subdued in all the shapes of sleep.          530
Here lay two sister twins in infancy;
　　There, a lone youth who in his dreams did weep;
Within, two lovers linkèd innocently
　　In their loose locks which over both did creep
Like ivy from one stem;—and there lay calm          535
Old age with snow-bright hair and folded palm.

### LXII

But other troubled forms of sleep she saw,
　　Not to be mirrored in a holy song—
Distortions foul of supernatural awe,
　　And pale imaginings of visioned wrong;          540
And all the code of Custom's lawless law
　　Written upon the brows of old and young:
'This,' said the wizard maiden, 'is the strife
Which stirs the liquid surface of man's life.'

### LXIII

And little did the sight disturb her soul.—          545
　　We, the weak mariners of that wide lake
Where'er its shores extend or billows roll,
　　Our course unpiloted and starless make
O'er its wild surface to an unknown goal:—
　　But she in the calm depths her way could take,          550
Where in bright bowers immortal forms abide
Beneath the weltering of the restless tide.

### LXIV

And she saw princes couched under the glow
　　Of sunlike gems; and round each temple-court
In dormitories ranged, row after row,          555
　　She saw the priests asleep—all of one sort—
For all were educated to be so.—
　　The peasants in their huts, and in the port
The sailors she saw cradled on the waves,
And the dead lulled within their dreamless graves.          560

LXV

And all the forms in which those spirits lay
   Were to her sight like the diaphanous
Veils, in which those sweet ladies oft array
   Their delicate limbs, who would conceal from us
Only their scorn of all concealment: they     565
   Move in the light of their own beauty thus.
But these and all now lay with sleep upon them,
And little thought a Witch was looking on them.

LXVI

She, all those human figures breathing there,
   Beheld as living spirits—to her eyes     570
The naked beauty of the soul lay bare,
   And often through a rude and worn disguise
She saw the inner form most bright and fair—
   And then she had a charm of strange device,
Which, murmured on mute lips with tender tone,     575
Could make that spirit mingle with her own.

LXVII

Alas! Aurora, what wouldst thou have given
   For such a charm when Tithon became gray?
Or how much, Venus, of thy silver heaven
   Wouldst thou have yielded, ere Proserpina     580
Had half (oh! why not all?) the debt forgiven
   Which dear Adonis had been doomed to pay,
To any witch who would have taught you it?
The Heliad doth not know its value yet.

LXVIII

'Tis said in after times her spirit free     585
   Knew what love was, and felt itself alone—
But holy Dian could not chaster be
   Before she stooped to kiss Endymion,
Than now this lady—like a sexless bee
   Tasting all blossoms, and confined to none,     590
Among those mortal forms, the wizard-maiden
Passed with an eye serene and heart unladen.

### LXIX

To those she saw most beautiful, she gave
　　Strange panacea in a crystal bowl:—
They drank in their deep sleep of that sweet wave,　　595
　　And lived thenceforward as if some control,
Mightier than life, were in them; and the grave
　　Of such, when death oppressed the weary soul,
Was as a green and overarching bower
Lit by the gems of many a starry flower.　　600

### LXX

For on the night when they were buried, she
　　Restored the embalmers' ruining, and shook
The light out of the funeral lamps, to be
　　A mimic day within that deathy nook;
And she unwound the woven imagery　　605
　　Of second childhood's swaddling bands, and took
The coffin, its last cradle, from its niche,
And threw it with contempt into a ditch.

### LXXI

And there the body lay, age after age,
　　Mute, breathing, beating, warm, and undecaying,　　610
Like one asleep in a green hermitage,
　　With gentle smiles about its eyelids playing,
And living in its dreams beyond the rage
　　Of death or life; while they were still arraying
In liveries ever new, the rapid, blind　　615
And fleeting generations of mankind.

### LXXII

And she would write strange dreams upon the brain
　　Of those who were less beautiful, and make
All harsh and crooked purposes more vain
　　Than in the desert is the serpent's wake　　620
Which the sand covers—all his evil gain
　　The miser in such dreams would rise and shake
Into a beggar's lap;—the lying scribe
Would his own lies betray without a bribe.

### LXXIII

The priests would write an explanation full,                   625
    Translating hieroglyphics into Greek,
How the God Apis really was a bull,
    And nothing more; and bid the herald stick
The same against the temple doors, and pull
    The old cant down; they licensed all to speak     630
Whate'er they thought of hawks, and cats, and geese,
By pastoral letters to each diocese.

### LXXIV

The king would dress an ape up in his crown
    And robes, and seat him on his glorious seat,
And on the right hand of the sunlike throne           635
    Would place a gaudy mock-bird to repeat
The chatterings of the monkey.—Every one
    Of the prone courtiers crawled to kiss the feet
Of their great Emperor, when the morning came,
And kissed—alas, how many kiss the same!              640

### LXXV

The soldiers dreamed that they were blacksmiths, and
    Walked out of quarters in somnambulism;
Round the red anvils you might see them stand
    Like Cyclopses in Vulcan's sooty abysm,
Beating their swords to ploughshares;—in a band      645
    The gaolers sent those of the liberal schism
Free through the streets of Memphis, much, I wis,
To the annoyance of king Amasis.

### LXXVI

And timid lovers who had been so coy,
    They hardly knew whether they loved or not,       650
Would rise out of their rest, and take sweet joy,
    To the fulfilment of their inmost thought;
And when next day the maiden and the boy
    Met one another, both, like sinners caught,
Blushed at the thing which each believed was done     655
Only in fancy—till the tenth moon shone;

### LXXVII

And then the Witch would let them take no ill:
　　Of many thousand schemes which lovers find,
The Witch found one,—and so they took their fill
　　Of happiness in marriage warm and kind.　　660
Friends who, by practice of some envious skill,
　　Were torn apart—a wide wound, mind from mind!—
She did unite again with visions clear
Of deep affection and of truth sincere.

### LXXVIII

These were the pranks she played among the cities　665
　　Of mortal men, and what she did to Sprites
And Gods, entangling them in her sweet ditties
　　To do her will, and show their subtle sleights,
I will declare another time; for it is
　　A tale more fit for the weird winter nights　　670
Than for these garish summer days, when we
Scarcely believe much more than we can see.

# EPIPSYCHIDION

## VERSES ADDRESSED TO THE NOBLE AND UNFORTUNATE LADY, EMILIA V——

### NOW IMPRISONED IN THE CONVENT OF ——

L'anima amante si slancia fuori del creato, e si crea nell' infinito un Mondo tutto per essa, diverso assai da questo oscuro e pauroso baratro.
HER OWN WORDS.

## ADVERTISEMENT

THE Writer of the following lines died at Florence, as he was preparing for a voyage to one of the wildest of the Sporades, which he had bought, and where he had fitted up the ruins of an old building, and where it was his hope to have realised a scheme of life, suited perhaps to that happier and better world of which he is now an inhabitant, but hardly practicable in this. His life was singular; less on account of the romantic vicissitudes which diversified it, than the ideal tinge which it received from his own character and feelings. The present Poem, like the *Vita Nuova* of Dante, is sufficiently intelligible to a certain class of readers without a matter-of-fact history of the circumstances to which it relates; and to a certain other class it must ever remain incomprehensible, from a defect of a common organ of perception for the ideas of which it treats. Not but that *gran vergogna sarebbe a colui, che rimasse cosa sotto veste di figura, o di colore rettorico: e domandato non sapesse denudare le sue parole da cotal veste, in guisa che avessero verace intendimento.*

The present poem appears to have been intended by the Writer as the dedication to some longer one. The stanza[1] is almost a literal translation from Dante's famous Canzone

*Voi, ch' intendendo, il terzo ciel movete, etc.*

The presumptuous application of the concluding lines to his own composition will raise a smile at the expense of my unfortunate friend: be it a smile not of contempt, but pity.   S.

> My Song, I fear that thou wilt find but few
> Who fitly shall conceive thy reasoning,
> Of such hard matter dost thou entertain;
> Whence, if by misadventure, chance should bring
> Thee to base company (as chance may do),                5
> Quite unaware of what thou dost contain,
> I prithee, comfort thy sweet self again,
> My last delight! tell them that they are dull,
> And bid them own that thou art beautiful.

# EPIPSYCHIDION

> Sweet Spirit! Sister of that orphan one,
> Whose empire is the name thou weepest on,
> In my heart's temple I suspend to thee
> These votive wreaths of withered memory.

[1] *i.e.* The nine lines below, beginning, "My Song, I fear."—Ed.

Poor captive bird! who, from thy narrow cage,          5
Pourest such music, that it might assuage
The ruggèd hearts of those who prisoned thee,
Were they not deaf to all sweet melody;
This song shall be thy rose: its petals pale
Are dead, indeed, my adored Nightingale!          10
But soft and fragrant is the faded blossom,
And it has no thorn left to wound thy bosom.

High, spirit-wingèd Heart! who dost for ever
Beat thine unfeeling bars with vain endeavour,
Till those bright plumes of thought, in which arrayed  15
It over-soared this low and worldly shade,
Lie shattered; and thy panting, wounded breast
Stains with dear blood its unmaternal nest!
I weep vain tears: blood would less bitter be,
Yet poured forth gladlier, could it profit thee.          20

Seraph of Heaven! too gentle to be human,
Veiling beneath that radiant form of Woman
All that is insupportable in thee
Of light, and love, and immortality!
Sweet Benediction in the eternal Curse!          25
Veiled Glory of this lampless Universe!
Thou Moon beyond the clouds! Thou living Form
Among the Dead! Thou Star above the Storm!
Thou Wonder, and thou Beauty, and thou Terror!
Thou Harmony of Nature's art! Thou Mirror          30
In whom, as in the splendour of the Sun,
All shapes look glorious which thou gazest on!
Ay, even the dim words which obscure thee now
Flash, lightning-like, with unaccustomed glow;
I pray thee that thou blot from this sad song          35
All of its much mortality and wrong,
With those clear drops, which start like sacred dew
From the twin lights thy sweet soul darkens through,
Weeping, till sorrow becomes ecstasy:
Then smile on it, so that it may not die.          40

I never thought before my death to see
Youth's vision thus made perfect. Emily,
I love thee; though the world by no thin name
Will hide that love from its unvalued shame.
Would we two had been twins of the same mother!          45
Or, that the name my heart lent to another
Could be a sister's bond for her and thee,
Blending two beams of one eternity!
Yet were one lawful and the other true,
These names, though dear, could paint not, as is due,     50
How beyond refuge I am thine. Ah me!
I am not thine: I am a part of *thee*.

Sweet Lamp! my moth-like Muse has burned its wings
Or, like a dying swan who soars and sings,
Young Love should teach Time, in his own gray style,      55
All that thou art. Art thou not void of guile,
A lovely soul formed to be blessed and bless?
A well of sealed and secret happiness,
Whose waters like blithe light and music are,
Vanquishing dissonance and gloom? A Star                  60
Which moves not in the moving heavens, alone?
A Smile amid dark frowns? a gentle tone
Amid rude voices? a belovèd light?
A Solitude, a Refuge, a Delight?
A Lute, which those whom Love has taught to play          65
Make music on, to soothe the roughest day
And lull fond Grief asleep? a buried treasure?
A cradle of young thoughts of wingless pleasure?
A violet-shrouded grave of Woe?—I measure
The world of fancies, seeking one like thee,              70
And find—alas! mine own infirmity.

She met me, Stranger, upon life's rough way,
And lured me towards sweet Death; as Night by Day,
Winter by Spring, or Sorrow by swift Hope,
Led into light, life, peace. An antelope,                 75
In the suspended impulse of its lightness,

Were less aethereally light: the brightness
Of her divinest presence trembles through
Her limbs, as underneath a cloud of dew
Embodied in the windless heaven of June      80
Amid the splendour-wingèd stars, the Moon
Burns, inextinguishably beautiful:
And from her lips, as from a hyacinth full
Of honey-dew, a liquid murmur drops,
Killing the sense with passion; sweet as stops      85
Of planetary music heard in trance.
In her mild lights the starry spirits dance,
The sunbeams of those wells which ever leap
Under the lightnings of the soul—too deep
For the brief fathom-line of thought or sense.      90
The glory of her being, issuing thence,
Stains the dead, blank, cold air with a warm shade
Of unentangled intermixture, made
By Love, of light and motion: one intense
Diffusion, one serene Omnipresence,      95
Whose flowing outlines mingle in their flowing,
Around her cheeks and utmost fingers glowing
With the unintermitted blood, which there
Quivers, (as in a fleece of snow-like air
The crimson pulse of living morning quiver,)      100
Continuously prolonged, and ending never,
Till they are lost, and in that Beauty furled
Which penetrates and clasps and fills the world;
Scarce visible from extreme loveliness.
Warm fragrance seems to fall from her light dress      105
And her loose hair; and where some heavy tress
The air of her own speed has disentwined.
The sweetness seems to satiate the faint wind;
And in the soul a wild odour is felt,
Beyond the sense, like fiery dews that melt      110
Into the bosom of a frozen bud.—
See where she stands! a mortal shape indued
With love and life and light and deity,
And motion which may change but cannot die;

An image of some bright Eternity;                    115
A shadow of some golden dream; a Splendour
Leaving the third sphere pilotless; a tender
Reflection of the eternal Moon of Love
Under whose motions life's dull billows move;
A Metaphor of Spring and Youth and Morning;          120
A Vision like incarnate April, warning,
With smiles and tears, Frost the Anatomy
Into his summer grave.
                            Ah, woe is me!
What have I dared? where am I lifted? how
Shall I descend, and perish not? I know              125
That Love makes all things equal: I have heard
By mine own heart this joyous truth averred:
The spirit of the worm beneath the sod
In love and worship, blends itself with God.

    Spouse! Sister! Angel! Pilot of the Fate         130
Whose course has been so starless! O too late
Belovèd! O too soon adored, by me!
For in the fields of Immortality
My spirit should at first have worshipped thine,
A divine presence in a place divine;                 135
Or should have moved beside it on this earth,
A shadow of that substance, from its birth;
But not as now:—I love thee; yes, I feel
That on the fountain of my heart a seal
Is set, to keep its waters pure and bright           140
For thee, since in those *tears* thou hast delight.
We—are we not formed, as notes of music are,
For one another, though dissimilar;
Such difference without discord, as can make
Those sweetest sounds, in which all spirits shake    145
As trembling leaves in a continuous air?

    Thy wisdom speaks in me, and bids me dare
Beacon the rocks on which high hearts are wrecked.
I never was attached to that great sect,

Whose doctrine is, that each one should select            150
Out of the crowd a mistress or a friend,
And all the rest, though fair and wise, commend
To cold oblivion, though it is in the code
Of modern morals, and the beaten road
Which those poor slaves with weary footsteps tread,   155
Who travel to their home among the dead
By the broad highway of the world, and so
With one chained friend, perhaps a jealous foe,
The dreariest and the longest journey go.

    True Love in this differs from gold and clay,            160
That to divide is not to take away.
Love is like understanding, that grows bright,
Gazing on many truths; 'tis like thy light,
Imagination! which from earth and sky,
And from the depths of human fantasy,                      165
As from a thousand prisms and mirrors, fills
The Universe with glorious beams, and kills
Error, the worm, with many a sun-like arrow
Of its reverberated lightning. Narrow
The heart that loves, the brain that contemplates,    170
The life that wears, the spirit that creates
One object, and one form, and builds thereby
A sepulchre for its eternity.

    Mind from its object differs most in this:
Evil from good; misery from happiness;                      175
The baser from the nobler; the impure
And frail, from what is clear and must endure.
If you divide suffering and dross, you may
Diminish till it is consumed away;
If you divide pleasure and love and thought,          180
Each part exceeds the whole; and we know not
How much, while any yet remains unshared,
Of pleasure may be gained, of sorrow spared:
This truth is that deep well, whence sages draw
The unenvied light of hope; the eternal law           185

By which those live, to whom this world of life
Is as a garden ravaged, and whose strife
Tills for the promise of a later birth
The wilderness of this Elysian earth.

There was a Being whom my spirit oft          190
Met on its visioned wanderings, far aloft,
In the clear golden prime of my youth's dawn,
Upon the fairy isles of sunny lawn,
Amid the enchanted mountains, and the caves
Of divine sleep, and on the air-like waves      195
Of wonder-level dream, whose tremulous floor
Paved her light steps;—on an imagined shore,
Under the gray beak of some promontory
She met me, robed in such exceeding glory,
That I beheld her not.  In solitudes            200
Her voice came to me through the whispering woods,
And from the fountains, and the odours deep
Of flowers, which, like lips murmuring in their sleep
Of the sweet kisses which had lulled them there,
Breathed but of *her* to the enamoured air;      205
And from the breezes whether low or loud,
And from the rain of every passing cloud,
And from the singing of the summer-birds,
And from all sounds, all silence.  In the words
Of antique verse and high romance,—in form,     210
Sound, colour—in whatever checks that Storm
Which with the shattered present chokes the past;
And in that best philosophy, whose taste
Makes this cold common hell, our life, a doom
As glorious as a fiery martyrdom;               215
Her Spirit was the harmony of truth.—

Then, from the caverns of my dreamy youth
I sprang, as one sandalled with plumes of fire,
And towards the lodestar of my one desire,
I flitted, like a dizzy moth, whose flight      220
Is as a dead leaf's in the owlet light,

When it would seek in Hesper's setting sphere
A radiant death, a fiery sepulchre,
As if it were a lamp of earthly flame.—
But She, whom prayers or tears then could not tame,   225
Passed, like a God throned on a wingèd planet,
Whose burning plumes to tenfold swiftness fan it,
Into the dreary cone of our life's shade;
And as a man with mighty loss dismayed,
I would have followed, though the grave between   230
Yawned like a gulf whose spectres are unseen:
When a voice said:—'O thou of hearts the weakest,
The phantom is beside thee whom thou seekest.'
Then I—'Where?'—the world's echo answered 'where?'
And in that silence, and in my despair,   235
I questioned every tongueless wind that flew
Over my tower of mourning, if it knew
Whither 'twas fled, this soul out of my soul;
And murmured names and spells which have control
Over the sightless tyrants of our fate;   240
But neither prayer nor verse could dissipate
The night which closed on her; nor uncreate
That world within this Chaos, mine and me,
Of which she was the veiled Divinity,
The world I say of thoughts that worshipped her:   245
And therefore I went forth, with hope and fear
And every gentle passion sick to death,
Feeding my course with expectation's breath,
Into the wintry forest of our life;
And struggling through its error with vain strife,   250
And stumbling in my weakness and my haste,
And half bewildered by new forms, I passed,
Seeking among those untaught foresters
If I could find one form resembling hers,
In which she might have masked herself from me.   255
There,—One, whose voice was venomed melody
Sate by a well, under blue nightshade bowers:
The breath of her false mouth was like faint flowers,
Her touch was as electric poison,—flame

Out of her looks into my vitals came,                    260
And from her living cheeks and bosom flew
A killing air, which pierced like honey-dew
Into the core of my green heart, and lay
Upon its leaves; until, as hair grown gray
O'er a young brow, they hid its unblown prime           265
With ruins of unseasonable time.

    In many mortal forms I rashly sought
The shadow of that idol of my thought.
And some were fair—but beauty dies away:
Others were wise—but honeyed words betray:              270
And One was true—oh! why not true to me?
Then, as a hunted deer that could not flee,
I turned upon my thoughts, and stood at bay,
Wounded and weak and panting; the cold day
Trembled, for pity of my strife and pain.               275
When, like a noonday dawn, there shone again
Deliverance. One stood on my path who seemed
As like the glorious shape which I had dreamed
As is the Moon, whose changes ever run
Into themselves, to the eternal Sun;                    280
The cold chaste Moon, the Queen of Heaven's bright
    isles,
Who makes all beautiful on which she smiles,
That wandering shrine of soft yet icy flame
Which ever is transformed, yet still the same,
And warms not but illumines. Young and fair             285
As the descended Spirit of that sphere,
She hid me, as the Moon may hide the night
From its own darkness, until all was bright
Between the Heaven and Earth of my calm mind,
And, as a cloud charioted by the wind,                  290
She led me to a cave in that wild place,
And sate beside me, with her downward face
Illumining my slumbers, like the Moon
Waxing and waning o'er Endymion.
And I was laid asleep, spirit and limb,                 295

And all my being became bright or dim
As the Moon's image in a summer sea,
According as she smiled or frowned on me;
And there I lay, within a chaste cold bed:
Alas, I then was nor alive nor dead:—                          300
For at her silver voice came Death and Life,
Unmindful each of their accustomed strife,
Masked like twin babes, a sister and a brother,
The wandering hopes of one abandoned mother,
And through the cavern without wings they flew,       305
And cried 'Away, he is not of our crew.'
I wept, and though it be a dream, I weep.

What storms then shook the ocean of my sleep,
Blotting that Moon, whose pale and waning lips
Then shrank as in the sickness of eclipse;—             310
And how my soul was as a lampless sea,
And who was then its Tempest; and when She,
The Planet of that hour, was quenched, what frost
Crept o'er those waters, till from coast to coast
The moving billows of my being fell                          315
Into a death of ice, immovable;—
And then—what earthquakes made it gape and split,
The white Moon smiling all the while on it,
These words conceal:—If not, each word would be
The key of staunchless tears. Weep not for me!       320

At length, into the obscure Forest came
The Vision I had sought through grief and shame.
Athwart that wintry wilderness of thorns
Flashed from her motion splendour like the Morn's,
And from her presence life was radiated                   325
Through the gray earth and branches bare and dead;
So that her way was paved, and roofed above
With flowers as soft as thoughts of budding love;
And music from her respiration spread
Like light,—all other sounds were penetrated           330
By the small, still, sweet spirit of that sound,

So that the savage winds hung mute around;
And odours warm and fresh fell from her hair
Dissolving the dull cold in the frore air:
Soft as an Incarnation of the Sun,                    335
When light is changed to love, this glorious One
Floated into the cavern where I lay,
And called my Spirit, and the dreaming clay
Was lifted by the thing that dreamed below
As smoke by fire, and in her beauty's glow          340
I stood, and felt the dawn of my long night
Was penetrating me with living light:
I knew it was the Vision veiled from me
So many years—that it was Emily.

Twin Spheres of light who rule this passive Earth,  345
This world of love, this *me*; and into birth
Awaken all its fruits and flowers, and dart
Magnetic might into its central heart;
And lifts its billows and its mists, and guide
By everlasting laws, each wind and tide             350
To its fit cloud, and its appointed cave;
And lull its storms, each in the craggy grave
Which was its cradle, luring to faint bowers
The armies of the rainbow-wingèd showers;
And, as those married lights, which from the towers 355
Of Heaven look forth and fold the wandering globe
In liquid sleep and splendour, as a robe;
And all their many-mingled influence blend,
If equal, yet unlike, to one sweet end;—
So ye, bright regents, with alternate sway          360
Govern my sphere of being, night and day!
Thou, not disdaining even a borrowed might;
Thou, not eclipsing a remoter light;
And, through the shadow of the seasons three,
From Spring to Autumn's sere maturity,              365
Light it into the Winter of the tomb,
Where it may ripen to a brighter bloom.
Thou too, O Comet beautiful and fierce,

Who drew the heart of this frail Universe
Towards thine own; till, wrecked in that convulsion,    370
Alternating attraction and repulsion,
Thine went astray and that was rent in twain;
Oh, float into our azure heaven again!
Be there Love's folding-star at thy return;
The living Sun will feed thee from its urn    375
Of golden fire; the Moon will veil her horn
In thy last smiles; adoring Even and Morn
Will worship thee with incense of calm breath
And lights and shadows; as the star of Death
And Birth is worshipped by those sisters wild    380
Called Hope and Fear—upon the heart are piled
Their offerings,—of this sacrifice divine
A World shall be the altar.
                              Lady mine,
Scorn not these flowers of thought, the fading birth
Which from its heart of hearts that plant puts forth    385
Whose fruit, made perfect by thy sunny eyes,
Will be as of the trees of Paradise.

The day is come, and thou wilt fly with me.
To whatsoe'er of dull mortality
Is mine, remain a vestal sister still;    390
To the intense, the deep, the imperishable,
Not mine but me, henceforth be thou united
Even as a bride, delighting and delighted.
The hour is come:—the destined Star has risen
Which shall descend upon a vacant prison.    395
The walls are high, the gates are strong, thick set
The sentinels—but true Love never yet
Was thus constrained: it overleaps all fence:
Like lightning, with invisible violence
Piercing its continents; like Heaven's free breath,    400
Which he who grasps can hold not; liker Death,
Who rides upon a thought, and makes his way
Through temple, tower, and palace, and the array
Of arms: more strength has Love than he or they;

JOHN KEATS

*From the painting by Joseph Severn. Now in the National Portrait Gallery, London.*

For it can burst his charnel, and make free                    405
The limbs in chains, the heart in agony,
The soul in dust and chaos.
                                        Emily,
A ship is floating in the harbour now,
A wind is hovering o'er the mountain's brow;
There is a path on the sea's azure floor,                    410
No keel has ever ploughed that path before;
The halcyons brood around the foamless isles;
The treacherous Ocean has forsworn its wiles;
The merry mariners are bold and free:
Say, my heart's sister, wilt thou sail with me?                    415
Our bark is as an albatross, whose nest
Is a far Eden of the purple East;
And we between her wings will sit, while Night,
And Day, and Storm, and Calm, pursue their flight,
Our ministers, along the boundless Sea,                    420
Treading each other's heels, unheededly.
It is an isle under Ionian skies,
Beautiful as a wreck of Paradise,
And, for the harbours are not safe and good,
This land would have remained a solitude                    425
But for some pastoral people native there,
Who from the Elysian, clear, and golden air
Draw the last spirit of the age of gold,
Simple and spirited; innocent and bold.
The blue Aegean girds this chosen home,                    430
With ever-changing sound and light and foam,
Kissing the sifted sands, and caverns hoar;
And all the winds wandering along the shore
Undulate with the undulating tide:
There are thick woods where sylvan forms abide;                    435
And many a fountain, rivulet, and pond,
As clear as elemental diamond,
Or serene morning air; and far beyond,
The mossy tracks made by the goats and deer
(Which the rough shepherd treads but once a year)                    440
Pierce into glades, caverns, and bowers, and halls

L

Built round with ivy, which the waterfalls
Illumining, with sound that never fails
Accompany the noonday nightingales;
And all the place is peopled with sweet airs;                445
The light clear element which the isle wears
Is heavy with the scent of lemon-flowers,
Which floats like mist laden with unseen showers,
And falls upon the eyelids like faint sleep;
And from the moss violets and jonquils peep,                450
And dart their arrowy odour through the brain
Till you might faint with that delicious pain.
And every motion, odour, beam, and tone,
With that deep music is in unison:
Which is a soul within the soul—they seem                   455
Like echoes of an antenatal dream.—
It is an isle 'twixt Heaven, Air, Earth, and Sea,
Cradled, and hung in clear tranquillity;
Bright as that wandering Eden Lucifer,
Washed by the soft blue Oceans of young air.               460
It is a favoured place. Famine or Blight,
Pestilence, War and Earthquake, never light
Upon its mountain-peaks; blind vultures, they
Sail onward far upon their fatal way:
The wingèd storms, chanting their thunder-psalm            465
To other lands, leave azure chasms of calm
Over this isle, or weep themselves in dew,
From which its fields and woods ever renew
Their green and golden immortality.
And from the sea there rise, and from the sky              470
There fall, clear exhalations, soft and bright,
Veil after veil, each hiding some delight,
Which Sun or Moon or zephyr draw aside;
Till the isle's beauty, like a naked bride
Glowing at once with love and loveliness,                 475
Blushes and trembles at its own excess:
Yet, like a buried lamp, a Soul no less
Burns in the heart of this delicious isle,
An atom of th' Eternal, whose own smile

Unfolds itself, and may be felt, not seen 480
O'er the gray rocks, blue waves, and forests green,
Filling their bare and void interstices.——
But the chief marvel of the wilderness
Is a lone dwelling, built by whom or how
None of the rustic island-people know: 485
'Tis not a tower of strength, though with its height
It overtops the woods; but for delight,
Some wise and tender Ocean-King, ere crime
Had been invented, in the world's young prime,
Reared it, a wonder of that simple time, 490
An envy of the isles, a pleasure-house
Made sacred to his sister and his spouse.
It scarce seems now a wreck of human art,
But, as it were Titanic; in the heart
Of Earth having assumed its form, then grown 495
Out of the mountains, from the living stone,
Lifting itself in caverns light and high:
For all the antique and learnèd imagery
Has been erased, and in the place of it
The ivy and the wild-vine interknit 500
The volumes of their many-twining stems;
Parasite flowers illume with dewy gems
The lampless halls, and when they fade, the sky
Peeps through their winter-woof of tracery
With moonlight patches, or star atoms keen, 505
Or fragments of the day's intense serene;——
Working mosaic on their Parian floors.
And, day and night, aloof, from the high towers
And terraces, the Earth and Ocean seem
To sleep in one another's arms, and dream 510
Of waves, flowers, clouds, woods, rocks, and all that we
Read in their smiles, and call reality.

This isle and house are mine, and I have vowed
Thee to be lady of the solitude.——
And I have fitted up some chambers there 515
Looking towards the golden Eastern air,

And level with the living winds, which flow
Like waves above the living waves below.—
I have sent books and music there, and all
Those instruments with which high Spirits call          520
The future from its cradle, and the past
Out of its grave, and make the present last
In thoughts and joys which sleep, but cannot die,
Folded within their own eternity.
Our simple life wants little, and true taste          525
Hires not the pale drudge Luxury, to waste
The scene it would adorn, and therefore still,
Nature with all her children haunts the hill.
The ring-dove, in the embowering ivy, yet
Keeps up her love-lament, and the owls flit          530
Round the evening tower, and the young stars glance
Between the quick bats in their twilight dance;
The spotted deer bask in the fresh moonlight
Before our gate, and the slow, silent night
Is measured by the pants of their calm sleep.          535
Be this our home in life, and when years heap
Their withered hours, like leaves, on our decay,
Let us become the overhanging day,
The living soul of this Elysian isle,
Conscious, inseparable, one. Meanwhile          540
We two will rise, and sit, and walk together,
Under the roof of blue Ionian weather,
And wander in the meadows, or ascend
The mossy mountains, where the blue heavens bend
With lightest winds, to touch their paramour;          545
Or linger, where the pebble-paven shore,
Under the quick, faint kisses of the sea
Trembles and sparkles as with ecstasy,—
Possessing and possessed by all that is
Within that calm circumference of bliss,          550
And by each other, till to love and live
Be one:—or, at the noontide hour, arrive
Where some old cavern hoar seems yet to keep
The moonlight of the expired night asleep,

Through which the awakened day can never peep;     555
A veil for our seclusion, close as night's,
Where secure sleep may kill thine innocent lights;
Sleep, the fresh dew of languid love, the rain
Whose drops quench kisses till they burn again.
And we will talk, until thought's melody           560
Become too sweet for utterance, and it die
In words, to live again in looks, which dart
With thrilling tone into the voiceless heart,
Harmonizing silence without a sound.
Our breath shall intermix, our bosoms bound,       565
And our veins beat together; and our lips
With other eloquence than words, eclipse
The soul that burns between them, and the wells
Which boil under our being's inmost cells,
The fountains of our deepest life, shall be         570
Confused in Passion's golden purity,
As mountain-springs under the morning sun.
We shall become the same, we shall be one
Spirit within two frames, oh! wherefore two?
One passion in twin-hearts, which grows and grew,  575
Till like two meteors of expanding flame,
Those spheres instinct with it become the same,
Touch, mingle, are transfigured; ever still
Burning, yet ever inconsumable:
In one another's substance finding food,            580
Like flames too pure and light and unimbued
To nourish their bright lives with baser prey,
Which point to Heaven and cannot pass away:
One hope within two wills, one will beneath
Two overshadowing minds, one life, one death,      585
One Heaven, one Hell, one immortality,
And one annihilation. Woe is me!
The wingèd words on which my soul would pierce
Into the height of Love's rare Universe,
Are chains of lead around its flight of fire—       590
I pant, I sink, I tremble, I expire!

Weak Verses, go, kneel at your Sovereign's feet,
And say:—'We are the masters of thy slave;
What wouldest thou with us and ours and thine?'
Then call your sisters from Oblivion's cave,      595
All singing loud: 'Love's very pain is sweet,
But its reward is in the world divine
Which, if not here, it builds beyond the grave.'
So shall ye live when I am there. Then haste
Over the hearts of men, until ye meet      600
Marina, Vanna, Primus, and the rest,
And bid them love each other and be blessed:
And leave the troop which errs, and which reproves,
And come and be my guest,—for I am Love's.


# ADONAIS

## AN ELEGY ON THE DEATH OF JOHN KEATS, AUTHOR OF ENDYMION, HYPERION, ETC.

Αστὴρ πρὶν μὲν ἔλαμπες ἐνὶ ζωοῖσιν Ἑῷος·
νῦν δὲ θανὼν λάμπεις Ἕσπερος ἐν φθιμένοις.—PLATO.

## PREFACE

Φάρμακον ἦλθε, Βίων, ποτὶ σὸν στόμα, φάρμακον εἶδες.
πῶς τευ τοῖς χείλεσσι ποτέδραμε, κοὐκ ἐγλυκάνθη;
τίς δὲ βροτὸς τοσσοῦτον ἀνάμερος, ἢ κεράσαι τοι,
ἢ δοῦναι λαλέοντι τὸ φάρμακον; ἔκφυγεν ᾠδάν.
    —MOSCHUS, EPITAPH. BION.

IT is my intention to subjoin to the London edition of this poem a criticism upon the claims of its lamented object to be classed among the writers of the highest genius who have adorned our age. My known repugnance to the narrow principles of taste on which several of his earlier compositions were modelled prove at least that I am an impartial judge. I consider the fragment of *Hyperion* as second to nothing that was ever produced by a writer of the same years.

John Keats died at Rome of a consumption, in his twenty-fourth year, on the —— of —— 1821;[1] and was buried in the romantic and lonely cemetery of the Protestants in that city, under the pyramid which is the tomb of Cestius, and the massy walls and towers, now mouldering and desolate, which formed the circuit of ancient Rome. The cemetery is an open space among the ruins, covered in winter with violets and daisies. It might make one in love with death, to think that one should be buried in so sweet a place.

The genius of the lamented person to whose memory I have dedicated these unworthy verses was not less delicate and fragile than it was beautiful; and where cankerworms abound, what wonder if its young flower was blighted in the bud? The savage criticism on his *Endymion*, which appeared in the *Quarterly Review*, produced the most violent effect on his susceptible mind; the agitation thus originated ended in the rupture of a blood-vessel in the lungs; a rapid consumption ensued, and the succeeding acknowledgements from more candid critics of the true greatness of his powers were ineffectual to heal the wound thus wantonly inflicted.

It may be well said that these wretched men know not what they do. They scatter their insults and their slanders without heed as to whether the poisoned shaft lights on a heart made callous by many blows or one like Keats's composed of more penetrable stuff. One of their associates is, to my knowledge, a most base and unprincipled calumniator. As to *Endymion*, was it a poem, whatever might be its defects, to be treated contemptuously by those who had celebrated, with various degrees of complacency and panegyric, *Paris*, and *Woman*, and a *Syrian Tale*, and Mrs. Lefanu, and Mr. Barrett, and Mr. Howard Payne, and a long list of the illustrious obscure? Are these the men who in their venal good nature presumed to draw a parallel between the Rev. Mr. Milman and Lord Byron? What gnat did they strain at here, after having swallowed all those camels? Against what woman taken in adultery dares the foremost of these literary prostitutes to cast his opprobrious stone? Miserable man! you, one of the meanest, have wantonly defaced one of the noblest specimens

[1] Keats died 23rd February 1821, in his twenty-sixth year.—ED.

of the workmanship of God. Nor shall it be your excuse, that, murderer as you are, you have spoken daggers, but used none.

The circumstances of the closing scene of poor Keats's life were not made known to me until the *Elegy* was ready for the press. I am given to understand that the wound which his sensitive spirit had received from the criticism of *Endymion* was exasperated by the bitter sense of unrequited benefits; the poor fellow seems to have been hooted from the stage of life, no less by those on whom he had wasted the promise of his genius, than those on whom he had lavished his fortune and his care. He was accompanied to Rome, and attended in his last illness by Mr. Severn, a young artist of the highest promise, who, I have been informed, 'almost risked his own life, and sacrificed every prospect to unwearied attendance upon his dying friend.' Had I known these circumstances before the completion of my poem, I should have been tempted to add my feeble tribute of applause to the more solid recompense which the virtuous man finds in the recollection of his own motives. Mr. Severn can dispense with a reward from 'such stuff as dreams are made of.' His conduct is a golden augury of the success of his future career—may the unextinguished Spirit of his illustrious friend animate the creations of his pencil, and plead against Oblivion for his name!

# ADONAIS

### I

I WEEP for Adonais—he is dead!
O, weep for Adonais! though our tears
Thaw not the frost which binds so dear a head!
And thou, sad Hour, selected from all years
To mourn our loss, rouse thy obscure compeers,          5
And teach them thine own sorrow, say: 'With me
Died Adonais; till the Future dares
Forget the Past, his fate and fame shall be
An echo and a light unto eternity!'

II

Where wert thou, mighty Mother, when he lay,                    10
When thy Son lay, pierced by the shaft which flies
In darkness? where was lorn Urania
When Adonais died? With veilèd eyes,
'Mid listening Echoes, in her Paradise
She sate, while one, with soft enamoured breath,                15
Rekindled all the fading melodies,
  With which, like flowers that mock the corse beneath,
He had adorned and hid the coming bulk of Death.

III

Oh, weep for Adonais—he is dead!
Wake, melancholy Mother, wake and weep!                         20
Yet wherefore? Quench within their burning bed
Thy fiery tears, and let thy loud heart keep
Like his, a mute and uncomplaining sleep;
For he is gone, where all things wise and fair
Descend;—oh, dream not that the amorous Deep                    25
  Will yet restore him to the vital air;
Death feeds on his mute voice, and laughs at our despair.

IV

Most musical of mourners, weep again!
Lament anew, Urania!—He died,
Who was the Sire of an immortal strain,                         30
Blind, old, and lonely, when his country's pride,
The priest, the slave, and the liberticide,
Trampled and mocked with many a loathèd rite
Of lust and blood; he went, unterrified,
  Into the gulf of death; but his clear Sprite                  35
Yet reigns o'er earth; the third among the sons of light.

V

Most musical of mourners, weep anew!
Not all to that bright station dared to climb;
And happier they their happiness who knew,
Whose tapers yet burn through that night of time                40

In which suns perished; others more sublime,
Struck by the envious wrath of man or god,
Have sunk, extinct in their refulgent prime;
And some yet live, treading the thorny road,
Which leads, through toil and hate, to Fame's serene abode.  45

### VI

But now, thy youngest, dearest one, has perished—
The nursling of thy widowhood, who grew,
Like a pale flower by some sad maiden cherished,
And fed with true-love tears, instead of dew;
Most musical of mourners, weep anew!                         50
Thy extreme hope, the loveliest and the last,
The bloom, whose petals nipped before they blew
Died on the promise of the fruit, is waste;
The broken lily lies—the storm is overpast.

### VII

To that high Capital, where kingly Death               55
Keeps his pale court in beauty and decay,
He came; and bought, with price of purest breath,
A grave among the eternal.—Come away!
Haste, while the vault of blue Italian day
Is yet his fitting charnel-roof! while still            60
He lies, as if in dewy sleep he lay;
Awake him not! surely he takes his fill
Of deep and liquid rest, forgetful of all ill.

### VIII

He will awake no more, oh, never more!—
Within the twilight chamber spreads apace               65
The shadow of white Death, and at the door
Invisible Corruption waits to trace
His extreme way to her dim dwelling-place;
The eternal Hunger sits, but pity and awe
Soothe her pale rage, nor dares she to deface           70
So fair a prey, till darkness, and the law
Of change, shall o'er his sleep the mortal curtain draw.

### IX

Oh, weep for Adonais!—The quick Dreams,
The passion-wingèd Ministers of thought,
Who were his flocks, whom near the living streams     75
Of his young spirit he fed, and whom he taught
The love which was its music, wander not,—
Wander no more, from kindling brain to brain,
But droop there, whence they sprung; and mourn their lot
Round the cold heart, where, after their sweet pain,     80
They ne'er will gather strength, or find a home again.

### X

And one with trembling hands clasps his cold head,
And fans him with her moonlight wings, and cries;
'Our love, our hope, our sorrow, is not dead;
See, on the silken fringe of his faint eyes,     85
Like dew upon a sleeping flower, there lies
A tear some Dream has loosened from his brain.'
Lost Angel of a ruined Paradise!
She knew not 'twas her own; as with no stain
She faded, like a cloud which had outswept its rain.     90

### XI

One from a lucid urn of starry dew
Washed his light limbs as if embalming them;
Another clipped her profuse locks, and threw
The wreath upon him, like an anadem,
Which frozen tears instead of pearls begem;     95
Another in her wilful grief would break
Her bow and wingèd reeds, as if to stem
A greater loss with one which was more weak;
And dull the barbèd fire against his frozen cheek.

### XII

Another Splendour on his mouth alit,     100
That mouth, whence it was wont to draw the breath
Which gave it strength to pierce the guarded wit,
And pass into the panting heart beneath

With lightning and with music: the damp death
Quenched its caress upon his icy lips; 105
And, as a dying meteor stains a wreath
Of moonlight vapour, which the cold night clips,
It flushed through his pale limbs, and passed to its eclipse.

### XIII

And others came . . . Desires and Adorations,
Wingèd Persuasions and veiled Destinies, 110
Splendours, and Glooms, and glimmering Incarnations
Of hopes and fears, and twilight Phantasies;
And Sorrow, with her family of Sighs,
And Pleasure, blind with tears, led by the gleam
Of her own dying smile instead of eyes, 115
Came in slow pomp;—the moving pomp might seem
Like pageantry of mist on an autumnal stream.

### XIV

All he had loved, and moulded into thought,
From shape, and hue, and odour, and sweet sound,
Lamented Adonais. Morning sought 120
Her eastern watch-tower, and her hair unbound,
Wet with the tears which should adorn the ground,
Dimmed the aëreal eyes that kindle day;
Afar the melancholy thunder moaned,
Pale Ocean in unquiet slumber lay, 125
And the wild Winds flew round, sobbing in their dismay.

### XV

Lost Echo sits amid the voiceless mountains,
And feeds her grief with his remembered lay,
And will no more reply to winds or fountains,
Or amorous birds perched on the young green spray, 130
Or herdsman's horn, or bell at closing day;
Since she can mimic not his lips, more dear
Than those for whose disdain she pined away
Into a shadow of all sounds:—a drear
Murmur, between their songs, is all the woodmen hear. 135

XVI

Grief made the young Spring wild, and she threw down
Her kindling buds, as if she Autumn were,
Or they dead leaves; since her delight is flown,
For whom should she have waked the sullen year?
To Phoebus was not Hyacinth so dear          140
Nor to himself Narcissus, as to both
Thou, Adonais: wan they stand and sere
Amid the faint companions of their youth,
With dew all turned to tears; odour, to sighing ruth.

XVII

Thy spirit's sister, the lorn nightingale          145
Mourns not her mate with such melodious pain;
Not so the eagle, who like thee could scale
Heaven, and could nourish in the sun's domain
Her mighty youth with morning, doth complain,
Soaring and screaming round her empty nest,          150
As Albion wails for thee: the curse of Cain
Light on his head who pierced thy innocent breast,
And scared the angel soul that was its earthly guest!

XVIII

Ah, woe is me! Winter is come and gone,
But grief returns with the revolving year;          155
The airs and streams renew their joyous tone;
The ants, the bees, the swallows reappear;
Fresh leaves and flowers deck the dead Seasons' bier;
The amorous birds now pair in every brake,
And build their mossy homes in field and brere;          160
And the green lizard, and the golden snake,
Like unimprisoned flames, out of their trance awake.

XIX

Through wood and stream and field and hill and Ocean
A quickening life from the Earth's heart has burst
As it has ever done, with change and motion,          165
From the great morning of the world when first

God dawned on Chaos; in its stream immersed,
The lamps of Heaven flash with a softer light;
All baser things pant with life's sacred thirst;
Diffuse themselves; and spend in love's delight,                    170
The beauty and the joy of their renewèd might.

### XX

The leprous corpse, touched by this spirit tender,
Exhales itself in flowers of gentle breath;
Like incarnations of the stars, when splendour
Is changed to fragrance, they illumine death                        175
And mock the merry worm that wakes beneath;
Nought we know, dies. Shall that alone which knows
Be as a sword consumed before the sheath
By sightless lightning?—the intense atom glows
A moment, then is quenched in a most cold repose.                    180

### XXI

Alas! that all we loved of him should be,
But for our grief, as if it had not been,
And grief itself be mortal! Woe is me!
Whence are we, and why are we? of what scene
The actors or spectators? Great and mean                            185
Meet massed in death, who lends what life must borrow.
As long as skies are blue, and fields are green,
Evening must usher night, night urge the morrow,
Month follow month with woe, and year wake year to sorrow.

### XXII

*He* will awake no more, oh, never more!                            190
'Wake thou,' cried Misery, 'childless Mother, rise
Out of thy sleep, and slake, in thy heart's core,
A wound more fierce than his, with tears and sighs.'
And all the Dreams that watched Urania's eyes,
And all the Echoes whom their sister's song                         195
Had held in holy silence, cried: 'Arise!'
Swift as a Thought by the snake Memory stung,
From her ambrosial rest the fading Splendour sprung.

### XXIII

She rose like an autumnal Night, that springs
Out of the East, and follows wild and drear                    200
The golden Day, which, on eternal wings,
Even as a ghost abandoning a bier,
Had left the Earth a corpse. Sorrow and fear
So struck, so roused, so rapt Urania;
So saddened round her like an atmosphere                        205
Of stormy mist; so swept her on her way
Even to the mournful place where Adonais lay.

### XXIV

Out of her secret Paradise she sped,
Through camps and cities rough with stone, and steel,
And human hearts, which to her aery tread                       210
Yielding not, wounded the invisible
Palms of her tender feet where'er they fell:
And barbèd tongues, and thoughts more sharp than they,
Rent the soft Form they never could repel,
Whose sacred blood, like the young tears of May,               215
Paved with eternal flowers that undeserving way.

### XXV

In the death-chamber for a moment Death,
Shamed by the presence of that living Might,
Blushed to annihilation, and the breath
Revisited those lips, and Life's pale light                     220
Flashed through those limbs, so late her dear delight.
'Leave me not wild and drear and comfortless,
As silent lightning leaves the starless night!
Leave me not!' cried Urania: her distress
Roused Death: Death rose and smiled, and met her vain caress.

### XXVI

'Stay yet awhile! speak to me once again;                       226
Kiss me, so long but as a kiss may live;
And in my heartless breast and burning brain
That word, that kiss, shall all thoughts else survive,

With food of saddest memory kept alive,                    230
Now thou art dead, as if it were a part
Of thee, my Adonais! I would give
All that I am to be as thou now art!
But I am chained to Time, and cannot thence depart!

#### XXVII

'O gentle child, beautiful as thou wert,                   235
Why didst thou leave the trodden paths of men
Too soon, and with weak hands though mighty heart
Dare the unpastured dragon in his den?
Defenceless as thou wert, oh, where was then
Wisdom the mirrored shield, or scorn the spear?           240
Or hadst thou waited the full cycle, when
Thy spirit should have filled its crescent sphere,
The monsters of life's waste had fled from thee like deer.

#### XXVIII

'The herded wolves, bold only to pursue;
The obscene ravens, clamorous o'er the dead;              245
The vultures to the conqueror's banner true
Who feed where Desolation first has fed,
And whose wings rain contagion;—how they fled,
When, like Apollo, from his golden bow
The Pythian of the age one arrow sped                     250
And smiled!—The spoilers tempt no second blow,
They fawn on the proud feet that spurn them lying low.

#### XXIX

'The sun comes forth, and many reptiles spawn;
He sets, and each ephemeral insect then
Is gathered into death without a dawn,                    255
And the immortal stars awake again;
So is it in the world of living men:
A godlike mind soars forth, in its delight
Making earth bare and veiling heaven, and when
It sinks, the swarms that dimmed or shared its light      260
Leave to its kindred lamps the spirit's awful night.'

### XXX

Thus ceased she: and the mountain shepherds came,
Their garlands sere, their magic mantles rent;
The Pilgrim of Eternity, whose fame
Over his living head like Heaven is bent,          265
An early but enduring monument,
Came, veiling all the lightnings of his song
In sorrow; from her wilds Ierne sent
The sweetest lyrist of her saddest wrong,
And Love taught Grief to fall like music from his tongue.   270

### XXXI

Midst others of less note, came one frail Form,
A phantom among men; companionless
As the last cloud of an expiring storm
Whose thunder is its knell; he, as I guess,
Had gazed on Nature's naked loveliness,            275
Actæon-like, and now he fled astray
With feeble steps o'er the world's wilderness,
And his own thoughts, along that rugged way,
Pursued, like raging hounds, their father and their prey.

### XXXII

A pardlike Spirit beautiful and swift—            280
A Love in desolation masked;—a Power
Girt round with weakness;—it can scarce uplift
The weight of the superincumbent hour;
It is a dying lamp, a falling shower,
A breaking billow;—even whilst we speak           285
Is it not broken?  On the withering flower
The killing sun smiles brightly: on a cheek
The life can burn in blood, even while the heart may break.

### XXXIII

His head was bound with pansies overblown,
And faded violets, white, and pied, and blue;     290
And a light spear topped with a cypress cone,
Round whose rude shaft dark ivy-tresses grew

Yet dripping with the forest's noonday dew,
Vibrated, as the ever-beating heart
Shook the weak hand that grasped it; of that crew    295
He came the last, neglected and apart;
A herd-abandoned deer struck by the hunter's dart.

### XXXIV

All stood aloof, and at his partial moan
Smiled through their tears; well knew that gentle band
Who in another's fate now wept his own,    300
As in the accents of an unknown land
He sung new sorrow; sad Urania scanned
The Stranger's mien, and murmured: 'Who art thou?'
He answered not, but with a sudden hand
Made bare his branded and ensanguined brow,    305
Which was like Cain's or Christ's—oh! that it should be so!

### XXXV

What softer voice is hushed over the dead?
Athwart what brow is that dark mantle thrown?
What form leans sadly o'er the white death-bed,
In mockery of monumental stone,    310
The heavy heart heaving without a moan?
If it be He, who, gentlest of the wise,
Taught, soothed, loved, honoured the departed one,
Let me not vex, with inharmonious sighs,
The silence of that heart's accepted sacrifice.    315

### XXXVI

Our Adonais has drunk poison—oh!
What deaf and viperous murderer could crown
Life's early cup with such a draught of woe?
The nameless worm would now itself disown:
It felt, yet could escape, the magic tone    320
Whose prelude held all envy, hate, and wrong,
But what was howling in one breast alone,
Silent with expectation of the song,
Whose master's hand is cold, whose silver lyre unstrung.

### XXXVII

Live thou, whose infamy is not thy fame!  325
Live! fear no heavier chastisement from me,
Thou noteless blot on a remembered name!
But be thyself, and know thyself to be!
And ever at thy season be thou free
To spill the venom when thy fangs o'erflow:  330
Remorse and Self-contempt shall cling to thee;
Hot Shame shall burn upon thy secret brow,
And like a beaten hound tremble thou shalt—as now.

### XXXVIII

Nor let us weep that our delight is fled
Far from these carrion kites that scream below;  335
He wakes or sleeps with the enduring dead;
Thou canst not soar where he is sitting now.—
Dust to the dust! but the pure spirit shall flow
Back to the burning fountain whence it came,
A portion of the Eternal, which must glow  340
Through time and change, unquenchably the same,
Whilst thy cold embers choke the sordid hearth of shame.

### XXXIX

Peace, peace! he is not dead, he doth not sleep—
He hath awakened from the dream of life—
'Tis we, who lost in stormy visions, keep  345
With phantoms an unprofitable strife,
And in mad trance, strike with our spirit's knife
Invulnerable nothings.—*We* decay
Like corpses in a charnel; fear and grief
Convulse us and consume us day by day,  350
And cold hopes swarm like worms within our living clay.

### XL

He has outsoared the shadow of our night;
Envy and calumny and hate and pain,
And that unrest which men miscall delight,
Can touch him not and torture not again;  355

From the contagion of the world's slow stain
He is secure, and now can never mourn
A heart grown cold, a head grown gray in vain;
Nor, when the spirit's self has ceased to burn,
With sparkless ashes load an unlamented urn.          360

### XLI

He lives, he wakes—'tis Death is dead, not he;
Mourn not for Adonais.—Thou young Dawn,
Turn all thy dew to splendour, for from thee
The spirit thou lamentest is not gone;
Ye caverns and ye forests, cease to moan!          365
Cease, ye faint flowers and fountains, and thou Air,
Which like a mourning veil thy scarf hadst thrown
O'er the abandoned Earth, now leave it bare
Even to the joyous stars which smile on its despair!

### XLII

He is made one with Nature: there is heard          370
His voice in all her music, from the moan
Of thunder, to the song of night's sweet bird;
He is a presence to be felt and known
In darkness and in light, from herb and stone,
Spreading itself where'er that Power may move          375
Which has withdrawn his being to its own;
Which wields the world with never-wearied love,
Sustains it from beneath, and kindles it above.

### XLIII

He is a portion of the loveliness
Which once he made more lovely: he doth bear          380
His part, while the one Spirit's plastic stress
Sweeps through the dull dense world, compelling there,
All new successions to the forms they wear;
Torturing th' unwilling dross that checks its flight
To its own likeness, as each mass may bear;          385
And bursting in its beauty and its might
From trees and beasts and men into the Heaven's light.

XLIV

The splendours of the firmament of time
May be eclipsed, but are extinguished not;
Like stars to their appointed height they climb,                    390
And death is a low mist which cannot blot
The brightness it may veil.  When lofty thought
Lifts a young heart above its mortal lair,
And love and life contend in it, for what
Shall be its earthly doom, the dead live there          395
And move like winds of light on dark and stormy air.

XLV

The inheritors of unfulfilled renown
Rose from their thrones, built beyond mortal thought,
Far in the Unapparent.  Chatterton
Rose pale,—his solemn agony had not                    400
Yet faded from him; Sidney, as he fought
And as he fell and as he lived and loved
Sublimely mild, a Spirit without spot,
Arose; and Lucan, by his death approved:
Oblivion as they rose shrank like a thing reproved.          405

XLVI

And many more, whose names on Earth are dark,
But whose transmitted effluence cannot die
So long as fire outlives the parent spark,
Rose, robed in dazzling immortality.
'Thou art become as one of us,' they cry,              410
'It was for thee yon kingless sphere has long
Swung blind in unascended majesty,
Silent alone amid an Heaven of Song.
Assume thy wingèd throne, thou Vesper of our throng!'

XLVII

Who mourns for Adonais?  Oh, come forth,          415
Fond wretch! and know thyself and him aright.
Clasp with thy panting soul the pendulous Earth;
As from a centre, dart thy spirit's light

Beyond all worlds, until its spacious might
Satiate the void circumference: then shrink          420
Even to a point within our day and night;
And keep thy heart light lest it make thee sink
When hope has kindled hope, and lured thee to the brink.


### XLVIII

Or go to Rome, which is the sepulchre,
Oh, not of him, but of our joy: 'tis nought          425
That ages, empires, and religions there
Lie buried in the ravage they have wrought;
For such as he can lend,—they borrow not
Glory from those who made the world their prey;
And he is gathered to the kings of thought          430
Who waged contention with their time's decay,
And of the past are all that cannot pass away.


### XLIX

Go thou to Rome,—at once the Paradise,
The grave, the city, and the wilderness;
And where its wrecks like shattered mountains rise,          435
And flowering weeds, and fragrant copses dress
The bones of Desolation's nakedness
Pass, till the spirit of the spot shall lead
Thy footsteps to a slope of green access
Where, like an infant's smile, over the dead          440
A light of laughing flowers along the grass is spread;


### L

And gray walls moulder round, on which dull Time
Feeds, like slow fire upon a hoary brand;
And one keen pyramid with wedge sublime,
Pavilioning the dust of him who planned          445
This refuge for his memory, doth stand
Like flame transformed to marble; and beneath,
A field is spread, on which a newer band
Have pitched in Heaven's smile their camp of death,
Welcoming him we lose with scarce extinguished breath.          450

LI

Here pause: these graves are all too young as yet
To have outgrown the sorrow which consigned
Its charge to each; and if the seal is set,
Here, on one fountain of a morning mind,
Break it not thou! too surely shalt thou find          455
Thine own well full, if thou returnest home,
Of tears and gall.  From the world's bitter wind
Seek shelter in the shadow of the tomb.
What Adonais is, why fear we to become?

LII

The One remains, the many change and pass;          460
Heaven's light forever shines, Earth's shadows fly;
Life, like a dome of many-coloured glass,
Stains the white radiance of Eternity,
Until Death tramples it to fragments.—Die,
If thou wouldst be with that which thou dost seek!     465
Follow where all is fled!—Rome's azure sky,
Flowers, ruins, statues, music, words, are weak
The glory they transfuse with fitting truth to speak.

LIII

Why linger, why turn back, why shrink, my Heart?
Thy hopes are gone before: from all things here        470
They have departed; thou shouldst now depart!
A light is passed from the revolving year,
And man, and woman; and what still is dear
Attracts to crush, repels to make thee wither.
The soft sky smiles,—the low wind whispers near:      475
'Tis Adonais calls! oh, hasten thither,
No more let Life divide what Death can join together.

LIV

That Light whose smile kindles the Universe,
That Beauty in which all things work and move,
That Benediction which the eclipsing Curse              480
Of birth can quench not, that sustaining Love

Which through the web of being blindly wove
By man and beast and earth and air and sea,
Burns bright or dim, as each are mirrors of
The fire for which all thirst; now beams on me,   485
Consuming the last clouds of cold mortality.

### LV

The breath whose might I have invoked in song
Descends on me; my spirit's bark is driven,
Far from the shore, far from the trembling throng
Whose sails were never to the tempest given;   490
The massy earth and spherèd skies are riven!
I am borne darkly, fearfully, afar;
Whilst, burning through the inmost veil of Heaven,
The soul of Adonais, like a star,
Beacons from the abode where the Eternal are.   495

# HELLAS

## A LYRICAL DRAMA

ΜΑΝΤΙΣ 'ΕΙΜ' 'ΕΣΘΛΩΝ 'ΑΓΩΝΩΝ.—Oedip. Colon.

TO HIS EXCELLENCY

### PRINCE ALEXANDER MAVROCORDATO

LATE SECRETARY FOR FOREIGN AFFAIRS TO THE HOSPODAR OF WALLACHIA

THE DRAMA OF HELLAS IS INSCRIBED AS AN
IMPERFECT TOKEN OF THE ADMIRATION,
SYMPATHY, AND FRIENDSHIP OF
THE AUTHOR

Pisa, *November* 1, 1821.

## PREFACE

THE poem of *Hellas*, written at the suggestion of the events
of the moment, is a mere improvise, and derives its interest
(should it be found to possess any) solely from the intense

sympathy which the Author feels with the cause he would celebrate.

The subject, in its present state, is insusceptible of being treated otherwise than lyrically, and if I have called this poem a drama from the circumstance of its being composed in dialogue, the licence is not greater than that which has been assumed by other poets who have called their productions epics, only because they have been divided into twelve or twenty-four books.

The *Persae* of Æschylus afforded me the first model of my conception, although the decision of the glorious contest now waging in Greece being yet suspended forbids a catastrophe parallel to the return of Xerxes and the desolation of the Persians. I have, therefore, contented myself with exhibiting a series of lyric pictures, and with having wrought upon the curtain of futurity, which falls upon the unfinished scene, such figures of indistinct and visionary delineation as suggest the final triumph of the Greek cause as a portion of the cause of civilisation and social improvement.

The drama (if drama it must be called) is, however, so inartificial that I doubt whether, if recited on the Thespian waggon to an Athenian village at the Dionysiaca, it would have obtained the prize of the goat. I shall bear with equanimity any punishment, greater than the loss of such a reward, which the Aristarchi of the hour may think fit to inflict.

The only *goat-song* which I have yet attempted has, I confess, in spite of the unfavourable nature of the subject, received a greater and a more valuable portion of applause than I expected or than it deserved.

Common fame is the only authority which I can allege for the details which form the basis of the poem, and I must trespass upon the forgiveness of my readers for the display of newspaper erudition to which I have been reduced. Undoubtedly, until the conclusion of the war, it will be impossible to obtain an account of it sufficiently authentic for historical materials; but poets have their privilege, and it is unquestionable that actions of the most exalted courage have been performed by the Greeks—that they have gained more than one naval victory, and that their defeat in Wallachia was signalized by circumstances of heroism more glorious even than victory.

The apathy of the rulers of the civilised world to the astonishing circumstance of the descendants of that nation to which they owe their civilisation, rising as it were from the ashes of their ruin, is something perfectly inexplicable to a mere spectator of the shows of this mortal scene. We are all Greeks. Our laws, our literature, our religion, our arts have their root in Greece. But for Greece—Rome, the instructor, the conqueror, or the metropolis of our ancestors, would have spread no illumination with their arms, and we might still have been savages and idolaters; or, what is worse, might have arrived at such a stagnant and miserable state of social institution as China and Japan possess.

The human form and the human mind attained to a perfection in Greece which has impressed its image on those faultless productions, whose very fragments are the despair of modern art, and has propagated impulses which cannot cease, through a thousand channels of manifest or imperceptible operation, to ennoble and delight mankind until the extinction of the race.

The modern Greek is the descendant of those glorious beings whom the imagination almost refuses to figure to itself as belonging to our kind, and he inherits much of their sensibility, their rapidity of conception, their enthusiasm, and their courage. If in many instances he is degraded by moral and political slavery to the practice of the basest vices it engenders—and that below the level of ordinary degradation—let us reflect that the corruption of the best produces the worst, and that habits which subsist only in relation to a peculiar state of social institution may be expected to cease as soon as that relation is dissolved. In fact, the Greeks, since the admirable novel of *Anastasius* could have been a faithful picture of their manners, have undergone most important changes; the flower of their youth, returning to their country from the universities of Italy, Germany, and France, have communicated to their fellow-citizens the latest results of that social perfection of which their ancestors were the original source. The University of Chios contained before the breaking out of the revolution eight hundred students, and among them several Germans and Americans. The munificence and energy of many of the Greek princes and merchants, directed to the renovation of their country with a spirit and a wisdom which has few examples, is above all praise.

The English permit their own oppressors to act according to their natural sympathy with the Turkish tyrant, and to brand upon their name the indelible blot of an alliance with the enemies of domestic happiness, of Christianity and civilisation.

Russia desires to possess, not to liberate Greece; and is contented to see the Turks, its natural enemies, and the Greeks, its intended slaves, enfeeble each other until one or both fall into its net. The wise and generous policy of England would have consisted in establishing the independence of Greece, and in maintaining it both against Russia and the Turk;—but when was the oppressor generous or just?

Should the English people ever become free, they will reflect upon the part which those who presume to represent their will have played in the great drama of the revival of liberty, with feelings which it would become them to anticipate. This is the age of the war of the oppressed against the oppressors, and every one of those ringleaders of the privileged gangs of murderers and swindlers, called Sovereigns, look to each other for aid against the common enemy, and suspend their mutual jealousies in the presence of a mightier fear. Of this holy alliance all the despots of the earth are virtual members. But a new race has arisen throughout Europe, nursed in the abhorrence of the opinions which are its chains, and she will continue to produce fresh generations to accomplish that destiny which tyrants foresee and dread.[1]

The Spanish peninsula is already free. France is tranquil in the enjoyment of a partial exemption from the abuses which its unnatural and feeble government are vainly attempting to revive. The seed of blood and misery has been sown in Italy, and

[1] This paragraph was suppressed by the publisher, Charles Ollier, in the edition of 1822; it was restored from a copy of the original proofs by H. Buxton Forman in his edition of Shelley's *Works*, 1892.

a more vigorous race is arising to go forth to the harvest. The world waits only the news of a revolution of Germany to see the tyrants who have pinnacled themselves on its supineness precipitated into the ruin from which they shall never arise. Well do these destroyers of mankind know their enemy, when they impute the insurrection in Greece to the same spirit before which they tremble throughout the rest of Europe, and that enemy well knows the power and the cunning of its opponents, and watches the moment of their approaching weakness and inevitable division to wrest the bloody sceptres from their grasp.

## PROLOGUE TO HELLAS[1]

*Herald of Eternity.* It is the day when all the sons of God
Wait in the roofless senate-house, whose floor
Is Chaos, and the immovable abyss
Frozen by His steadfast word to hyaline

. . . . . . . . . . .

The shadow of God, and delegate 5
Of that before whose breath the universe
Is as a print of dew.
                    Hierarchs and kings
Who from your thrones pinnacled on the past
Sway the reluctant present, ye who sit
Pavilioned on the radiance or the gloom 10
Of mortal thought, which like an exhalation
Steaming from earth, conceals the      of heaven
Which gave it birth,          assemble here
Before your Father's throne; the swift decree
Yet hovers, and the fiery incarnation 15
Is yet withheld, clothèd in which it shall
                    annul
The fairest of those wandering isles that gem
The sapphire space of interstellar air,
That green and azure sphere, that earth enwrapped 20
Less in the beauty of its tender light

[1] First published in R. S. Garnett's *Relics of Shelley*, 1862.

Than in an atmosphere of living spirit
Which interpenetrating all the . . .
       it rolls from realm to realm
And age to age, and in its ebb and flow     25
Impels the generations
To their appointed place,
Whilst the high Arbiter
Beholds the strife, and at the appointed time
Sends His decrees veiled in eternal . . .     30

Within the circuit of this pendent orb
There lies an antique region, on which fell
The dews of thought in the world's golden dawn
Earliest and most benign, and from it sprung
Temples and cities and immortal forms     35
And harmonies of wisdom and of song,
And thoughts, and deeds worthy of thoughts so fair.
And when the sun of its dominion failed,
And when the winter of its glory came,
The winds that stripped it bare blew on and swept     40
That dew into the utmost wildernesses
In wandering clouds of sunny rain that thawed
The unmaternal bosom of the North.
Haste, sons of God,        for ye beheld,
Reluctant, or consenting, or astonished,     45
The stern decrees go forth, which heaped on Greece
Ruin and degradation and despair.
A fourth now waits: assemble, sons of God,
To speed or to prevent or to suspend,
If, as ye dream, such power be not withheld,     50
The unaccomplished destiny.

   ·   ·   ·   ·   ·   ·   ·   ·   ·

*Chorus.*

The curtain of the Universe
   Is rent and shattered,
The splendour-wingèd worlds disperse
   Like wild doves scattered.     55

Space is roofless and bare,
And in the midst a cloudy shrine,
   Dark amid thrones of light.
In the blue glow of hyaline
Golden worlds revolve and shine.                             60
   In                                  flight
   From every point of the Infinite,
   Like a thousand dawns on a single night
The splendours rise and spread;
And through thunder and darkness dread          65
Light and music are radiated,
And in their pavilioned chariots led
By living wings high overhead
   The giant Powers move,
Gloomy or bright as the thrones they fill.           70

   A chaos of light and motion
   Upon that glassy ocean.

.    .    .    .

   The senate of the Gods is met,
   Each in his rank and station set;
     There is silence in the spaces—          75
   Lo! Satan, Christ, and Mahomet
   Start from their places!

*Christ.*                                              Almighty Father!
Low-kneeling at the feet of Destiny

.   .   .   .   .   .

There are two fountains in which spirits weep          80
When mortals err, Discord and Slavery named,
And with their bitter dew two Destinies
Filled each their irrevocable urns; the third,
Fiercest and mightiest, mingled both, and added

Chaos and Death, and slow Oblivion's lymph,      85
And hate and terror, and the poisoned rain

·        ·        ·        ·        ·        ·        ·

. The Aurora of the nations.  By this brow
Whose pores wept tears of blood, by these wide wounds,
By this imperial crown of agony,
By infamy and solitude and death,              90
For this I underwent, and by the pain
Of pity for those who would        for me
The unremembered joy of a revenge,
For this I felt—by Plato's sacred light,
Of which my spirit was a burning morrow—       95
By Greece and all she cannot cease to be,
Her quenchless words, sparks of immortal truth,
Stars of all night—her harmonies and forms,
Echoes and shadows of what Love adores
In thee, I do compel thee, send forth Fate,    100
Thy irrevocable child: let her descend,
A seraph-wingèd Victory [arrayed]
In tempest of the omnipotence of God
Which sweeps through all things.

From hollow leagues, from Tyranny which arms    105
Adverse miscreeds and emulous anarchies
To stamp, as on a wingèd serpent's seed,
Upon the name of Freedom; from the storm
Of faction, which like earthquake shakes and sickens
The solid heart of enterprise; from all         110
By which the holiest dreams of highest spirits
Are stars beneath the dawn . . . .
                            She shall arise
Victorious as the world arose from Chaos!
And as the Heavens and the Earth arrayed
Their presence in the beauty and the light      115
Of Thy first smile, O Father,—as they gather
The spirit of Thy love which paves for them

Their path o'er the abyss, till every sphere
Shall be one living Spirit,—so shall Greece—
   *Satan.*  Be as all things beneath the empyrean,     120
Mine! Art thou eyeless like old Destiny,
Thou mockery-king, crowned with a wreath of thorns?
Whose sceptre is a reed, the broken reed
Which pierces thee! whose throne a chair of scorn;
For seest thou not beneath this crystal floor     125
The innumerable worlds of golden light
Which are my empire, and the least of them
     which thou wouldst redeem from me?
Know'st thou not them my portion?
Or wouldst rekindle the         strife     130
Which our great Father then did arbitrate
Which he assigned to his competing sons
Each his apportioned realm?
                    Thou Destiny,
Thou who art mailed in the omnipotence
Of Him who sends thee forth, whate'er thy task,     135
Speed, spare not to accomplish, and be mine
Thy trophies, whether Greece again become
The fountain in the desert whence the earth
Shall drink of freedom, which shall give it strength
To suffer, or a gulf of hollow death     140
To swallow all delight, all life, all hope.
Go, thou Vicegerent of my will, no less
Than of the Father's; but less thou shouldst faint,
The wingèd hounds, Famine and Pestilence,
Shall wait on thee, the hundred-forkèd snake     145
Insatiate Superstition still shall . . .
The earth behind thy steps, and War shall hover
Above, and Fraud shall gape below, and Change
Shall flit before thee on her dragon wings,
Convulsing and consuming, and I add     150
Three vials of the tears which daemons weep
When virtuous spirits through the gate of Death
Pass triumphing over the thorns of life,
Sceptres and crowns, mitres and swords and snares,

THOMAS LOVE PEACOCK

*From the painting by Henry Wallis. Now in the National Portrait Gallery, London.*

Trampling in scorn, like Him and Socrates.                     155
The first is Anarchy; when Power and Pleasure,
Glory and science and security,
On Freedom hang like fruit on the green tree,
Then pour it forth, and men shall gather ashes.
The second Tyranny—
   *Christ.*              Obdurate spirit!                 160
Thou seest but the Past in the To-come.
Pride is thy error and thy punishment.
Boast not thine empire, dream not that thy worlds
Are more than furnace-sparks or rainbow-drops
Before the Power that wields and kindles them.                 165
True greatness asks not space, true excellence
Lives in the Spirit of all things that live,
Which lends it to the worlds thou callest thine.

.   .   .   .   .   .

   *Mahomet.* . . . Haste thou and fill the waning crescent
With beams as keen as those which pierced the shadow         170
Of Christian night rolled back upon the West,
When the orient moon of Islam rode in triumph
From Tmolus to the Acroceraunian snow.

.   .   .   .   .   .

                        Wake, thou Word
Of God, and from the throne of Destiny                          175
Even to the utmost limit of thy way
May Triumph

.   .   .   .   .   .

    Be thou a curse on them whose creed
Divides and multiplies the most high God.

M

# HELLAS

## *DRAMATIS PERSONÆ*

MAHMUD.                          DAOOD.
HASSAN.                          AHASUERUS, *a Jew.*

CHORUS *of Greek Captive Women. The Phantom of Mahomet II.
Messengers, Slaves, and Attendants.* SCENE, *Constantinople.*
TIME, *Sunset.*

SCENE.—*A Terrace on the Seraglio.* MAHMUD *sleeping, an
Indian Slave sitting beside his Couch.*

*Chorus of Greek Captive Women.*

WE strew these opiate flowers
    On thy restless pillow,—
They were stripped from Orient bowers,
    By the Indian billow,
        Be thy sleep                             5
        Calm and deep,
Like theirs who fell—not ours who weep!


*Indian.*

Away, unlovely dreams!
    Away, false shapes of sleep!
Be his, as Heaven seems,                         10
    Clear, and bright, and deep!
Soft as love, and calm as death,
Sweet as a summer night without a breath.


*Chorus.*

Sleep, sleep! our song is laden
    With the soul of slumber;                    15
It was sung by a Samian maiden,
    Whose lover was of the number
        Who now keep
        That calm sleep
Whence none may wake, where none shall weep.    20

*Indian.*

I touch thy temples pale!
    I breathe my soul on thee!
And could my prayers avail,
    All my joy should be
Dead, and I would live to weep,                    25
So thou mightst win one hour of quiet sleep.

*Chorus.*

Breathe low, low
    The spell of the mighty mistress now!
When Conscience lulls her sated snake,
And Tyrants sleep, let Freedom wake.               30
    Breathe low—low
The words which, like secret fire, shall flow
Through the veins of the frozen earth—low, low!

*Semichorus I.*

Life may change, but it may fly not;
Hope may vanish, but can die not;                  35
Truth be veiled, but still it burneth;
Love repulsed,—but it returneth!

*Semichorus II.*

Yet were life a charnel where
Hope lay coffined with Despair;
Yet were truth a sacred lie,                       40
Love were lust—

*Semichorus I.*

           If Liberty
Lent not life its soul of light,
Hope its iris of delight,
Truth its prophet's robe to wear,
Love its power to give and bear.                   45

## Chorus.

In the great morning of the world,
The Spirit of God with might unfurled
The flag of Freedom over Chaos,
   And all its banded anarchs fled,
Like vultures frighted from Imaus,                    50
   Before an earthquake's tread.—
So from Time's tempestuous dawn
Freedom's splendour burst and shone:—
Thermopylae and Marathon
Caught, like mountains, beacon-lighted,               55
   The springing Fire.—The wingèd glory
On Philippi half-alighted,
   Like an eagle on a promontory.
Its unwearied wings could fan
The quenchless ashes of Milan.                        60
From age to age, from man to man,
   It lived; and lit from land to land
   Florence, Albion, Switzerland.

Then night fell; and, as from night,
Reassuming fiery flight,                              65
From the West swift Freedom came,
   Against the course of Heaven and doom,
A second sun arrayed in flame,
   To burn, to kindle, to illume.
From far Atlantis its young beams                     70
Chased the shadows and the dreams.
France, with all her sanguine steams,
   Hid, but quenched it not; again
   Through clouds its shafts of glory rain
From utmost Germany to Spain.                         75
As an eagle fed with morning
Scorns the embattled tempest's warning,
When she seeks her aerie hanging
   In the mountain-cedar's hair,
And her brood expect the clanging                     80

Of her wings through the wild air,
Sick with famine:—Freedom, so
To what of Greece remaineth now
Returns; her hoary ruins glow
Like Orient mountains lost in day;                    85
    Beneath the safety of her wings
Her renovated nurslings prey,
    And in the naked lightenings
Of truth they purge their dazzled eyes.
Let Freedom leave—where'er she flies,                90
A Desert, or a Paradise:
    Let the beautiful and the brave
    Share her glory, or a grave.

*Semichorus I.*

With the gifts of gladness
    Greece did thy cradle strew;                      95

*Semichorus II.*

With tears of sadness
    Greece did thy shroud bedew!

*Semichorus I.*

With an orphan's affection
    She followed thy bier through Time;

*Semichorus II.*

And at thy resurrection                               100
    Reappeareth, like thou, sublime!

*Semichorus I.*

If Heaven should resume thee,
    To Heaven shall her spirit ascend;

*Semichorus II.*

If Hell should entomb thee,
    To Hell shall her high hearts bend.               105

*Semichorus I.*

If Annihilation——

*Semichorus II.*

Dust let her glories be!
And a name and a nation
Be forgotten, Freedom, with thee!

*Indian.*

His brow grows darker—breathe not—move not!    110
He starts—he shudders—ye that love not,
    With your panting loud and fast,
    Have awakened him at last.

*Mahmud (starting from his sleep).* Man the Seraglio-guard!
    make fast the gate!
What! from a cannonade of three short hours?    115
'Tis false! that breach towards the Bosphorus
Cannot be practicable yet—who stirs?
Stand to the match; that when the foe prevails
One spark may mix in reconciling ruin
The conqueror and the conquered! Heave the tower    120
Into the gap—wrench off the roof!
    *(Enter* HASSAN.)                    Ha! what!
The truth of day lightens upon my dream
And I am Mahmud still.
    *Hassan.*                    Your Sublime Highness
Is strangely moved.
    *Mahmud.*            The times do cast strange shadows
On those who watch and who must rule their course,    125
Lest they, being first in peril as in glory,
Be whelmed in the fierce ebb:—and these are of them.
Thrice has a gloomy vision hunted me
As thus from sleep into the troubled day;
It shakes me as the tempest shakes the sea,    130
Leaving no figure upon memory's glass.
Would that——no matter. Thou didst say thou knewest

A Jew, whose spirit is a chronicle
Of strange and secret and forgotten things.
I bade thee summon him:—'tis said his tribe                135
Dream, and are wise interpreters of dreams.

   *Hassan.* The Jew of whom I spake is old,—so old
He seems to have outlived a world's decay;
The hoary mountains and the wrinkled ocean
Seem younger still than he;—his hair and beard            140
Are whiter than the tempest-sifted snow;
His cold pale limbs and pulseless arteries
Are like the fibres of a cloud instinct
With light, and to the soul that quickens them
Are as the atoms of the mountain-drift                    145
To the winter wind:—but from his eye looks forth
A life of unconsumèd thought which pierces
The Present, and the Past, and the To-come.
Some say that this is he whom the great prophet
Jesus, the son of Joseph, for his mockery,                150
Mocked with the curse of immortality.
Some feign that he is Enoch: others dream
He was pre-adamite and has survived
Cycles of generation and of ruin.
The sage, in truth, by dreadful abstinence                155
And conquering penance of the mutinous flesh,
Deep contemplation, and unwearied study,
In years outstretched beyond the date of man,
May have attained to sovereignty and science
Over those strong and secret things and thoughts          160
Which others fear and know not.

   *Mahmud.*                                   I would talk
With this old Jew.

   *Hassan.*                        Thy will is even now
Made known to him, where he dwells in a sea-cavern
'Mid the Demonesi, less accessible
Than thou or God! He who would question him               165
Must sail alone at sunset, where the stream
Of Ocean sleeps around those foamless isles,
When the young moon is westering as now,

And evening airs wander upon the wave;
And when the pines of that bee-pasturing isle,                        170
Green Erebinthus, quench the fiery shadow
Of this gilt prow within the sapphire water,
Then must the lonely helmsman cry aloud
'Ahasuerus!' and the caverns round
Will answer 'Ahasuerus!' If his prayer                                175
Be granted, a faint meteor will arise
Lighting him over Marmora, and a wind
Will rush out of the sighing pine-forest,
And with the wind a storm of harmony
Unutterably sweet, and pilot him                                      180
Through the soft twilight to the Bosphorus:
Thence at the hour and place and circumstance
Fit for the matter of their conference
The Jew appears. Few dare, and few who dare
Win the desired communion—but that shout                             185
Bodes——                              [*A shout within.*
    *Mahmud.* Evil, doubtless; like all human sounds.
Let me converse with spirits.
    *Hassan.*                          That shout again.
    *Mahmud.* This Jew whom thou hast summoned—
    *Hassan.*                          Will be here—
    *Mahmud.* When the omnipotent hour to which are yoked
He, I, and all things shall compel—enough!                           190
Silence those mutineers—that drunken crew,
That crowd about the pilot in the storm.
Ay! strike the foremost shorter by a head!
They weary me, and I have need of rest.
Kings are like stars—they rise and set, they have                    195
The worship of the world, but no repose.     [*Exeunt severally.*

### Chorus.

Worlds on worlds are rolling ever
    From creation to decay,
Like the bubbles on a river
    Sparkling, bursting, borne away.                                 200
    But they are still immortal

Who, through birth's orient portal
And death's dark chasm hurrying to and fro,
   Clothe their unceasing flight
   In the brief dust and light 205
Gathered around their chariots as they go;
   New shapes they still may weave,
   New gods, new laws receive,
Bright or dim are they as the robes they last
   On Death's bare ribs had cast. 210

A power from the unknown God,
   A Promethean conqueror, came;
Like a triumphal path he trod
   The thorns of death and shame.
   A mortal shape to him 215
   Was like the vapour dim
Which the orient planet animates with light;
   Hell, Sin, and Slavery came,
   Like bloodhounds mild and tame,
Nor preyed, until their Lord had taken flight; 220
   The moon of Mahomet
   Arose, and it shall set:
While blazoned as on Heaven's immortal noon
   The cross leads generations on.

Swift as the radiant shapes of sleep 225
   From one whose dreams are Paradise
Fly, when the fond wretch wakes to weep,
   And Day peers forth with her blank eyes;
   So fleet, so faint, so fair,
   The Powers of earth and air 230
Fled from the folding-star of Bethlehem:
   Apollo, Pan, and Love,
   And even Olympian Jove
Grew weak, for killing Truth had glared on them;
   Our hills and seas and streams, 235
   Dispeopled of their dreams,
Their waters turned to blood, their dew to tears,
   Wailed for the golden years.

*Enter* MAHMUD, HASSAN, DAOOD, *and others.*

*Mahmud.* More gold? our ancestors bought gold with victory,
And shall I sell it for defeat?

    *Daood.*            The Janizars       240
Clamour for pay.

    *Mahmud.*       Go! bid them pay themselves
With Christian blood! Are there no Grecian virgins
Whose shrieks and spasms and tears they may enjoy?
No infidel children to impale on spears?
No hoary priests after that Patriarch        245
Who bent the curse against his country's heart,
Which clove his own at last? Go! bid them kill,
Blood is the seed of gold.

    *Daood.*           It has been sown,
And yet the harvest to the sicklemen
Is as a grain to each.

    *Mahmud*       Then, take this signet,      250
Unlock the seventh chamber in which lie
The treasures of victorious Solyman,—
An empire's spoil stored for a day of ruin.
O spirit of my sires! is it not come?
The prey-birds and the wolves are gorged and sleep;   255
But these, who spread their feast on the red earth,
Hunger for gold, which fills not.—See them fed;
Then, lead them to the rivers of fresh death.    [*Exit* DAOOD.
O miserable dawn, after a night
More glorious than the day which it usurped!    260
O faith in God! O power on earth! O word
Of the great prophet, whose o'ershadowing wings
Darkened the thrones and idols of the West,
Now bright!—For thy sake cursèd be the hour,
Even as a father by an evil child,    265
When the orient moon of Islam rolled in triumph
From Caucasus to White Ceraunia!
Ruin above, and anarchy below;
Terror without, and treachery within;
The Chalice of destruction full, and all    270

Thirsting to drink; and who among us dares
To dash it from his lips? and where is Hope?

*Hassan.* The lamp of our dominion still rides high;
One God is God—Mahomet is His prophet.
Four hundred thousand Moslems, from the limits        275
Of utmost Asia, irresistibly
Throng, like full clouds at the Sirocco's cry;
But not like them to weep their strength in tears:
They bear destroying lightning, and their step
Wakes earthquake to consume and overwhelm,           280
And reign in ruin. Phrygian Olympus,
Tmolus, and Latmos, and Mycale, roughen
With horrent arms; and lofty ships even now,
Like vapours anchored to a mountain's edge,
Freighted with fire and whirlwind, wait at Scala       285
The convoy of the ever-veering wind.
Samos is drunk with blood;—the Greek has paid
Brief victory with swift loss and long despair.
The false Moldavian serfs fled fast and far.
When the fierce shout of 'Allah-illa-Allah!'           290
Rose like the war-cry of the northern wind
Which kills the sluggish clouds, and leaves a flock
Of wild swans struggling with the naked storm.
So were the lost Greeks on the Danube's day!
If night is mute, yet the returning sun                295
Kindles the voices of the morning birds;
Nor at thy bidding less exultingly
Than birds rejoicing in the golden day,
The Anarchies of Africa unleash
Their tempest-wingèd cities of the sea,                300
To speak in thunder to the rebel world.
Like sulphurous clouds, half-scattered by the storm,
They sweep the pale Aegean, while the Queen
Of Ocean, bound upon her island-throne,
Far in the West, sits mourning that her sons           305
Who frown on Freedom spare a smile for thee:
Russia still hovers, as an eagle might
Within a cloud, near which a kite and crane

Hang tangled in inextricable fight,
To stoop upon the victor;—for she fears        310
The name of Freedom, even as she hates thine.
But recreant Austria loves thee as the Grave
Loves Pestilence, and her slow dogs of war
Fleshed with the chase, come up from Italy,
And howl upon their limits; for they see        315
The panther, Freedom, fled to her old cover,
Amid seas and mountains, and a mightier brood
Crouch round. What Anarch wears a crown or mitre,
Or bears the sword, or grasps the key of gold,
Whose friends are not thy friends, whose foes thy foes?        320
Our arsenals and our armouries are full;
Our forts defy assault; ten thousand cannon
Lie ranged upon the beach, and hour by hour
Their earth-convulsing wheels affright the city;
The galloping of fiery steeds makes pale        325
The Christian merchant; and the yellow Jew
Hides his hoard deeper in the faithless earth.
Like clouds, and like the shadows of the clouds,
Over the hills of Anatolia,
Swift in wide troops the Tartar chivalry        330
Sweep;—the far flashing of their starry lances
Reverberates the dying light of day.
We have one God, one King, one Hope, one Law;
But many-headed Insurrection stands
Divided in itself, and soon must fall.        335
    *Mahmud.* Proud words, when deeds come short, are season-
        able:
Look, Hassan, on yon crescent moon, emblazoned
Upon that shattered flag of fiery cloud
Which leads the rear of the departing day;
Wan emblem of an empire fading now!        340
See how it trembles in the blood-red air,
And like a mighty lamp whose oil is spent
Shrinks on the horizon's edge, while, from above,
One star with insolent and victorious light
Hovers above its fall, and with keen beams,        345

Like arrows through a fainting antelope,
Strikes its weak form to death.
    *Hassan.*             Even as that moon
Renews itself—
    *Mahmud.*       Shall we be not renewed!
Far other bark than ours were needed now
To stem the torrent of descending time:       350
The Spirit that lifts the slave before his lord
Stalks through the capitals of armèd kings,
And spreads his ensign in the wilderness:
Exults in chains; and, when the rebel falls,
Cries like the blood of Abel from the dust;    355
And the inheritors of the earth, like beasts
When earthquake is unleashed, with idiot fear
Cower in their kingly dens—as I do now.
What were Defeat when Victory must appal?
Or Danger, when Security looks pale?—     360
How said the messenger—who, from the fort
Islanded in the Danube, saw the battle
Of Bucharest?—that—
    *Hassan.*          Ibrahim's scimitar
Drew with its gleam swift victory from Heaven,
To burn before him in the night of battle—   365
A light and a destruction.
    *Mahmud.*           Ay! the day
Was ours: but how?——
    *Hassan.*          The light Wallachians,
The Arnaut, Servian, and Albanian allies
Fled from the glance of our artillery
Almost before the thunderstone alit.      370
One half the Grecian army made a bridge
Of safe and slow retreat, with Moslem dead;
The other—
    *Mahmud.*   Speak—tremble not.—
    *Hassan.*            Islanded
By victor myriads, formed in hollow square
With rough and steadfast front, and thrice flung back  375
The deluge of our foaming cavalry;

Thrice their keen wedge of battle pierced our lines.
Our baffled army trembled like one man
Before a host, and gave them space; but soon,
From the surrounding hills, the batteries blazed,          380
Kneading them down with fire and iron rain:
Yet none approached; till, like a field of corn
Under the hook of the swart sickleman,
The band, intrenched in mounds of Turkish dead,
Grew weak and few.—Then said the Pacha, 'Slaves,          385
Render yourselves—they have abandoned you—
What hope of refuge, or retreat, or aid?
We grant your lives.' 'Grant that which is thine own!'
Cried one, and fell upon his sword and died!
Another—'God, and man, and hope abandon me;              390
But I to them, and to myself, remain
Constant:'—he bowed his head, and his heart burst.
A third exclaimed, 'There is a refuge, tyrant,
Where thou darest not pursue, and canst not harm
Shouldst thou pursue; there we shall meet again.'         395
Then held his breath, and, after a brief spasm,
The indignant spirit cast its mortal garment
Among the slain—dead earth upon the earth!
So these survivors, each by different ways,
Some strange, all sudden, none dishonourable,             400
Met in triumphant death; and when our army
Closed in, while yet wonder, and awe, and shame
Held back the base hyaenas of the battle
That feed upon the dead and fly the living,
One rose out of the chaos of the slain:                   405
And if it were a corpse which some dread spirit
Of the old saviours of the land we rule
Had lifted in its anger, wandering by;—
Or if there burned within the dying man
Unquenchable disdain of death, and faith                  410
Creating what it feigned;—I cannot tell—
But he cried, 'Phantoms of the free, we come!
Armies of the Eternal, ye who strike
To dust the citadels of sanguine kings,

And shake the souls throned on their stony hearts,     415
And thaw their frostwork diadems like dew;—
O ye who float around this clime, and weave
The garment of the glory which it wears,
Whose fame, though earth betray the dust it clasped,
Lies sepulchred in monumental thought;—     420
Progenitors of all that yet is great,
Ascribe to your bright senate, O accept
In your high ministrations, us, your sons—
Us first, and the more glorious yet to come!
And ye, weak conquerors! giants who look pale     425
When the crushed worm rebels beneath your tread,
The vultures and the dogs, your pensioners tame,
Are overgorged; but, like oppressors, still
They crave the relic of Destruction's feast.
The exhalations and the thirsty winds     430
Are sick with blood; the dew is foul with death;
Heaven's light is quenched in slaughter: thus, where'er
Upon your camps, cities, or towers, or fleets,
The obscene birds the reeking remnants cast
Of these dead limbs,—upon your streams and mountains,     435
Upon your fields, your gardens, and your housetops,
Where'er the winds shall creep, or the clouds fly,
Or the dews fall, or the angry sun look down
With poisoned light—Famine, and Pestilence,
And Panic, shall wage war upon our side!     440
Nature from all her boundaries is moved
Against ye: Time has found ye light as foam.
The Earth rebels; and Good and Evil stake
Their empire o'er the unborn world of men
On this one cast;—but ere the die be thrown,     445
The renovated genius of our race,
Proud umpire of the impious game, descends,
A seraph-wingèd Victory, bestriding
The tempest of the Omnipotence of God,
Which sweeps all things to their appointed doom,     450
And you to oblivion!'—More he would have said,
But—

*Mahmud.* Died—as thou shouldest ere thy lips had painted
Their ruin in the hues of our success.
A rebel's crime, gilt with a rebel's tongue!
Your heart is Greek, Hassan.

   *Hassan.*             It may be so:   455
A spirit not my own wrenched me within,
And I have spoken words I fear and hate;
Yet would I die for—

   *Mahmud.*          Live! oh live! outlive
Me and this sinking empire. But the fleet—

   *Hassan.* Alas!—

   *Mahmud.*     The fleet which, like a flock of clouds  460
Chased by the wind, flies the insurgent banner!
Our wingèd castles from their merchant ships!
Our myriads before their weak pirate bands!
Our arms before their chains! our years of empire
Before their centuries of servile fear!         465
Death is awake! Repulse is on the waters!
They own no more the thunder-bearing banner
Of Mahmud; but, like hounds of a base breed,
Gorge from a stranger's hand, and rend their master.

   *Hassan.* Latmos, and Ampelos, and Phanae saw  470
The wreck—

   *Mahmud.*      The caves of the Icarian isles
Told each to the other in loud mockery,
And with the tongue as of a thousand echoes,
First of the sea-convulsing fight—and, then,—
Thou darest to speak—senseless are the mountains:  475
Interpret thou their voice!

   *Hassan.*           My presence bore
A part in that day's shame. The Grecian fleet
Bore down at daybreak from the North, and hung
As multitudinous on the ocean line,
As cranes upon the cloudless Thracian wind.   480
Our squadron, convoying ten thousand men,
Was stretching towards Nauplia when the battle
Was kindled.—
First through the hail of our artillery

The agile Hydriote barks with press of sail          485
Dashed:—ship to ship, cannon to cannon, man
To man were grappled in the embrace of war,
Inextricable but by death or victory.
The tempest of the raging fight convulsed
To its crystàlline depths that stainless sea,          490
And shook Heaven's roof of golden morning clouds,
Poised on an hundred azure mountain-isles.
In the brief trances of the artillery
One cry from the destroyed and the destroyer
Rose, and a cloud of desolation wrapped          495
The unforeseen event, till the north wind
Sprung from the sea, lifting the heavy veil
Of battle-smoke—then victory—victory!
For, as we thought, three frigates from Algiers
Bore down from Naxos to our aid, but soon          500
The abhorrèd cross glimmered behind, before,
Among, around us; and that fatal sign
Dried with its beams the strength in Moslem hearts,
As the sun drinks the dew.—What more? We fled!—
Our noonday path over the sanguine foam          505
Was beaconed,—and the glare struck the sun pale,—
By our consuming transports: the fierce light
Made all the shadows of our sails blood-red,
And every countenance blank. Some ships lay feeding
The ravening fire, even to the water's level;          510
Some were blown up; some, settling heavily,
Sunk; and the shrieks of our companions died
Upon the wind, that bore us fast and far,
Even after they were dead. Nine thousand perished!
We met the vultures legioned in the air          515
Stemming the torrent of the tainted wind;
They, screaming from their cloudy mountain-peaks,
Stooped through the sulphurous battle-smoke and perched
Each on the weltering carcase that we loved,
Like its ill angel or its damnèd soul,          520
Riding upon the bosom of the sea.
We saw the dog-fish hastening to their feast.

Joy waked the voiceless people of the sea,
And ravening Famine left his ocean cave
To dwell with War, with us, and with Despair. 525
We met night three hours to the west of Patmos,
And with night, tempest——

   *Mahmud.*                         Cease!

*Enter a Messenger.*

   *Messenger.*                 Your Sublime Highness,
That Christian hound, the Muscovite Ambassador,
Has left the city.—If the rebel fleet
Had anchored in the port, had victory 530
Crowned the Greek legions in the Hippodrome,
Panic were tamer.—Obedience and Mutiny,
Like giants in contention planet-struck,
Stand gazing on each other.—There is peace
In Stamboul.—

   *Mahmud.*    Is the grave not calmer still? 535
Its ruins shall be mine.

   *Hassan.*              Fear not the Russian:
The tiger leagues not with the stag at bay
Against the hunter.—Cunning, base, and cruel,
He crouches, watching till the spoil be won,
And must be paid for his reserve in blood. 540
After the war is fought, yield the sleek Russian
That which thou canst not keep, his deserved portion
Of blood, which shall not flow through streets and fields,
Rivers and seas, like that which we may win,
But stagnate in the veins of Christian slaves! 545

*Enter second Messenger.*

   *Second Messenger.*  Nauplia, Tripolizza, Mothon, Athens,
Navarin, Artas, Monembasia,
Corinth, and Thebes are carried by assault,
And every Islamite who made his dogs
Fat with the flesh of Galilean slaves 550
Passed at the edge of the sword: the lust of blood,
Which made our warriors drunk, is quenched in death;

But like a fiery plague breaks out anew
In deeds which make the Christian cause look pale
In its own light. The garrison of Patras          555
Has store but for ten days, nor is there hope
But from the Briton: at once slave and tyrant,
His wishes still are weaker than his fears,
Or he would sell what faith may yet remain
From the oaths broke in Genoa and in Norway;      560
And if you buy him not, your treasury
Is empty even of promises—his own coin.
The freedman of a western poet-chief
Holds Attica with seven thousand rebels,
And has beat back the Pacha of Negropont:         565
The agèd Ali sits in Yanina
A crownless metaphor of empire:
His name, that shadow of his withered might,
Holds our besieging army like a spell
In prey to famine, pest, and mutiny;              570
He, bastioned in his citadel, looks forth
Joyless upon the sapphire lake that mirrors
The ruins of the city where he reigned
Childless and sceptreless. The Greek has reaped
The costly harvest his own blood matured,         575
Not the sower, Ali—who has bought a truce
From Ypsilanti with ten camel-loads
Of Indian gold.

*Enter a third Messenger.*

*Mahmud.*          What more?
*Third Messenger.*                The Christian tribes
Of Lebanon and the Syrian wilderness
Are in revolt;—Damascus, Hems, Aleppo             580
Tremble;—the Arab menaces Medina,
The Aethiop has intrenched himself in Sennaar,
And keeps the Egyptian rebel well employed,
Who denies homage, claims investiture
As price of tardy aid. Persia demands             585
The cities on the Tigris, and the Georgians

Refuse their living tribute. Crete and Cyprus,
Like mountain-twins that from each other's veins
Catch the volcano-fire and earthquake-spasm,
Shake in the general fever. Through the city,          590
Like birds before a storm, the Santons shriek,
And prophesyings horrible and new
Are heard among the crowd: that sea of men
Sleeps on the wrecks it made, breathless and still.
A Dervise, learnèd in the Koran, preaches             595
That it is written how the sins of Islam
Must raise up a destroyer even now.
The Greeks expect a Saviour from the West,
Who shall not come, men say, in clouds and glory,
But in the omnipresence of that Spirit                600
In which all live and are. Ominous signs
Are blazoned broadly on the noonday sky:
One saw a red cross stamped upon the sun;
It has rained blood; and monstrous births declare
The secret wrath of Nature and her Lord.              605
The army encamped upon the Cydaris
Was roused last night by the alarm of battle,
And saw two hosts conflicting in the air,
The shadows doubtless of the unborn time
Cast on the mirror of the night. While yet            610
The fight hung balanced, there arose a storm
Which swept the phantoms from among the stars.
At the third watch the Spirit of the Plague
Was heard abroad flapping among the tents;
Those who relieved watch found the sentinels dead.    615
The last news from the camp is, that a thousand
Have sickened, and——

*Enter a fourth Messenger.*

*Mahmud.*                  And thou, pale ghost, dim shadow
Of some untimely rumour, speak!
       *Fourth Messenger.*                      One comes
Fainting with toil, covered with foam and blood:
He stood, he says, on Chelonites'                     620

Promontory, which o'erlooks the isles that groan
Under the Briton's frown, and all their waters
Then trembling in the splendour of the moon,
When as the wandering clouds unveiled or hid
Her boundless light, he saw two adverse fleets          625
Stalk through the night in the horizon's glimmer,
Mingling fierce thunders and sulphureous gleams,
And smoke which strangled every infant wind
That soothed the silver clouds through the deep air.
At length the battle slept, but the Sirocco              630
Awoke, and drove his flock of thunder-clouds
Over the sea-horizon, blotting out
All objects—save that in the faint moon-glimpse
He saw, or dreamed he saw, the Turkish admiral
And two the loftiest of our ships of war,                635
With the bright image of that Queen of Heaven
Who hid, perhaps, her face for grief, reversed;
And the abhorrèd cross—

Enter an Attendant.

Attendant.                    Your Sublime Highness,
The Jew, who——
　　Mahmud.          Could not come more seasonably:
Bid him attend. I'll hear no more! too long          640
We gaze on danger through the mist of fear,
And multiply upon our shattered hopes
The images of ruin. Come what will!
To-morrow and to-morrow are as lamps
Set in our path to light us to the edge                645
Through rough and smooth, nor can we suffer aught
Which He inflicts not in whose hand we are.      [Exeunt.

Semichorus I.

Would I were the wingèd cloud
Of a tempest swift and loud!
　　I would scorn                                 650
　　The smile of morn
And the wave where the moonrise is born!

I would leave
The spirits of eve
A shroud for the corpse of the day to weave          655
From other threads than mine!
Bask in the deep blue noon divine.
Who would?   Not I.

*Semichorus II.*

Whither to fly?

*Semichorus I.*

Where the rocks that gird th' Aegean          660
Echo to the battle paean
Of the free—
I would flee
A tempestuous herald of victory!
My golden rain          665
For the Grecian slain
Should mingle in tears with the bloody main,
And my solemn thunder-knell
Should ring to the world the passing-bell
Of Tyranny!          670

*Semichorus II.*

Ah king! wilt thou chain
The rack and the rain?
Wilt thou fetter the lightning and hurricane?
The storms are free,
But we—          675

*Chorus.*

O Slavery! thou frost of the world's prime,
Killing its flowers and leaving its thorns bare!
Thy touch has stamped these limbs with crime,
These brows thy branding garland bear,
But the free heart, the impassive soul          680
Scorn thy control!

*Semichorus I.*

Let there be light! said Liberty,
And like sunrise from the sea,
Athens arose!—Around her born,
Shone like mountains in the morn                    685
Glorious states;—and are they now
Ashes, wrecks, oblivion?

*Semichorus II.*

Go,
Where Thermae and Asopus swallowed
    Persia, as the sand does foam;
Deluge upon deluge followed,                        690
    Discord, Macedon, and Rome:
And lastly thou!

*Semichorus I.*

Temples and towers,
    Citadels and marts, and they
Who live and die there, have been ours,
    And may be thine, and must decay;              695
But Greece and her foundations are
Built below the tide of war,
Based on the crystàlline sea
Of thought and its eternity;
Her citizens, imperial spirits,                     700
    Rule the present from the past,
On all this world of men inherits
    Their seal is set.

*Semichorus II.*

Hear ye the blast,
Whose Orphic thunder thrilling calls
From ruin her Titanian walls?                       705

Whose spirit shakes the sapless bones
　　Of Slavery?  Argos, Corinth, Crete
Hear, and from their mountain thrones
　　The daemons and the nymphs repeat
The harmony.

### Semichorus I.

　　　　I hear! I hear!                                    710

### Semichorus II.

The world's eyeless charioteer,
　　Destiny, is hurrying by!
What faith is crushed, what empire bleeds
Beneath her earthquake-footed steeds?
What eagle-wingèd victory sits                              715
At her right hand? what shadow flits
　　Before? what splendour rolls behind?
　　　　Ruin and renovation cry
'Who but We?'

### Semichorus I.

　　　　I hear! I hear!
The hiss as of a rushing wind,                              720
The roar as of an ocean foaming,
The thunder as of earthquake coming
　　　　　　I hear! I hear!
The crash as of an empire falling,
The shrieks as of a people calling                          725
'Mercy! mercy!'—How they thrill!
Then a shout of 'kill! kill! kill!'
And then a small still voice, thus—

### Semichorus II.

　　　　　　For
Revenge and Wrong bring forth their kind,
　　The foul cubs like their parents are,                   730
Their den is in the guilty mind,
　　And Conscience feeds them with despair.

*Semichorus I.*

In sacred Athens, near the fane
  Of Wisdom, Pity's altar stood:
Serve not the unknown God in vain,                735
But pay that broken shrine again,
  Love for hate and tears for blood.

*Enter* MAHMUD *and* AHASUERUS.

*Mahmud.*  Thou art a man, thou sayest, even as we.
*Ahasuerus.*  No more!
*Mahmud.*             But raised above thy fellow-men
By thought, as I by power.
*Ahasuerus.*             Thou sayest so.        740
*Mahmud.*  Thou art an adept in the difficult lore
Of Greek and Frank philosophy; thou numberest
The flowers, and thou measurest the stars;
Thou severest element from element;
Thy spirit is present in the Past, and sees      745
The birth of this old world through all its cycles
Of desolation and of loveliness,
And when man was not, and how man became
The monarch and the slave of this low sphere,
And all its narrow circles—it is much—           750
I honour thee, and would be what thou art
Were I not what I am; but the unborn hour,
Cradled in fear and hope, conflicting storms,
Who shall unveil? Nor thou, nor I, nor any
Mighty or wise. I apprehended not                755
What thou hast taught me, but I now perceive
That thou art no interpreter of dreams;
Thou dost not own that art, device, or God,
Can make the Future present—let it come!
Moreover thou disdainest us and ours;            760
Thou art as God, whom thou contemplatest.

*Ahasuerus.*  Disdain thee?—not the worm beneath thy feet!
The Fathomless has care for meaner things
Than thou canst dream, and has made pride for those

Who would be what they may not, or would seem        765
That which they are not. Sultan! talk no more
Of thee and me, the Future and the Past;
But look on that which cannot change—the One,
The unborn and the undying. Earth and ocean,
Space, and the isles of life or light that gem        770
The sapphire floods of interstellar air,
This firmament pavilioned upon chaos,
With all its cressets of immortal fire,
Whose outwall, bastioned impregnably
Against the escape of boldest thoughts, repels them   775
As Calpe the Atlantic clouds—this Whole
Of suns, and worlds, and men, and beasts, and flowers,
With all the silent or tempestuous workings
By which they have been, are, or cease to be,
Is but a vision;—all that it inherits                 780
Are motes of a sick eye, bubbles and dreams;
Thought is its cradle and its grave, nor less
The Future and the Past are idle shadows
Of thought's eternal flight—they have no being:
Nought is but that which feels itself to be.          785
    *Mahmud.* What meanest thou? Thy words stream like a
        tempest
Of dazzling mist within my brain—they shake
The earth on which I stand, and hang like night
On Heaven above me. What can they avail?
They cast on all things surest, brightest, best,      790
Doubt, insecurity, astonishment.
    *Ahasuerus.* Mistake me not! All is contained in each.
Dodona's forest to an acorn's cup
Is that which has been, or will be, to that
Which is—the absent to the present. Thought          795
Alone, and its quick elements. Will, Passion,
Reason, Imagination, cannot die;
They are, what that which they regard appears,
The stuff whence mutability can weave
All that it hath dominion o'er, worlds, worms,        800
Empires, and superstitions. What has thought

To do with time, or place, or circumstance?
Wouldst thou behold the Future?—ask and have!
Knock and it shall be opened—look, and lo!
The coming age is shadowed on the Past                    805
As on a glass.
    *Mahmud.*       Wild, wilder thoughts convulse
My spirit—Did not Mahomet the Second
Win Stamboul?
    *Ahasuerus.*      Thou wouldst ask that giant spirit
The written fortunes of thy house and faith.
Thou wouldst cite one out of the grave to tell            810
How what was born in blood must die.
    *Mahmud.*           Thy words
Have power on me! I see——
    *Ahasuerus.*      What hearest thou?
    *Mahmud.*  A far whisper——
Terrible silence.
    *Ahasuerus.*    What succeeds?
    *Mahmud.*         The sound
As of the assault of an imperial city,                    815
The hiss of inextinguishable fire,
The roar of giant cannon; the earthquaking
Fall of vast bastions and precipitous towers,
The shock of crags shot from strange enginery,
The clash of wheels, and clang of armèd hoofs,            820
And crash of brazen mail as of the wreck
Of adamantine mountains—the mad blast
Of trumpets, and the neigh of raging steeds,
The shrieks of women whose thrill jars the blood,
And one sweet laugh, most horrible to hear,               825
As of a joyous infant waked and playing
With its dead mother's breast, and now more loud
The mingled battle-cry,—ha! hear I not
"Ἐν τούτῳ νίκη!'   'Allah-illa-Allah!'?
    *Ahasuerus.*  The sulphurous mist is raised—thou seest—
    *Mahmud.*           A chasm       830
As of two mountains, in the wall of Stamboul;
And in that ghastly breach the Islamites,

Like giants on the ruins of a world,
Stand in the light of sunrise. In the dust
Glimmers a kingless diadem, and one                      835
Of regal port has cast himself beneath
The stream of war. Another proudly clad
In golden arms spurs a Tartarian barb
Into the gap, and with his iron mace
Directs the torrent of that tide of men,                 840
And seems—he is—Mahomet!

   *Ahasuerus.*                          What thou seest
Is but the ghost of thy forgotten dream.
A dream itself, yet less, perhaps, than that
Thou call'st reality. Thou mayst behold
How cities, on which Empire sleeps enthroned,            845
Bow their towered crests to mutability.
Poised by the flood, e'en on the height thou holdest,
Thou mayst now learn how the full tide of power
Ebbs to its depths—Inheritor of glory,
Conceived in darkness, born in blood, and nourished      850
With tears and toil, thou seest the mortal throes
Of that whose birth was but the same. The Past
Now stands before thee like an Incarnation
Of the To-come; yet wouldst thou commune with
That portion of thyself which was ere thou               855
Didst start for this brief race whose crown is death,
Dissolve with that strong faith and fervent passion
Which called it from the uncreated deep,
Yon cloud of war, with its tempestuous phantoms
Of raging death; and draw with mighty will               860
The imperial shade hither.

                       *[Exit* AHASUERUS. *The
Phantom of* MAHOMET THE SECOND *appears.*

*Mahmud.*                          Approach!
*Phantom.*                                    I come
Thence whither thou must go! The grave is fitter
To take the living than give up the dead;
Yet has thy faith prevailed, and I am here.
The heavy fragments of the power which fell              865

When I arose, like shapeless crags and clouds,
Hang round my throne on the abyss, and voices
Of strange lament soothe my supreme repose,
Wailing for glory never to return.—
    A later Empire nods in its decay:                    870
The autumn of a greener faith is come,
And wolfish change, like winter, howls to strip
The foliage in which Fame, the eagle, built
Her aerie, while Dominion whelped below.
The storm is in its branches, and the frost        875
Is on its leaves, and the blank deep expects
Oblivion on oblivion, spoil on spoil,
Ruin on ruin:—Thou art slow, my son;
The Anarchs of the world of darkness keep
A throne for thee, round which thine empire lies    880
Boundless and mute; and for thy subjects thou,
Like us, shalt rule the ghosts of murdered life,
The phantoms of the powers who rule thee now—
Mutinous passions, and conflicting fears,
And hopes that sate themselves on dust, and die!—   885
Stripped of their mortal strength, as thou of thine.
Islam must fall, but we will reign together
Over its ruins in the world of death:—
And if the trunk be dry, yet shall the seed
Unfold itself even in the shape of that            890
Which gathers birth in its decay. Woe! woe!
To the weak people tangled in the grasp
Of its last spasms.
    *Mahmud.*              Spirit, woe to all!
Woe to the wronged and the avenger! Woe
To the destroyer, woe to the destroyed!            895
Woe to the dupe, and woe to the deceiver!
Woe to the oppressed, and woe to the oppressor!
Woe both to those that suffer and inflict;
Those who are born and those who die! but say,
Imperial shadow of the thing I am,                 900
When, how, by whom, Destruction must accomplish
Her consummation!

 *Phantom.*    Ask the cold pale Hour,
Rich in reversion of impending death,
When *he* shall fall upon whose ripe gray hairs
Sit Care, and Sorrow, and Infirmity—
The weight which Crime, whose wings are plumed with years,  905
Leaves in his flight from ravaged heart to heart
Over the heads of men, under which burthen
They bow themselves unto the grave: fond wretch!
He leans upon his crutch, and talks of years    910
To come, and how in hours of youth renewed
He will renew lost joys, and——
 *Voice without.*      Victory! Victory!

            [*The Phantom vanishes.*

 *Mahmud.* What sound of the importunate earth has broken
My mighty trance?
 *Voice without.*   Victory! Victory!
 *Mahmud.* Weak lightning before darkness! poor faint smile
Of dying Islam! Voice which art the response   916
Of hollow weakness! Do I wake and live?
Were there such things, or may the unquiet brain,
Vexed by the wise mad talk of the old Jew,
Have shaped itself these shadows of its fear?   920
It matters not!—for nought we see or dream,
Possess, or lose, or grasp at, can be worth
More than it gives or teaches. Come what may,
The Future must become the Past, and I
As they were to whom once this present hour,   925
This gloomy crag of time to which I cling,
Seemed an Elysian isle of peace and joy
Never to be attained.—I must rebuke
This drunkenness of triumph ere it die,
And dying, bring despair. Victory! poor slaves!   930

              [*Exit* MAHMUD.

 *Voice without.* Shout in the jubilee of death! The Greeks
Are as a brood of lions in the net
Round which the kingly hunters of the earth
Stand smiling. Anarchs, ye whose daily food

Are curses, groans, and gold, the fruit of death, 935
From Thule to the girdle of the world,
Come feast! the board groans with the flesh of men;
The cup is foaming with a nation's blood,
Famine and Thirst await! eat, drink, and die!

### Semichorus I.

   Victorious Wrong, with vulture scream, 940
Salutes the rising sun, pursues the flying day!
   I saw her, ghastly as a tyrant's dream,
Perch on the trembling pyramid of night
Beneath which earth and all her realms pavilioned lay
   In visions of the dawning undelight. 945
      Who shall impede her flight?
      Who rob her of her prey?

*Voice without.* Victory! Victory! Russia's famished eagles
Dare not to prey beneath the crescent's light.
Impale the remnant of the Greeks! despoil! 950
Violate! make their flesh cheaper than dust!

### Semichorus II.

   Thou voice which art
The herald of the ill in splendour hid!
   Thou echo of the hollow heart
Of monarchy, bear me to thine abode 955
   When desolation flashes o'er a world destroyed:
Oh, bear me to those isles of jaggèd cloud
   Which float like mountains on the earthquake, mid
The momentary oceans of the lightning,
   Or to some toppling promontory proud 960
   Of solid tempest whose black pyramid,
Riven, overhangs the founts intensely bright'ning
   Of those dawn-tinted deluges of fire
   Before their waves expire,
When heaven and earth are light, and only light 965
      In the thunder-night!

*Voice without.*  Victory! Victory! Austria, Russia, England,
And that tame serpent, that poor shadow, France,
Cry peace, and that means death when monarchs speak.
Ho, there! bring torches, sharpen those red stakes,            970
These chains are light, fitter for slaves and poisoners
Than Greeks.  Kill! plunder! burn! let none remain.

### Semichorus I.

>     Alas! for Liberty!
If numbers, wealth, or unfulfilling years
    Or fate, can quell the free!                               975
>         Alas! for Virtue, when
Torments, or contumely, or the sneers
        Of erring judging men
    Can break the heart where it abides.
Alas! if Love, whose smile makes this obscure world splendid,
    Can change with its false times and tides,                981
        Like hope and terror,—
            Alas for Love!
And Truth, who wanderest lone and unbefriended,
If thou canst veil thy lie-consuming mirror                    985
    Before the dazzled eyes of Error,
    Alas for thee!  Image of the Above.

### Semichorus II.

>     Repulse, with plumes from conquest torn,
Led the ten thousand from the limits of the morn
        Through many an hostile Anarchy!                       990
At length they wept aloud, and cried, 'The Sea! the Sea!'
    Through exile, persecution, and despair,
        Rome was, and young Atlantis shall become
        The wonder, or the terror, or the tomb
Of all whose step wakes Power lulled in her savage lair:       995
    But Greece was as a hermit-child,
        Whose fairest thoughts and limbs were built
    To woman's growth, by dreams so mild,
        She knew not pain or guilt;
And now, O Victory, blush! and Empire, tremble                 1000

When ye desert the free—
    If Greece must be
A wreck, yet shall its fragments reassemble,
And build themselves again impregnably
    In a diviner clime,                                      1005
To Amphionic music on some Cape sublime,
Which frowns above the idle foam of Time.

### Semichorus I.

Let the tyrants rule the desert they have made;
    Let the free possess the Paradise they claim;
Be the fortune of our fierce oppressors weighed         1010
    With our ruin, our resistance, and our name!

### Semichorus II.

Our dead shall be the seed of their decay,
    Our survivors be the shadow of their pride,
Our adversity a dream to pass away—
    Their dishonour a remembrance to abide!            1015

*Voice without.* Victory! Victory! The bought Briton sends
The keys of ocean to the Islamite—
Now shall the blazon of the cross be veiled,
And British skill directing Othman might
Thunder-strike rebel victory. Oh, keep holy            1020
This jubilee of unrevengèd blood!
Kill! crush! despoil! Let not a Greek escape!

### Semichorus I.

Darkness has dawned in the East
    On the noon of time:
The death-birds descend to their feast                  1025
    From the hungry clime.
Let Freedom and Peace flee far
    To a sunnier strand,
And follow Love's folding-star
    To the Evening land!                                1030

N

*Semichorus II.*

The young moon has fed
  Her exhausted horn
    With the sunset's fire:
  The weak day is dead,
    But the night is not born;                                    1035
And, like loveliness panting with wild desire
  While it trembles with fear and delight,
  Hesperus flies from awakening night,
And pants in its beauty and speed with light
    Fast-flashing, soft, and bright.                             1040
Thou beacon of love! thou lamp of the free!
    Guide us far, far away,
To climes where now veiled by the ardour of day
    Thou art hidden
  From waves on which weary Noon                                 1045
  Faints in her summer swoon,
  Between kingless continents sinless as Eden,
  Around mountains and islands inviolably
    Pranked on the sapphire sea.

*Semichorus I.*

Through the sunset of hope,                                      1050
  Like the shapes of a dream.
What Paradise islands of glory gleam!
  Beneath Heaven's cope,
  Their shadows more clear float by—
The sound of their oceans, the light of their sky,              1055
The music and fragrance their solitudes breathe
Burst, like morning on dream, or like Heaven on death,
    Through the walls of our prison;
  And Greece, which was dead, is arisen!

*Chorus.*

The world's great age begins anew,                              1060
  The golden years return,
  The earth doth like a snake renew
    Her winter weeds outworn:

Heaven smiles, and faiths and empires gleam,
Like wrecks of a dissolving dream.                    1065

A brighter Hellas rears its mountains
    From waves serener far;
A new Peneus rolls his fountains
    Against the morning star.
Where fairer Tempes bloom, there sleep               1070
Young Cyclads on a sunnier deep.

A loftier Argo cleaves the main,
    Fraught with a later prize;
Another Orpheus sings again,
    And loves, and weeps, and dies.                   1075
A new Ulysses leaves once more
Calypso for his native shore.

Oh, write no more the tale of Troy,
    If earth Death's scroll must be!
Nor mix with Laian rage the joy                       1080
    Which dawns upon the free:
Although a subtler Sphinx renew
Riddles of death Thebes never knew.

Another Athens shall arise,
    And to remoter time                               1085
Bequeath, like sunset to the skies,
    The splendour of its prime;
And leave, if nought so bright may live,
All earth can take or Heaven can give.

Saturn and Love their long repose                     1090
    Shall burst, more bright and good
Than all who fell, than One who rose,
    Than many unsubdued:
Not gold, not blood, their altar dowers,
But votive tears and symbol flowers.                  1095

Oh, cease! must hate and death return?
　　Cease! must men kill and die?
Cease! drain not to its dregs the urn
　　Of bitter prophecy.
The world is weary of the past,                    1100
Oh, might it die or rest at last!

# SONG FROM CHARLES THE FIRST

HEIGHO! the lark and the owl!
　　One flies the morning, and one lulls the night:—
Only the nightingale, poor fond soul,
　　Sings like the fool through darkness and light.

'A widow bird sate mourning for her love                    5
　　Upon a wintry bough;
The frozen wind crept on above,
　　The freezing stream below.

'There was no leaf upon the forest bare,
　　No flower upon the ground,                    10
And little motion in the air
　　Except the mill-wheel's sound.'

# THE TRIUMPH OF LIFE

SWIFT as a spirit hastening to his task
Of glory and of good, the Sun sprang forth
Rejoicing in his splendour, and the mask

Of darkness fell from the awakened Earth—
The smokeless altars of the mountain snows                    5
Flamed above crimson clouds, and at the birth

Of light, the Ocean's orison arose,
To which the birds tempered their matin lay.
All flowers in field or forest which unclose

Their trembling eyelids to the kiss of day,　　　10
Swinging their censers in the element,
With orient incense lit by the new ray

Burned slow and inconsumably, and sent
Their odorous sighs up to the smiling air;
And, in succession due, did continent,　　　15

Isle, ocean, and all things that in them wear
The form and character of mortal mould,
Rise as the Sun their father rose, to bear

Their portion of the toil, which he of old
Took as his own, and then imposed on them:　　　20
But I, whom thoughts which must remain untold

Had kept as wakeful as the stars that gem
The cone of night, now they were laid asleep
Stretched my faint limbs beneath the hoary stem

Which an old chestnut flung athwart the steep　　　25
Of a green Apennine: before me fled
The night; behind me rose the day; the deep

Was at my feet, and Heaven above my head,—
When a strange trance over my fancy grew
Which was not slumber, for the shade it spread　　　30

Was so transparent, that the scene came through
As clear as when a veil of light is drawn
O'er evening hills they glimmer; and I knew

That I had felt the freshness of that dawn
Bathe in the same cold dew my brow and hair,                35
And sate as thus upon that slope of lawn

Under the self-same bough, and heard as there
The birds, the fountains and the ocean hold
Sweet talk in music through the enamoured air,
And then a vision on my brain was rolled.                    40


As in that trance of wondrous thought I lay,
This was the tenour of my waking dream:—
Methought I sate beside a public way

Thick strewn with summer dust, and a great stream
Of people there was hurrying to and fro,                     45
Numerous as gnats upon the evening gleam,

All hastening onward, yet none seemed to know
Whither he went, or whence he came, or why
He made one of the multitude, and so

Was borne amid the crowd, as through the sky                 50
One of the million leaves of summer's bier;
Old age and youth, manhood and infancy,

Mixed in one mighty torrent did appear,
Some flying from the thing they feared, and some
Seeking the object of another's fear;                        55

And others, as with steps towards the tomb,
Pored on the trodden worms that crawled beneath,
And others mournfully within the gloom

Of their own shadow walked, and called it death;
And some fled from it as it were a ghost,                    60
Half fainting in the affliction of vain breath:

But more, with motions which each other crossed,
Pursued or shunned the shadows the clouds threw,
Or birds within the noonday aether lost,

Upon that path where flowers never grew,—          65
And, weary with vain toil and faint for thirst,
Heard not the fountains, whose melodious dew

Out of their mossy cells forever burst;
Nor felt the breeze which from the forest told
Of grassy paths and wood-lawns interspersed          70

With overarching elms and caverns cold,
And violet banks where sweet dreams brood, but they
Pursued their serious folly as of old.

And as I gazed, methought that in the way
The throng grew wilder, as the woods of June          75
When the south wind shakes the extinguished day,

And a cold glare, intenser than the noon,
But icy cold, obscured with blinding light
The sun, as he the stars. Like the young moon—

When on the sunlit limits of the night          80
Her white shell trembles amid crimson air,
And whilst the sleeping tempest gathers might—

Doth, as the herald of its coming, bear
The ghost of its dead mother, whose dim form
Bends in dark aether from her infant's chair,—          85

So came a chariot on the silent storm
Of its own rushing splendour, and a Shape
So sate within, as one whom years deform,

Beneath a dusky hood and double cape,
Crouching within the shadow of a tomb;
And o'er what seemed the head a cloud-like crape                    90

Was bent, a dun and faint aethereal gloom
Tempering the light.  Upon the chariot-beam
A Janus-visaged Shadow did assume

The guidance of that wonder-wingèd team;                            95
The shapes which drew it in thick lightenings
Were lost:—I heard alone on the air's soft stream

The music of their ever-moving wings.
All the four faces of that Charioteer
Had their eyes banded; little profit brings                         100

Speed in the van and blindness in the rear,
Nor then avail the beams that quench the sun,—
Or that with banded eyes could pierce the sphere

Of all that is, has been or will be done;
So ill was the car guided—but it passed                            105
With solemn speed majestically on.

The crowd gave way, and I arose aghast,
Or seemed to rise, so mighty was the trance,
And saw, like clouds upon the thunder-blast,

The million with fierce song and maniac dance                      110
Raging around—such seemed the jubilee
As when to greet some conqueror's advance

Imperial Rome poured forth her living sea
From senate-house, and forum, and theatre,
When                          upon the free                         115

Had bound a yoke, which soon they stooped to bear.
Nor wanted here the just similitude
Of a triumphal pageant, for where'er


The chariot rolled, a captive multitude
Was driven;—all those who had grown old in power   120
Or misery,—all who had their age subdued


By action or by suffering, and whose hour
Was drained to its last sand in weal or woe,
So that the trunk survived both fruit and flower;—


All those whose fame or infamy must grow          125
Till the great winter lay the form and name
Of this green earth with them for ever low;—


All but the sacred few who could not tame
Their spirits to the conquerors—but as soon
As they had touched the world with living flame,   130


Fled back like eagles to their native noon,
Or those who put aside the diadem
Of earthly thrones or gems . . .


Were there, of Athens or Jerusalem,
Were neither mid the mighty captives seen,        135
Nor mid the ribald crowd that followed them,


Nor those who went before fierce and obscene.
The wild dance maddens in the van, and those
Who lead it—fleet as shadows on the green,


Outspeed the chariot, and without repose          140
Mix with each other in tempestuous measure
To savage music, wilder as it grows,

They, tortured by their agonizing pleasure,
Convulsed and on the rapid whirlwinds spun
Of that fierce Spirit, whose unholy leisure　　145

Was soothed by mischief since the world begun,
Throw back their heads and loose their streaming hair;
And in their dance round her who dims the sun,

Maidens and youths fling their wild arms in air
As their feet twinkle; they recede, and now　　150
Bending within each other's atmosphere,

Kindle invisibly—and as they glow,
Like moths by light attracted and repelled,
Oft to their bright destruction come and go,

Till like two clouds into one vale impelled,　　155
That shake the mountains when their lightnings mingle
And die in rain—the fiery band which held

Their natures, snaps—while the shock still may tingle;
One falls and then another in the path
Senseless—nor is the desolation single,　　160

Yet ere I can say *where*—the chariot hath
Passed over them—nor other trace I find
But as of foam after the ocean's wrath

Is spent upon the desert shore;—behind,
Old men and women foully disarrayed,　　165
Shake their gray hairs in the insulting wind,

And follow in the dance, with limbs decayed,
Seeking to reach the light which leaves them still
Farther behind and deeper in the shade.

But not the less with impotence of will  170
They wheel, though ghastly shadows interpose
Round them and round each other, and fulfil

Their work, and in the dust from whence they rose
Sink, and corruption veils them as they lie,
And past in these performs what  in those.  175

Struck to the heart by this sad pageantry,
Half to myself I said—'And what is this?
Whose shape is that within the car? And why—'

I would have added—'is all here amiss?—'
But a voice answered—'Life!'—I turned, and knew 180
(O Heaven, have mercy on such wretchedness!)

That what I thought was an old root which grew
To strange distortion out of the hill side,
Was indeed one of those deluded crew,

And that the grass, which methought hung so wide 185
And white, was but his thin discoloured hair,
And that the holes he vainly sought to hide,

Were or had been eyes:—'If thou canst, forbear
To join the dance, which I had well forborne!'
Said the grim Feature (of my thought aware).  190

'I will unfold that which to this deep scorn
Led me and my companions, and relate
The progress of the pageant since the morn;

'If thirst of knowledge shall not then abate,
Follow it thou even to the night, but I  195
Am weary.'—Then like one who with the weight

Of his own words is staggered, wearily
He paused; and ere he could resume, I cried:
'First, who art thou?'—'Before thy memory,

'I feared, loved, hated, suffered, did and died,    200
And if the spark with which Heaven lit my spirit
Had been with purer nutriment supplied,

'Corruption would not now thus much inherit
Of what was once Rousseau,—nor this disguise
Stain that which ought to have disdained to wear it; 205

'If I have been extinguished, yet there rise
A thousand beacons from the spark I bore'—
'And who are those chained to the car?'—'The wise,

'The great, the unforgotten,—they who wore
Mitres and helms and crowns, or wreaths of light,    210
Signs of thought's empire over thought—their lore

'Taught them not this, to know themselves; their might
Could not repress the mystery within,
And for the morn of truth they feigned, deep night

'Caught them ere evening.'—'Who is he with chin    215
Upon his breast, and hands crossed on his chain?'—
'The child of a fierce hour; he sought to win

'The world, and lost all that it did contain
Of greatness, in its hope destroyed; and more
Of fame and peace than virtue's self can gain    220

'Without the opportunity which bore
Him on its eagle pinions to the peak
From which a thousand climbers have before

'Fallen, as Napoleon fell.'—I felt my cheek
Alter, to see the shadow pass away,     225
Whose grasp had left the giant world so weak

That every pigmy kicked it as it lay;
And much I grieved to think how power and will
In opposition rule our mortal day,

And why God made irreconcilable     230
Good and the means of good; and for despair
I half disdained mine eyes' desire to fill

With the spent vision of the times that were
And scarce have ceased to be.—'Dost thou behold,'
Said my guide, 'those spoilers spoiled, Voltaire,     235

'Frederick, and Paul, Catherine, and Leopold,
And hoary anarchs, demagogues, and sage—
    names which the world thinks always old,

'For in the battle Life and they did wage,
She remained conqueror. I was overcome     240
By my own heart alone, which neither age,

'Nor tears, nor infamy, nor now the tomb
Could temper to its object.'—'Let them pass,'
I cried, 'the world and its mysterious doom

'Is not so much more glorious than it was,     245
That I desire to worship those who drew
New figures on its false and fragile glass

'As the old faded.'—'Figures ever new
Rise on the bubble, paint them as you may;
We have but thrown, as those before us threw,     250

'Our shadows on it as it passed away.
But mark how chained to the triumphal chair
The mighty phantoms of an elder day;

'All that is mortal of great Plato there
Expiates the joy and woe his master knew not;        255
The star that ruled his doom was far too fair,

'And life, where long that flower of Heaven grew not,
Conquered that heart by love, which gold, or pain,
Or age, or sloth, or slavery could subdue not.

'And near him walk the    twain,        260
The tutor and his pupil, whom Dominion
Followed as tame as vulture in a chain.

'The world was darkened beneath either pinion
Of him whom from the flock of conquerors
Fame singled out for her thunder-bearing minion;        265

'The other long outlived both woes and wars,
Throned in the thoughts of men, and still had kept
The jealous key of Truth's eternal doors,

'If Bacon's eagle spirit had not lept
Like lightning out of darkness—he compelled        270
The Proteus shape of Nature, as it slept

'To wake, and lead him to the caves that held
The treasure of the secrets of its reign.
See the great bards of elder time, who quelled

'The passions which they sung, as by their strain        275
May well be known: their living melody
Tempers its own contagion to the vein

'Of those who are infected with it—I
Have suffered what I wrote, or viler pain!
And so my words have seeds of misery—          280

'Even as the deeds of others, not as theirs.'
And then he pointed to a company,

'Midst whom I quickly recognized the heirs
Of Caesar's crime, from him to Constantine;
The anarch chiefs, whose force and murderous snares   285

Had founded many a sceptre-bearing line,
And spread the plague of gold and blood abroad:
And Gregory and John, and men divine,

Who rose like shadows between man and God;
Till that eclipse, still hanging over heaven,          290
Was worshipped by the world o'er which they strode,

For the true sun it quenched—'Their power was given
But to destroy,' replied the leader:—'I
Am one of those who have created, even

'If it be but a world of agony.'—                      295
'Whence camest thou? and whither goest thou?
How did thy course begin?' I said, 'and why?

'Mine eyes are sick of this perpetual flow
Of people, and my heart sick of one sad thought—
Speak!'—'Whence I am, I partly seem to know,          300

'And how and by what paths I have been brought
To this dread pass, methinks even thou mayst guess;—
Why this should be, my mind can compass not;

'Whither the conqueror hurries me, still less;—
But follow thou, and from spectator turn              305
Actor or victim in this wretchedness,

'And what thou wouldst be taught I then may learn
From thee. Now listen:—In the April prime,
When all the forest-tips began to burn

'With kindling green, touched by the azure clime     310
Of the young season, I was laid asleep
Under a mountain, which from unknown time

'Had yawned into a cavern, high and deep;
And from it came a gentle rivulet,
Whose water, like clear air, in its calm sweep     315

'Bent the soft grass, and kept for ever wet
The stems of the sweet flowers, and filled the grove
With sounds, which whoso hears must needs forget

'All pleasure and all pain, all hate and love,
Which they had known before that hour of rest;     320
A sleeping mother then would dream not of

'Her only child who died upon the breast
At eventide—a king would mourn no more
The crown of which his brows were dispossessed

'When the sun lingered o'er his ocean floor     325
To gild his rival's new prosperity.
Thou wouldst forget thus vainly to deplore

'Ills, which if ills can find no cure from thee,
The thought of which no other sleep will quell,
Nor other music blot from memory,     330

'So sweet and deep is the oblivious spell;
And whether life had been before that sleep
The Heaven which I imagine, or a Hell

'Like this harsh world in which I wake to weep,
I know not. I arose, and for a space          335
The scene of woods and waters seemed to keep,

'Though it was now broad day, a gentle trace
Of light diviner than the common sun
Sheds on the common earth, and all the place

'Was filled with magic sounds woven into one     340
Oblivious melody, confusing sense
Amid the gliding waves and shadows dun;

'And, as I looked, the bright omnipresence
Of morning through the orient cavern flowed,
And the sun's image radiantly intense          345

'Burned on the waters of the well that glowed
Like gold, and threaded all the forest's maze
With winding paths of emerald fire; there stood

'Amid the sun, as he amid the blaze
Of his own glory, on the vibrating            350
Floor of the fountain, paved with flashing rays,

'A Shape all light, which with one hand did fling
Dew on the earth, as if she were the dawn,
And the invisible rain did ever sing

'A silver music on the mossy lawn;           355
And still before me on the dusky grass,
Iris her many-coloured scarf had drawn:

'In her right hand she bore a crystal glass,
Mantling with bright Nepenthe; the fierce splendour
Fell from her as she moved under the mass         360

'Of the deep cavern, and with palms so tender,
Their tread broke not the mirror of its billow,
Glided along the river, and did bend her

'Head under the dark boughs, till like a willow
Her fair hair swept the bosom of the stream    365
That whispered with delight to be its pillow.

'As one enamoured is upborne in dream
O'er lily-paven lakes, mid silver mist,
To wondrous music, so this shape might seem

'Partly to tread the waves with feet which kissed    370
The dancing foam; partly to glide along
The air which roughened the moist amethyst,

'Or the faint morning beams that fell among
The trees, or the soft shadows of the trees;
And her feet, ever to the ceaseless song    375

'Of leaves, and winds, and waves, and birds, and bees,
And falling drops, moved in a measure new
Yet sweet, as on the summer evening breeze,

'Up from the lake a shape of golden dew
Between two rocks, athwart the rising moon,    380
Dances i' the wind, where never eagle flew;

'And still her feet, no less than the sweet tune
To which they moved, seemed as they moved to blot
The thoughts of him who gazed on them; and soon

'All that was, seemed as if it had been not;    385
And all the gazer's mind was strewn beneath
Her feet like embers; and she, thought by thought,

'Trampled its sparks into the dust of death;
As day upon the threshold of the east
Treads out the lamps of night, until the breath    390

'Of darkness re-illumine even the least
Of heaven's living eyes—like day she came,
Making the night a dream; and ere she ceased

'To move, as one between desire and shame
Suspended, I said—If, as it doth seem,    395
Thou comest from the realm without a name

'Into this valley of perpetual dream,
Show whence I came, and where I am, and why—
Pass not away upon the passing stream.

'Arise and quench thy thirst, was her reply.    400
And as a shut lily stricken by the wand
Of dewy morning's vital alchemy,

'I rose; and, bending at her sweet command,
Touched with faint lips the cup she raised,
And suddenly my brain became as sand    405

'Where the first wave had more than half erased
The track of deer on desert Labrador;
Whilst the wolf, from which they fled amazed·

'Leaves his stamp visibly upon the shore,
Until the second bursts;—so on my sight    410
Burst a new vision, never seen before,

'And the fair shape waned in the coming light,
As veil by veil the silent splendour drops
From Lucifer, amid the chrysolite

'Of sunrise, ere it tinge the mountain-tops;        415
And as the presence of that fairest planet,
Although unseen, is felt by one who hopes

'That his day's path may end as he began it,
In that star's smile, whose light is like the scent
Of a jonquil when evening breezes fan it,        420

'Or the soft note in which his dear lament
The Brescian shepherd breathes, or the caress
That turned his weary slumber to content;

'So knew I in that light's severe excess
The presence of that Shape which on the stream        425
Moved, as I moved along the wilderness,

'More dimly than a day-appearing dream,
The ghost of a forgotten form of sleep;
A light of heaven, whose half-extinguished beam

'Through the sick day in which we wake to weep        430
Glimmers, for ever sought, for ever lost;
So did that shape its obscure tenour keep

'Beside my path, as silent as a ghost;
But the new Vision, and the cold bright car,
With solemn speed and stunning music, crossed        435

'The forest, and as if from some dread war
Triumphantly returning, the loud million
Fiercely extolled the fortune of her star.

'A moving arch of victory, the vermilion
And green and azure plumes of Iris had        440
Built high over her wind-wingèd pavilion,

'And underneath aethereal glory clad
The wilderness, and far before her flew
The tempest of the splendour, which forbade


'Shadow to fall from leaf and stone; the crew          445
Seemed in that light, like atomies to dance
Within a sunbeam;—some upon the new


'Embroidery of flowers, that did enhance
The grassy vesture of the desert, played,
Forgetful of the chariot's swift advance;          450


'Others stood gazing, till within the shade
Of the great mountain its light left them dim;
Others outspeeded it; and others made


'Circles around it, like the clouds that swim
Round the high moon in a bright sea of air;          455
And more did follow, with exulting hymn,


'The chariot and the captives fettered there:—
But all like bubbles on an eddying flood
Fell into the same track at last, and were


'Borne onward.—I among the multitude          460
Was swept—me, sweetest flowers delayed not long;
Me, not the shadow nor the solitude;


'Me, not that falling stream's Lethean song;
Me, not the phantom of that early Form
Which moved upon its motion—but among          465


'The thickest billows of that living storm
I plunged, and bared my bosom to the clime
Of that cold light, whose airs too soon deform.

'Before the chariot had begun to climb
The opposing steep of that mysterious dell,        470
Behold a wonder worthy of the rhyme


'Of him who from the lowest depths of hell,
Through every paradise and through all glory,
Love led serene, and who returned to tell


'The words of hate and awe; the wondrous story        475
How all things are transfigured except Love;
For deaf as is a sea, which wrath makes hoary,


'The world can hear not the sweet notes that move
The sphere whose light is melody to lovers—
A wonder worthy of his rhyme.—The grove        480


'Grew dense with shadows to its inmost covers,
The earth was gray with phantoms, and the air
Was peopled with dim forms, as when there hovers


'A flock of vampire-bats before the glare
Of the tropic sun, bringing, ere evening,        485
Strange night upon some Indian isle;—thus were


'Phantoms diffused around; and some did fling
Shadows of shadows, yet unlike themselves,
Behind them; some like eaglets on the wing


'Were lost in the white day; others like elves        490
Danced in a thousand unimagined shapes
Upon the sunny streams and grassy shelves;


'And others sate chattering like restless apes
On vulgar hands, . . .
Some made a cradle of the ermined capes        495

'Of kingly mantles; some across the tiar
Of pontiffs sate like vultures; others played
Under the crown which girt with empire

'A baby's or an idiot's brow, and made
Their nests in it.  The old anatomies            500
Sate hatching their bare broods under the shade

'Of daemon wings, and laughed from their dead eyes
To reassume the delegated power,
Arrayed in which those worms did monarchize,

'Who made this earth their charnel.  Others more   505
Humble, like falcons, sate upon the fist
Of common men, and round their heads did soar;

'Or like small gnats and flies, as thick as mist
On evening marshes, thronged about the brow
Of lawyers, statesmen, priest and theorist;—     510

'And others, like discoloured flakes of snow
On fairest bosoms and the sunniest hair,
Fell, and were melted by the youthful glow

'Which they extinguished; and, like tears, they were
A veil to those from whose faint lids they rained   515
In drops of sorrow.  I became aware

'Of whence those forms proceeded which thus stained
The track in which we moved.  After brief space,
From every form the beauty slowly waned;

'From every firmest limb and fairest face            520
The strength and freshness fell like dust, and left
The action and the shape without the grace

'Of life. The marble brow of youth was cleft
    With care; and in those eyes where once hope shone,
    Desire, like a lioness bereft                                    525

'Of her last cub, glared ere it died; each one
    Of that great crowd sent forth incessantly
    These shadows, numerous as the dead leaves blown

'In autumn evening from a poplar tree.
    Each like himself and like each other were            530
    At first; but some distorted seemed to be

'Obscure clouds, moulded by the casual air;
    And of this stuff the car's creative ray
    Wrought all the busy phantoms that were there,

'As the sun shapes the clouds; thus on the way      535
    Mask after mask fell from the countenance
    And form of all; and long before the day

'Was old, the joy which waked like heaven's glance
    The sleepers in the oblivious valley, died;
    And some grew weary of the ghastly dance,          540

'And fell, as I have fallen, by the wayside;—
    Those soonest from whose forms most shadows passed,
    And least of strength and beauty did abide.

'Then, what is life? I cried.'—

# EARLY POEMS [1814, 1815]
## STANZAS.—APRIL, 1814

AWAY! the moor is dark beneath the moon,
    Rapid clouds have drank the last pale beam of even:
Away! the gathering winds will call the darkness soon,
    And profoundest midnight shroud the serene lights of heaven.

Pause not! The time is past! Every voice cries, Away!    5
    Tempt not with one last tear thy friend's ungentle mood:
Thy lover's eye, so glazed and cold, dares not entreat thy stay;
    Duty and dereliction guide thee back to solitude.

Away, away! to thy sad and silent home;
    Pour bitter tears on its desolated hearth;    10
Watch the dim shades as like ghosts they go and come,
    And complicate strange webs of melancholy mirth.

The leaves of wasted autumn woods shall float around thine
        head:
    The blooms of dewy spring shall gleam beneath thy feet:
But thy soul or this world must fade in the frost that binds the
        dead,    15
    Ere midnight's frown and morning's smile, ere thou and
        peace may meet.

The cloud shadows of midnight possess their own repose,
    For the weary winds are silent, or the moon is in the deep:
Some respite to its turbulence unresting ocean knows;
    Whatever moves, or toils, or grieves, hath its appointed
        sleep.    20

Thou in the grave shalt rest—yet till the phantoms flee
    Which that house and heath and garden made dear to thee
        erewhile,
Thy remembrance, and repentance, and deep musings are not
        free
    From the music of two voices and the light of one sweet
        smile.

# TO MARY WOLLSTONECRAFT GODWIN

### I

MINE eyes were dim with tears unshed;
    Yes, I was firm—thus wert not thou;—
My baffled looks did fear yet dread
    To meet thy looks—I could not know
How anxiously they sought to shine     5
With soothing pity upon mine.

### II

To sit and curb the soul's mute rage
    Which preys upon itself alone;
To curse the life which is the cage
    Of fettered grief that dares not groan,     10
Hiding from many a careless eye
The scornèd load of agony.

### III

Whilst thou alone, then not regarded,
    The         thou alone should be,
To spend years thus, and be rewarded,     15
    As thou, sweet love, requited me
When none were near—Oh! I did wake
From torture for that moment's sake.

### IV

Upon my heart thy accents sweet
    Of peace and pity fell like dew     20
On flowers half dead;—thy lips did meet
    Mine tremblingly; thy dark eyes threw
Their soft persuasion on my brain,
Charming away its dream of pain.

### V

We are not happy, sweet! our state          25
  Is strange and full of doubt and fear;
More need of words that ills abate;—
  Reserve or censure come not near
Our sacred friendship, lest there be
No solace left for thee and me.             30

### VI

Gentle and good and mild thou art,
  Nor can I live if thou appear
Aught but thyself, or turn thine heart
  Away from me, or stoop to wear
The mask of scorn, although it be           35
To hide the love thou feel'st for me.

## MUTABILITY

WE are as clouds that veil the midnight moon;
  How restlessly they speed, and gleam, and quiver.
Streaking the darkness radiantly!—yet soon
  Night closes round, and they are lost for ever:

Or like forgotten lyres, whose dissonant strings      5
  Give various response to each varying blast,
To whose frail frame no second motion brings
  One mood or modulation like the last.

We rest.—A dream has power to poison sleep;
  We rise.—One wandering thought pollutes the day;
We feel, conceive or reason, laugh or weep;          11
  Embrace fond woe, or cast our cares away:

It is the same!—For, be it joy or sorrow,
  The path of its departure still is free:
Man's yesterday may ne'er be like his morrow;        15
  Nought may endure but Mutability.

# A SUMMER EVENING CHURCHYARD

## LECHLADE, GLOUCESTERSHIRE

THE wind has swept from the wide atmosphere
Each vapour that obscured the sunset's ray;
And pallid Evening twines its beaming hair
In duskier braids around the languid eyes of Day:
Silence and Twilight, unbeloved of men,                    5
Creep hand in hand from yon obscurest glen.

They breathe their spells towards the departing day,
Encompassing the earth, air, stars, and sea;
Light, sound, and motion own the potent sway,
Responding to the charm with its own mystery.             10
The winds are still, or the dry church-tower grass
Knows not their gentle motions as they pass.

Thou too, aëreal Pile! whose pinnacles
Point from one shrine like pyramids of fire,
Obeyest in silence their sweet solemn spells,              15
Clothing in hues of heaven thy dim and distant spire,
Around whose lessening and invisible height
Gather among the stars the clouds of night.

The dead are sleeping in their sepulchres:
And, mouldering as they sleep, a thrilling sound,          20
Half sense, half thought, among the darkness stirs,
Breathed from their wormy beds all living things around,
And mingling with the still night and mute sky
Its awful hush is felt inaudibly.

Thus solemnized and softened, death is mild                25
And terrorless as this serenest night:
Here could I hope, like some inquiring child
Sporting on graves, that death did hide from human sight
Sweet secrets, or beside its breathless sleep
That loveliest dreams perpetual watch did keep.           30

# TO ——[1]

ΔΑΚΡΥΣΙ ΔΙΟΙΣΩ ΠΟΤΜΟΝ 'ΑΠΟΤΜΟΝ.

OH! there are spirits of the air,
  And genii of the evening breeze,
And gentle ghosts, with eyes as fair
  As star-beams among twilight trees:—
Such lovely ministers to meet    5
Oft hast thou turned from men thy lonely feet.

With mountain winds, and babbling springs,
  And moonlight seas, that are the voice
Of these inexplicable things,
  Thou didst hold commune, and rejoice    10
When they did answer thee; but they
Cast, like a worthless boon, thy love away.

And thou hast sought in starry eyes
  Beams that were never meant for thine,
Another's wealth:—tame sacrifice    15
  To a fond faith! still dost thou pine?
Still dost thou hope that greeting hands,
Voice, looks, or lips, may answer thy demands?

Ah! wherefore didst thou build thine hope
  On the false earth's inconstancy?    20
Did thine own mind afford no scope
  Of love, or moving thoughts to thee?
That natural scenes or human smiles
Could steal the power to wind thee in their wiles?

Yes, all the faithless smiles are fled    25
  Whose falsehood left thee broken-hearted;
The glory of the moon is dead;
  Night's ghosts and dreams have now departed;
Thine own soul still is true to thee,
But changed to a foul fiend through misery.    30

[1] Mrs. Shelley suggested that in this poem Shelley was addressing Coleridge, but Edward Dowden, in his *Life of Shelley*, wonders "whether it was
not rather addressed in a despondent mood by Shelley to his own spirit.—ED.

This fiend, whose ghastly presence ever
    Beside thee like thy shadow hangs,
Dream not to chase;—the mad endeavour
    Would scourge thee to severer pangs.
Be as thou art. Thy settled fate,        35
Dark as it is, all change would aggravate.

## TO WORDSWORTH

POET of Nature, thou hast wept to know
That things depart which never may return:
Childhood and youth, friendship and love's first glow,
Have fled like sweet dreams, leaving thee to mourn.
These common woes I feel. One loss is mine     5
Which thou too feel'st, yet I alone deplore.
Thou wert as a lone star, whose light did shine
On some frail bark in winter's midnight roar:
Thou hast like to a rock-built refuge stood
Above the blind and battling multitude:     10
In honoured poverty thy voice did weave
Songs consecrate to truth and liberty,—
Deserting these, thou leavest me to grieve,
Thus having been, that thou shouldst cease to be.

## FEELINGS OF A REPUBLICAN ON THE FALL OF BONAPARTE

I HATED thee, fallen tyrant! I did groan
To think that a most unambitious slave,
Like thou, shouldst dance and revel on the grave
Of Liberty. Thou mightst have built thy throne
Where it had stood even now: thou didst prefer     5
A frail and bloody pomp which Time has swept
In fragments towards Oblivion. Massacre,
For this I prayed, would on thy sleep have crept,
Treason and Slavery, Rapine, Fear, and Lust,
And stifled thee, their minister. I know     10

Too late, since thou and France are in the dust,
That Virtue owns a more eternal foe
Than Force or Fraud: old Custom, legal Crime.
And bloody Faith the foulest birth of Time.


## LINES: NOVEMBER 1815

### I

THE cold earth slept below,
　Above the cold sky shone;
And all around, with a chilling sound,
　From caves of ice and fields of snow,
　The breath of night like death did flow　　5
　　Beneath the sinking moon.

### II

The wintry hedge was black,
　The green grass was not seen,
The birds did rest on the bare thorn's breast,
　Whose roots, beside the pathway track,　　10
　Had bound their folds o'er many a crack
　　Which the frost had made between.

### III

Thine eyes glowed in the glare
　Of the moon's dying light;
As a fen-fire's beam on a sluggish stream　　15
　Gleams dimly, so the moon shone there,
　And it yellowed the strings of thy raven hair,
　　That shook in the wind of night.

### IV

The moon made thy lips pale, beloved—
　The wind made thy bosom chill—　　20
The night did shed on thy dear head
　Its frozen dew, and thou didst lie
　Where the bitter breath of the naked sky
　　Might visit thee at will.

# POEMS WRITTEN IN 1816
## HYMN TO INTELLECTUAL BEAUTY

I

THE awful shadow of some unseen Power
   Floats though unseen among us,—visiting
   This various world with as inconstant wing
As summer winds that creep from flower to flower,—
Like moonbeams that behind some piny mountain shower,
     It visits with inconstant glance       6
     Each human heart and countenance;
Like hues and harmonies of evening,—
     Like clouds in starlight widely spread,—
     Like memory of music fled,—      10
     Like aught that for its grace may be
Dear, and yet dearer for its mystery.

II

Spirit of BEAUTY, that dost consecrate
   With thine own hues all thou dost shine upon
   Of human thought or form,—where art thou gone? 15
Why dost thou pass away and leave our state,
This dim vast vale of tears, vacant and desolate?
     Ask why the sunlight not for ever
     Weaves rainbows o'er yon mountain-river,
Why aught should fail and fade that once is shown,   20
     Why fear and dream and death and birth
     Cast on the daylight of this earth
     Such gloom,—why man has such a scope
For love and hate, despondency and hope?

III

No voice from some sublimer world hath ever     25
     To sage or poet these responses given—
     Therefore the names of Demon, Ghost, and Heaven,
Remain the records of their vain endeavour,

**BYRON**

*From a painting of 1825, after Richard Westall. Now in the National Portrait Gallery, London.*

Frail spells—whose uttered charm might not avail to sever,
  From all we hear and all we see,      30
  Doubt, chance, and mutability.
Thy light alone—like mist o'er mountains driven,
  Or music by the night-wind sent
  Through strings of some still instrument,
  Or moonlight on a midnight stream,     35
Gives grace and truth to life's unquiet dream.


IV

Love, Hope, and Self-esteem, like clouds depart
  And come, for some uncertain moments lent.
  Man were immortal, and omnipotent,
Didst thou, unknown and awful as thou art,    40
Keep with thy glorious train firm state within his heart.
  Thou messenger of sympathies,
  That wax and wane in lovers' eyes—
Thou—that to human thought art nourishment,
  Like darkness to a dying flame!      45
  Depart not as thy shadow came,
  Depart not—lest the grave should be,
Like life and fear, a dark reality.


V

While yet a boy I sought for ghosts, and sped
  Through many a listening chamber, cave and ruin, 50
  And starlight wood, with fearful steps pursuing
Hopes of high talk with the departed dead.
I called on poisonous names with which our youth is fed;
  I was not heard—I saw them not—
  When musing deeply on the lot      55
Of life, at that sweet time when winds are wooing
  All vital things that woke to bring
  News of birds and blossoming,—
  Sudden, thy shadow fell on me;
I shrieked, and clasped my hands in ecstasy!    60

o

## VI

I vowed that I would dedicate my powers
   To thee and thine—have I not kept the vow?
   With beating heart and streaming eyes, even now
I call the phantoms of a thousand hours
Each from his voiceless grave: they have in visioned bowers
      Of studious zeal or love's delight      66
      Outwatched with me the envious night—
They know that never joy illumed my brow
      Unlinked with hope that thou wouldst free
      This world from its dark slavery,      70
      That thou—O awful LOVELINESS,
Wouldst give whate'er these words cannot express.

## VII

The day becomes more solemn and serene
   When noon is past—there is a harmony
   In autumn, and a lustre in its sky,      75
Which through the summer is not heard or seen,
As if it could not be, as if it had not been!
      Thus let thy power, which like the truth
      Of nature on my passive youth
   Descended, to my onward life supply      80
      Its calm—to one who worships thee,
      And every form containing thee,
      Whom, SPIRIT fair, thy spells did bind
   To fear himself, and love all human kind.

# MONT BLANC

### LINES WRITTEN IN THE VALE OF CHAMOUNI

## I

THE everlasting universe of things
Flows through the mind, and rolls its rapid waves,
Now dark—now glittering—now reflecting gloom—

Now lending splendour, where from secret springs
The source of human thought its tribute brings 5
Of waters, — with a sound but half its own,
Such as a feeble brook will oft assume
In the wild woods, among the mountains lone,
Where waterfalls around it leap for ever,
Where woods and winds contend, and a vast river 10
Over its rocks ceaselessly bursts and raves.

II

Thus thou, Ravine of Arve—dark, deep Ravine—
Thou many-coloured, many-voicèd vale,
Over whose pines, and crags, and caverns sail
Fast cloud-shadows and sunbeams: awful scene, 15
Where Power in likeness of the Arve comes down
From the ice-gulfs that gird his secret throne,
Bursting through these dark mountains like the flame
Of lightning through the tempest;—thou dost lie,
Thy giant brood of pines around thee clinging, 20
Children of elder time, in whose devotion
The chainless winds still come and ever came
To drink their odours, and their mighty swinging
To hear—an old and solemn harmony;
Thine earthly rainbows stretched across the sweep 25
Of the aethereal waterfall, whose veil
Robes some unsculptured image; the strange sleep
Which when the voices of the desert fail
Wraps all in its own deep eternity;—
Thy caverns echoing to the Arve's commotion, 30
A loud, lone sound no other sound can tame;
Thou art pervaded with that ceaseless motion,
Thou art the path of that unresting sound—
Dizzy Ravine! and when I gaze on thee
I seem as in a trance sublime and strange 35
To muse on my own separate fantasy,
My own, my human mind, which passively
Now renders and receives fast influencings,
Holding an unremitting interchange

With the clear universe of things around;                    40
One legion of wild thoughts, whose wandering wings
Now float above thy darkness, and now rest
Where that or thou art no unbidden guest,
In the still cave of the witch Poesy,
Seeking among the shadows that pass by                       45
Ghosts of all things that are, some shade of thee,
Some phantom, some faint image; till the breast
From which they fled recalls them, thou art there!

III
Some say that gleams of a remoter world
Visit the soul in sleep,—that death is slumber,             50
And that its shapes the busy thoughts outnumber
Of those who wake and live.—I look on high;
Has some unknown omnipotence unfurled
The veil of life and death? or do I lie
In dream, and does the mightier world of sleep              55
Spread far around and inaccessibly
Its circles? For the very spirit fails,
Driven like a homeless cloud from steep to steep
That vanishes among the viewless gales!
Far, far above, piercing the infinite sky,                  60
Mont Blanc appears,—still, snowy, and serene—
Its subject mountains their unearthly forms
Pile around it, ice and rock; broad vales between
Of frozen floods, unfathomable deeps,
Blue as the overhanging heaven, that spread                 65
And wind among the accumulated steeps;
A desert peopled by the storms alone,
Save when the eagle brings some hunter's bone,
And the wolf tracks her there—how hideously
Its shapes are heaped around! rude, bare, and high,         70
Ghastly, and scarred, and riven.—Is this the scene
Where the old Earthquake-daemon taught her young
Ruin? Were these their toys? or did a sea
Of fire envelop once this silent snow?
None can reply—all seems eternal now.                       75

The wilderness has a mysterious tongue
Which teaches awful doubt, or faith so mild,
So solemn, so serene, that man may be,
But for such faith, with nature reconciled;
Thou hast a voice, great Mountain, to repeal          80
Large codes of fraud and woe; not understood
By all, but which the wise, and great, and good
Interpret, or make felt, or deeply feel.

IV

The fields, the lakes, the forests, and the streams,
Ocean, and all the living things that dwell          85
Within the daedal earth; lightning, and rain,
Earthquake, and fiery flood, and hurricane,
The torpor of the year when feeble dreams
Visit the hidden buds, or dreamless sleep
Holds every future leaf and flower;—the bound        90
With which from that detested trance they leap;
The works and ways of man, their death and birth,
And that of him and all that his may be;
All things that move and breathe with toil and sound
Are born and die; revolve, subside, and swell.       95
Power dwells apart in its tranquillity,
Remote, serene, and inaccessible:
And *this*, the naked countenance of earth,
On which I gaze, even these primaeval mountains
Teach the adverting mind. The glaciers creep         100
Like snakes that watch their prey, from their far fountains,
Slow rolling on; there, many a precipice,
Frost and the Sun in scorn of mortal power
Have piled: dome, pyramid, and pinnacle,
A city of death, distinct with many a tower          105
And wall impregnable of beaming ice.
Yet not a city, but a flood of ruin
Is there, that from the boundaries of the sky
Rolls its perpetual stream; vast pines are strewing
Its destined path, or in the mangled soil            110
Branchless and shattered stand; the rocks, drawn down

From yon remotest waste, have overthrown
The limits of the dead and living world,
Never to be reclaimed.  The dwelling-place
Of insects, beasts, and birds, becomes its spoil;        115
Their food and their retreat for ever gone,
So much of life and joy is lost.  The race
Of man flies far in dread; his work and dwelling
Vanish, like smoke before the tempest's stream,
And their place is not known.  Below, vast caves        120
Shine in the rushing torrent's restless gleam,
Which from those secret chasms in tumult welling
Meet in the vale, and one majestic River,
The breath and blood of distant lands, for ever
Rolls its loud waters to the ocean-waves,               125
Breathes its swift vapours to the circling air.

v

Mont Blanc yet gleams on high:—the power is there,
The still and solemn power of many sights,
And many sounds, and much of life and death.
In the calm darkness of the moonless nights,            130
In the lone glare of day, the snows descend
Upon that Mountain; none beholds them there,
Nor when the flakes burn in the sinking sun,
Or the star-beams dart through them:—Winds contend
Silently there, and heap the snow with breath           135
Rapid and strong, but silently!  Its home
The voiceless lightning in these solitudes
Keeps innocently, and like vapour broods
Over the snow.  The secret Strength of things
Which governs thought, and to the infinite dome         140
Of Heaven is as a law, inhabits thee!
And what were thou, and earth, and stars, and sea,
If to the human mind's imaginings
Silence and solitude were vacancy?

　　*July* 23, 1816.

# POEMS WRITTEN IN 1817

## TO CONSTANTIA, SINGING

### I

Thus to be lost and thus to sink and die,
  Perchance were death indeed!—Constantia, turn!
In thy dark eyes a power like light doth lie,
  Even though the sounds which were thy voice, which burn
Between thy lips, are laid to sleep;                    5
  Within thy breath, and on thy hair, like odour, it is yet,
And from thy touch like fire doth leap.
  Even while I write, my burning cheeks are wet,
  Alas, that the torn heart can bleed, but not forget!

### II

A breathless awe, like the swift change            10
  Unseen, but felt in youthful slumbers,
Wild, sweet, but uncommunicably strange,
  Thou breathest now in fast ascending numbers.
The cope of heaven seems rent and cloven
  By the enchantment of thy strain,                15
And on my shoulders wings are woven,
  To follow its sublime career
Beyond the mighty moons that wane
  Upon the verge of Nature's utmost sphere,
  Till the world's shadowy walls are past and disappear.   20

### III

Her voice is hovering o'er my soul—it lingers
  O'ershadowing it with soft and lulling wings,
The blood and life within those snowy fingers
  Teach witchcraft to the instrumental strings.

My brain is wild, my breath comes quick—        25
  The blood is listening in my frame,
And thronging shadows, fast and thick,
  Fall on my overflowing eyes;
My heart is quivering like a flame;
  As morning dew, that in the sunbeam dies,      30
  I am dissolved in these consuming ecstasies.


### IV

I have no life, Constantia, now, but thee,
  Whilst, like the world-surrounding air, thy song
Flows on, and fills all things with melody.—
  Now is thy voice a tempest swift and strong,     35
On which, like one in trance upborne,
  Secure o'er rocks and waves I sweep,
Rejoicing like a cloud of morn.
  Now 'tis the breath of summer night,
Which when the starry waters sleep,      40
  Round western isles, with incense-blossoms bright,
  Lingering, suspends my soul in its voluptuous flight.


## TO THE LORD CHANCELLOR

### I

THY country's curse is on thee, darkest crest
  Of that foul, knotted, many-headed worm
Which rends our Mother's bosom—Priestly Pest!
  Masked Resurrection of a buried Form!


### II

Thy country's curse is on thee! Justice sold,     5
  Truth trampled, Nature's landmarks overthrown,
And heaps of fraud-accumulated gold,
  Plead, loud as thunder, at Destruction's throne.

### III

And, whilst that sure slow Angel which aye stands
  Watching the beck of Mutability        10
Delays to execute her high commands,
  And, though a nation weeps, spares thine and thee,

### IV

Oh, let a father's curse be on thy soul,
  And let a daughter's hope be on thy tomb;
Be both, on thy gray head, a leaden cowl      15
  To weigh thee down to thine approaching doom!

### V

I curse thee by a parent's outraged love,
  By hopes long cherished and too lately lost,
By gentle feelings thou couldst never prove,
  By griefs which thy stern nature never crossed;    20

### VI

By those infantine smiles of happy light,
  Which were a fire within a stranger's hearth,
Quenched even when kindled, in untimely night
  Hiding the promise of a lovely birth:

### VII

By those unpractised accents of young speech,    25
  Which he who is a father thought to frame
To gentlest lore, such as the wisest teach—
  *Thou* strike the lyre of mind!—oh, grief and shame!

### VIII

By all the happy see in children's growth—
  That undeveloped flower of budding years—    30
Sweetness and sadness interwoven both,
  Source of the sweetest hopes and saddest fears—

### IX

By all the days, under an hireling's care,
    Of dull constraint and bitter heaviness,—
O wretched ye if ever any were,—        35
    Sadder than orphans, yet not fatherless!


### X

By the false cant which on their innocent lips
    Must hang like poison on an opening bloom,
By the dark creeds which cover with eclipse
    Their pathway from the cradle to the tomb—    40


### XI

By thy most impious Hell, and all its terror;
    By all the grief, the madness, and the guilt
Of thine impostures, which must be their error—
    That sand on which thy crumbling power is built—


### XII

By thy complicity with lust and hate—    45
    Thy thirst for tears—thy hunger after gold—
The ready frauds which ever on thee wait—
    The servile arts in which thou hast grown old—


### XIII

By thy most killing sneer, and by thy smile—
    By all the arts and snares of thy black den,    50
And—for thou canst outweep the crocodile—
    By thy false tears—those millstones braining men—


### XIV

By all the hate which checks a father's love—
    By all the scorn which kills a father's care—
By those most impious hands which dared remove    55
    Nature's high bounds—by thee—and by despair—

### XV

Yes, the despair which bids a father groan,
 And cry, 'My children are no longer mine—
The blood within those veins may be mine own,
 But—Tyrant—their polluted souls are thine;—'  60

### XVI

I curse thee—though I hate thee not.—O slave!
 If thou couldst quench the earth-consuming Hell
Of which thou art a daemon, on thy grave
 This curse should be a blessing.  Fare thee well!

## TO WILLIAM SHELLEY

### I

THE billows on the beach are leaping around it,
 The bark is weak and frail,
The sea looks black, and the clouds that bound it
 Darkly strew the gale.
Come with me, thou delightful child,   5
Come with me, though the wave is wild,
And the winds are loose, we must not stay,
Or the slaves of the law may rend thee away.

### II

They have taken thy brother and sister dear,
 They have made them unfit for thee;  10
They have withered the smile and dried the tear
 Which should have been sacred to me.
To a blighting faith and a cause of crime
They have bound them slaves in youthly prime,
And they will curse my name and thee  15
Because we fearless are and free.

### III

Come thou, belovèd as thou art;
  Another sleepeth still
Near thy sweet mother's anxious heart,
  Which thou with joy shalt fill,                              20
With fairest smiles of wonder thrown
On that which is indeed our own,
And which in distant lands will be
The dearest playmate unto thee.

### IV

Fear not the tyrants will rule for ever,                      25
  Or the priests of the evil faith;
They stand on the brink of that raging river,
  Whose waves they have tainted with death.
It is fed from the depth of a thousand dells,
Around them it foams and rages and swells;                    30
And their swords and their sceptres I floating see,
Like wrecks on the surge of eternity.

### V

Rest, rest, and shriek not, thou gentle child!
  The rocking of the boat thou fearest,
And the cold spray and the clamour wild?—                     35
  There, sit between us two, thou dearest—
Me and thy mother—well we know
The storm at which thou tremblest so,
With all its dark and hungry graves,
Less cruel than the savage slaves                             40
Who hunt us o'er these sheltering waves.

### VI

This hour will in thy memory
  Be a dream of days forgotten long,
We soon shall dwell by the azure sea
Of serene and golden Italy,                                   45
Or Greece, the Mother of the free;

And I will teach thine infant tongue
To call upon those heroes old
In their own language, and will mould
Thy growing spirit in the flame     50
Of Grecian lore, that by such name
A patriot's birthright thou mayst claim!


## ON FANNY GODWIN

HER voice did quiver as we parted,
   Yet knew I not that heart was broken
From which it came, and I departed
   Heeding not the words then spoken.
     Misery—O Misery,     5
     This world is all too wide for thee.


## LINES

### I

THAT time is dead for ever, child!
Drowned, frozen, dead for ever!
   We look on the past
   And stare aghast
At the spectres wailing, pale and ghast,     5
Of hopes which thou and I beguiled
   To death on life's dark river.

### II

The stream we gazed on then rolled by;
Its waves are unreturning;
   But we yet stand     10
   In a lone land,
Like tombs to mark the memory
Of hopes and fears, which fade and flee
   In the light of life's dim morning.

# DEATH

### I

THEY die—the dead return not—Misery
  Sits near an open grave and calls them over,
A Youth with hoary hair and haggard eye—
  They are the names of kindred, friend and lover,
Which he so feebly calls—they all are gone—                    5
Fond wretch, all dead! those vacant names alone,
    This most familiar scene, my pain—
    These tombs—alone remain.

### II

Misery, my sweetest friend—oh, weep no more!
  Thou wilt not be consoled—I wonder not!                      10
For I have seen thee from thy dwelling's door
  Watch the calm sunset with them, and this spot
Was even as bright and calm, but transitory,
And now thy hopes are gone, thy hair is hoary;
    This most familiar scene, my pain—                         15
    These tombs—alone remain.


# OZYMANDIAS

I MET a traveller from an antique land
Who said: Two vast and trunkless legs of stone
Stand in the desert . . . Near them, on the sand,
Half sunk, a shattered visage lies, whose frown,
And wrinkled lip, and sneer of cold command,                   5
Tell that its sculptor well those passions read
Which yet survive, stamped on these lifeless things,
The hand that mocked them, and the heart that fed:
And on the pedestal these words appear:
'My name is Ozymandias, king of kings:                         10
Look on my works, ye Mighty, and despair!'
Nothing beside remains. Round the decay
Of that colossal wreck, boundless and bare
The lone and level sands stretch far away.

# POEMS WRITTEN IN 1818

## TO THE NILE

MONTH after month the gathered rains descend
Drenching yon secret Aethiopian dells,
And from the desert's ice-girt pinnacles
Where Frost and Heat in strange embraces blend
On Atlas, fields of moist snow half depend.                    5
Girt there with blasts and meteors Tempest dwells
By Nile's aëreal urn, with rapid spells
Urging those waters to their mighty end.
O'er Egypt's land of Memory floods are level
And they are thine, O Nile—and well thou knowest   10
That soul-sustaining airs and blasts of evil
And fruits and poisons spring where'er thou flowest.
Beware, O Man—for knowledge must to thee,
Like the great flood to Egypt, ever be.

## PASSAGE OF THE APENNINE

LISTEN, listen, Mary mine,
To the whisper of the Apennine,
It bursts on the roof like the thunder's roar,
Or like the sea on a northern shore,
Heard in its raging ebb and flow                               5
By the captives pent in the cave below.
The Apennine in the light of day
Is a mighty mountain dim and gray,
Which between the earth and sky doth lay;
But when night comes, a chaos dread                            10
On the dim starlight then is spread,
And the Apennine walks abroad with the storm.

## THE PAST

### I

WILT thou forget the happy hours
Which we buried in Love's sweet bowers,
Heaping over their corpses cold
Blossoms and leaves, instead of mould?
  Blossoms which were the joys that fell,      5
    And leaves, the hopes that yet remain.

### II

Forget the dead, the past? Oh, yet
There are ghosts that may take revenge for it,
Memories that make the heart a tomb,
Regrets which glide through the spirit's gloom,      10
  And with ghastly whispers tell
    That joy, once lost, is pain.

## ON A FADED VIOLET

### I

THE odour from the flower is gone
  Which like thy kisses breathed on me;
The colour from the flower is flown
  Which glowed of thee and only thee!

### II

A shrivelled, lifeless, vacant form,      5
  It lies on my abandoned breast,
And mocks the heart which yet is warm,
  With cold and silent rest.

### III

I weep,—my tears revive it not!
  I sigh,—it breathes no more on me      10
Its mute and uncomplaining lot
  Is such as mine should be.

# LINES WRITTEN AMONG THE EUGANEAN HILLS

### OCTOBER, 1818.

MANY a green isle needs must be
In the deep wide sea of Misery,
Or the mariner, worn and wan,
Never thus could voyage on—
Day and night, and night and day,     5
Drifting on his dreary way,
With the solid darkness black
Closing round his vessel's track;
Whilst above the sunless sky,
Big with clouds, hangs heavily,     10
And behind the tempest fleet
Hurries on with lightning feet,
Riving sail, and cord, and plank,
Till the ship has almost drank
Death from the o'er-brimming deep;     15
And sinks down, down, like that sleep
When the dreamer seems to be
Weltering through eternity;
And the dim low line before
Of a dark and distant shore     20
Still recedes, as ever still
Longing with divided will,
But no power to seek or shun,
He is ever drifted on
O'er the unreposing wave     25
To the haven of the grave.
What, if there no friends will greet;
What, if there no heart will meet
His with love's impatient beat;
Wander wheresoe'er he may,     30
Can he dream before that day

To find refuge from distress
In friendship's smile, in love's caress?
Then 'twill wreak him little woe
Whether such there be or no:                          35
Senseless is the breast, and cold,
Which relenting love would fold;
Bloodless are the veins and chill
Which the pulse of pain did fill;
Every little living nerve                              40
That from bitter words did swerve
Round the tortured lips and brow,
Are like sapless leaflets now
Frozen upon December's bough.

On the beach of a northern sea                        45
Which tempests shake eternally,
As once the wretch there lay to sleep
Lies a solitary heap,
One white skull and seven dry bones,
On the margin of the stones,                          50
Where a few gray rushes stand,
Boundaries of the sea and land:
Nor is heard one voice of wail
But the sea-mews, as they sail
O'er the billows of the gale;                         55
Or the whirlwind up and down
Howling, like a slaughtered town,
When a king in glory rides
Through the pomp of fratricides:
Those unburied bones around                           60
There is many a mournful sound;
There is no lament for him,
Like a sunless vapour, dim,
Who once clothed with life and thought
What now moves nor murmurs not.                       65

Ay, many flowering islands lie
In the waters of wide Agony:

To such a one this morn was led,
My bark by soft winds piloted:
'Mid the mountains Euganean                        70
I stood listening to the paean
With which the legioned rooks did hail
The sun's uprise majestical;
Gathering round with wings all hoar,
Through the dewy mist they soar                    75
Like gray shades, till the eastern heaven
Bursts, and then, as clouds of even,
Flecked with fire and azure, lie
In the unfathomable sky,
So their plumes of purple grain,                   80
Starred with drops of golden rain,
Gleam above the sunlight woods,
As in silent multitudes
On the morning's fitful gale
Through the broken mist they sail,                 85
And the vapours cloven and gleaming
Follow, down the dark steep streaming,
Till all is bright, and clear, and still,
Round the solitary hill.

Beneath is spread like a green sea                 90
The waveless plain of Lombardy,
Bounded by the vaporous air,
Islanded by cities fair;
Underneath Day's azure eyes
Ocean's nursling, Venice lies,                     95
A peopled labyrinth of walls,
Amphitrite's destined halls,
Which her hoary sire now paves
With his blue and beaming waves.
Lo! the sun upsprings behind,                      100
Broad, red, radiant, half-reclined
On the level quivering line
Of the waters crystalline;
And before that chasm of light,

As within a furnace bright,                105
Column, tower, and dome, and spire,
Shine like obelisks of fire,
Pointing with inconstant motion
From the altar of dark ocean
To the sapphire-tinted skies;              110
As the flames of sacrifice
From the marble shrines did rise,
As to pierce the dome of gold
Where Apollo spoke of old.

Sun-girt City, thou hast been              115
Ocean's child, and then his queen;
Now is come a darker day,
And thou soon must be his prey,
If the power that raised thee here
Hallow so thy watery bier.                 120
A less drear ruin then than now,
With thy conquest-branded brow
Stooping to the slave of slaves
From thy throne, among the waves
Wilt thou be, when the sea-mew             125
Flies, as once before it flew,
O'er thine isles depopulate,
And all is in its ancient state,
Save where many a palace gate
With green sea-flowers overgrown           130
Like a rock of Ocean's own,
Topples o'er the abandoned sea
As the tides change sullenly.
The fisher on his watery way,
Wandering at the close of day,             135
Will spread his sail and seize his oar
Till he pass the gloomy shore,
Lest thy dead should, from their sleep
Bursting o'er the starlight deep,
Lead a rapid masque of death               140
O'er the waters of his path.

Those who alone thy towers behold
Quivering through aëreal gold,
As I now behold them here,
Would imagine not they were          145
Sepulchres, where human forms,
Like pollution-nourished worms,
To the corpse of greatness cling,
Murdered, and now mouldering:
But if Freedom should awake          150
In her omnipotence, and shake
From the Celtic Anarch's hold
All the keys of dungeons cold,
Where a hundred cities lie
Chained like thee, ingloriously,     155
Thou and all thy sister band
Might adorn this sunny land,
Twining memories of old time
With new virtues more sublime;
If not, perish thou and they!—       160
Clouds which stain truth's rising day
By her sun consumed away—
Earth can spare ye: while like flowers,
In the waste of years and hours,
From your dust new nations spring    165
With more kindly blossoming.


Perish—let there only be
Floating o'er thy hearthless sea
As the garment of thy sky
Clothes the world immortally,        170
One remembrance, more sublime
Than the tattered pall of time,
Which scarce hides thy visage wan;—
That a tempest-cleaving Swan
Of the songs of Albion,              175
Driven from his ancestral streams
By the might of evil dreams,

Found a nest in thee; and Ocean
Welcomed him with such emotion
That its joy grew his, and sprung                    180
From his lips like music flung
O'er a mighty thunder-fit,
Chastening terror:—what though yet
Poesy's unfailing River,
Which through Albion winds forever                  185
Lashing with melodious wave
Many a sacred Poet's grave,
Mourn its latest nursling fled?
What though thou with all thy dead
Scarce can for this fame repay                       190
Aught thine own? oh, rather say
Though thy sins and slaveries foul
Overcloud a sunlike soul?
As the ghost of Homer clings
Round Scamander's wasting springs;                  195
As divinest Shakespeare's might
Fills Avon and the world with light
Like omniscient power which he
Imaged 'mid mortality;
As the love from Petrarch's urn,                    200
Yet amid yon hills doth burn,
A quenchless lamp by which the heart
Sees things unearthly;—so thou art,
Mighty spirit—so shall be
The City that did refuge thee.                      205


Lo, the sun floats up the sky
Like thought-wingèd Liberty,
Till the universal light
Seems to level plain and height;
From the sea a mist has spread,                     210
And the beams of morn lie dead
On the towers of Venice now,
Like its glory long ago.

By the skirts of that gray cloud
Many-domèd Padua proud                                    215
Stands, a peopled solitude,
'Mid the harvest-shining plain,
Where the peasant heaps his grain
In the garner of his foe,
And the milk-white oxen slow                              220
With the purple vintage strain,
Heaped upon the creaking wain,
That the brutal Celt may swill
Drunken sleep with savage will;
And the sickle to the sword                               225
Lies unchanged, though many a lord,
Like a weed whose shade is poison,
Overgrows this region's foison,
Sheaves of whom are ripe to come
To destruction's harvest-home:                            230
Men must reap the things they sow,
Force from force must ever flow,
Or worse; but 'tis a bitter woe
That love or reason cannot change
The despot's rage, the slave's revenge.                   235
Padua, thou within whose walls
Those mute guests at festivals,
Son and Mother, Death and Sin,
Played at dice for Ezzelin,
Till Death cried, "I win, I win!"                         240
And Sin cursed to lose the wager
But Death promised, to assuage her,
That he would petition for
Her to be made Vice-Emperor,
When the destined years were o'er,                        245
Over all between the Po
And the eastern Alpine snow,
Under the mighty Austrian.
Sin smiled so as Sin only can.
And since that time, ay, long before,                     250
Both have ruled from shore to shore,—

That incestuous pair, who follow
Tyrants as the sun the swallow,
As Repentance follows Crime,
And as changes follow Time.                          255


In thine halls the lamp of learning,
Padua, now no more is burning;
Like a meteor, whose wild way
Is lost over the grave of day,
It gleams betrayed and to betray:                    260
Once remotest nations came
To adore that sacred flame,
When it lit not many a hearth
On this cold and gloomy earth:
Now new fires from antique light                      265
Spring beneath the wide world's might;
But their spark lies dead in thee,
Trampled out by Tyranny.
As the Norway woodman quells,
In the depth of piny dells,                           270
One light flame among the brakes,
While the boundless forest shakes,
And its mighty trunks are torn
By the fire thus lowly born:
The spark beneath his feet is dead,                   275
He starts to see the flames it fed
Howling through the darkened sky
With a myriad tongues victoriously,
And sinks down in fear: so thou,
O Tyranny, beholdest now                              280
Light around thee, and thou hearest
The loud flames ascend, and fearest:
Grovel on the earth; ay, hide
In the dust thy purple pride!


Noon descends around me now:                          285
'Tis the noon of autumn's glow,

When a soft and purple mist
Like a vaporous amethyst,
Or an air-dissolvèd star
Mingling light and fragrance, far     290
From the curved horizon's bound
To the point of Heaven's profound,
Fills the overflowing sky;
And the plains that silent lie
Underneath, the leaves unsodden     295
Where the infant Frost has trodden
With his morning-wingèd feet,
Whose bright print is gleaming yet;
And the red and golden vines,
Piercing with their trellised lines     300
The rough, dark-skirted wilderness;
The dun and bladed grass no less,
Pointing from this hoary tower
In the windless air; the flower
Glimmering at my feet; the line     305
Of the olive-sandalled Apennine
In the south dimly islanded;
And the Alps, whose snows are spread
High between the clouds and sun;
And of living things each one;     310
And my spirit which so long
Darkened this swift stream of song,—
Interpenetrated lie
By the glory of the sky:
Be it love, light, harmony,     315
Odour, or the soul of all
Which from Heaven like dew doth fall,
Or the mind which feeds this verse
Peopling the lone universe.


Noon descends, and after noon     320
Autumn's evening meets me soon,
Leading the infantine moon,

And that one star, which to her
Almost seems to minister
Half the crimson light she brings                325
From the sunset's radiant springs:
And the soft dreams of the morn
(Which like wingèd winds had borne
To that silent isle, which lies
Mid remembered agonies,                          330
The frail bark of this lone being)
Pass, to other sufferers fleeing,
And its ancient pilot, Pain,
Sits beside the helm again.

Other flowering isles must be                    335
In the sea of Life and Agony:
Other spirits float and flee
O'er that gulf: even now, perhaps,
On some rock the wild wave wraps,
With folded wings they waiting sit               340
For my bark, to pilot it
To some calm and blooming cove,
Where for me, and those I love,
May a windless bower be built,
Far from passion, pain, and guilt,               345
In a dell mid lawny hills,
Which the wild sea-murmur fills,
And soft sunshine, and the sound
Of old forests echoing round,
And the light and smell divine                   350
Of all flowers that breathe and shine:
We may live so happy there,
That the Spirits of the Air,
Envying us, may even entice
To our healing Paradise                          355
The polluting multitude;
But their rage would be subdued
By that clime divine and calm,
And the winds whose wings rain balm

On the uplifted soul, and leaves 360
Under which the bright sea heaves;
While each breathless interval
In their whisperings musical
The inspired soul supplies
With its own deep melodies, 365
And the love which heals all strife
Circling, like the breath of life,
All things in that sweet abode
With its own mild brotherhood:
They, not it, would change; and soon 370
Every sprite beneath the moon
Would repent its envy vain,
And the earth grow young again.

## SONG FOR 'TASSO'

### I

I LOVED—alas! our life is love;
But when we cease to breathe and move
I do suppose love ceases too.
I thought, but not as now I do,
Keen thoughts and bright of linkèd lore, 5
Of all that men had thought before,
And all that Nature shows, and more.

### II

And still I love and still I think,
But strangely, for my heart can drink
The dregs of such despair, and live, 10
And love; . . .
And if I think, my thoughts come fast,
I mix the present with the past,
And each seems uglier than the last.

### III

Sometimes I see before me flee
A silver spirit's form, like thee, 15

O Leonora, and I sit
. . . still watching it,
Till by the grated casement's ledge
It fades, with such a sigh, as sedge                    20
Breathes o'er the breezy streamlet's edge.


## STANZAS

### WRITTEN IN DEJECTION, NEAR NAPLES

#### I

THE sun is warm, the sky is clear,
    The waves are dancing fast and bright,
Blue isles and snowy mountains wear
    The purple noon's transparent might,
    The breath of the moist earth is light        5
Around its unexpanded buds;
    Like many a voice of one delight,
The winds, the birds, the ocean floods,
The City's voice itself, is soft like Solitude's.

#### II

I see the Deep's untrampled floor               10
    With green and purple seaweeds strown;
I see the waves upon the shore,
    Like light dissolved in star-showers, thrown:
    I sit upon the sands alone,—
The lightning of the noontide ocean             15
    Is flashing round me, and a tone
Arises from its measured motion,
How sweet! did any heart now share in my emotion.

#### III

Alas! I have nor hope nor health,
    Nor peace within nor calm around,           20
Nor that content surpassing wealth
    The sage in meditation found,

And walked with inward glory crowned—
Nor fame, nor power, nor love, nor leisure.
Others I see whom these surround—
Smiling they live, and call life pleasure;—
To me that cup has been dealt in another measure.

IV

Yet now despair itself is mild,
Even as the winds and waters are;
I could lie down like a tired child,
And weep away the life of care
Which I have borne and yet must bear,
Till death like sleep might steal on me,
And I might feel in the warm air
My cheek grow cold, and hear the sea
Breathe o'er my dying brain its last monotony.

V

Some might lament that I were cold,
As I, when this sweet day is gone,
Which my lost heart, too soon grown old,
Insults with this untimely moan;
They might lament—for I am one
Whom men love not,—and yet regret,
Unlike this day, which, when the sun
Shall on its stainless glory set,
Will linger, though enjoyed, like joy in memory yet.

## SONNET

LIFT not the painted veil which those who live
Call Life: though unreal shapes be pictured there,
And it but mimic all we would believe
With colours idly spread,—behind, lurk Fear
And Hope, twin Destinies; who ever weave
Their shadows, o'er the chasm, sightless and drear.

I knew one who had lifted it—he sought,
For his lost heart was tender, things to love,
But found them not, alas! nor was there aught
The world contains, the which he could approve.    10
Through the unheeding many he did move,
A splendour among shadows, a bright blot
Upon this gloomy scene, a Spirit that strove
For truth, and like the Preacher found it not.

# POEMS WRITTEN IN 1819

## SONG TO THE MEN OF ENGLAND

### I

MEN of England, wherefore plough
For the lords who lay ye low?
Wherefore weave with toil and care
The rich robes your tyrants wear?

### II

Wherefore feed, and clothe, and save,    5
From the cradle to the grave,
Those ungrateful drones who would
Drain your sweat—nay, drink your blood?

### III

Wherefore, Bees of England, forge
Many a weapon, chain, and scourge,    10
That these stingless drones may spoil
The forced produce of your toil?

### IV

Have ye leisure, comfort, calm,
Shelter, food, love's gentle balm?
Or what is it ye buy so dear    15
With your pain and with your fear?

### V

The seed ye sow, another reaps;
The wealth ye find, another keeps;
The robes ye weave, another wears;
The arms ye forge, another bears.    20

### VI

Sow seed,—but let no tyrant reap;
Find wealth,—let no impostor heap;
Weave robes,—let not the idle wear;
Forge arms,—in your defence to bear.

### VII

Shrink to your cellars, holes, and cells;    25
In halls ye deck another dwells.
Why shake the chains ye wrought? Ye see
The steel ye tempered glance on ye.

### VIII

With plough and spade, and hoe and loom,
Trace your grave and build your tomb,    30
And weave your winding-sheet, till fair
England be your sepulchre.


# SIMILES FOR TWO
# POLITICAL CHARACTERS OF 1819

## SIDMOUTH AND CASTLEREAGH

### I

As from an ancestral oak
  Two empty ravens sound their clarion,
Yell by yell, and croak by croak,
When they scent the noonday smoke
  Of fresh human carrion:—    5

### II

As two gibbering night-birds flit
  From their bowers of deadly yew
Through the night to frighten it,
When the moon is in a fit,
    And the stars are none, or few:—          10

### III

As a shark and dog-fish wait
  Under an Atlantic isle,
For the negro-ship, whose freight
Is the theme of their debate,
    Wrinkling their red gills the while—          15

### IV

Are ye, two vultures sick for battle,
  Two scorpions under one wet stone,
Two bloodless wolves whose dry throats rattle,
Two crows perched on the murrained cattle,
    Two vipers tangled into one.          20


## SONNET: ENGLAND IN 1819

An old, mad, blind, despised, and dying king,—
Princes, the dregs of their dull race, who flow
Through public scorn,—mud from a muddy spring,—
Rulers who neither see, nor feel, nor know,
But leech-like to their fainting country cling,          5
Till they drop, blind in blood, without a blow,—
A people starved and stabbed in the untilled field,—
An army, which liberticide and prey
Makes as a two-edged sword to all who wield,—
Golden and sanguine laws which tempt and slay;          10

THE FUNERAL OF SHELLEY

*From the painting by Fournier which differs in some details from Trelawny's*

Religion Christless, Godless—a book sealed;
A Senate,—Time's worst statute unrepealed,—
Are graves, from which a glorious Phantom may
Burst, to illumine our tempestuous day.


# ODE TO HEAVEN

### CHORUS OF SPIRITS

*First Spirit.*

PALACE-ROOF of cloudless nights!
Paradise of golden lights!
  Deep, immeasurable, vast,
Which art now, and which wert then
  Of the Present and the Past,          5
Of the eternal Where and When,
  Presence-chamber, temple, home,
  Ever-canopying dome,
  Of acts and ages yet to come!


Glorious shapes have life in thee,          10
Earth, and all earth's company;
  Living globes which ever throng
Thy deep chasms and wildernesses;
  And green worlds that glide along;
And swift stars with flashing tresses;          15
  And icy moons most cold and bright,
  And mighty suns beyond the night,
  Atoms of intensest light.


Even thy name is as a god,
Heaven! for thou art the abode          20
  Of that Power which is the glass
Wherein man his nature sees.
  Generations as they pass
Worship thee with bended knees.

P

Their unremaining gods and they                    25
Like a river roll away:
Thou remainest such—alway!—

*Second Spirit.*

Thou art but the mind's first chamber,
Round which its young fancies clamber,
    Like weak insects in a cave,                    30
Lighted up by stalactites;
    But the portal of the grave,
Where a world of new delights
    Will make thy best glories seem
    But a dim and noonday gleam                    35
From the shadow of a dream!

*Third Spirit.*

Peace! the abyss is wreathed with scorn
At your presumption, atom-born!
    What is Heaven? and what are ye
Who its brief expanse inherit?                    40
    What are suns and spheres which flee
    With the instinct of that Spirit
    Of which ye are but a part?
    Drops which Nature's mighty heart
Drives through thinnest veins! Depart!            45

What is Heaven? a globe of dew
Filling in the morning new
    Some eyed flower whose young leaves waken
On an unimagined world:
    Constellated suns unshaken,                    50
Orbits measureless, are furled
    In that frail and fading sphere,
    With ten millions gathered there,
    To tremble, gleam and disappear.

# ODE TO THE WEST WIND[1]

### I

O WILD West Wind, thou breath of Autumn's being,
Thou, from whose unseen presence the leaves dead
Are driven, like ghosts from an enchanter fleeing,

Yellow, and black, and pale, and hectic red,
Pestilence-stricken multitudes: O thou,                    5
Who chariotest to their dark wintry bed

The wingèd seeds, where they lie cold and low,
Each like a corpse within its grave, until
Thine azure sister of the Spring shall blow

Her clarion o'er the dreaming earth, and fill           10
(Driving sweet buds like flocks to feed in air)
With living hues and odours plain and hill:

Wild Spirit, which art moving everywhere;
Destroyer and preserver; hear, oh, hear!

### II

Thou on whose stream, mid the steep sky's commotion, 15
Loose clouds like earth's decaying leaves are shed,
Shook from the tangled boughs of Heaven and Ocean,

[1] This poem was conceived and chiefly written in a wood that skirts the Arno, near Florence, and on a day when that tempestuous wind, whose temperature is at once mild and animating, was collecting the vapours which pour down the autumnal rains. They began, as I foresaw, at sunset with a violent tempest of hail and rain, attended by that magnificent thunder and lightning peculiar to the Cisalpine regions.

The phenomenon alluded to at the conclusion of the third stanza is well known to naturalists. The vegetation at the bottom of the sea, of rivers, and of lakes, sympathizes with that of the land in the change of seasons, and is consequently influenced by the winds which announce it.—
[SHELLEY'S NOTE.]

Angels of rain and lightning: there are spread
On the blue surface of thine aëry surge,
Like the bright hair uplifted from the head 20

Of some fierce Maenad, even from the dim verge
Of the horizon to the zenith's height,
The locks of the approaching storm. Thou dirge

Of the dying year, to which this closing night
Will be the dome of a vast sepulchre, 25
Vaulted with all thy congregated might

Of vapours, from whose solid atmosphere
Black rain, and fire, and hail will burst: oh, hear!

III

Thou who didst waken from his summer dreams
The blue Mediterranean, where he lay,
Lulled by the coil of his crystàlline streams, 30

Beside a pumice isle in Baiae's bay,
And saw in sleep old palaces and towers
Quivering within the wave's intenser day,

All overgrown with azure moss and flowers 35
So sweet, the sense faints picturing them! Thou
For whose path the Atlantic's level powers

Cleave themselves into chasms, while far below
The sea-blooms and the oozy woods which wear
The sapless foliage of the ocean, know 40

Thy voice, and suddenly grow gray with fear,
And tremble and despoil themselves: oh, hear!

IV

If I were a dead leaf thou mightest bear;
If I were a swift cloud to fly with thee;
A wave to pant beneath thy power, and share     45

The impulse of thy strength, only less free
Than thou, O uncontrollable! If even
I were as in my boyhood, and could be

The comrade of thy wanderings over Heaven,
As then, when to outstrip thy skiey speed     50
Scarce seemed a vision; I would ne'er have striven

As thus with thee in prayer in my sore need.
Oh, lift me as a wave, a leaf, a cloud!
I fall upon the thorns of life! I bleed!

A heavy weight of hours has chained and bowed     55
One too like thee: tameless, and swift, and proud.


V

Make me thy lyre, even as the forest is:
What if my leaves are falling like its own!
The tumult of thy mighty harmonies

Will take from both a deep, autumnal tone,     60
Sweet though in sadness. Be thou, Spirit fierce,
My spirit! Be thou me, impetuous one!

Drive my dead thoughts over the universe
Like withered leaves to quicken a new birth!
And, by the incantation of this verse,     65

Scatter, as from an unextinguished hearth
Ashes and sparks, my words among mankind!
Be through my lips to unawakened earth

The trumpet of a prophecy! O, wind,
If Winter comes, can Spring be far behind?          70

## AN EXHORTATION

CHAMELEONS feed on light and air:
    Poets' food is love and fame:
If in this wide world of care
    Poets could but find the same
With as little toil as they,          5
    Would they ever change their hue
    As the light chameleons do,
Suiting it to every ray
    Twenty times a day?

Poets are on this cold earth,          10
    As chameleons might be,
Hidden from their early birth
    In a cave beneath the sea;
Where light is, chameleons change:
    Where love is not, poets do:          15
    Fame is love disguised: if few
Find either, never think it strange
    That poets range.

Yet dare not stain with wealth or power
    A poet's free and heavenly mind:          20
If bright chameleons should devour
    Any food but beams and wind,
They would grow as earthly soon
    As their brother lizards are.
    Children of a sunnier star,          25
Spirits from beyond the moon,
    Oh, refuse the boon!

# THE INDIAN SERENADE

### I

I ARISE from dreams of thee
In the first sweet sleep of night,
When the winds are breathing low,
And the stars are shining bright:
I arise from dreams of thee,                    5
And a spirit in my feet
Hath led me—who knows how?
To thy chamber window, Sweet!

### II

The wandering airs they faint
On the dark, the silent stream—                 10
And the Champak odours fail
Like sweet thoughts in a dream;
The nightingale's complaint,
It dies upon her heart;—
As I must on thine,                             15
Oh, belovèd as thou art!

### III

Oh lift me from the grass!
I die! I faint! I fail!
Let thy love in kisses rain
On my lips and eyelids pale.                    20
My cheek is cold and white, alas!
My heart beats loud and fast;—
Oh! press it to thine own again,
Where it will break at last.

## TO SOPHIA (MISS STACEY)

### I

THOU art fair, and few are fairer
   Of the Nymphs of earth or ocean;
They are robes that fit the wearer—
   Those soft limbs of thine, whose motion
Ever falls and shifts and glances      5
As the life within them dances.

### II

Thy deep eyes, a double Planet,
   Gaze the wisest into madness
With soft clear fire,—the winds that fan it
   Are those thoughts of tender gladness      10
Which, like zephyrs on the billow,
Make thy gentle soul their pillow.

### III

If, whatever face thou paintest
   In those eyes, grows pale with pleasure,
If the fainting soul is faintest      15
   When it hears thy harp's wild measure,
Wonder not that when thou speakest
Of the weak my heart is weakest.

### IV

As dew beneath the wind of morning,
   As the sea which whirlwinds waken,
As the birds at thunder's warning,      20
   As aught mute yet deeply shaken,
As one who feels an unseen spirit
Is my heart when thine is near it.

## TO WILLIAM SHELLEY

(With what truth may I say—
Roma! Roma! Roma!
Non è più come era prima!)

### I

My lost William, thou in whom
    Some bright spirit lived, and did
That decaying robe consume
    Which its lustre faintly hid,—
Here its ashes find a tomb,                    5
    But beneath this pyramid
Thou art not—if a thing divine
Like thee can die, thy funeral shrine
Is thy mother's grief and mine.

### II

Where art thou, my gentle child?            10
    Let me think thy spirit feeds,
With its life intense and mild,
    The love of living leaves and weeds
Among these tombs and ruins wild;—
    Let me think that through low seeds      15
Of sweet flowers and sunny grass
Into their hues and scents may pass
A portion——

## TO WILLIAM SHELLEY

THY little footsteps on the sands
    Of a remote and lonely shore;
The twinkling of thine infant hands,
    Where now the worm will feed no more;
Thy mingled look of love and glee            5
When we returned to gaze on thee—

## TO MARY SHELLEY

My dearest Mary, wherefore hast thou gone,
And left me in this dreary world alone?
Thy form is here indeed—a lovely one—
But thou art fled, gone down the dreary road,
That leads to Sorrow's most obscure abode;        5
Thou sittest on the hearth of pale despair,
                                             Where
For thine own sake I cannot follow thee.


## ON THE MEDUSA OF LEONARDO DA VINCI IN THE FLORENTINE GALLERY

### I

It lieth, gazing on the midnight sky,
    Upon the cloudy mountain-peak supine;
Below, far lands are seen tremblingly;
    Its horror and its beauty are divine.
Upon its lips and eyelids seems to lie        5
    Loveliness like a shadow, from which shine,
Fiery and lurid, struggling underneath,
The agonies of anguish and of death.


### II

Yet it is less the horror than the grace
    Which turns the gazer's spirit into stone,        10
Whereon the lineaments of that dead face
    Are graven, till the characters be grown
Into itself, and thought no more can trace;
    'Tis the melodious hue of beauty thrown
Athwart the darkness and the glare of pain,        15
Which humanize and harmonize the strain.

### III

And from its head as from one body grow,
 As  grass out of a watery rock,
Hairs which are vipers, and they curl and flow
 And their long tangles in each other lock,   20
And with unending involutions show
 Their mailèd radiance, as it were to mock
The torture and the death within, and saw
The solid air with many a raggèd jaw.


### IV

And, from a stone beside, a poisonous eft   25
 Peeps idly into those Gorgonian eyes;
Whilst in the air a ghastly bat, bereft
 Of sense, has flitted with a mad surprise
Out of the cave this hideous light had cleft,
 And he comes hastening like a moth that hies  30
After a taper; and the midnight sky
Flares, a light more dread than obscurity.


### V

'Tis the tempestuous loveliness of terror;
 For from the serpents gleams a brazen glare
Kindled by that inextricable error,   35
 Which makes a thrilling vapour of the air
Become a  and ever-shifting mirror
 Of all the beauty and the terror there—
A woman's countenance, with serpent-locks,
Gazing in death on Heaven from those wet rocks. 40


## LOVE'S PHILOSOPHY

### I

THE fountains mingle with the river
 And the rivers with the Ocean,
The winds of Heaven mix for ever
 With a sweet emotion;

Nothing in the world is single;     5
   All things by a law divine
In one spirit meet and mingle.
   Why not I with thine?—

II

See the mountains kiss high Heaven
   And the waves clasp one another;     10
No sister-flower would be forgiven
   If it disdained its brother;
And the sunlight clasps the earth
   And the moonbeams kiss the sea:
What is all this sweet work worth     15
   If thou kiss not me?


# FRAGMENT: SUFFICIENT UNTO THE DAY

Is not to-day enough? Why do I peer
   Into the darkness of the day to come?
Is not to-morrow even as yesterday?
   And will the day that follows change thy doom?
Few flowers grow upon thy wintry way;     5
   And who waits for thee in that cheerless home
Whence thou hast fled, whither thou must return
Charged with the load that makes thee faint and mourn?


# FRAGMENT: 'YE GENTLE VISITATIONS OF CALM THOUGHT'

Ye gentle visitations of calm thought—
   Moods like the memories of happier earth,
   Which come arrayed in thoughts of little worth,
Like stars in clouds by the weak winds enwrought,—
   But that the clouds depart and stars remain,     5
While they remain, and ye, alas, depart!

## FRAGMENT: THE SEPULCHRE OF MEMORY

AND where is truth? On tombs? for such to thee
Has been my heart—and thy dead memory
Has lain from childhood, many a changeful year,
Unchangingly preserved and buried there.

## FRAGMENT: 'WAKE THE SERPENT NOT'

WAKE the serpent not—lest he
Should not know the way to go,—
Let him crawl which yet lies sleeping
Through the deep grass of the meadow!
Not a bee shall hear him creeping,  5
Not a may-fly shall awaken
From its cradling blue-bell shaken,
Not the starlight as he's sliding
Through the grass with silent gliding.

## FRAGMENT: WINE OF THE FAIRIES

I AM drunk with the honey wine
Of the moon-unfolded eglantine,
Which fairies catch in hyacinth bowls.
The bats, the dormice, and the moles
Sleep in the walls or under the sward  5
Of the desolate castle yard;
And when 'tis spilt on the summer earth
 Or its fumes arise among the dew,
Their jocund dreams are full of mirth,
 They gibber their joy in sleep; for few  10
 Of the fairies bear those bowls so new!

# POEMS WRITTEN IN 1820
## THE SENSITIVE PLANT

### PART FIRST

A SENSITIVE Plant in a garden grew,
And the young winds fed it with silver dew,
And it opened its fan-like leaves to the light,
And closed them beneath the kisses of Night.

And the Spring arose on the garden fair,                5
Like the Spirit of Love felt everywhere;
And each flower and herb on Earth's dark breast
Rose from the dreams of its wintry rest.

But none ever trembled and panted with bliss
In the garden, the field, or the wilderness,           10
Like a doe in the noontide with love's sweet want,
As the companionless Sensitive Plant.

The snowdrop, and then the violet,
Arose from the ground with warm rain wet,
And their breath was mixed with fresh odour, sent      15
From the turf, like the voice and the instrument.

Then the pied wind-flowers and the tulip tall,
And narcissi, the fairest among them all,
Who gaze on their eyes in the stream's recess,
Till they die of their own dear loveliness;            20

And the Naiad-like lily of the vale,
Whom youth makes so fair and passion so pale
That the light of its tremulous bells is seen
Through their pavilions of tender green;

And the hyacinth purple, and white, and blue, 25
Which flung from its bells a sweet peal anew
Of music so delicate, soft, and intense,
It was felt like an odour within the sense;

And the rose like a nymph to the bath addressed,
Which unveiled the depth of her glowing breast, 30
Till, fold after fold, to the fainting air
The soul of her beauty and love lay bare:

And the wand-like lily, which lifted up,
As a Maenad, its moonlight-coloured cup,
Till the fiery star, which is its eye, 35
Gazed through clear dew on the tender sky;

And the jessamine faint, and the sweet tuberose,
The sweetest flower for scent that blows;
And all rare blossoms from every clime
Grew in that garden in perfect prime. 40

And on the stream whose inconstant bosom
Was pranked, under boughs of embowering blossom,
With golden and green light, slanting through
Their heaven of many a tangled hue,

Broad water-lilies lay tremulously, 45
And starry river-buds glimmered by,
And around them the soft stream did glide and dance
With a motion of sweet sound and radiance.

And the sinuous paths of lawn and of moss,
Which led through the garden along and across, 50
Some open at once to the sun and the breeze,
Some lost among bowers of blossoming trees,

Were all paved with daisies and delicate bells
As fair as the fabulous asphodels,
And flow'rets which, drooping as day drooped too,      55
Fell into pavilions, white, purple, and blue,
To roof the glow-worm from the evening dew.

And from this undefilèd Paradise
The flowers (as an infant's awakening eyes
Smile on its mother, whose singing sweet      60
Can first lull, and at last must awaken it),

When Heaven's blithe winds had unfolded them,
As mine-lamps enkindle a hidden gem,
Shone smiling to Heaven, and every one
Shared joy in the light of the gentle sun;      65

For each one was interpenetrated
With the light and the odour its neighbour shed,
Like young lovers whom youth and love make dear
Wrapped and filled by their mutual atmosphere.

But the Sensitive Plant which could give small fruit      70
Of the love which it felt from the leaf to the root,
Received more than all, it loved more than ever,
Where none wanted but it, could belong to the giver,—

For the Sensitive Plant has no bright flower;
Radiance and odour are not its dower;      75
It loves, even like Love, its deep heart is full,
It desires what it has not, the Beautiful!

The light winds which from unsustaining wings
Shed the music of many murmurings;
The beams which dart from many a star      80
Of the flowers whose hues they bear afar;

The plumèd insects swift and free,
Like golden boats on a sunny sea,
Laden with light and odour, which pass
Over the gleam of the living grass;                    85

The unseen clouds of the dew, which lie
Like fire in the flowers till the sun rides high,
Then wander like spirits among the spheres,
Each cloud faint with the fragrance it bears;

The quivering vapours of dim noontide,                 90
Which like a sea o'er the warm earth glide,
In which every sound, and odour, and beam,
Move, as reeds in a single stream;

Each and all like ministering angels were
For the Sensitive Plant sweet joy to bear,             95
Whilst the lagging hours of the day went by
Like windless clouds o'er a tender sky.

And when evening descended from Heaven above,
And the Earth was all rest, and the air was all love,
And delight, though less bright, was far more deep,   100
And the day's veil fell from the world of sleep,

And the beasts, and the birds, and the insects were drowned
In an ocean of dreams without a sound;
Whose waves never mark, though they ever impress
The light sand which paves it, consciousness;         105

(Only overhead the sweet nightingale
Ever sang more sweet as the day might fail,
And snatches of its Elysian chant
Were mixed with the dreams of the Sensitive Plant);—

The Sensitive Plant was the earliest          110
Upgathered into the bosom of rest;
A sweet child weary of its delight,
The feeblest and yet the favourite,
Cradled within the embrace of Night.

### Part Second

There was a Power in this sweet place,
An Eve in this Eden; a ruling Grace
Which to the flowers, did they waken or dream,
Was as God is to the starry scheme.

A Lady, the wonder of her kind,          5
Whose form was upborne by a lovely mind
Which, dilating, had moulded her mien and motion
Like a sea-flower unfolded beneath the ocean,

Tended the garden from morn to even:
And the meteors of that sublunar Heaven,          10
Like the lamps of the air when Night walks forth,
Laughed round her footsteps up from the Earth!

She had no companion of mortal race,
But her tremulous breath and her flushing face
Told, whilst the morn kissed the sleep from her eyes,          15
That her dreams were less slumber than Paradise:

As if some bright Spirit for her sweet sake
Had deserted Heaven while the stars were awake,
As if yet around her he lingering were,
Though the veil of daylight concealed him from her.          20

Her step seemed to pity the grass it pressed;
You might hear by the heaving of her breast,
That the coming and going of the wind
Brought pleasure there and left passion behind.

And wherever her aëry footsteps trod,          25
Her trailing hair from the grassy sod
Erased its light vestige, with shadowy sweep,
Like a sunny storm o'er the dark green deep.


I doubt not the flowers of that garden sweet
Rejoiced in the sound of her gentle feet;          30
I doubt not they felt the spirit that came
From her glowing fingers through all their frame.


She sprinkled bright water from the stream
On those that were faint with the sunny beam;
And out of the cups of the heavy flowers          35
She emptied the rain of the thunder-showers.


She lifted their heads with her tender hands,
And sustained them with rods and osier-bands;
If the flowers had been her own infants, she
Could never have nursed them more tenderly.          40


And all killing insects and gnawing worms,
And things of obscene and unlovely forms,
She bore, in a basket of Indian woof,
Into the rough woods far aloof,—


In a basket, of grasses and wild-flowers full,          45
The freshest her gentle hands could pull
For the poor banished insects, whose intent,
Although they did ill, was innocent.


But the bee and the beamlike ephemeris
Whose path is the lightning's, and soft moths that kiss 50
The sweet lips of the flowers, and harm not, did she
Make her attendant angels be.

And many an antenatal tomb,
Where butterflies dream of the life to come,
She left clinging round the smooth and dark          55
Edge of the odorous cedar bark.


This fairest creature from earliest Spring
Thus moved through the garden ministering
All the sweet season of Summertide,
And ere the first leaf looked brown—she died!          60


## PART THIRD

Three days the flowers of the garden fair,
Like stars when the moon is awakened, were,
Or the waves of Baiae, ere luminous
She floats up through the smoke of Vesuvius.


And on the fourth, the Sensitive Plant          5
Felt the sound of the funeral chant,
And the steps of the bearers, heavy and slow,
And the sobs of the mourners, deep and low;


The weary sound and the heavy breath,
And the silent motions of passing death,          10
And the smell, cold, oppressive, and dank,
Sent through the pores of the coffin-plank;


The dark grass, and the flowers among the grass,
Were bright with tears as the crowd did pass;
From their sighs the wind caught a mournful tone,          15
And sate in the pines, and gave groan for groan.


The garden, once fair, became cold and foul,
Like the corpse of her who had been its soul,
Which at first was lovely as if in sleep,
Then slowly changed, till it grew a heap          20
To make men tremble who never weep.

Swift Summer into the Autumn flowed,
And frost in the mist of the morning rode,
Though the noonday sun looked clear and bright,
Mocking the spoil of the secret night.                    25


The rose-leaves, like flakes of crimson snow,
Paved the turf and the moss below.
The lilies were drooping, and white, and wan,
Like the head and the skin of a dying man.


And Indian plants, of scent and hue                       30
The sweetest that ever were fed on dew,
Leaf by leaf, day after day,
Were massed into the common clay.


And the leaves, brown, yellow, and gray, and red,
And white with the whiteness of what is dead,             35
Like troops of ghosts on the dry wind passed;
Their whistling noise made the birds aghast.


And the gusty winds waked the wingèd seeds,
Out of their birthplace of ugly weeds,
Till they clung round many a sweet flower's stem,         40
Which rotted into the earth with them.


The water-blooms under the rivulet
Fell from the stalks on which they were set;
And the eddies drove them here and there,
As the winds did those of the upper air.                  45


Then the rain came down, and the broken stalks
Were bent and tangled across the walks;
And the leafless network of parasite bowers
Massed into ruin; and all sweet flowers.

Between the time of the wind and the snow          50
All loathliest weeds began to grow,
Whose coarse leaves were splashed with many a speck,
Like the water-snake's belly and the toad's back.


And thistles, and nettles, and darnels rank,
And the dock, and henbane, and hemlock dank,          55
Stretched out its long and hollow shank,
And stifled the air till the dead wind stank.


And plants, at whose names the verse feels loath,
Filled the place with a monstrous undergrowth,
Prickly, and pulpous, and blistering, and blue,          60
Livid, and starred with a lurid dew.


And agarics, and fungi, with mildew and mould
Started like mist from the wet ground cold;
Pale, fleshy, as if the decaying dead
With a spirit of growth had been animated!          65


Spawn, weeds, and filth, a leprous scum,
Made the running rivulet thick and dumb,
And at its outlet flags huge as stakes
Dammed it up with roots knotted like water-snakes.


And hour by hour, when the air was still,          70
The vapours arose which have strength to kill;
At morn they were seen, at noon they were felt,
At night they were darkness no star could melt.


And unctuous meteors from spray to spray
Crept and flitted in broad noonday          75
Unseen; every branch on which they alit
By a venomous blight was burned and bit.

The Sensitive Plant, like one forbid,
Wept, and the tears within each lid
Of its folded leaves, which together grew,        80
Were changed to a blight of frozen glue.


For the leaves soon fell, and the branches soon
By the heavy axe of the blast were hewn;
The sap shrank to the root through every pore
As blood to a heart that will beat no more.        85


For Winter came: the wind was his whip:
One choppy finger was on his lip:
He had torn the cataracts from the hills
And they clanked at his girdle like manacles;


His breath was a chain which without a sound        90
The earth, and the air, and the water bound;
He came, fiercely driven, in his chariot-throne
By the tenfold blasts of the Arctic zone.


Then the weeds which were forms of living death
Fled from the frost to the earth beneath.        95
Their decay and sudden flight from frost
Was but like the vanishing of a ghost!


And under the roots of the Sensitive Plant
The moles and the dormice died for want:
The birds dropped stiff from the frozen air        100
And were caught in the branches naked and bare.


First there came down a thawing rain
And its dull drops froze on the boughs again;
Then there steamed up a freezing dew
Which to the drops of the thaw-rain grew;        105

And a northern whirlwind, wandering about
Like a wolf that had smelt a dead child out,
Shook the boughs thus laden, and heavy, and stiff,
And snapped them off with his rigid griff.


When Winter had gone and Spring came back          110
The Sensitive Plant was a leafless wreck;
But the mandrakes, and toadstools, and docks, and darnels,
Rose like the dead from their ruined charnels.


### CONCLUSION

Whether the Sensitive Plant, or that
Which within its boughs like a Spirit sat,          115
Ere its outward form had known decay,
Now felt this change, I cannot say.


Whether that Lady's gentle mind,
No longer with the form combined
Which scattered love, as stars do light,          120
Found sadness, where it left delight,


I dare not guess; but in this life
Of error, ignorance, and strife,
Where nothing is, but all things seem,
And we the shadows of the dream,          125


It is a modest creed, and yet
Pleasant if one considers it,
To own that death itself must be,
Like all the rest, a mockery.


That garden sweet, that lady fair,          130
And all sweet shapes and odours there,
In truth have never passed away:
'Tis we, 'tis ours, are changed; not they.

For love, and beauty, and delight,
There is no death nor change: their might          135
Exceeds our organs, which endure
No light, being themselves obscure.

# THE CLOUD

I BRING fresh showers for the thirsting flowers,
 From the seas and the streams;
I bear light shade for the leaves when laid
 In their noonday dreams.
From my wings are shaken the dews that waken          5
 The sweet buds every one,
When rocked to rest on their mother's breast,
 As she dances about the sun.
I wield the flail of the lashing hail,
 And whiten the green plains under,          10
And then again I dissolve it in rain,
 And laugh as I pass in thunder.

I sift the snow on the mountains below,
 And their great pines groan aghast;
And all the night 'tis my pillow white,          15
 While I sleep in the arms of the blast.
Sublime on the towers of my skiey bowers,
 Lightning my pilot sits;
In a cavern under is fettered the thunder,
 It struggles and howls at fits;          20
Over earth and ocean, with gentle motion,
 This pilot is guiding me,
Lured by the love of the genii that move
 In the depths of the purple sea;
Over the rills, and the crags, and the hills,          25
 Over the lakes and the plains,
Wherever he dream, under mountain or stream,
 The Spirit he loves remains;
And I all the while bask in Heaven's blue smile,
 Whilst he is dissolving in rains.          30

The sanguine Sunrise, with his meteor eyes,
    And his burning plumes outspread,
Leaps on the back of my sailing rack,
    When the morning star shines dead;
As on the jag of a mountain crag,       35
    Which an earthquake rocks and swings,
An eagle alit one moment may sit
    In the light of its golden wings.
And when Sunset may breathe, from the lit sea beneath,
    Its ardours of rest and of love,      40
And the crimson pall of eve may fall
    From the depth of Heaven above,
With wings folded I rest, on mine aëry nest,
    As still as a brooding dove.

That orbèd maiden with white fire laden,      45
    Whom mortals call the Moon,
Glides glimmering o'er my fleece-like floor,
    By the midnight breezes strewn;
And wherever the beat of her unseen feet,
    Which only the angels hear,      50
May have broken the woof of my tent's thin roof,
    The stars peep behind her and peer;
And I laugh to see them whirl and flee,
    Like a swarm of golden bees,
When I widen the rent in my wind-built tent,      55
    Till the calm rivers, lakes, and seas,
Like strips of the sky fallen through me on high,
    Are each paved with the moon and these.

I bind the Sun's throne with a burning zone,
    And the Moon's with a girdle of pearl;      60
The volcanoes are dim, and the stars reel and swim,
    When the whirlwinds my banner unfurl.
From cape to cape, with a bridge-like shape,
    Over a torrent sea,
Sunbeam-proof, I hang like a roof,—      65
    The mountains its columns be.

The triumphal arch through which I march
    With hurricane, fire, and snow,
When the Powers of the air are chained to my chair,
    Is the million-coloured bow;        70
The sphere-fire above its soft colours wove,
    While the moist Earth was laughing below.

I am the daughter of Earth and Water,
    And the nursling of the Sky;
I pass through the pores of the ocean and shores;   75
    I change, but I cannot die.
For after the rain when with never a stain
    The pavilion of Heaven is bare,
And the winds and sunbeams with their convex gleams
    Build up the blue dome of air,      80
I silently laugh at my own cenotaph,
    And out of the caverns of rain,
Like a child from the womb, like a ghost from the tomb,
    I arise and unbuild it again.

## TO A SKYLARK

Hail to thee, blithe Spirit!
    Bird thou never wert,
That from Heaven, or near it,
    Pourest thy full heart
In profuse strains of unpremeditated art.      5

Higher still and higher
    From the earth thou springest
Like a cloud of fire;
    The blue deep thou wingest,
And singing still dost soar, and soaring ever singest.   10

In the golden lightning
    Of the sunken sun,
O'er which clouds are bright'ning,
    Thou dost float and run;
Like an unbodied joy whose race is just begun.   15

The pale purple even
   Melts around thy flight;
Like a star of Heaven,
   In the broad daylight
Thou art unseen, but yet I hear thy shrill delight,    20

Keen as are the arrows
   Of that silver sphere,
Whose intense lamp narrows
   In the white dawn clear
Until we hardly see—we feel that it is there.    25

All the earth and air
   With thy voice is loud,
As, when night is bare,
   From one lonely cloud
The moon rains out her beams, and Heaven is overflowed.    30

What thou art we know not;
   What is most like thee?
From rainbow clouds there flow not
   Drops so bright to see
As from thy presence showers a rain of melody.    35

Like a Poet hidden
   In the light of thought,
Singing hymns unbidden,
   Till the world is wrought
To sympathy with hopes and fears it heeded not:    40

Like a high-born maiden
   In a palace-tower,
Soothing her love-laden
   Soul in secret hour
With music sweet as love, which overflows her bower:    45

Like a glow-worm golden
   In a dell of dew,
Scattering unbeholden
   Its aëreal hue
Among the flowers and grass, which screen it from the view! 50


Like a rose embowered
   In its own green leaves,
By warm winds deflowered,
   Till the scent it gives
Makes faint with too much sweet those heavy-wingèd thieves:


Sound of vernal showers                56
   On the twinkling grass,
Rain-awakened flowers,
   All that ever was
Joyous, and clear, and fresh, thy music doth surpass:   60


Teach us, Sprite or Bird,
   What sweet thoughts are thine:
I have never heard
   Praise of love or wine
That panted forth a flood of rapture so divine.    65


Chorus Hymeneal,
   Or triumphal chant,
Matched with thine would be all
   But an empty vaunt,
A thing wherein we feel there is some hidden want.   70


What objects are the fountains
   Of thy happy strain?
What fields, or waves, or mountains?
   What shapes of sky or plain?
What love of thine own kind? what ignorance of pain?   75

With thy clear keen joyance
   Languor cannot be:
Shadow of annoyance
   Never came near thee:
Thou lovest—but ne'er knew love's sad satiety.          80

Waking or asleep,
   Thou of death must deem
Things more true and deep
   Than we mortals dream,
Or how could thy notes flow in such a crystal stream?          85

We look before and after,
   And pine for what is not:
Our sincerest laughter
   With some pain is fraught;
Our sweetest songs are those that tell of saddest thought.          90

Yet if we could scorn
   Hate, and pride, and fear;
If we were things born
   Not to shed a tear,
I know not how thy joy we ever should come near.          95

Better than all measures
   Of delightful sound,
Better than all treasures
   That in books are found,
Thy skill to poet were, thou scorner of the ground!          100

Teach me half the gladness
   That thy brain must know,
Such harmonious madness
   From my lips would flow
The world should listen then—as I am listening now.          105

## ODE TO LIBERTY

Yet, Freedom, yet, thy banner, torn but flying,
Streams like a thunder-storm against the wind.—BYRON.

### I

A GLORIOUS people vibrated again
    The lightning of the nations: Liberty
From heart to heart, from tower to tower, o'er Spain,
    Scattering contagious fire into the sky,
Gleamed.  My soul spurned the chains of its dismay,        5
        And in the rapid plumes of song
        Clothed itself, sublime and strong,
(As a young eagle soars the morning clouds among,)
    Hovering in verse o'er its accustomed prey;
        Till from its station in the Heaven of fame        10
    The Spirit's whirlwind rapt it, and the ray
        Of the remotest sphere of living flame
Which paves the void was from behind it flung,
    As foam from a ship's swiftness, when there came
    A voice out of the deep: I will record the same.        15

### II

The Sun and the serenest Moon sprang forth:
    The burning stars of the abyss were hurled
Into the depths of Heaven.  The daedal earth,
    That island in the ocean of the world,
Hung in its cloud of all-sustaining air:        20
        But this divinest universe
        Was yet a chaos and a curse,
For thou wert not: but, power from worst producing worse,
    The spirit of the beasts was kindled there,
        And of the birds, and of the watery forms,        25
    And there was war among them, and despair
        Within them, raging without truce or terms:
The bosom of their violated nurse
    Groaned, for beasts warred on beasts, and worms on worms,
    And men on men; each heart was as a hell of storms.  30

### III

Man, the imperial shape, then multiplied
  His generations under the pavilion
Of the Sun's throne: palace and pyramid,
  Temple and prison, to many a swarming million
Were, as to mountain-wolves their raggèd caves.    35
      This human living multitude
      Was savage, cunning, blind, and rude,
For thou wert not; but o'er the populous solitude,
  Like one fierce cloud over a waste of waves,
    Hung Tyranny; beneath, sate deified    40
  The sister-pest, congregator of slaves;
    Into the shadow of her pinions wide
Anarchs and priests, who feed on gold and blood
  Till with the stain their inmost souls are dyed,
  Drove the astonished herds of men from every side.    45

### IV

The nodding promontories, and blue isles,
  And cloud-like mountains, and dividuous waves
Of Greece, basked glorious in the open smiles
  Of favouring Heaven: from their enchanted caves
Prophetic echoes flung dim melody.    50
      On the unapprehensive wild
      The vine, the corn, the olive mild,
Grew savage yet, to human use unreconciled;
  And, like unfolded flowers beneath the sea,
    Like the man's thought dark in the infant's brain,    55
  Like aught that is which wraps what is to be,
    Art's deathless dreams lay veiled by many a vein
Of Parian stone; and, yet a speechless child,
  Verse murmured, and Philosophy did strain
  Her lidless eyes for thee; when o'er the Aegean main    60

### V

Athens arose: a city such as vision
  Builds from the purple crags and silver towers

Of battlemented cloud, as in derision
  Of kingliest masonry: the ocean-floors
Pave it; the evening sky pavilions it;         65
    Its portals are inhabited
    By thunder-zonèd winds, each head
Within its cloudy wings with sun-fire garlanded,—
  A divine work! Athens, diviner yet,
    Gleamed with its crest of columns, on the will   70
  Of man, as on a mount of diamond, set;
   For thou wert, and thine all-creative skill
Peopled, with forms that mock the eternal dead
  In marble immortality, that hill
  Which was thine earliest throne and latest oracle.   75

### VI

Within the surface of Time's fleeting river
  Its wrinkled image lies, as then it lay
Immovably unquiet, and for ever
  It trembles, but it cannot pass away!
The voices of thy bards and sages thunder       80
    With an earth-awakening blast
    Through the caverns of the past:
(Religion veils her eyes; Oppression shrinks aghast:)
  A wingèd sound of joy, and love, and wonder,
    Which soars where Expectation never flew,   85
  Rending the veil of space and time asunder!
    One ocean feeds the clouds, and streams, and dew;
One Sun illumines Heaven; one Spirit vast
  With life and love makes chaos ever new,
  As Athens doth the world with thy delight renew.   90

### VII

Then Rome was, and from thy deep bosom fairest,
  Like a wolf-cub from a Cadmaean Maenad,[1]
She drew the milk of greatness, though thy dearest
  From that Elysian food was yet unweanèd;
And many a deed of terrible uprightness      95

[1] See the *Bacchae* of Euripides.—[SHELLEY'S NOTE.]

Ω

By thy sweet love was sanctified;
   And in thy smile, and by thy side,
Saintly Camillus lived, and firm Atilius died.
   But when tears stained thy robe of vestal whiteness,
      And gold profaned thy Capitolian throne,      100
   Thou didst desert, with spirit-wingèd lightness,
      The senate of the tyrants: they sunk prone
Slaves of one tyrant: Palatinus sighed
   Faint echoes of Ionian song; that tone
   Thou didst delay to hear, lamenting to disown.     105

### VIII

From what Hyrcanian glen or frozen hill,
   Or piny promontory of the Arctic main,
Or utmost islet inaccessible,
   Didst thou lament the ruin of thy reign,
Teaching the woods and waves, and desert rocks,     110
      And every Naiad's ice-cold urn,
      To talk in echoes sad and stern
Of that sublimest lore which man had dared unlearn?
   For neither didst thou watch the wizard flocks
      Of the Scald's dreams, nor haunt the Druid's sleep.  115
   What if the tears rained through thy shattered locks
      Were quickly dried? for thou didst groan, not weep,
When from its sea of death, to kill and burn,
   The Galilean serpent forth did creep,
   And made thy world an undistinguishable heap.     120

### IX

A thousand years the Earth cried, 'Where art thou?'
   And then the shadow of thy coming fell
On Saxon Alfred's olive-cinctured brow:
   And many a warrior-peopled citadel,
Like rocks which fire lifts out of the flat deep,     125
      Arose in sacred Italy,
      Frowning o'er the tempestuous sea
Of kings, and priests, and slaves, in tower-crowned majesty;
   That multitudinous anarchy did sweep

And burst around their walls, like idle foam,      130
  Whilst from the human spirit's deepest deep
    Strange melody with love and awe struck dumb
Dissonant arms; and Art, which cannot die,
  With divine wand traced on our earthly home
Fit imagery to pave Heaven's everlasting dome.      135

X

Thou huntress swifter than the Moon! thou terror
  Of the world's wolves! thou bearer of the quiver,
Whose sunlike shafts pierce tempest-wingèd Error,
  As light may pierce the clouds when they dissever
In the calm regions of the orient day!             140
    Luther caught thy wakening glance;
    Like lightning, from his leaden lance
Reflected, it dissolved the visions of the trance
  In which, as in a tomb, the nations lay;
    And England's prophets hailed thee as their queen,  145
  In songs whose music cannot pass away,
    Though it must flow forever: not unseen
Before the spirit-sighted countenance
  Of Milton didst thou pass, from the sad scene
Beyond whose night he saw, with a dejected mien.    150

XI

The eager hours and unreluctant years
  As on a dawn-illumined mountain stood,
Trampling to silence their loud hopes and fears,
  Darkening each other with their multitude,
And cried aloud, 'Liberty!' Indignation           155
    Answered Pity from her cave;
    Death grew pale within the grave,
And Desolation howled to the destroyer, Save!
  When like Heaven's Sun girt by the exhalation
    Of its own glorious light, thou didst arise,    160
  Chasing thy foes from nation unto nation
    Like shadows: as if day had cloven the skies
At dreaming midnight o'er the western wave,

Men started, staggering with a glad surprise,
Under the lightnings of thine unfamiliar eyes.        165

### XII

Thou Heaven of earth! what spells could pall thee then
    In ominous eclipse? a thousand years
Bred from the slime of deep Oppression's den,
    Dyed all thy liquid light with blood and tears,
Till thy sweet stars could weep the stain away;        170
        How like Bacchanals of blood
        Round France, the ghastly vintage, stood
Destruction's sceptred slaves, and Folly's mitred brood!
    When one, like them, but mightier far than they,
        The Anarch of thine own bewildered powers,        175
    Rose: armies mingled in obscure array,
        Like clouds with clouds, darkening the sacred bowers
Of serene Heaven. He, by the past pursued,
    Rests with those dead, but unforgotten hours,
    Whose ghosts scare victor kings in their ancestral towers. 180

### XIII

England yet sleeps: was she not called of old?
    Spain calls her now, as with its thrilling thunder
Vesuvius wakens Aetna, and the cold
    Snow-crags by its reply are cloven in sunder:
O'er the lit waves every Aeolian isle        185
        From Pithecusa to Pelorus
        Howls, and leaps, and glares in chorus:
They cry, 'Be dim; ye lamps of Heaven suspended o'er us!'
    Her chains are threads of gold, she need but smile
        And they dissolve; but Spain's were links of steel,   190
    Till bit to dust by virtue's keenest file.
        Twins of a single destiny! appeal
To the eternal years enthroned before us
    In the dim West; impress us from a seal,
    All ye have thought and done! Time cannot dare conceal.

### XIV

Tomb of Arminius! render up thy dead     196
  Till, like a standard from a watch-tower's staff,
His soul may stream over the tyrant's head;
  Thy victory shall be his epitaph,
Wild Bacchanal of truth's mysterious wine,     200
     King-deluded Germany,
     His dead spirit lives in thee.
Why do we fear or hope? thou art already free!
  And thou, lost Paradise of this divine
    And glorious world! thou flowery wilderness!     205
  Thou island of eternity! thou shrine
    Where Desolation, clothed with loveliness,
Worships the thing thou wert! O Italy,
  Gather thy blood into thy heart; repress
  The beasts who make their dens thy sacred palaces.   210

### XV

Oh, that the free would stamp the impious name
  Of KING into the dust! or write it there,
So that this blot upon the page of fame
  Were as a serpent's path, which the light air
Erases, and the flat sands close behind!     215
     Ye the oracle have heard:
     Lift the victory-flashing sword,
And cut the snaky knots of this foul gordian word,
  Which, weak itself as stubble, yet can bind
    Into a mass, irrefragably firm,     220
  The axes and the rods which awe mankind;
    The sound has poison in it, 'tis the sperm
Of what makes life foul, cankerous, and abhorred;
  Disdain not thou, at thine appointed term,
  To set thine armèd heel on this reluctant worm.   225

### XVI

Oh, that the wise from their bright minds would kindle
  Such lamps within the dome of this dim world,

That the pale name of PRIEST might shrink and dwindle
  Into the hell from which it first was hurled,
A scoff of impious pride from fiends impure;     230
      Till human thoughts might kneel alone,
      Each before the judgement-throne
Of its own aweless soul, or of the Power unknown!
  Oh, that the words which make the thoughts obscure
    From which they spring, as clouds of glimmering dew
From a white lake blot Heaven's blue portraiture,   236
    Were stripped of their thin masks and various hue
And frowns and smiles and splendours not their own,
  Till in the nakedness of false and true
  They stand before their Lord, each to receive its due! 240

### XVII

He who taught man to vanquish whatsoever
  Can be between the cradle and the grave
Crowned him the King of Life. Oh, vain endeavour!
  If on his own high will, a willing slave,
He has enthroned the oppression and the oppressor.   245
      What if earth can clothe and feed
      Amplest millions at their need,
And power in thought be as the tree within the seed?
  Or what if Art, an ardent intercessor,
    Driving on fiery wings to Nature's throne,     250
  Checks the great mother stooping to caress her,
    And cries: 'Give me, thy child, dominion
Over all height and depth'? if Life can breed
  New wants, and wealth from those who toil and groan,
  Rend of thy gifts and hers a thousandfold for one!  255

### XVIII

Come thou, but lead out of the inmost cave
  Of man's deep spirit, as the morning-star
Beckons the Sun from the Eoan wave,
  Wisdom. I hear the pennons of her car
Self-moving, like cloud charioted by flame;     260

Comes she not, and come ye not,
   Rulers of eternal thought,
To judge, with solemn truth, life's ill-apportioned lot?
  Blind Love, and equal Justice, and the Fame
    Of what has been, the Hope of what will be?   265
  O Liberty! if such could be thy name
   Wert thou disjoined from these, or they from thee:
If thine or theirs were treasures to be bought
  By blood or tears, have not the wise and free
  Wept tears, and blood like tears?—The solemn harmony

### XIX

Paused, and the Spirit of that mighty singing   271
  To its abyss was suddenly withdrawn;
Then, as a wild swan, when sublimely winging
  Its path athwart the thunder-smoke of dawn,
Sinks headlong through the aëreal golden light   275
    On the heavy-sounding plain,
    When the bolt has pierced its brain;
As summer clouds dissolve, unburthened of their rain;
  As a far taper fades with fading night,
    As a brief insect dies with dying day,—   280
  My song, its pinions disarrayed of might,
    Drooped; o'er it closed the echoes far away
Of the great voice which did its flight sustain,
  As waves which lately paved his watery way
  Hiss round a drowner's head in their tempestuous play. 285

### TO——

#### I

I FEAR thy kisses, gentle maiden,
  Thou needest not fear mine;
My spirit is too deeply laden
  Ever to burthen thine.

II

I fear thy mien, thy tones, thy motion,          5
    Thou needest not fear mine;
Innocent is the heart's devotion
    With which I worship thine.


## ARETHUSA

I

ARETHUSA arose
From her couch of snows
In the Acroceraunian mountains,—
    From cloud and from crag,
    With many a jag,          5
Shepherding her bright fountains.
    She leapt down the rocks,
    With her rainbow locks
Streaming among the streams;—
    Her steps paved with green.          10
    The downward ravine
Which slopes to the western gleams;
    And gliding and springing
    She went, ever singing,
In murmurs as soft as sleep;          15
    The Earth seemed to love her,
    And Heaven smiled above her,
As she lingered towards the deep.


II

    Then Alpheus bold,
    On his glacier cold,          20
With his trident the mountains strook;
    And opened a chasm
    In the rocks—with the spasm
All Erymanthus shook.
    And the black south wind          25

It unsealed behind
The urns of the silent snow,
  And earthquake and thunder
  Did rend in sunder
The bars of the springs below.        30
  And the beard and the hair
  Of the River-god were
Seen through the torrent's sweep,
  As he followed the light
  Of the fleet nymph's flight       35
To the brink of the Dorian deep.

### III

'Oh, save me! Oh, guide me!
  And bid the deep hide me,
For he grasps me now by the hair!'
  The loud Ocean heard,       40
  To its blue depth stirred,
And divided at her prayer;
  And under the water
  The Earth's white daughter
Fled like a sunny beam;       45
  Behind her descended
  Her billows, unblended
With the brackish Dorian stream:--
  Like a gloomy stain
  On the emerald main       50
Alpheus rushed behind,--
  As an eagle pursuing
  A dove to its ruin
Down the streams of the cloudy wind.

### IV

Under the bowers       55
Where the Ocean Powers
Sit on their pearlèd thrones;

Through the coral woods
Of the weltering floods,
Over heaps of unvalued stones;                    60
Through the dim beams
Which amid the streams
Weave a network of coloured light;
And under the caves,
Where the shadowy waves                    65
Are as green as the forest's night:—
Outspeeding the shark,
And the sword-fish dark,
Under the Ocean's foam,
And up through the rifts                    70
Of the mountain clifts
They passed to their Dorian home.


                    V

And now from their fountains
In Enna's mountains,
Down one vale where the morning basks,                    75
Like friends once parted
Grown single-hearted,
They ply their watery tasks.
At sunrise they leap
From their cradles steep                    80
In the cave of the shelving hill;
At noontide they flow
Through the woods below
And the meadows of asphodel;
And at night they sleep                    85
In the rocking deep
Beneath the Ortygian shore;—
Like spirits that lie
In the azure sky
When they love but live no more.                    90

# SONG OF PROSERPINE

## WHILE GATHERING FLOWERS ON THE PLAIN OF ENNA

### I

SACRED Goddess, Mother Earth,
   Thou from whose immortal bosom
Gods, and men, and beasts have birth,
   Leaf and blade, and bud and blossom,
Breathe thine influence most divine      5
On thine own child, Proserpine.

### II

If with mists of evening dew
   Thou dost nourish these young flowers
Till they grow, in scent and hue,
   Fairest children of the Hours,      10
Breathe thine influence most divine
On thine own child, Proserpine.

# HYMN OF APOLLO

### I

THE sleepless Hours who watch me as I lie,
   Curtained with star-inwoven tapestries
From the broad moonlight of the sky,
   Fanning the busy dreams from my dim eyes,—
Waken me when their Mother, the gray Dawn,      5
Tells them that dreams and that the moon is gone.

### II

Then I arise, and climbing Heaven's blue dome,
   I walk over the mountains and the waves,
Leaving my robe upon the ocean foam;
   My footsteps pave the clouds with fire; the caves      10
Are filled with my bright presence, and the air
Leaves the green Earth to my embraces bare.

### III

The sunbeams are my shafts, with which I kill
   Deceit, that loves the night and fears the day:
All men who do or even imagine ill                    15
   Fly me, and from the glory of my ray
Good minds and open actions take new might,
Until diminished by the reign of Night.

### IV

I feed the clouds, the rainbows and the flowers
   With their aethereal colours; the moon's globe    20
And the pure stars in their eternal bowers
   Are cinctured with my power as with a robe;
Whatever lamps on Earth or Heaven may shine
Are portions of one power, which is mine.

### V

I stand at noon upon the peak of Heaven,             25
   Then with unwilling steps I wander down
Into the clouds of the Atlantic even;
   For grief that I depart they weep and frown:
What look is more delightful than the smile
With which I soothe them from the western isle?      30

### VI

I am the eye with which the Universe
   Beholds itself and knows itself divine;
All harmony of instrument or verse,
   All prophecy, all medicine is mine,
All light of art or nature;—to my song               35
Victory and praise in its own right belong.

## HYMN OF PAN

### I

From the forests and highlands
   We come, we come;

From the river-girt islands,
　Where loud waves are dumb
　　Listening to my sweet pipings. 5
The wind in the reeds and the rushes,
　The bees on the bells of thyme,
The birds on the myrtle bushes,
　The cicale above in the lime,
And the lizards below in the grass, 10
Were as silent as ever old Tmolus was,
　　Listening to my sweet pipings.

II

Liquid Peneus was flowing,
　And all dark Tempe lay
In Pelion's shadow, outgrowing 15
　The light of the dying day,
　　Speeded by my sweet pipings.
The Sileni, and Sylvans, and Fauns,
　And the Nymphs of the woods and the waves,
To the edge of the moist river-lawns, 20
　And the brink of the dewy caves,
And all that did then attend and follow,
Were silent with love, as you now, Apollo,
　　With envy of my sweet pipings.

III

I sang of the dancing stars, 25
　I sang of the daedal Earth,
And of Heaven—and the giant wars,
　And Love, and Death, and Birth,—
　　And then I changed my pipings,—
Singing how down the vale of Maenalus 30
　I pursued a maiden and clasped a reed.
Gods and men, we are all deluded thus!
　It breaks in our bosom and then we bleed:
All wept, as I think both ye now would,
If envy or age had not frozen your blood, 35
　　At the sorrow of my sweet pipings.

# THE QUESTION

### I

I DREAMED that, as I wandered by the way,
　Bare Winter suddenly was changed to Spring,
And gentle odours led my steps astray,
　Mixed with a sound of waters murmuring
Along a shelving bank of turf, which lay          5
　Under a copse, and hardly dared to fling
Its green arms round the bosom of the stream,
But kissed it and then fled, as thou mightest in dream.

### II

There grew pied wind-flowers and violets,
　Daisies, those pearled Arcturi of the earth,          10
The constellated flower that never sets;
　Faint oxslips; tender bluebells, at whose birth
The sod scarce heaved; and that tall flower that wets—
　Like a child, half in tenderness and mirth—
Its mother's face with Heaven's collected tears,          15
When the low wind, its playmate's voice, it hears.

### III

And in the warm hedge grew lush eglantine,
　Green cowbind and the moonlight-coloured may,
And cherry-blossoms, and white cups, whose wine
　Was the bright dew, yet drained not by the day;          20
And wild roses, and ivy serpentine,
　With its dark buds and leaves, wandering astray;
And flowers azure, black, and streaked with gold,
Fairer than any wakened eyes behold.

### IV

And nearer to the river's trembling edge          25
　There grew broad flag-flowers, purple pranked with
　　white,

And starry river buds among the sedge,
   And floating water-lilies, broad and bright,
Which lit the oak that overhung the hedge
   With moonlight beams of their own watery light;   30
And bulrushes, and reeds of such deep green
As soothed the dazzled eye with sober sheen.

v

Methought that of these visionary flowers
   I made a nosegay, bound in such a way
That the same hues, which in their natural bowers   35
   Were mingled or opposed, the like array
Kept these imprisoned children of the Hours
   Within my hand,—and then, elate and gay,
I hastened to the spot whence I had come,
That I might there present it!—Oh! to whom?   40

# THE TWO SPIRITS: AN ALLEGORY

*First Spirit.*

O THOU, who plumed with strong desire
   Wouldst float above the earth, beware!
A Shadow tracks thy flight of fire—
     Night is coming!
   Bright are the regions of the air,   5
And among the winds and beams
   It were delight to wander there—
     Night is coming!

*Second Spirit.*

The deathless stars are bright above;
   If I would cross the shade of night,   10
Within my heart is the lamp of love,
     And that is day!
And the moon will smile with gentle light
On my golden plumes where'er they move;
   The meteors will linger round my flight,   15
     And make night day.

*First Spirit.*

But if the whirlwinds of darkness waken
  Hail, and lightning, and stormy rain;
See, the bounds of the air are shaken—
      Night is coming!                                          20
  The red swift clouds of the hurricane
Yon declining sun have overtaken,
    The clash of the hail sweeps over the plain—
        Night is coming!

*Second Spirit.*

I see the light, and I hear the sound;                         25
  I'll sail on the flood of the tempest dark,
With the calm within and the light around
      Which makes night day:
  And thou, when the gloom is deep and stark,
Look from thy dull earth, slumber-bound,                       30
    My moon-like flight thou then mayst mark
        On high, far away.

———————————

Some say there is a precipice
  Where one vast pine is frozen to ruin
O'er piles of snow and chasms of ice                           35
      Mid Alpine mountains;
  And that the languid storm pursuing
That wingèd shape, for ever flies
    Round those hoar branches, aye renewing
        Its aëry fountains.                                     40

Some say when nights are dry and clear,
  And the death-dews sleep on the morass,
Sweet whispers are heard by the traveller,
      Which make night day:
  And a silver shape like his early love doth pass             45
Upborne by her wild and glittering hair,
    And when he awakes on the fragrant grass,
        He finds night day.

# ODE TO NAPLES[1]

## EPODE I α

I STOOD within the City disinterred[2];
    And heard the autumnal leaves like light footfalls
    Of spirits passing through the streets; and heard
The Mountain's slumberous voice at intervals
      Thrill through those roofless halls:        5
The oracular thunder penetrating shook
    The listening soul in my suspended blood;
I felt that Earth out of her deep heart spoke—
    I felt, but heard not:—through white columns glowed
      The isle-sustaining ocean-flood,      10
A plane of light between two heavens of azure!
    Around me gleamed many a bright sepulchre
Of whose pure beauty, Time, as if his pleasure
Were to spare Death, had never made erasure;
    But every living lineament was clear      15
    As in the sculptor's thought; and there
The wreaths of stony myrtle, ivy, and pine,
    Like winter leaves o'ergrown by moulded snow,
    Seemed only not to move and grow
Because the crystal silence of the air      20
    Weighed on their life; even as the Power divine
    Which then lulled all things, brooded upon mine.

## EPODE II α

    Then gentle winds arose
    With many a mingled close
Of wild Aeolian sound, and mountain-odours keen;      25

[1] The Author has connected many recollections of his visit to Pompeii and Baiae with the enthusiasm excited by the intelligence of the proclamation of a Constitutional Government at Naples. This has given a tinge of picturesque and descriptive imagery to the introductory Epodes which depicture these scenes, and some of the majestic feelings permanently connected with the scene of this animating event.—[SHELLEY'S NOTE.]

[2] Pompeii.—[SHELLEY'S NOTE.]

And where the Baian ocean
Welters with airlike motion,
Within, above, around its bowers of starry green,
 Moving the sea-flowers in those purple caves,
  Even as the ever stormless atmosphere   30
   Floats o'er the Elysian realm,
 It bore me, like an Angel, o'er the waves
  Of sunlight, whose swift pinnace of dewy air
   No storm can overwhelm.
   I sailed, where ever flows   35
   Under the calm Serene
   A spirit of deep emotion
   From the unknown graves
   Of the dead Kings of Melody[1].

Shadowy Aornos darkened o'er the helm   40
The horizontal aether; Heaven stripped bare
Its depths over Elysium, where the prow
Made the invisible water white as snow;
From that Typhaean mount, Inarime,
 There streamed a sunbright vapour, like the standard 45
  Of some aethereal host;
   Whilst from all the coast,
 Louder and louder, gathering round, there wandered
Over the oracular woods and divine sea
Prophesyings which grew articulate—   50
They seize me—I must speak them!—be they fate!

### STROPHE I

Naples! thou Heart of men which ever pantest
 Naked, beneath the lidless eye of Heaven!
Elysian City, which to calm enchantest
 The mutinous air and sea! they round thee, even 55
 As sleep round Love, are driven!
Metropolis of a ruined Paradise
 Long lost, late won, and yet but half regained!
Bright Altar of the bloodless sacrifice,

[1] Homer and Virgil.—[SHELLEY's NOTE.]

Which armèd Victory offers up unstained          60
 To Love, the flower-enchainèd!
Thou which wert once, and then didst cease to be,
Now art, and henceforth ever shalt be, free,
 If Hope, and Truth, and Justice can avail,—
  Hail, hail, all hail!          65

STROPHE II

  Thou youngest giant birth
  Which from the groaning earth
Leap'st, clothed in armour of impenetrable scale!
  Last of the Intercessors!
  Who 'gainst the Crowned Transgressors          70
Pleadest before God's love!  Arrayed in Wisdom's mail,
  Wave thy lightning lance in mirth
  Nor let thy high heart fail,
Though from their hundred gates the leagued Oppressors
  With hurried legions move!          75
  Hail, hail, all hail!

ANTISTROPHE Iα

What though Cimmerian Anarchs dare blaspheme
 Freedom and thee? thy shield is as a mirror
To make their blind slaves see, and with fierce gleam
 To turn his hungry sword upon the wearer;          80
  A new Actaeon's error
Shall theirs have been—devoured by their own hounds!
 Be thou like the imperial Basilisk
Killing thy foe with unapparent wounds!
 Gaze on Oppression, till at that dread risk          85
 Aghast she pass from the Earth's disk:
Fear not, but gaze—for freemen mightier grow,
And slaves more feeble, gazing on their foe:—
 If Hope, and Truth, and Justice may avail,
  Thou shalt be great—All hail!          90

ANTISTROPHE II α

From Freedom's form divine,
From Nature's inmost shrine,
Strip every impious gawd, rend Error veil by veil;
    O'er Ruin desolate,
    O'er Falsehood's fallen state,         95
Sit thou sublime, unawed; be the Destroyer pale!
    And equal laws be thine,
    And wingèd words let sail,
Freighted with truth even from the throne of God:
    That wealth, surviving fate,        100
    Be thine.—All hail!

ANTISTROPHE I β

Didst thou not start to hear Spain's thrilling paean
  From land to land re-echoed solemnly,
Till silence became music? From the Aeaean[1]
    To the cold Alps, eternal Italy        105
    Starts to hear thine! The Sea
Which paves the desert streets of Venice laughs
  In light and music; widowed Genoa wan
By moonlight spells ancestral epitaphs,
    Murmuring, 'Where is Doria?' fair Milan,    110
    Within whose veins long ran
The viper's[2] palysing venom, lifts her heel
To bruise his head. The signal and the seal
  (If Hope and Truth and Justice can avail)
    Art thou of all these hopes.—O hail!     115

ANTISTROPHE II β

Florence! beneath the sun,
Of cities fairest one,
Blushes within her bower for Freedom's expectation:
    From eyes of quenchless hope

---

[1] Aeaea, the island of Circe.—[SHELLEY'S NOTE.]
[2] The viper was the armorial device of the Visconti, tyrants of Milan.
—[SHELLEY'S NOTE.]

  Rome tears the priestly cope,     120
As ruling once by power, so now by admiration,—
   An athlete stripped to run
   From a remoter station
For the high prize lost on Philippi's shore:—
  As then Hope, Truth, and Justice did avail,  125
  So now may Fraud and Wrong! O hail!

EPODE I β

Hear ye the march as of the Earth-born Forms
  Arrayed against the ever-living Gods?
The crash and darkness of a thousand storms
  Bursting their inaccessible abodes   130
   Of crags and thunder-clouds?
See ye the banners blazoned to the day,
  Inwrought with emblems of barbaric pride?
Dissonant threats kill Silence far away,
  The serene Heaven which wraps our Eden wide  135
   With iron light is dyed;
The Anarchs of the North lead forth their legions
   Like Chaos o'er creation, uncreating;
An hundred tribes nourished on strange religions
And lawless slaveries,—down the aëreal regions  140
   Of the white Alps, desolating,
   Famished wolves that bide no waiting,
Blotting the glowing footsteps of old glory,
Trampling our columned cities into dust,
   Their dull and savage lust   145
  On Beauty's corse to sickness satiating—
They come! The fields they tread look black and hoary
With fire—from their red feet the streams run gory!

EPODE II β

  Great Spirit, deepest Love!
  Which rulest and dost move   150
All things which live and are, within the Italian shore;
  Who spreadest Heaven around it,
  Whose woods, rocks, waves, surround it;

Who sittest in thy star, o'er Ocean's western floor;
Spirit of beauty! at whose soft command                    155
  The sunbeams and the showers distil its foison
      From the earth's bosom chill;
Oh, bid those beams be each a blinding brand
  Of lightning! bid those showers be dews of poison!
      Bid the Earth's plenty kill!                 160
      Bid thy bright Heaven above,
      Whilst light and darkness bound it,
      Be their tomb who planned
      To make it ours and thine!
  Or, with thine harmonizing ardours fill             165
And raise thy sons, as o'er the prone horizon
Thy lamp feeds every twilight wave with fire—
Be man's high hope and unextinct desire
The instrument to work thy will divine!
  Then clouds from sunbeams, antelopes from leopards,   170
      And frowns and fears from thee,
      Would not more swiftly flee
  Than Celtic wolves from the Ausonian shepherds.—
Whatever, Spirit, from thy starry shrine
  Thou yieldest or withholdest, oh, let be              175
  This city of thy worship ever free!

## AUTUMN: A DIRGE

### I

THE warm sun is failing, the bleak wind is wailing,
The bare boughs are sighing, the pale flowers are dying,
      And the Year
On the earth her death-bed, in a shroud of leaves dead,
        Is lying.                             5
      Come, Months, come away,
      From November to May,
      In your saddest array;
      Follow the bier
      Of the dead cold Year,                       10
And like dim shadows watch by her sepulchre.

II

The chill rain is falling, the nipped worm is crawling,
The rivers are swelling, the thunder is knelling
      For the Year;
The blithe swallows are flown, and the lizards each gone    15
        To his dwelling;
        Come, Months, come away;
        Put on white, black, and gray;
        Let your light sisters play—
        Ye, follow the bier            20
        Of the dead cold Year,
And make her grave green with tear on tear.

## THE WANING MOON

    AND like a dying lady, lean and pale,
    Who totters forth, wrapped in a gauzy veil
    Out of her chamber, led by the insane
    And feeble wanderings of her fading brain,
    The moon arose up in the murky East,       5
    A white and shapeless mass—

## TO THE MOON

I

    ART thou pale for weariness
Of climbing heaven and gazing on the earth,
    Wandering companionless
Among the stars that have a different birth,—
And ever changing, like a joyless eye       5
That finds no object worth its constancy?

## THE TOWER OF FAMINE

AMID the desolation of a city,
Which was the cradle, and is now the grave
Of an extinguished people,—so that Pity

Weeps o'er the shipwrecks of Oblivion's wave,
There stands the Tower of Famine.    It is built          5
Upon some prison-homes, whose dwellers rave

For bread, and gold, and blood: Pain, linked to Guilt,
Agitates the light flame of their hours,
Until its vital oil is spent or spilt.

There stands the pile, a tower amid the towers          10
And sacred domes; each marble-ribbèd roof,
The brazen-gated temples, and the bowers

Of solitary wealth,—the tempest-proof
Pavilions of the dark Italian air,—
Are by its presence dimmed—they stand aloof,          15

And are withdrawn—so that the world is bare;
As if a spectre wrapped in shapeless terror
Amid a company of ladies fair

Should glide and glow, till it became a mirror
Of all their beauty, and their hair and hue,          20
The life of their sweet eyes, with all its error,
Should be absorbed, till they to marble grew.

# AN ALLEGORY

### I

A PORTAL as of shadowy adamant
    Stands yawning on the highway of the life
Which we all tread, a cavern huge and gaunt;
    Around it rages an unceasing strife
Of shadows, like the restless clouds that haunt          5
The gap of some cleft mountain, lifted high
Into the whirlwinds of the upper sky.

II

And many pass it by with careless tread,
  Not knowing that a shadowy . . .
Tracks every traveller even to where the dead          10
  Wait peacefully for their companion new;
But others, by more curious humour led,
  Pause to examine;—these are very few,
And they learn little there, except to know
That shadows follow them where'er they go.             15

## SONNET

YE hasten to the grave! What seek ye there,
Ye restless thoughts and busy purposes
Of the idle brain, which the world's livery wear?
O thou quick heart, which pantest to possess
All that pale Expectation feigneth fair!               5
Thou vainly curious mind which wouldest guess
Whence thou didst come, and whither thou must go,
And all that never yet was known would know—
Oh, whither hasten ye, that thus ye press,
With such swift feet life's green and pleasant path,   10
Seeking, alike from happiness and woe,
A refuge in the cavern of gray death?
O heart, and mind, and thoughts! what thing do you
Hope to inherit in the grave below?

## GOOD-NIGHT

I

GOOD-NIGHT? ah! no; the hour is ill
  Which severs those it should unite;
Let us remain together still,
  Then it will be *good* night.

## II

How can I call the lone night good,     5
    Though thy sweet wishes wing its flight?
Be it not said, thought, understood—
    Then it will be—*good* night.

## III

To hearts which near each other move
    From evening close to morning light,     10
The night is good; because, by love,
    They never *say* good-night.

# TIME LONG PAST

## I

LIKE the ghost of a dear friend dead
    Is Time long past.
A tone which is now forever fled
A hope which is now forever past,
A love so sweet it could not last,     5
    Was Time long past.

## II

There were sweet dreams in the night
    Of Time long past:
And, was it sadness or delight,
Each day a shadow onward cast     10
Which made us wish it yet might last—
    That Time long past.

## III

There is regret, almost remorse,
    For Time long past.
'Tis like a child's belovèd corse     15
A father watches, till at last
Beauty is like remembrance, cast
    From Time long past.

# FRAGMENT: 'ALAS! THIS IS NOT WHAT I THOUGHT LIFE WAS'

ALAS! this is not what I thought life was.
I knew that there were crimes and evil men,
Misery and hate; nor did I hope to pass
Untouched by suffering, through the rugged glen.
In mine own heart I saw as in a glass 5
The hearts of others        And when
I went among my kind, with triple brass
Of calm endurance my weak breast I armed,
To bear scorn, fear, and hate, a woful mass!

# POEMS WRITTEN IN 1821

## DIRGE FOR THE YEAR

### I

ORPHAN Hours, the Year is dead,
   Come and sigh, come and weep!
Merry Hours, smile instead,
   For the Year is but asleep.
See, it smiles as it is sleeping, 5
Mocking your untimely weeping.

### II

As an earthquake rocks a corse
   In its coffin in the clay,
So White Winter, that rough nurse,
   Rocks the death-cold Year to-day; 10
Solemn Hours! wail aloud
For your mother in her shroud.

### III

As the wild air stirs and sways
   The tree-swung cradle of a child,
So the breath of these rude days 15
   Rocks the Year:—be calm and mild,

Trembling Hours, she will arise
With new love within her eyes.

IV

January gray is here,
    Like a sexton by her grave;          20
February bears the bier,
    March with grief doth howl and rave,
And April weeps—but, O ye Hours!
Follow with May's fairest flowers.

## TO NIGHT

I

SWIFTLY walk o'er the western wave,
        Spirit of Night!
Out of the misty eastern cave,
Where, all the long and lone daylight,
Thou wovest dreams of joy and fear,          5
Which make thee terrible and dear,—
        Swift be thy flight!

II

Wrap thy form in a mantle gray,
        Star-inwrought!
Blind with thine hair the eyes of Day;          10
Kiss her until she be wearied out,
Then wander o'er city, and sea, and land,
Touching all with thine opiate wand—
        Come, long-sought!

III

When I arose and saw the dawn          15
        I sighed for thee;
When light rode high, and the dew was gone,
And noon lay heavy on flower and tree
And the weary Day turned to his rest,
Lingering like an unloved guest,          20
        I sighed for thee.

IV

Thy brother Death came, and cried,
    Wouldst thou me?
Thy sweet child Sleep, the filmy-eyed,
Murmured like a noontide bee,           25
Shall I nestle near thy side?
Wouldst thou me?—And I replied,
    No, not thee!

V

Death will come when thou art dead,
    Soon, too soon—           30
Sleep will come when thou art fled ;
Of neither would I ask the boon
I ask of thee, belovèd Night—
Swift be thine approaching flight,
    Come soon, soon!           35

# TIME

UNFATHOMABLE Sea! whose waves are years,
  Ocean of Time, whose waters of deep woe
Are brackish with the salt of human tears!
  Thou shoreless flood, which in thy ebb and flow
Claspest the limits of mortality,          5
And sick of prey, yet howling on for more,
Vomitest thy wrecks on its inhospitable shore;
  Treacherous in calm, and terrible in storm,
    Who shall put forth on thee,
    Unfathomable Sea?          10

# LINES

I

FAR, far away, O ye
Halcyons of Memory,

Seek some far calmer nest
Than this abandoned breast!
No news of your false spring                    5
To my heart's winter bring,
Once having gone, in vain
        Ye come again.


II

Vultures, who build your bowers
High in the Future's towers,                    10
Withered hopes on hopes are spread!
Dying joys, choked by the dead,
Will serve your beaks for prey
        Many a day.


# FROM THE ARABIC: AN IMITATION

I

My faint spirit was sitting in the light
        Of thy looks, my love;
It panted for thee like the hind at noon
        For the brooks, my love.
Thy barb whose hoofs outspeed the tempest's flight    5
        Bore thee far from me;
My heart, for my weak feet were weary soon
        Did companion thee.


II

Ah! fleeter far than fleetest storm or steed,
        Or the death they bear,                 10
The heart which tender thought clothes like a dove
        With the wings of care;
In the battle, in the darkness, in the need,
        Shall mine cling to thee,
Nor claim one smile for all the comfort, love,      15
        It may bring to thee.

# TO EMILIA VIVIANI

### I

MADONNA, wherefore hast thou sent to me
  Sweet-basil and mignonette?
Embleming love and health, which never yet
In the same wreath might be.
  Alas, and they are wet!                                         5
Is it with thy kisses or thy tears?
    For never rain or dew
    Such fragrance drew
From plant or flower—the very doubt endears
    My sadness ever new,                                         10
The sighs I breathe, the tears I shed for thee.


### II

Send the stars light, but send not love to me,
  In whom love ever made
Health like a heap of embers soon to fade—


## TO ——

Music, when soft voices die,
Vibrates in the memory—
Odours, when sweet violets sicken,
Live within the sense they quicken.


Rose leaves, when the rose is dead,                               5
Are heaped for the belovèd's bed;
And so thy thoughts, when thou art gone,
Love itself shall slumber on.

# SONG

## I

RARELY, rarely, comest thou,
  Spirit of Delight!
Wherefore hast thou left me now
  Many a day and night?
Many a weary night and day          5
'Tis since thou art fled away.

## II

How shall ever one like me
  Win thee back again?
With the joyous and the free
  Thou wilt scoff at pain.          10
Spirit false! thou hast forgot
All but those who need thee not.

## III

As a lizard with the shade
  Of a trembling leaf,
Thou with sorrow art dismayed;          15
  Even the sighs of grief
Reproach thee, that thou art not near,
And reproach thou wilt not hear.

## IV

Let me set my mournful ditty
  To a merry measure;
Thou wilt never come for pity,          20
  Thou wilt come for pleasure;
Pity then will cut away
Those cruel wings, and thou wilt stay.

V

I love all that thou lovest,                     25
    Spirit of Delight!
The fresh Earth in new leaves dressed,
    And the starry night;
Autumn evening, and the morn
When the golden mists are born.                  30

VI

I love snow, and all the forms
    Of the radiant frost;
I love waves, and winds, and storms,
    Everything almost
Which is Nature's, and may be                    35
Untainted by man's misery.

VII

I love tranquil solitude,
    And such society
As is quiet, wise, and good;
    Between thee and me
What difference? but thou dost possess           40
The things I seek, not love them less.

VIII

I love Love—though he has wings,
    And like light can flee,
But above all other things,                      45
    Spirit, I love thee—
Thou art love and life! Oh, come,
Make once more my heart thy home.

## MUTABILITY

I

THE flower that smiles to-day
    To-morrow dies;

R

All that we wish to stay
    Tempts and then flies.
What is this world's delight?          5
Lightning that mocks the night,
    Brief even as bright.

II

Virtue, how frail it is!
    Friendship how rare!
Love, how it sells poor bliss          10
    For proud despair!
But we, though soon they fall,
Survive their joy, and all
    Which ours we call.

III

Whilst skies are blue and bright,          15
    Whilst flowers are gay,
Whilst eyes that change ere night
    Make glad the day;
Whilst yet the calm hours creep,
Dream thou—and from thy sleep          20
    Then wake to weep.

# LINES WRITTEN ON HEARING THE NEWS OF THE DEATH OF NAPOLEON

WHAT! alive and so bold, O Earth?
  Art thou not overbold?
  What! leapest thou forth as of old
In the light of thy morning mirth,
The last of the flock of the starry fold?          5
Ha! leapest thou forth as of old?
Are not the limbs still when the ghost is fled,
And canst thou move, Napoleon being dead?

How! is not thy quick heart cold?
  What spark is alive on thy hearth?          10
  How! is not *his* death-knell knolled?
And livest *thou* still, Mother Earth?
Thou wert warming thy fingers old
O'er the embers covered and cold
Of that most fiery spirit, when it fled—          15
What, Mother, do you laugh now he is dead?


'Who has known me of old,' replied Earth,
  'Or who has my story told?
  It is thou who art overbold.'
And the lightning of scorn laughed forth          20
As she sung, 'To my bosom I fold
All my sons when their knell is knolled,
And so with living motion all are fed,
And the quick spring like weeds out of the dead.


'Still alive and still bold,' shouted Earth,          25
  'I grow bolder and still more bold.
  The dead fill me ten thousandfold
Fuller of speed, and splendour, and mirth.
I was cloudy and sullen, and cold,
Like a frozen chaos uprolled.
Till by the spirit of the mighty dead          30
My heart grew warm. I feed on whom I fed.


'Ay, alive and still bold,' muttered Earth,
  'Napoleon's fierce spirit rolled,
  In terror and blood and gold,          35
A torrent of ruin to death from his birth.
Leave the millions who follow to mould
The metal before it be cold;
And weave into his shame, which like the dead
Shrouds me, the hopes that from his glory fled.'          40

## SONNET : POLITICAL GREATNESS

Nor happiness, nor majesty, nor fame,
Nor peace, nor strength, nor skill in arms or arts,
Shepherd those herds whom tyranny makes tame;
Verse echoes not one beating of their hearts,
History is but the shadow of their shame,                    5
Art veils her glass, or from the pageant starts
As to oblivion their blind millions fleet,
Staining that Heaven with obscene imagery
Of their own likeness.  What are numbers knit
By force or custom?  Man who man would be,            10
Must rule the empire of himself; in it
Must be supreme, establishing his throne
On vanquished will, quelling the anarchy
Of hopes and fears, being himself alone.

## THE AZIOLA

### I

'Do you not hear the Aziola cry?
    Methinks she must be nigh,'
        Said Mary, as we sate
In dusk, ere stars were lit, or candles brought;
        And I, who thought                            5
    This Aziola was some tedious woman,
        Asked, 'Who is Aziola?'  How elate
I felt to know that it was nothing human,
    No mockery of myself to fear or hate:
        And Mary saw my soul,                        10
And laughed, and said, 'Disquiet yourself not;
    'Tis nothing but a little downy owl.'

### II

Sad Aziola! many an eventide
    Thy music I had heard
By wood and stream, meadow and mountain-side,   15
    And fields and marshes wide,—

Such as nor voice, nor lute, nor wind, nor bird,
 The soul ever stirred;
Unlike and far sweeter than them all.
Sad Aziola! from that moment I    20
 Loved thee and thy sad cry.


## A LAMENT

### I

O WORLD! O life! O time!
On whose last steps I climb,
 Trembling at that where I had stood before;
When will return the glory of your prime?
  No more—Oh, never more!   5

### II

Out of the day and night
A joy has taken flight;
 Fresh spring, and summer, and winter hoar,
Move my faint heart with grief, but with delight
  No more—Oh, never more!   10


## REMEMBRANCE

### I

 SWIFTER far than summer's flight—
 Swifter far than youth's delight—
 Swifter far than happy night,
  Art thou come and gone—
 As the earth when leaves are dead,   5
 As the night when sleep is sped,
 As the heart when joy is fled,
  I am left alone, alone.

### II

 The swallow summer comes again—
 The owlet night resumes her reign—
 But the wild-swan youth is fain   10

To fly with thee, false as thou.—
My heart each day desires the morrow;
Sleep itself is turned to sorrow;
Vainly would my winter borrow          15
        Sunny leaves from any bough.

### III

Lilies for a bridal bed—
Roses for a matron's head—
Violets for a maiden dead—
        Pansies let *my* flowers be:          20
On the living grave I bear
Scatter them without a tear—
Let no friend, however dear,
        Waste one hope, one fear for me.

## TO EDWARD WILLIAMS

### I

THE serpent is shut out from Paradise.
        The wounded deer must seek the herb no more
        In which its heart-cure lies:
        The widowed dove must cease to haunt a bower
Like that from which its mate with feignèd sighs          5
        Fled in the April hour.
        I too must seldom seek again
Near happy friends a mitigated pain.

### II

Of hatred I am proud,—with scorn content;
        Indifference, that once hurt me, now is grown          10
        Itself indifferent;
        But, not to speak of love, pity alone
Can break a spirit already more than bent.
        The miserable one
        Turns the mind's poison into food,—          15
Its medicine is tears,—its evil good.

### III

Therefore, if now I see you seldomer,
    Dear friends, dear *friend*! know that I only fly
      Your looks, because they stir
    Griefs that should sleep, and hopes that cannot die: 20
The very comfort that they minister
      I scarce can bear, yet I,
      So deeply is the arrow gone,
Should quickly perish if it were withdrawn.

### IV

When I return to my cold home, you ask     25
    Why I am not as I have ever been.
      *You* spoil me for the task
Of acting a forced part in life's dull scene,—
Of wearing on my brow the idle mask
      Of author, great or mean,     30
      In the world's carnival. I sought
Peace thus, and but in you I found it not.

### V

Full half an hour, to-day, I tried my lot
    With various flowers, and every one still said,
      'She loves me—loves me not.'     35
    And if this meant a vision long since fled—
If it meant fortune, fame, or peace of thought—
      If it meant,—but I dread
      To speak what you may know too well:
Still there was truth in the sad oracle.     40

### VI

The crane o'er seas and forests seeks her home;
    No bird so wild but has its quiet nest,
      When it no more would roam;
    The sleepless billows on the ocean's breast

Break like a bursting heart, and die in foam,　　　45
　　　　And thus at length find rest:
　　　　　　Doubtless there is a place of peace
Where *my* weak heart and all its throbs will cease

### VII

I asked her, yesterday, if she believed
　　　　That I had resolution.  One who *had*　　　50
　　　　　　Would ne'er have thus relieved
　　　　His heart with words,—but what his judgement bade
Would do, and leave the scorner unrelieved.
　　　　　　These verses are too sad
　　　　To send to you, but that I know,　　　55
Happy yourself, you feel another's woe.

### TO ——

### I

ONE word is too often profaned
　　　　For me to profane it,
One feeling too falsely disdained
　　　　For thee to disdain it;
One hope is too like despair　　　5
　　　　For prudence to smother,
And pity from thee more dear
　　　　Than that from another.

### II

I can give not what men call love,
　　　　But wilt thou accept not　　　10
The worship the heart lifts above
　　　　And the Heavens reject not,—
The desire of the moth for the star,
　　　　Of the night for the morrow,
The devotion to something afar　　　15
　　　　From the sphere of our sorrow?

## TO ——

### I

WHEN passion's trance is overpast,
If tenderness and truth could last,
Or live, whilst all wild feelings keep
Some mortal slumber, dark and deep,
I should not weep, I should not weep!                    5

### II

It were enough to feel, to see,
Thy soft eyes gazing tenderly,
And dream the rest—and burn and be
The secret food of fires unseen,
Couldst thou but be as thou hast been.                   10

### III

After the slumber of the year
The woodland violets reappear;
All things revive in field or grove,
And sky and sea, but two, which move
And form all others, life and love.                      15

## A BRIDAL SONG

### I

THE golden gates of Sleep unbar
  Where Strength and Beauty, met together,
Kindle their image like a star
  In a sea of glassy weather!
Night, with all thy stars look down,—                    5
  Darkness, weep thy holiest dew,—
Never smiled the inconstant moon
     On a pair so true.
Let eyes not see their own delight;—
Haste, swift Hour, and thy flight                        10
     Oft renew.

II

Fairies, sprites, and angels, keep her!
  Holy stars, permit no wrong!
And return to wake the sleeper,
      Dawn—ere it be long!
O joy! O fear! what will be done
In the absence of the sun!
      Come along!

# GINEVRA

WILD, pale, and wonder-stricken, even as one
Who staggers forth into the air and sun
From the dark chamber of a mortal fever,
Bewildered, and incapable, and ever
Fancying strange comments in her dizzy brain
Of usual shapes, till the familiar train
Of objects and of persons passed like things
Strange as a dreamer's mad imaginings,
Ginevra from the nuptial altar went;
The vows to which her lips had sworn assent
Rung in her brain still with a jarring din,
Deafening the lost intelligence within.

And so she moved under the bridal veil,
Which made the paleness of her cheek more pale,
And deepened the faint crimson of her mouth,
And darkened her dark locks, as moonlight doth,—
And of the gold and jewels glittering there
She scarce felt conscious,—but the weary glare
Lay like a chaos of unwelcome light,
Vexing the sense with gorgeous undelight,
A moonbeam in the shadow of a cloud
Was less heavenly fair—her face was bowed,
And as she passed, the diamonds in her hair
Were mirrored in the polished marble stair

Which led from the cathedral to the street;   25
And ever as she went her light fair feet
Erased these images.

The bride-maidens who round her thronging came,
Some with a sense of self-rebuke and shame,
Envying the unenviable; and others   30
Making the joy which should have been another's
Their own by gentle sympathy; and some
Sighing to think of an unhappy home:
Some few admiring what can ever lure
Maidens to leave the heaven serene and pure   35
Of parents' smiles for life's great cheat; a thing
Bitter to taste, sweet in imagining.

But they are all dispersed—and, lo! she stands
Looking in idle grief on her white hands,
Alone within the garden now her own;   40
And through the sunny air, with jangling tone,
The music of the merry marriage-bells,
Killing the azure silence, sinks and swells;—
Absorbed like one within a dream who dreams
That he is dreaming, until slumber seems   45
A mockery of itself—when suddenly
Antonio stood before her, pale as she.
With agony, with sorrow, and with pride,
He lifted his wan eyes upon the bride,
And said—'Is this thy faith?' and then as one   50
Whose sleeping face is stricken by the sun
With light like a harsh voice, which bids him rise
And look upon his day of life with eyes
Which weep in vain that they can dream no more,
Ginevra saw her lover, and forbore   55
To shriek or faint, and checked the stifling blood
Rushing upon her heart, and unsubdued
Said—'Friend, if earthly violence or ill,
Suspicion, doubt, or the tyrannic will
Of parents, chance or custom, time or change,   60

Or circumstance, or terror, or revenge,
Or bewildered looks, or words, or evil speech,
With all their stings and venom can impeach
Our love,—we love not:—if the grave which hides
The victim from the tyrant, and divides                                65
The cheek that whitens from the eyes that dart
Imperious inquisition to the heart
That is another's, could dissever ours,
We love not.'—'What! do not the silent hours
Beckon thee to Gherardi's bridal bed?                                  70
Is not that ring'—a pledge, he would have said,
Of broken vows, but she with patient look
The golden circle from her finger took,
And said—'Accept this token of my faith,
The pledge of vows to be absolved by death;                            75
And I am dead or shall be soon—my knell
Will mix its music with that merry bell,
Does it not sound as if they sweetly said
"We toll a corpse out of the marriage-bed"?
The flowers upon my bridal chamber strewn                              80
Will serve unfaded for my bier—so soon
That even the dying violet will not die
Before Ginevra.' The strong fantasy
Had made her accents weaker and more weak,
And quenched the crimson life upon her cheek,                          85
And glazed her eyes, and spread an atmosphere
Round her, which chilled the burning noon with fear,
Making her but an image of the thought
Which, like a prophet or a shadow, brought
News of the terrors of the coming time.                                90
Like an accuser branded with the crime
He would have cast on a belovèd friend,
Whose dying eyes reproach not to the end
The pale betrayer—he then with vain repentance
Would share, he cannot now avert, the sentence—                        95
Antonio stood and would have spoken, when
The compound voice of women and of men
Was heard approaching; he retired, while she

Was led amid the admiring company
Back to the palace,—and her maidens soon 100
Changed her attire for the afternoon,
And left her at her own request to keep
An hour of quiet and rest:—like one asleep
With open eyes and folded hands she lay,
Pale in the light of the declining day. 105

Meanwhile the day sinks fast, the sun is set,
And in the lighted hall the guests are met;
The beautiful looked lovelier in the light
Of love, and admiration, and delight
Reflected from a thousand hearts and eyes, 110
Kindling a momentary Paradise.
This crowd is safer than the silent wood,
Where love's own doubts disturb the solitude;
On frozen hearts the fiery rain of wine
Falls, and the dew of music more divine 115
Tempers the deep emotions of the time
To spirits cradled in a sunny clime:—
How many meet, who never yet have met,
To part too soon, but never to forget,
How many saw the beauty, power and wit 120
Of looks and words which ne'er enchanted yet;
But life's familiar veil was now withdrawn,
As the world leaps before an earthquake's dawn,
And unprophetic of the coming hours,
The matin winds from the expanded flowers 125
Scatter their hoarded incense, and awaken
The earth, until the dewy sleep is shaken
From every living heart which it possesses,
Through seas and winds, cities and wildernesses,
As if the future and the past were all 130
Treasured i' the instant;—so Gherardi's hall
Laughed in the mirth of its lord's festival,
Till some one asked—'Where is the Bride?' And then
A bridesmaid went,—and ere she came again
A silence fell upon the guests—a pause 135

s

Of expectation, as when beauty awes
All hearts with its approach, though unbeheld;
Then wonder, and then fear that wonder quelled;—
For whispers passed from mouth to ear which drew
The colour from the hearer's cheeks, and flew          140
Louder and swifter round the company;
And then Gherardi entered with an eye
Of ostentatious trouble, and a crowd
Surrounded him, and some were weeping loud.

They found Ginevra dead! if it be death          145
To lie without motion, or pulse, or breath,
With waxen cheeks, and limbs cold, stiff, and white,
And open eyes, whose fixed and glassy light
Mocked at the speculation they had owned.
If it be death, when there is felt around          150
A smell of clay, a pale and icy glare,
And silence, and a sense that lifts the hair
From the scalp to the ankles, as it were
Corruption from the spirit passing forth,
And giving all it shrouded to the earth,          155
And leaving as swift lightning in its flight
Ashes, and smoke, and darkness: in our night
Of thought we know thus much of death,—no more
Than the unborn dream of our life before
Their barks are wrecked on its inhospitable shore.          160
The marriage feast and its solemnity
Was turned to funeral pomp—the company,
With heavy hearts and looks, broke up; nor they
Who loved the dead went weeping on their way
Alone, but sorrow mixed with sad surprise          165
Loosened the springs of pity in all eyes,
On which that form, whose fate they weep in vain,
Will never, thought they, kindle smiles again.
The lamps which, half extinguished in their haste,
Gleamed few and faint o'er the abandoned feast,          170
Showed as it were within the vaulted room
A cloud of sorrow hanging, as if gloom

Had passed out of men's minds into the air.
Some few yet stood around Gherardi there,
Friends and relations of the dead,—and he,                     175
A loveless man, accepted torpidly
The consolation that he wanted not;
Awe in the place of grief within him wrought.
Their whispers made the solemn silence seem
More still—some wept, . . .                                    180
Some melted into tears without a sob,
And some with hearts that might be heard to throb
Leaned on the table, and at intervals
Shuddered to hear through the deserted halls
And corridors the thrilling shrieks which came                185
Upon the breeze of night, that shook the flame
Of every torch and taper as it swept
From out the chamber where the women kept;—
Their tears fell on the dear companion cold
Of pleasures now departed; then was knolled                   190
The bell of death, and soon the priests arrived,
And finding Death their penitent had shrived,
Returned like ravens from a corpse whereon
A vulture has just feasted to the bone.
And then the mourning women came.—                            195

.    .    .    .    .    .

### THE DIRGE

            Old winter was gone
In his weakness back to the mountains hoar,
            And the spring came down
From the planet that hovers upon the shore
        Where the sea of sunlight encroaches                  200
On the limits of wintry night;—
If the land, and the air, and the sea,
        Rejoice not when spring approaches,
We did not rejoice in thee,
                Ginevra!                                      205

She is still, she is cold
        On the bridal couch,
One step to the white deathbed,
        And one to the bier,
And one to the charnel—and one, oh where?    210
        The dark arrow fled
        In the noon.

Ere the sun through heaven once more has rolled,
The rats in her heart
Will have made their nest,    215
And the worms be alive in her golden hair,
While the Spirit that guides the sun,
Sits throned in his flaming chair,
        She shall sleep.

## EVENING: PONTE AL MARE, PISA

### I

THE sun is set; the swallows are asleep;
    The bats are flitting fast in the gray air;
The slow soft toads out of damp corners creep,
    And evening's breath, wandering here and there
Over the quivering surface of the stream,    5
Wakes not one ripple from its summer dream.

### II

There is no dew on the dry grass to-night,
    Nor damp within the shadow of the trees;
The wind is intermitting, dry, and light;
    And in the inconstant motion of the breeze    10
The dust and straws are driven up and down,
And whirled about the pavement of the town.

### III

Within the surface of the fleeting river
    The wrinkled image of the city lay,
Immovably unquiet, and forever    15

It trembles, but it never fades away;
Go to the . . .
You, being changed, will find it then as now.

IV

The chasm in which the sun has sunk is shut
   By darkest barriers of cinereous cloud,         20
Like mountain over mountain huddled—but
   Growing and moving upwards in a crowd,
And over it a space of watery blue,
Which the keen evening star is shining through.

## THE BOAT ON THE SERCHIO

OUR boat is asleep on Serchio's stream,
Its sails are folded like thoughts in a dream,
The helm sways idly, hither and thither;
   Dominic, the boatsman, has brought the mast,
   And the oars, and the sails; but 'tis sleeping fast,    5
Like a beast, unconscious of its tether.

The stars burnt out in the pale blue air,
And the thin white moon lay withering there;
To tower, and cavern, and rift, and tree,
The owl and the bat fled drowsily.          10
Day had kindled the dewy woods,
   And the rocks above and the stream below,
And the vapours in their multitudes,
   And the Apennines' shroud of summer snow,
And clothed with light of aëry gold      15
The mists in their eastern caves uprolled.

Day had awakened all things that be,
The lark and the thrush and the swallow free,
   And the milkmaid's song and the mower's scythe,
And the matin-bell and the mountain bee:    20
Fireflies were quenched on the dewy corn,

Glow-worms went out on the river's brim,
  Like lamps which a student forgets to trim:
The beetle forgot to wind his horn,
  The crickets were still in the meadow and hill:     25
Like a flock of rooks at a farmer's gun
Night's dreams and terrors, every one,
Fled from the brains which are their prey
From the lamp's death to the morning ray.

All rose to do the task He set to each,     30
  Who shaped us to His ends and not our own;
The million rose to learn, and one to teach
  What none yet ever knew or can be known.
    And many rose
  Whose woe was such that fear became desire;—     35
Melchior and Lionel were not among those;
They from the throng of men had stepped aside,
And made their home under the green hill-side.
It was that hill, whose intervening brow
  Screens Lucca from the Pisan's envious eye,     40
Which the circumfluous plain waving below,
  Like a wide lake of green fertility,
With streams and fields and marshes bare,
  Divides from the far Apennines—which lie
Islanded in the immeasurable air.     45

'What think you, as she lies in her green cove,
Our little sleeping boat is dreaming of?'
'If morning dreams are true, why I should guess
That she was dreaming of our idleness,
And of the miles of watery way     50
We should have led her by this time of day.'—

  'Never mind,' said Lionel,
  'Give care to the winds, they can bear it well
  About yon poplar-tops; and see
  The white clouds are driving merrily,     55
  And the stars we miss this morn will light

More willingly our return to-night.—
How it whistles, Dominic's long black hair!
List, my dear fellow; the breeze blows fair:
Hear how it sings into the air—'                                    60

—'Of us and of our lazy motions,'
    Impatiently said Melchior,
'If I can guess a boat's emotions;
    And how we ought, two hours before,
To have been the devil knows where.'                                65
And then, in such transalpine Tuscan
As would have killed a Della-Cruscan,

    .     .     .

So, Lionel according to his art
    Weaving his idle words, Melchior said:
'She dreams that we are not yet out of bed;                         70
We'll put a soul into her, and a heart
Which like a dove chased by a dove shall beat.'

    .     .

    'Ay, heave the ballast overboard,
    And stow the eatables in the aft locker.'
'Would not this keg be best a little lowered?'                      75

'No, now all's right.' 'Those bottles of warm tea—
(Give me some straw)—must be stowed tenderly;
Such as we used, in summer after six,
To cram in greatcoat pockets, and to mix
Hard eggs and radishes and rolls at Eton,                          80
And, couched on stolen hay in those green harbours
Farmers called gaps, and we schoolboys called arbours,
Would feast till eight.'

    .     .     .     .

    With a bottle in one hand,
As if his very soul were at a stand,                                85
Lionel stood—when Melchior brought him steady:—
'Sit at the helm—fasten this sheet—all ready!'

The chain is loosed, the sails are spread,
  The living breath is fresh behind,
As, with dews and sunrise fed,                          90
  Comes the laughing morning wind;—
The sails are full, the boat makes head
Against the Serchio's torrent fierce,
Then flags with intermitting course,
  And hangs upon the wave, and stems     95
  The tempest of the . . .
Which fervid from its mountain source
Shallow, smooth and strong doth come,—
Swift as fire, tempestuously
It sweeps into the affrighted sea;                     100
In morning's smile its eddies coil,
Its billows sparkle, toss and boil,
Torturing all its quiet light
Into columns fierce and bright.

  The Serchio, twisting forth            105
Between the marble barriers which it clove
  At Ripafratta, leads through the dread chasm
The wave that died the death which lovers love,
  Living in what it sought; as if this spasm
Had not yet passed, the toppling mountains cling,    110
  But the clear stream in full enthusiasm
Pours itself on the plain, then wandering
  Down one clear path of effluence crystalline
Sends its superfluous waves, that they may fling
  At Arno's feet tribute of corn and wine;   115
Then, through the pestilential deserts wild
  Of tangled marsh and woods of stunted pine,
It rushes to the Ocean.

## MUSIC

### I

I PANT for the music which is divine,
  My heart in its thirst is a dying flower;

Pour forth the sound like enchanted wine,
　　Loosen the notes in a silver shower;
Like a herbless plain, for the gentle rain, 5
I gasp, I faint, till they wake again.

II

Let me drink of the spirit of that sweet sound,
　　More, oh more,—I am thirsting yet;
It loosens the serpent which care has bound
　　Upon my heart to stifle it; 10
The dissolving strain, through every vein,
Passes into my heart and brain. . . .

## SONNET TO BYRON

[I AM afraid these verses will not please you, but]
If I esteemed you less, Envy would kill
Pleasure, and leave to Wonder and Despair
The ministration of the thoughts that fill
My mind, which, like a worm whose life may share
A portion of the Unapproachable, 5
Marks your creations rise as fast and fair
As perfect worlds at the creator's will,
And bows itself before the godhead there.
But such is my regard, that, nor your fame
Cast on the present by the coming hour, 10
Nor your well-won prosperity and power
Move one regret for his unhonoured name
Who dares these words,—the worm beneath the sod
May lift itself in worship to the God.

## FRAGMENT: ON KEATS

WHO DESIRED THAT ON HIS TOMB SHOULD BE INSCRIBED—

'HERE lieth One whose name was writ on water.'
　　But, ere the breath that could erase it blew,

Death in remorse for that fell slaughter,
　　Death, the immortalizing winter, flew
　　Athwart the stream,—and time's printless torrent grew 5
A scroll of crystal, blazoning the name
　　Of Adonais!

## TO-MORROW

WHERE art thou, beloved To-morrow?
　　When young and old, and strong and weak,
Rich and poor, through joy and sorrow,
　　Thy sweet smiles we ever seek,—
In thy place—ah! well-a-day!　　　　　　　　　5
We find the thing we fled—To-day.


If I walk in Autumn's even
　　While the dead leaves pass,
If I look on Spring's soft heaven,—
　　Something is not there which was.　　　　　　10
Winter's wondrous frost and snow,
Summer's clouds, where are they now?


## FRAGMENT: 'WE BEGIN IN WHAT WE END'

THE babe is at peace within the womb;
The corpse is at rest within the tomb:
　　We begin in what we end.


## FRAGMENT: THE LADY OF THE SOUTH

FAINT with love, the Lady of the South
　　Lay in the paradise of Lebanon
Under a heaven of cedar boughs: the drouth
　　Of love was on her lips; the light was gone
Out of her eyes—　　　　　　　　　　　　　　5

# FRAGMENT: 'O THOU IMMORTAL DEITY'

O THOU immortal deity
Whose throne is in the depth of human thought,
   I do adjure thy power and thee
By all that man may be, by all that he is not,
By all that he has been and yet must be!      5

# POEMS WRITTEN IN 1822

## LINES: 'WHEN THE LAMP IS SHATTERED'

### I

WHEN the lamp is shattered
The light in the dust lies dead—
   When the cloud is scattered
The rainbow's glory is shed.
   When the lute is broken,      5
Sweet tones are remembered not;
   When the lips have spoken,
Loved accents are soon forgot.

### II

As music and splendour
Survive not the lamp and the lute,      10
   The heart's echoes render
No song when the spirit is mute:—
   No song but sad dirges,
Like the wind through a ruined cell,
   Or the mournful surges      15
That ring the dead seaman's knell.

### III

When hearts have once mingled
Love first leaves the well-built nest;
   The weak one is singled
To endure what it once possessed.      20

O Love! who bewailest
The frailty of all things here,
　Why choose you the frailest
For your cradle, your home, and your bier?

### IV

　Its passions will rock thee　　　　　25
As the storms rock the ravens on high;
　Bright reason will mock thee,
Like the sun from a wintry sky.
　From the nest every rafter
Will rot, and thine eagle home　　　　30
　Leave thee naked to laughter,
When leaves fall and cold winds come.


# TO JANE: THE INVITATION

BEST and brightest, come away!
Fairer far than this fair Day,
Which, like thee to those in sorrow,
Comes to bid a sweet good-morrow
To the rough Year just awake　　　　5
In its cradle on the brake.
The brightest hour of unborn Spring,
Through the winter wandering,
Found, it seems, the halcyon Morn
To hoar February born.　　　　　10
Bending from Heaven, in azure mirth,
It kissed the forehead of the Earth,
And smiled upon the silent sea,
And bade the frozen streams be free,
And waked to music all their fountains,　15
And breathed upon the frozen mountains,
And like a prophetess of May
Strewed flowers upon the barren way,
Making the wintry world appear
Like one on whom thou smiles dear.　　20

Away, away, from men and towns,
To the wild wood and the downs—
To the silent wilderness
Where the soul need not repress
Its music lest it should not find 25
An echo in another's mind,
While the touch of Nature's art
Harmonizes heart to heart.
I leave this notice on my door
For each accustomed visitor:— 30
'I am gone into the fields
To take what this sweet hour yields;—
Reflection, you may come to-morrow,
Sit by the fireside with Sorrow.—
You with the unpaid bill, Despair,— 35
You tiresome verse-reciter, Care,—
I will pay you in the grave,—
Death will listen to your stave.
Expectation too, be off!
To-day is for itself enough; 40
Hope, in pity mock not Woe
With smiles, nor follow where I go;
Long having lived on thy sweet food,
At length I find one moment's good
After long pain—with all your love, 45
This you never told me of.'

Radiant Sister of the Day,
Awake! arise! and come away!
To the wild woods and the plains,
And the pools where winter rains 50
Image all their roof of leaves,
Where the pine its garland weaves
Of sapless green and ivy dun
Round stems that never kiss the sun;
Where the lawns and pastures be, 55
And the sandhills of the sea;—
Where the melting hoar-frost wets

The daisy-star that never sets,
And wind-flowers, and violets,
Which yet join not scent to hue,                    60
Crown the pale year weak and new;
When the night is left behind
In the deep east, dun and blind,
And the blue noon is over us,
And the multitudinous                               65
Billows murmur at our feet,
Where the earth and ocean meet,
And all things seem only one
In the universal sun.

## TO JANE: THE RECOLLECTION

### I

Now the last day of many days,
   All beautiful and bright as thou,
      The loveliest and the last, is dead,
Rise, Memory, and write its praise!
      Up,—to thy wonted work! come, trace          5
      The epitaph of glory fled,—
For now the Earth has changed its face,
   A frown is on the Heaven's brow.

### II

We wandered to the Pine Forest
   That skirts the Ocean's foam,
The lightest wind was in its nest,                  10
   The tempest in its home.
The whispering waves were half asleep,
   The clouds were gone to play,
And on the bosom of the deep                        15
   The smile of Heaven lay;
It seemed as if the hour were one
   Sent from beyond the skies,
Which scattered from above the sun
   A light of Paradise.                          20

### III

We paused amid the pines that stood
    The giants of the waste,
Tortured by storms to shapes as rude
    As serpents interlaced,
And soothed by every azure breath,         25
    That under Heaven is blown,
To harmonies and hues beneath,
    As tender as its own;
Now all the tree-tops lay asleep,
    Like green waves on the sea,        30
As still as in the silent deep
    The ocean woods may be.

### IV

How calm it was!—the silence there
    By such a chain was bound
That even the busy woodpecker        35
    Made stiller by her sound
The inviolable quietness;
    The breath of peace we drew
With its soft motion made not less
    The calm that round us grew.        40
There seemed from the remotest seat
    Of the white mountain waste,
To the soft flower beneath our feet,
    A magic circle traced,—
A spirit interfused around,        45
    A thrilling, silent life,—
To momentary peace it bound
    Our mortal nature's strife;
And still I felt the centre of
    The magic circle there        50
Was one fair form that filled with love
    The lifeless atmosphere.

V

We paused beside the pools that lie
  Under the forest bough,—
Each seemed as 'twere a little sky          55
  Gulfed in a world below;
A firmament of purple light
  Which in the dark earth lay,
More boundless than the depth of night,
  And purer than the day—          60
In which the lovely forests grew,
  As in the upper air,
More perfect both in shape and hue
  Than any spreading there.
There lay the glade and neighbouring lawn,  65
  And through the dark green wood
The white sun twinkling like the dawn
  Out of a speckled cloud.
Sweet views which in our world above
  Can never well be seen,          70
Were imaged by the water's love
  Of that fair forest green.
And all was interfused beneath
  With an Elysian glow,
An atmosphere without a breath,          75
  A softer day below.
Like one beloved the scene had lent
  To the dark water's breast,
Its every leaf and lineament
  With more than truth expressed;      80
Until an envious wind crept by,
  Like an unwelcome thought,
Which from the mind's too faithful eye
  Blots one dear image out.
Though thou art ever fair and kind,      85
  The forests ever green,
Less oft is peace in Shelley's mind,
  Than calm in waters, seen.

# WITH A GUITAR, TO JANE

ARIEL to Miranda:—Take
This slave of Music, for the sake
Of him who is the slave of thee,
And teach it all the harmony
In which thou canst, and only thou,          5
Make the delighted spirit glow,
Till joy denies itself again,
And, too intense, is turned to pain;
For by permission and command
Of thine own Prince Ferdinand,               10
Poor Ariel sends this silent token
Of more than ever can be spoken;
Your guardian spirit, Ariel, who,
From life to life, must still pursue
Your happiness;—for thus alone              15
Can Ariel ever find his own.
From Prospero's enchanted cell,
As the mighty verses tell,
To the throne of Naples, he
Lit you o'er the trackless sea,              20
Flitting on, your prow before,
Like a living meteor.
When you die, the silent Moon,
In her interlunar swoon,
Is not sadder in her cell                    25
Than deserted Ariel.
When you live again on earth,
Like an unseen star of birth,
Ariel guides you o'er the sea
Of life from your nativity.                   30
Many changes have been run
Since Ferdinand and you begun
Your course of love, and Ariel still
Has tracked your steps, and served your will;
Now, in humbler, happier lot,                35

This is all remembered not;
And now, alas! the poor sprite is
Imprisoned, for some fault of his,
In a body like a grave;—
From you he only dares to crave,                    40
For his service and his sorrow,
A smile to-day, a song to-morrow.

The artist who this idol wrought,
To echo all harmonious thought,
Felled a tree, while on the steep                   45
The woods were in their winter sleep,
Rocked in that repose divine
On the wind-swept Apennine;
And dreaming, some of Autumn past,
And some of Spring approaching fast,                50
And some of April buds and showers,
And some of songs in July bowers,
And all of love; and so this tree,—
O that such our death may be!—
Died in sleep, and felt no pain,                    55
To live in happier form again:
From which, beneath Heaven's fairest star,
The artist wrought this loved Guitar,
And taught it justly to reply,
To all who question skilfully,                      60
In language gentle as thine own;
Whispering in enamoured tone
Sweet oracles of woods and dells,
And summer winds in sylvan cells;
For it had learned all harmonies                    65
Of the plains and of the skies,
Of the forests and the mountains,
And the many-voicèd fountains;
The clearest echoes of the hills,
The softest notes of falling rills,                 70
The melodies of birds and bees,
The murmuring of summer seas,

And pattering rain, and breathing dew,
And airs of evening; and it knew
That seldom-heard mysterious sound, 75
Which, driven on its diurnal round,
As it floats through boundless day,
Our world enkindles on its way.—
All this it knows, but will not tell
To those who cannot question well 80
The Spirit that inhabits it;
It talks according to the wit
Of its companions; and no more
Is heard than has been felt before,
By those who tempt it to betray 85
These secrets of an elder day:
But, sweetly as its answers will
Flatter hands of perfect skill,
It keeps its highest, holiest tone
For our belovèd Jane alone. 90

# TO JANE: 'THE KEEN STARS WERE
## TWINKLING'

### I

THE keen stars were twinkling,
And the fair moon was rising among them,
Dear Jane!
The guitar was tinkling,
But the notes were not sweet till you sung them 5
Again.

### II

As the moon's soft splendour
O'er the faint cold starlight of Heaven
Is thrown,
So your voice most tender 10
To the strings without soul had then given
Its own.

### III

The stars will awaken,
Though the moon sleep a full hour later,
  To-night;      15
 No leaf will be shaken
Whilst the dews of your melody scatter
  Delight.

### IV

 Though the sound overpowers,
Sing again, with your dear voice revealing  20
  A tone
 Of some world far from ours,
Where music and moonlight and feeling
  Are one.


## A DIRGE

Rough  wind, that moanest loud
 Grief too sad for song;
Wild wind, when sullen cloud
 Knells all the night long;
Sad storm, whose tears are vain,     5
Bare woods, whose branches strain,
Deep caves and dreary main,—
 Wail, for the world's wrong!


## LINES WRITTEN IN THE BAY OF LERICI

She left me at the silent time
When the moon had ceased to climb
The azure path of Heaven's steep,
And like an albatross asleep,
Balanced on her wings of light,     5
Hovered in the purple night,
Ere she sought her ocean nest

In the chambers of the West.
She left me, and I stayed alone
Thinking over every tone                                    10
Which, though silent to the ear,
The enchanted heart could hear,
Like notes which die when born, but still
Haunt the echoes of the hill;
And feeling ever—oh, too much!—                             15
The soft vibration of her touch,
As if her gentle hand, even now,
Lightly trembled on my brow;
And thus, although she absent were,
Memory gave me all of her                                   20
That even Fancy dares to claim:—
Her presence had made weak and tame
All passions, and I lived alone
In the time which is our own;
The past and future were forgot,                            25
As they had been, and would be, not.
But soon, the guardian angel gone,
The daemon reassumed his throne
In my faint heart. I dare not speak
My thoughts, but thus disturbed and weak    30
I sat and saw the vessels glide
Over the ocean bright and wide,
Like spirit-wingèd chariots sent
O'er some serenest element
For ministrations strange and far;                          35
As if to some Elysian star
Sailed for drink to medicine
Such sweet and bitter pain as mine.
And the wind that winged their flight
From the land came fresh and light,                         40
And the scent of wingèd flowers,
And the coolness of the hours
Of dew, and sweet warmth left by day,
Were scattered o'er the twinkling bay.
And the fisher with his lamp                                45

And spear about the low rocks damp
Crept, and struck the fish which came
To worship the delusive flame.
Too happy they, whose pleasure sought
Extinguishes all sense and thought        50
Of the regret that pleasure leaves,
Destroying life alone, not peace!

# LINES: 'WE MEET NOT AS WE PARTED'

### I

We meet not as we parted,
    We feel more than all may see;
My bosom is heavy-hearted,
    And thine full of doubt for me:—
    One moment has bound the free.        5

### II

That moment is gone for ever,
    Like lightning that flashed and died—
Like a snowflake upon the river—
    Like a sunbeam upon the tide,
    Which the dark shadows hide.        10

### III

That moment from time was singled
    As the first of a life of pain;
The cup of its joy was mingled
    —Delusion too sweet though vain!
    Too sweet to be mine again.        15

### IV

Sweet lips, could my heart have hidden
    That its life was crushed by you,
Ye would not have then forbidden
    The death which a heart so true
    Sought in your briny dew.        20

## THE ISLE

THERE was a little lawny islet
By anemone and violet,
  Like mosaic, paven:
And its roof was flowers and leaves
Which the summer's breath enweaves,　　5
Where nor sun nor showers nor breeze
Pierce the pines and tallest trees,
  Each a gem engraven;—
Girt by many an azure wave
With which the clouds and mountains pave　10
  A lake's blue chasm.

# TRANSLATIONS

## FROM THE CYCLOPS OF EURIPIDES

### THE CREED OF THE CYCLOPS

*Cyclops.*  Wealth, my good fellow, is the wise man's God,
All other things are a pretence and boast.
What are my father's ocean promontories,
The sacred rocks whereon he dwells, to me?
Stranger, I laugh to scorn Jove's thunderbolt,　　5
I know not that his strength is more than mine.
As to the rest I care not.—When he pours
Rain from above, I have a close pavilion
Under this rock, in which I lie supine,
Feasting on a roast calf or some wild beast,　　10
And d  king pans of milk, and gloriously
Emulating the thunder of high Heaven.
And when the Thracian wind pours down the snow,
I wrap my body in the skins of beasts,
Kindle a fire, and bid the snow whirl on.　　15
The earth, by force, whether it will or no,
Bringing forth grass, fattens my flocks and herds,
Which, to what other God but to myself
And this great belly, first of deities,

Should I be bound to sacrifice? I well know                         20
The wise man's only Jupiter is this,
To eat and drink during his little day,
And give himself no care. And as for those
Who complicate with laws the life of man,
I freely give them tears for their reward.                          25
I will not cheat my soul of its delight,
Or hesitate in dining upon you:—
And that I may be quit of all demands,
These are my hospitable gifts;—fierce fire
And yon ancestral caldron, which o'er-bubbling                      30
Shall finely cook your miserable flesh.
Creep in!—

.   .   .   .   .   .   .   .   .

# PAN, ECHO, AND THE SATYR

### FROM THE GREEK OF MOSCHUS

PAN loved his neighbour Echo—but that child
  Of Earth and Air pined for the Satyr leaping;
The Satyr loved with wasting madness wild
  The bright nymph Lyda,—and so three went weeping.
As Pan loved Echo, Echo loved the Satyr,                            5
  The Satyr, Lyda; and so love consumed them.—
And thus to each—which was a woful matter—
  To bear what they inflicted Justice doomed them;
For, inasmuch as each might hate the lover,
  Each, loving, so was hated.—Ye that love not                     10
Be warned—in thought turn this example over,
  That when ye love, the like return ye prove not.

# EPIGRAM: TO STELLA

### FROM THE GREEK OF PLATO

THOU wert the morning star among the living,
  Ere thy fair light had fled;—
Now, having died, thou art as Hesperus, giving
  New splendour to the dead.

# INDEX OF FIRST LINES

# INDEX OF FIRST LINES

521

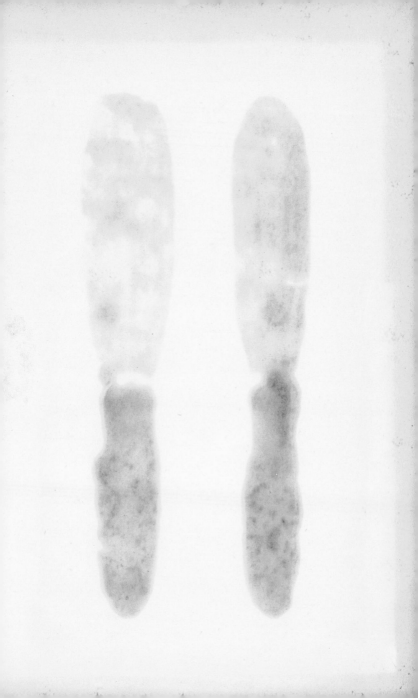

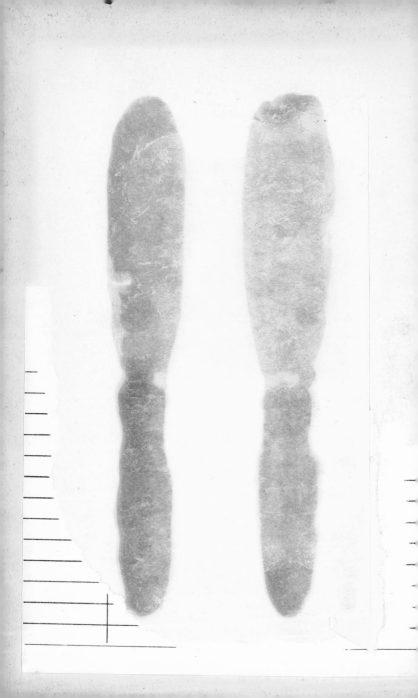